Avizandum Statutes on

The Scots Law of Obligations

Second edition

Avizandum Statutes on

The Scots Law of Obligations

Second edition

Editor

Laura J Macgregor LLM, Solicitor
Senior lecturer in commercial law,
University of Edinburgh

Avizandum Publishing Ltd
Edinburgh
2005

Published by
Avizandum Publishing Ltd
58 Candlemaker Row
Edinburgh EH1 2QE

First published 2003
2nd edition   2005

© Avizandum Publishing Ltd

ISBN 1-904968-06-6

British Library Cataloguing in Publication Data
A catalogue record for this book is available from the British Library

Typeset by AFS Image Setters Ltd, Glasgow
Printed and bound by Bell & Bain Ltd, Glasgow

EDITOR'S PREFACE

The aim of *Avizandum Statutes on the Scots Law of Obligations* remains unchanged: it has been produced for the use of students at undergraduate level studying obligations as part of a law degree in Scotland. The form and content of obligations courses in the different Scottish universities differ. Nevertheless, it is hoped that the volume contains the materials which are essential to an understanding of the subject as a whole.

As with the first edition, one of the guiding principles has been keeping the length, and therefore the cost to the student, to a minimum. With this in mind, the editor's most difficult task is to decide how much or how little of a particular statute to reproduce. The first edition reproduced all the most important statutes in full, and this remains the case with the second edition. However, one difference of approach in this edition is that more statutes appear in their entirety. In this way the student is provided with a more comprehensive picture of the legislation. To accommodate this, some of the less relevant material has been excised. The end result is, we think, a more focused set of materials.

This edition has a companion volume: *Avizandum Statutes on Scots Commercial and Consumer Law*. As a general rule, statutes appear either in this volume or in the companion volume and not in both. There are exceptions; certain statutes, such as the Sale of Goods Act 1979, are so important as to merit a place in both volumes. A debate on which pieces of legislation are part of the law of obligations and which are part of commercial law would ultimately be a fruitless one. As a general rule, legislation which has a consumer-protection flavour has been reproduced in the *Commercial and Consumer Law Statutes*, reflecting the fact that consumer law tends to be taught as part of a commercial law course. The availability of the *Commercial and Consumer Law Statutes* should be borne in mind particularly by students of the law of contract.

As stated above, the statutes are produced for the use of undergraduate students. More specifically, they are intended for use principally at ordinary rather than honours level. It has, however, been possible to include some material which facilitates the study of obligations at a deeper level, including certain international 'codes' such as the Principles of European Contract Law produced by the Lando Commission and the Unidroit Principles for International Commercial Contracts.

Grateful thanks must go primarily to Margaret Cherry, whose hard work has enabled this volume, and the others in the series, to be produced. I am also very grateful to Dot Reid of the University of Strathclyde for her assistance in deciding what the new edition should include. This edition has benefited from the input of many lecturers, but those at Strathclyde University deserve a special mention. Comments on the contents would be most gratefully received, and should be sent to L.Macgregor@ed.ac.uk.

Materials are in general up to date to 31 July 2005 but it has been possible to include the General Product Safety Regulations 2005, which come into effect on 1 October 2005.

Laura Macgregor
University of Edinburgh
September 2005

CONTENTS

Part II   Statutory Instruments

Part III   EC Materials

Part IV   Codes

PART I

STATUTES

LAWBURROWS ACT 1429

5 ITEM it is ſtatute ande ordanit þat quhare a borgh is fundyn in a courte apoñ a weir of law þat þe pty defendour as to þat borgh ſal haf fredome to be aviſit and aſk leve þarto ande ſal haf leve ande quheþ' he wil be aviſit w'in courte or oute of courte findande borowis of his entre 't his anſuer witħin the hour of cauſe at the conſid'acioun of the Juge 't the courte.

LAWBURROWS ACT 1581

Additioun to the act of Lawborrowis.

FORSAMEKILL / as ſindrie guid actis hes bene maid anent finding of Lawborrowis for preferuatioun of the trew and obedient ſubiectis from iniuſt force / and violence / and laitlie for þair greitter confort It wes weill ordanit / þat þe panes of lawborrowis ſuld be deuidit betuix þe king and þe pairte offendit vnto. Neuerþeles / ſeing þe panes of lawborrowis hes extendit onlie in tyme bigane in ſaulftie of bodilie harme from þe perfone of þe complenar / The malice of [the] wickit ſa increſſis as þei ceiſ' not be indirect meanis / and hunding out of lȳmaris / vagaboundis / and vþeris not reſponſall / to Inuaid þe Innocent perſonis / not onlie in þair bodeis bot to reif / ſteill hoch / or ſlay þair oxin / and vþeris cattell / cut or diſtroy þair coirnis / or to cauſ' eit þe famȳ wᵗʰ beſtiall / to hund and ſlay þair ſcheip wᵗʰ doggis / boiſt þame ſelf in ſic fort as þai dar not ly in þair awin houſſ' / or to manas þair ſeruādℓ to leve pair ſernice / quhairthrow þair ground may be lyed waiſt / to þe vttir wrak and depaupering of þe Innocentℓ Quhairfoir oure ſouerane lord wᵗʰ aduiſe of his thre eſtatis in þis preſent parliament / Ordanis þat all letteris of lawborrowis ſalbe direct in tyme cūing at þe inſtance of þe pairteis complenand / chargeing þe perſonis cōplenit vpoun to find ſicker ſouertie and lawborrowis / that þe complenaris / thair wyffis bairnis / tenentis and ſeruandis / ſalbe harmeles and ſkaithles / in þair bodeis landis / takkis / poſſeſſionis / guidis / and geir / and on na wayis to be moleſtit or trublit thairin be þe perſonis complenit vpoun / nor na vþeris of þair cauſing / ſending hunding out reſetting cōmand / aſſiſtance / and ratihabitioun / quhome þai may ſtop or let direclie or Indireclie / vþirwayis nor be þe ordoure of law and iuſtice vnder greit panes to be modifeit be þe lordis of ſeſſioun / Or vþeris ordinar Judges / Be quhome in caiſ' þe ſaid lawborrowis / ſalbe dewlie tryit / to be brokin / the ane half of þe pane fall pertene to oure ſouerane lord / and þe vþir half to þe pairte grevit / according to þe effect' 't meaning of þe ſaid act' / maid to þat effect' of befoir.

COMPENSATION ACT 1592

THAT Compenſatioun de liquido ad liquidum be admittit in all Jugementis.

OURE SOUERANE LORD and eſtaitis of parliament ſtatutis and Ordanis that ony debt de liquido ad liquidum inſtantlie verifiet be wreit or aith of the partie befoir the geving of decreit be admittit be all Jugis w^{th}in this realme be way of exceptioun Bot no' eftir the geving thairof ⫽ In the ſuſpenſioun or in reductioun of þe fame decreit.

PARLIAMENTARY PAPERS ACT 1840
(3 & 4 Vict, c 9)

Whereas it is essential to the due and effectual exercise and discharge of the functions and duties of Parliament, and to the promotion of wise legislation, that no obstructions or impediments should exist to the publication of such of the reports, papers, votes, or proceedings of either House of Parliament as such House of Parliament may deem fit or necessary to be published: And whereas obstructions or impediments to such publication have arisen, and hereafter may arise, by means of civil or criminal proceedings being taken against persons employed by or acting under the authority of the Houses of Parliament, or one of them, in the publication of such reports, papers, votes, or proceedings; by reason and for remedy whereof it is expedient that more speedy protection should be afforded to all persons acting under the authority aforesaid, and that all such civil or criminal proceedings should be summarily put an end to and determined in manner herein-after mentioned: Be it therefore enacted by the Queen's most excellent Majesty, by and with the advice and consent of the lords spiritual and temporal, and commons, in this present Parliament assembled, and by the authority of the same, that

1   Proceedings, criminal or civil, against persons for publication of papers printed by order of Parliament, to be stayed upon delivery of a certificate and affidavit to the effect that such publication is by order of either House of Parliament
It shall and may be lawful for any person or persons who now is or are, or hereafter shall be, a defendant or defendants in any civil or criminal proceeding commenced or prosecuted in any manner soever, for or on account or in respect of the publication of any such report, paper, votes, or proceedings by such person or persons, or by his, her, or their servant or servants, by or under the authority of either House of Parliament, to bring before the court in which such proceeding shall have been or shall be so commenced or prosecuted, or before any judge of the same (if one of the superior courts at Westminster), first giving twenty-four hours notice of his intention so to do to the prosecutor or plaintiff in such proceeding, a certificate under the hand of the lord high chancellor of Great Britain, or the lord keeper of the great seal, or of the speaker of the House of Lords, for the time being, or of the clerk of the Parliaments, or of the speaker of the House of Commons, or of the clerk of the same house, stating that the report, paper, votes, or proceedings, as the case may be, in respect whereof such civil or criminal proceeding shall have been commenced or prosecuted, was published by such person or persons, or by his, her, or their servant or servants, by order or under the authority of the House of Lords or of the House of Commons, as the case may be, together with an affidavit verifying such certificate; and such court or judge shall thereupon immediately stay such civil or criminal proceeding; and the same, and every writ or process issued therein, shall be and shall be deemed and taken to be finally put an end to, determined, and superseded by virtue of this Act.

2 Proceedings to be stayed when commenced in respect of a copy of an authenticated report, &c

And be it enacted, that in case of any civil or criminal proceeding hereafter to be commenced or prosecuted for or on account or in respect of the publication of any copy of such report, paper, votes, or proceedings, it shall be lawful for the defendant or defendants at any stage of the proceedings to lay before the court or judge such report, paper, votes, or proceedings, and such copy, with an affidavit verifying such report, paper, votes, or proceedings, and the correctness of such copy, and the court or judge shall immediately stay such civil or criminal proceeding; and the same, and every writ or process issued therein, shall be and shall be deemed and taken to be finally put an end to, determined, and superseded by virtue of this Act.

3 In proceedings for printing any extract or abstract of a paper, it may be shewn that such extract was bonâ fide made

And be it enacted, that it shall be lawful in any civil or criminal proceeding to be commenced or prosecuted for printing any extract from or abstract of such report, paper, votes, or proceedings, to give in evidence . . . such report, paper, votes, or proceedings, and to show that such extract or abstract was published bonâ fide and without malice; and if such shall be the opinion of the jury, a verdict of not guilty shall be entered for the defendant or defendants.

4 Act not to affect the privileges of Parliament

Provided always, and it is hereby expressly declared and enacted, that nothing herein contained shall be deemed or taken, or held or construed, directly or indirectly, by implication or otherwise, to affect the privileges of Parliament in any manner whatsoever.

TRESPASS (SCOTLAND) ACT 1865
(1865, c lvi)

I Short Title

This Act may be cited for all Purposes as 'The Trespass (*Scotland*) Act, 1865.'

II Interpretation of Terms

In this Act the following Words shall have the Meanings hereby assigned to them:

'Premises' shall mean and include any House, Barn, Stable, Shed, Loft, Granary, Outhouse, Garden, Stackyard, Court, Close, or inclosed Place:

'Magistrate' shall mean and include the Sheriff and Sheriff Substitute, or any One or more Justice or Justices of the Peace, or any One or more Magistrate or Magistrates, having Jurisdiction respectively in the County or Burgh where any Offence against the Provisions of this Act is committed, or where any Person charged with such Offence is found or brought to Trial:

'Procurator Fiscal' shall mean and include the Procurator Fiscal of the Court having such Jurisdiction.

['Road' shall mean and include any way, other than—
  (a) a waterway; or
  (b) without prejudice to section 100(c) (damage to roads by fire) or 129(4) (camping in a road) of the Roads (Scotland) Act 1984, a road within the meaning of that Act.]

III Parties lodging in Premises or encamping on Land, without Permission, guilty of an Offence

[(1)] Every Person who lodges in any Premises, or occupies or encamps on any Land, being private Property, without the Consent and Permission of the Owner or legal Occupier of such Premises or Land, and every Person who encamps or lights a Fire on or near any [. . .] Road or inclosed or cultivated Land, or in or near any Plantation, without the Consent and Permission of the Owner or Legal Occupier of such Road, Land, or Plantation, [. . .] shall be guilty of an Offence punishable as herein-after provided.

[(2) Subsection (1) above does not extend to anything done by a person in the exercise of the access rights created by the Land Reform (Scotland) Act 2003 (asp 2).]

IV Apprehension and Punishment of Offenders

Every Person who commits any Offence against the Provisions of this Act may, if found in the Act of committing the same by any Officer of Police or Constable, be apprehended by such Officer or Constable, and detained in any Prison, Police Station, Lock-up, or other Place of safe Custody, and not later than in the course of the next lawful Day after he shall have been so taken into Custody shall be brought before a Magistrate; and every Person charged with the Commission of any such Offence may, if not so taken into Custody, or if he shall have been liberated on Bail or Pledge, be summoned to appear before a Magistrate, [and every person committing an offence against the provisions of this Act shall be liable, on summary conviction, to a fine not exceeding level 1 on the standard scale.]

V As to Prosecutions under Act

Every Prosecution for an Offence against the Provisions of this Act shall be raised and proceeded in at the Instance of the Procurator Fiscal, and shall be heard and determined by One or more Magistrate or Magistrates in a summary Form; and every such Prosecution shall be commenced within One Month after the Offence has been committed.

BILLS OF EXCHANGE ACT 1882
(1882, c 61)

3 Bill of exchange defined

(1) A bill of exchange is an unconditional order in writing, addressed by one person to another, signed by the person giving it, requiring the person to whom it is addressed to pay on demand or at a fixed or determinable future time a sum certain in money to or to the order of a specified person, or to bearer.

(2) An instrument which does not comply with these conditions, or which orders any act to be done in addition to the payment of money, is not a bill of exchange.

(3) An order to pay out of a particular fund is not unconditional within the meaning of this section; but an unqualified order to pay, coupled with (a) an indication of a particular fund out of which the drawee is to re-imburse himself or a particular account to be debited with the amount, or (b) a statement of the transaction which gives rise to the bill, is unconditional.

(4) A bill is not invalid by reason—

   (a) That it is not dated;

   (b) That it does not specify the value given, or that any value has been given therefor;

   (c) That it does not specify the place where it is drawn or the place where it is payable.

73 Cheque defined

A cheque is a bill of exchange drawn on a banker payable on demand. Except as otherwise provided in this Part, the provisions of this Act applicable to a bill of exchange payable on demand apply to a cheque.

83 Promissory note defined

(1) A promissory note is an unconditional promise in writing made by one person to another signed by the maker, engaging to pay, on demand, or at a fixed or determinable future time, a sum certain in money, to, or to the order of, a specified person or to bearer.

(2)   An instrument in the form of a note payable to maker's order is not a note within the meaning of this section unless and until it is indorsed by the maker.

(3)   A note is not invalid by reason only that it contains also a pledge of collateral security with authority to sell or dispose thereof.

(4)   A note which is, or on the face of it purports to be, both made and payable within the British Islands is an inland note. Any other note is a foreign note.

FACTORS ACT 1889
(1889, c 45)

Preliminary

1 Definitions

For the purposes of this Act—

(1)   The expression 'mercantile agent' shall mean a mercantile agent having in the customary course of his business as such agent authority either to sell goods or to consign goods for the purpose of sale, or to buy goods, or to raise money on the security of goods:

(2)   A person shall be deemed to be in possession of goods or of the documents of title to goods, where the goods or documents are in the actual custody or are held by any other person subject to his control or for him or on his behalf:

(3)   The expression 'goods' shall include wares and merchandise:

(4)   The expression 'document of title' shall include any bill of lading, dock warrant, warehouse-keeper's certificate, and warrant or order for the delivery of goods, and any other document used in the ordinary course of business as proof of the possession or control of goods, or authorising or purporting to authorise, either by endorsement or by delivery, the possessor of the document to transfer or receive goods thereby represented:

(5)   The expression 'pledge' shall include any contract pledging, or giving a lien or security on, goods, whether in consideration of an original advance or of any further or continuing advance or of any pecuniary liability:

(6)   The expression 'person' shall include any body of persons corporate or unincorporate.

Dispositions by mercantile agents

2 Powers of mercantile agent with respect to disposition of goods

(1)   Where a mercantile agent is, with the consent of the owner, in possession of goods or of the documents of title to goods, any sale, pledge, or other disposition of the goods, made by him when acting in the ordinary course of business of a mercantile agent, shall, subject to the provisions of this Act, be as valid as if he were expressly authorised by the owner of the goods to make the same; provided that the person taking under the disposition acts in good faith, and has not at the time of the disposition notice that the person making the disposition has not authority to make the same.

(2)   Where a mercantile agent has, with the consent of the owner, been in possession of goods or of the documents of title to goods, any sale, pledge, or other disposition, which would have been valid if the consent had continued, shall be valid notwithstanding the determination of the consent; provided that the person taking under the disposition has not at the time thereof notice that the consent has been determined.

(3)   Where a mercantile agent has obtained possession of any documents of title to goods by reason of his being or having been, with the consent of the owner, in possession of the goods represented thereby, or of any other documents of title to the goods, his possession of the first-mentioned documents shall, for the purposes of this Act, be deemed to be with the consent of the owner.

(4)   For the purposes of this Act the consent of the owner shall be presumed in the absence of evidence to the contrary.

3   Effect of pledges of documents of title
A pledge of the documents of title to goods shall be deemed to be a pledge of the goods.

4   Pledge for antecedent debt
Where a mercantile agent pledges goods as security for a debt or liability due from the pledgor to the pledgee before the time of the pledge, the pledgee shall acquire no further right to the goods than could have been enforced by the pledgor at the time of the pledge.

5   Rights acquired by exchange of goods or documents
The consideration necessary for the validity of a sale, pledge, or other disposition of goods, in pursuance of this Act, may be either a payment in cash, or the delivery or transfer of other goods, or of a document of title to goods, or of a negotiable security, or any other valuable consideration; but where goods are pledged by a mercantile agent in consideration of the delivery or transfer of other goods, or of a document of title to goods, or of a negotiable security, the pledgee shall acquire no right or interest in the goods so pledged in excess of the value of the goods, documents, or security when so delivered or transferred in exchange.

6   Agreements through clerks, &c
For the purposes of this Act an agreement made with a mercantile agent through a clerk or other person authorised in the ordinary course of business to make contracts of sale or pledge on his behalf shall be deemed to be an agreement with the agent.

7   Provisions as to consignors and consignees
(1)   Where the owner of goods has given possession of the goods to another person for the purpose of consignment or sale, or has shipped the goods in the name of another person, and the consignee of the goods has not had notice that such person is not the owner of the goods, the consignee shall, in respect of advances made to or for the use of such person, have the same lien on the goods as if such person were the owner of the goods, and may transfer any such lien to another person.

(2)   Nothing in this section shall limit or affect the validity of any sale, pledge, or disposition, by a mercantile agent.

Dispositions by sellers and buyers of goods

8   Disposition by seller remaining in possession
Where a person, having sold goods, continues, or is, in possession of the goods or of the documents of title to the goods, the delivery or transfer by that person, or by a mercantile agent acting for him, of the goods or documents of title under any sale, pledge, or other disposition thereof, or under any agreement for sale, pledge, or other disposition thereof, to any person receiving the same in good faith and without notice of the previous sale, shall have the same effect as if the person making the delivery or transfer were expressly authorised by the owner of the goods to make the same.

9   Disposition by buyer obtaining possession
Where a person, having bought or agreed to buy goods, obtains with the consent of the seller possession of the goods or the documents of title to the goods, the delivery or transfer, by that person or by a mercantile agent acting for him, of the goods or documents of title under any sale, pledge, or other disposition thereof, or under any agreement for sale, pledge, or other disposition thereof, to any person receiving the same in good faith and without notice of any lien or other right of

the original seller in respect of the goods, shall have the same effect as if the person making the delivery or transfer were a mercantile agent in possession of the goods or documents of title with the consent of the owner.

[For the purposes of this section—

(i) the buyer under a conditional sale agreement shall be deemed not to be a person who has bought or agreed to buy goods, and

(ii) 'conditional sale agreement' means an agreement for the sale of goods which is a consumer credit agreement within the meaning of the Consumer Credit Act 1974 under which the purchase price or part of it is payable in instalments, and the property in the goods is to remain in the seller (notwithstanding that the buyer is to be in possession of the goods) until such conditions as to the payment of instalments or otherwise as may be specified in the agreement are fulfilled.]

10 Effect of transfer of documents on vendor's lien or right of stoppage in transitu

Where a document of title to goods has been lawfully transferred to a person as a buyer or owner of the goods, and that person transfers the document to a person who takes the document in good faith and for valuable consideration, the last-mentioned transfer shall have the same effect for defeating any vendor's lien or right of stoppage in transitu as the transfer of a bill of lading has for defeating the right of stoppage in transitu.

Supplemental

11 Mode of transferring documents

For the purposes of this Act, the transfer of a document may be by endorsement, or, where the document is by custom or by its express terms transferable by delivery or makes the goods deliverable to the bearer, then by delivery.

12 Saving for rights of true owner

(1) Nothing in this Act shall authorise an agent to exceed or depart from his authority as between himself and his principal, or exempt him from any liability, civil or criminal, for so doing.

(2) Nothing in this Act shall prevent the owner of goods from recovering the goods from any agent or his trustee in bankruptcy at any time before the sale or pledge thereof, or shall prevent the owner of goods pledged by an agent from having the right to redeem the goods at any time before the sale thereof, on satisfying the claim for which the goods were pledged, and paying to the agent, if by him required, any money in respect of which the agent would by law be entitled to retain the goods or the documents of title thereto, or any of them, by way of lien as against the owner, or from recovering from any person with whom the goods have been pledged any balance of money remaining in his hands as the produce of the sale of the goods after deducting the amount of his lien.

(3) Nothing in this Act shall prevent the owner of goods sold by an agent from recovering from the buyer the price agreed to be paid for the same, or any part of that price, subject to any right of set off on the part of the buyer against the agent.

13 Saving for common law powers of agent

The provisions of this Act shall be construed in amplification and not in derogation of the powers exercisable by an agent independently of this Act.

[. . .]

16 Extent of Act

This Act shall not extend to Scotland.

17 Short title

This Act may be cited as the Factors Act, 1889.

FACTORS (SCOTLAND) ACT 1890
(1890, c 40)

1 Application of 52 & 53 Vict c 45 to Scotland
Subject to the following provisions, the Factors Act, 1889, shall apply to Scotland:—

(1) The expression 'lien' shall mean and include right of retention; the expression 'vendor's lien' shall mean and include any right of retention competent to the original owner or vendor; and the expression 'set off' shall mean and include compensation.

(2) In the application of section five of the recited Act, a sale, pledge, or other disposition of goods shall not be valid unless made for valuable consideration.

2 Short title
This Act may be cited as the Factors (Scotland) Act, 1890.

LAW REFORM (MISCELLANEOUS PROVISIONS) (SCOTLAND) ACT 1940
(1940, c 42)

1 Amendment of the law as to enforcement of decrees ad factum praestandum
(1) No person shall be apprehended or imprisoned on account of his failure to comply with a decree ad factum praestandum except in accordance with the following provisions—

(i) On an application by the person in right of such a decree (hereinafter referred to as the applicant) to the court by which the decree was granted, the court may, if it is satisfied that the person against whom such decree was granted (hereinafter referred to as the respondent) is wilfully refusing to comply with the decree, grant warrant for his imprisonment for any period not exceeding six months;

(ii) Where the court is satisfied that a person undergoing imprisonment in pursuance of a warrant granted under this section has complied, or is no longer wilfully refusing to comply, with the decree, the court shall, notwithstanding any period specified in the warrant, order the immediate liberation of such person, and it shall be the duty of the applicant, as soon as he is satisfied that the decree has been complied with, forthwith to inform the clerk of the court of such compliance;

(iii) Imprisonment under a warrant granted under this subsection shall not operate to extinguish the obligation imposed by the decree on which the application proceeds;

(iv) The person on whose application a warrant for imprisonment has been granted under this subsection shall not be liable to aliment, or to contribute to the aliment of, the respondent while in prison.

(2) On any application in pursuance of the foregoing subsection, the court may, in lieu of granting warrant for imprisonment, recall the decree on which the application proceeds and make an order for the payment by the respondent to the applicant of a specified sum or make such other order as appears to the court to be just and equitable in the circumstances, including, in the case where the decree on which the application proceeds is a decree for delivery of corporeal moveables, a warrant to officers of court to search any premises in the occupation of the respondent or of such other person as may be named in the warrant, and to take possession of, and deliver to the applicant, any such moveables which may be found in such premises.

(3) Any warrant granted under the last foregoing subsection shall be deemed to include authority to open shut and lockfast places for the purpose of carrying the warrant into lawful execution.

3 Contribution among joint wrongdoers

(1) Where in any action of damages in respect of loss or damage arising from any wrongful acts or negligent acts or omissions two or more persons are, in pursuance of the verdict of a jury or the judgment of a court found jointly and severally liable in damages or expenses, they shall be liable *inter se* to contribute to such damages or expenses in such proportions as the jury or the court, as the case may be, may deem just: Provided that nothing in this subsection shall affect the right of the person to whom such damages or expenses have been awarded to obtain a joint and several decree therefor against the persons so found liable.

(2) Where any person has paid any damages or expenses in which he has been found liable in any such action as aforesaid, he shall be entitled to recover from any other person who, if sued, might also have been held liable in respect of the loss or damage on which the action was founded, such contribution, if any, as the court may deem just.

(3) Nothing in this section shall—

(a) apply to any action in respect of loss or damage suffered before the commencement of this Act; or

(b) affect any contractual or other right of relief or indemnity or render enforceable any agreement for indemnity which could not have been enforced if this section had not been enacted.

LAW REFORM (CONTRIBUTORY NEGLIGENCE) ACT 1945
(1945, c 28)

1 Apportionment of liability in case of contributory negligence

(1) Where any person suffers damage as the result partly of his own fault and partly of the fault of any other person or persons, a claim in respect of that damage shall not be defeated by reason of the fault of the person suffering the damage, but the damages recoverable in respect thereof shall be reduced to such extent as the court thinks just and equitable having regard to the claimant's share in the responsibility for the damage:

Provided that—

(a) this subsection shall not operate to defeat any defence arising under a contract;

(b) where any contract or enactment providing for the limitation of liability is applicable to the claim, the amount of damages recoverable by the claimant by virtue of this subsection shall not exceed the maximum limit so applicable.

(2) Where damages are recoverable by any person by virtue of the foregoing subsection subject to such reduction as is therein mentioned, the court shall find and record the total damages which would have been recoverable if the claimant had not been at fault.

[. . .]

(4) Where any person dies as the result partly of his own fault and partly of the fault of any other person or persons, a claim by any dependant of the first mentioned person for damages or solatium in respect of that person's death shall not be defeated by reason of his fault, but the damages or solatium recoverable shall be reduced to such extent as the court thinks just and equitable having regard to the share of the said person in the responsibility for his death.

(5) Where, in any case to which subsection (1) of this section applies, one of the persons at fault avoids liability to any other such person or his personal representative by pleading the Limitation Act, 1939, or any other enactment limiting the time within which proceedings may be taken, he shall not be entitled to recover any damages [. . .] from that other person or representative by virtue of the said subsection.

(6) Where any case to which subsection (1) of this section applies is tried with a jury, the jury shall determine the total damages which would have been recover-

able if the claimant had not been at fault and the extent to which those damages are to be reduced.

2 Provisions as to workmen and employers

(1)   Where, within the time limited for the taking of proceedings under the Workmen's Compensation Acts, 1925 to 1943, an action is brought to recover damages independently of the said Acts in respect of an injury or disease giving rise to a claim for compensation under the said Acts, and it is determined in that action that—

(a)   damages are recoverable independently of the said Acts subject to such reduction as is mentioned in subsection (1) of the foregoing section of this Act; and

(b)   the employer would have been liable to pay compensation under the Workmen's Compensation Acts, 1925 to 1943;

subsection (2) of section twenty-nine of the Workmen's Compensation Act, 1925, (which enables the court, on the dismissal of an action to recover damages independently of the said Acts, to assess and award compensation under the said Acts) shall apply in all respects as if the action had been dismissed, and, if the claimant chooses to have compensation assessed and awarded in accordance with the said subsection (2), no damages shall be recoverable in the said action.

This subsection shall apply, with the necessary adaptations, in any case where compensation is recoverable under a scheme certified or made under the Workmen's Compensation Acts, 1925 to 1943, or under the Workmen's Compensation and Benefit (Byssinosis) Act, 1940, if the scheme applies section twenty-nine of the Workmen's Compensation Act, 1925, or contains any provision similar to that section.

(2)   Where a workman or his personal representative or dependant has recovered compensation under the Workmen's Compensation Acts, 1925 to 1943, or under any scheme certified under the Workmen's Compensation Act, 1925, in respect of an injury caused under circumstances which would give a right to recover reduced damages in respect thereof by virtue of section one of this Act from some person other than the employer (hereinafter referred to as 'the third party'), any right conferred by section thirty of the Workmen's Compensation Act, 1925, on the person by whom the compensation was paid, or on any person called on to pay an indemnity under section six of that Act, to be indemnified by the third party shall be limited to a right to be indemnified in respect of such part only of the sum paid or payable by the said person as bears to the total sum so paid or payable the same proportion as the said reduced damages bear to the total damages which would have been recoverable if the workman had not been at fault.

3 Saving for Maritime Conventions Act, 1911, and past cases

(1)   This Act shall not apply to any claim to which section one of the Maritime Conventions Act, 1911, applies and that Act shall have effect as if this Act had not passed.

(2)   This Act shall not apply to any case where the acts or omissions giving rise to the claim occurred before the passing of this Act.

4 Interpretation

The following expressions have the meanings hereby respectively assigned to them, that is to say—

'court' means, in relation to any claim, the court or arbitrator by or before whom the claim falls to be determined;

'damage' includes loss of life and personal injury;

[. . .]

'employer' and 'workman' have the same meaning as in the Workmen's Compensation Act, 1925, as amended by any subsequent enactment;

'fault' means negligence, breach of statutory duty or other act or omission which gives rise to a liability in tort or would, apart from this Act, give rise to the defence of contributory negligence.

5 Application to Scotland
In the application of this Act to Scotland—

(a) the expression 'dependant' means, in relation to any person, any person who would in the event of such first mentioned person's death through the fault of a third party be entitled to sue that third party for damages or solatium; and the expression 'fault' means wrongful act, breach of statutory duty or negligent act or omission which gives rise to liability in damages, or would apart from this Act, give rise to the defence of contributory negligence;

[(b) section 3 of the Law Reform (Miscellaneous Provisions) (Scotland) Act 1940 (contribution among joint wrongdoers) shall apply in any case where two or more persons are liable, or would if they had all been sued be liable, by virtue of section 1(1) of this Act in respect of the damage suffered by any person;]

(c) [*substitutes s 1(4) above*]

6 Provisions as to Northern Ireland
(2) This Act shall not extend to Northern Ireland.

7 Short title and extent
This Act may be cited as the Law Reform (Contributory Negligence) Act, 1945.

DEFAMATION ACT 1952
(1952, c 66)

3 Actions for verbal injury
In any action for verbal injury it shall not be necessary for the pursuer to aver or prove special damage if the words on which the action is founded are calculated to cause pecuniary damage to the pursuer.

[. . .]

5 Justification
In an action for libel or slander in respect of words containing two or more distinct charges against the plaintiff, a defence of justification shall not fail by reason only that the truth of every charge is not proved if the words not proved to be true do not materially injure the plaintiff's reputation having regard to the truth of the remaining charges.

6 Fair comment
In an action for libel or slander in respect of words consisting partly of allegations of fact and partly of expression of opinion, a defence of fair comment shall not fail by reason only that the truth of every allegation or fact is not proved if the expression of opinion is fair comment having regard to such of the facts alleged or referred to in the words complained of as are proved.

[. . .]

9 Extension of certain defences to broadcasting
(1) Section three of the Parliamentary Papers Act, 1840 (which confers protection in respect of proceedings for printing extracts from or abstracts of parliamentary papers) shall have effect as if the reference to printing included a reference to broadcasting by means of wireless telegraphy.

[. . .]

10 Limitation on privilege at elections
A defamatory statement published by or on behalf of a candidate in any election to local government authority [, to the Scottish Parliament] or to Parliament shall not

be deemed to be published on a privileged occasion on the ground that it is material to a question in issue in the election, whether or not the person by whom it is published is qualified to vote at the election.

11   Agreements for indemnity
An agreement for indemnifying any person against civil liability for libel in respect of the publication of any matter shall not be unlawful unless at the time of the publication that person knows that the matter is defamatory, and does not reasonably believe that there is a good defence to any action brought upon it.

12   Evidence of other damages recovered by plaintiff
In any action for libel or slander the defendant may give evidence in mitigation of damages that the plaintiff has recovered damages, or has brought actions for damages, for libel or slander in respect of the publication of words to the same effect as the words on which the action is founded, or has received or agreed to receive compensation in respect of any such publication.

14   Application of Act to Scotland
This Act shall apply to Scotland subject to the following modifications, that is to say—
   (a)   sections one, two, eight and thirteen shall be omitted;
   (b)   for section three there shall be substituted the following section [*see s 3 above*];
   [. . .]
   (d)   for any reference to libel, or to libel or slander, there shall be substituted a reference to defamation; the expression 'plaintiff' means pursuer; the expression 'defendant' means defender; for any reference to an affidavit made by any person there shall be substituted a reference to a written declaration signed by that person; for any reference to the High Court there shall be substituted a reference to the Court of Session or, if an action of defamation is depending in the sheriff court in respect of the publication in question, the sheriff; the expression 'costs' means expenses; and for any reference to a defence of justification there shall be substituted a reference to a defence of veritas.

16   Interpretation
   (1)   Any reference in this Act to words shall be construed as including a reference to pictures, visual images, gestures and other methods of signifying meaning.

17   Proceedings affected and savings
   (2)   Nothing in this Act affects the law relating to criminal libel.

INTEREST ON DAMAGES (SCOTLAND) ACT 1958
(1958, c 61)

1   Power of courts to grant interest on damages
   [(1)   Where a court pronounces an interlocutor decerning for payment by any person of a sum of money as damages, the interlocutor may include decree for payment by that person of interest, at such rate or rates as may be specified in the interlocutor, on the whole or any part of that sum for the whole or any part of the period between the date when the right of action arose and the date of the interlocutor.
   (1A)   Where a court pronounces an interlocutor decerning for payment of a sum which consists of or includes damages or solatium in respect of personal injuries sustained by the pursuer or any other person, then (without prejudice to the exercise of the power conferred by subsection (1) of this section in relation to any part of that sum which does not represent such damages or solatium) the court shall exercise that power so as to include in that sum interest on those damages and on that solatium or on such part of each as the court considers appropriate,

unless the court is satisfied that there are reasons special to the case why no interest should be given in respect thereof.

(1B)   For the avoidance of doubt, it is hereby declared that where, in any action in which it is competent for the court to award interest under this Act, a tender is made in the course of the action, the tender shall, unless otherwise stated therein, be in full satisfaction of any claim to interest thereunder by any person in whose favour the tender is made; and in considering in any such action whether an award is equal to or greater than an amount tendered in the action, the court shall take account of the amount of any interest awarded under this Act, or such part of that interest as the court considers appropriate.]

(2)   Nothing in this section shall—

(a)   authorise the granting of interest upon interest, or

(b)   prejudice any other power of the court as to the granting of interest, or

(c)   affect the running of any interest which apart from this section would run by virtue of any enactment or rule of law.

2   Amendment of s 31 of Sheriff Courts (Scotland) Act, 1907

Section thirty-one of the Sheriff Courts (Scotland) Act, 1907 (which among other things specifies the grounds on which an interlocutor of a sheriff entering judgment under that section may be appealed to the Court of Session) shall have effect as if after head (4) thereof there were inserted the following head—

'(5) That no grant of interest on the damages (if any) has been included in the interlocutor or that any such grant so included is inadequate or is excessive.'

and as if there were added at the end of the section the words 'and upon any such appeal so far as based on the ground specified in head (5) of this section the court may make such order as to it seems just.'

3   Citation, interpretation, extent and commencement

(1)   This Act may be cited as the Interest on Damages (Scotland) Act, 1958.

[(2)   In this Act, 'personal injuries' includes any disease and any impairment of a person's physical or mental condition.]

(3)   This Act shall extend to Scotland only, and shall not apply to any action commenced against any person before the passing of this Act.

OCCUPIERS' LIABILITY (SCOTLAND) ACT 1960
(1960, c 30)

1   Variation of rules of common law as to duty of care owed by occupiers

(1)   The provisions of the next following section of this Act shall have effect, in place of the rules of the common law, for the purpose of determining the care which a person occupying or having control of land or other premises (in this Act referred to as an 'occupier of premises') is required, by reason of such occupation or control, to show towards persons entering on the premises in respect of dangers which are due to the state of the premises or to anything done or omitted to be done on them and for which he is in law responsible.

(2)   Nothing in those provisions shall be taken to alter the rules of the common law which determine the person on whom in relation to any premises a duty to show care as aforesaid towards persons entering thereon is incumbent.

(3)   Those provisions shall apply, in like manner and to the same extent as they do in relation to an occupier of premises and to persons entering thereon,—

(a)   in relation to a person occupying or having control of any fixed or moveable structure, including any vessel, vehicle or aircraft, and to persons entering thereon; and

(b)   in relation to an occupier of premises or a person occupying or having control of any such structure and to property thereon, including the property of persons who have not themselves entered on the premises or structure.

2 Extent of occupier's duty to show care

(1) The care which an occupier of premises is required, by reason of his occupation or control of the premises, to show towards a person entering thereon in respect of dangers which are due to the state of the premises or to anything done or omitted to be done on them and for which the occupier is in law responsible shall, except in so far as he is entitled to and does extend, restrict, modify or exclude by agreement his obligations towards that person, be such care as in all the circumstances of the case is reasonable to see that that person will not suffer injury or damage by reason of any such danger.

(2) Nothing in the foregoing subsection shall relieve an occupier of premises of any duty to show in any particular case any higher standard of care which in that case is incumbent on him by virtue of any enactment or rule of law imposing special standards of care on particular classes of persons.

(3) Nothing in the foregoing provisions of this Act shall be held to impose on an occupier any obligation to a person entering on his premises in respect of risks which that person has willingly accepted as his; and any question whether a risk was so accepted shall be decided on the same principles as in other cases in which one person owes to another a duty to show care.

3 Landlord's liability by virtue of responsibility for repairs

(1) Where premises are occupied or used by virtue of a tenancy under which the landlord is responsible for the maintenance or repair of the premises, it shall be the duty of the landlord to show towards any persons who or whose property may from time to time be on the premises the same care in respect of dangers arising from any failure on his part in carrying out his responsibility aforesaid as is required by virtue of the foregoing provisions of this Act to be shown by an occupier of premises towards persons entering on them.

(2) Where premises are occupied or used by virtue of a subtenancy, the foregoing subsection shall apply to any landlord who is responsible for the maintenance or repair of the premises comprised in the sub-tenancy.

(3) Nothing in this section shall relieve a landlord of any duty which he is under apart from this section.

(4) For the purposes of this section, any obligation imposed on a landlord by any enactment by reason of the premises being subject to a tenancy shall be treated as if it were an obligation imposed on him by the tenancy, 'tenancy' includes a statutory tenancy which does not in law amount to a tenancy and includes also any contract conferring a right of occupation, and 'landlord' shall be construed accordingly.

(5) This section shall apply to tenancies created before the commencement of this Act as well as to tenancies created after its commencement.

4 Application to Crown

This Act shall bind the Crown, but as regards the liability of the Crown for any wrongful or negligent act or omission giving rise to liability in reparation shall not bind the Crown any further than the Crown is made liable in respect of such acts or omissions by the Crown Proceedings Act, 1947, and that Act and in particular section two thereof shall apply in relation to duties under section two or section three of this Act as statutory duties.

5 Short title, extent and commencement

(1) This Act may be cited as the Occupiers' Liability (Scotland) Act 1960, and shall extend to Scotland only.

(2) This Act shall come into operation at the end of the period of three months beginning with the day on which it is passed.

LAW REFORM (HUSBAND AND WIFE) ACT 1962
(1962, c 48)

2   Proceedings between husband and wife in respect of delict

(1)   Subject to the provisions of this section, each of the parties to a marriage shall have the like right to bring proceedings against the other in respect of a wrongful or negligent act or omission, or for the prevention of a wrongful act, as if they were not married.

(2)   Where any such proceedings are brought by one of the parties to a marriage against the other during the subsistence of the marriage, the court may dismiss the proceedings if it appears that no substantial benefit would accrue to either party from the continuation thereof; and it shall be the duty of the court to consider at an early stage of the proceedings whether the power to dismiss the proceedings under this subsection should or should not be exercised.

(3)   This section extends to Scotland only.

HIRE-PURCHASE ACT 1964
(1964, c 53)

[PART III
TITLE TO MOTOR VEHICLES ON HIRE-PURCHASE OR CONDITIONAL SALE

27   Protection of purchasers of motor vehicles

(1)   This section applies where a motor vehicle has been bailed or (in Scotland) hired under a hire-purchase agreement, or has been agreed to be sold under a conditional sale agreement, and, before the property in the vehicle has become vested in the debtor, he disposes of the vehicle to another person.

(2)   Where the disposition referred to in subsection (1) above is to a private purchaser, and he is a purchaser of the motor vehicle in good faith without notice of the hire-purchase or conditional sale agreement (the 'relevant agreement') that disposition shall have effect as if the creditor's title to the vehicle has been vested in the debtor immediately before that disposition.

(3)   Where the person to whom the disposition referred to in subsection (1) above is made (the 'original purchaser') is a trade or finance purchaser, then if the person who is the first private purchaser of the motor vehicle after that disposition (the 'first private purchaser') is a purchaser of the vehicle in good faith without notice of the relevant agreement, the disposition of the vehicle to the first private purchaser shall have effect as if the title of the creditor to the vehicle had been vested in the debtor immediately before he disposed of it to the original purchaser.

(4)   Where, in a case within subsection (3) above—

(a)   the disposition by which the first private purchaser becomes a purchaser of the motor vehicle in good faith without notice of the relevant agreement is itself a bailment or hiring under a hire-purchase agreement, and

(b)   the person who is the creditor in relation to that agreement disposes of the vehicle to the first private purchaser, or a person claiming under him, by transferring to him the property in the vehicle in pursuance of a provision in the agreement in that behalf, the disposition referred to in paragraph (b) above (whether or not the person to whom it is made is a purchaser in good faith without notice of the relevant agreement) shall as well as the disposition referred to in paragraph (a) above, have effect as mentioned in subsection (3) above.

(5)   The preceding provisions of this section apply—

(a)   notwithstanding anything in [section 21 of the Sale of Goods Act 1979] (sale of goods by a person not the owner), but

(b)   without prejudice to the provisions of the Factors Acts (as defined by [section 61(1) of the said Act of 1979]) or any other enactment enabling the apparent owner of goods to dispose of them as if he were the true owner.

(6) Nothing in this section shall exonerate the debtor from any liability (whether criminal or civil) to which he would be subject apart from this section; and, in a case where the debtor disposes of the motor vehicle to a trade or finance purchaser, nothing in this section shall exonerate—

(a)   that trade or finance purchaser, or

(b)   any other trade or finance purchaser who becomes a purchaser of the vehicle and is not a person claiming under the first private purchaser,

from any liability (whether criminal or civil) to which he would be subject apart from this section.

28   Presumptions relating to dealings with motor vehicles

(1)   Where in any proceedings (whether criminal or civil) relating to a motor vehicle it is proved—

(a)   that the vehicle was bailed or (in Scotland) hired under a hire-purchase agreement, or was agreed to be sold under a conditional sale agreement, and

(b)   that a person (whether a party to the proceedings or not) became a private purchaser of the vehicle in good faith without notice of the hire-purchase or conditional sale agreement (the 'relevant agreement'), this section shall have effect for the purposes of the operation of section 27 of this Act in relation to those proceedings.

(2)   It shall be presumed for those purposes unless the contrary is proved, that the disposition of the vehicle to the person referred to in subsection (1)(b) above (the 'relevant purchaser') was made by the debtor.

(3)   If it is proved that that disposition was not made by the debtor, then it shall be presumed for those purposes, unless the contrary is proved—

(a)   that the debtor disposed of the vehicle to a private purchaser purchasing in good faith without notice of the relevant agreement, and

(b)   that the relevant purchaser is or was a person claiming under the person to whom the debtor so disposed of the vehicle.

(4)   If it is proved that the disposition of the vehicle to the relevant purchaser was not made by the debtor, and that the person to whom the debtor disposed of the vehicle (the 'original purchaser') was a trade or finance purchaser, then it shall be presumed for those purposes, unless the contrary is proved—

(a)   that the person who, after the disposition of the vehicle to the original purchaser, first became a private purchaser of the vehicle was a purchaser in good faith without notice of the relevant agreement, and

(b)   that the relevant purchaser is or was a person claiming under the original purchaser.

(5)   Without prejudice to any other method of proof, where in any proceedings a party thereto admits a fact, that fact shall, for the purposes of this section, be taken as against him to be proved in relation to those proceedings.

29   Interpretation of Part III

(1)   In this Part of this Act—

'conditional sale agreement' means an agreement for the sale of goods under which the purchase price or part of it is payable by instalments, and the property in the goods is to remain in the seller (notwithstanding that the buyer is to be in possession of the goods) until such conditions as to the payment of instalments or otherwise as may be specified in the agreement are fulfilled;

'creditor' means the person by whom goods are bailed or (in Scotland) hired under a hire-purchase agreement or as the case may be, the seller under a conditional sale agreement, or the person to whom his rights and duties have passed by assignment or operation of law;

'disposition' means any sale or contract of sale (including a conditional sale agreement), any bailment or (in Scotland) hiring under a hire-purchase agreement and any transfer of the property of goods in pursuance of a provision in that behalf contained in a hire-purchase agreement, and includes any transaction purporting to be a disposition (as so defined), and 'dispose of' shall be construed accordingly;

'hire-purchase agreement' means an agreement, other than a conditional sale agreement, under which—

(a)   goods are bailed or (in Scotland) hired in return for periodical payments by the person to whom they are bailed or hired, and

(b)   the property in the goods will pass to that person if the terms of the agreement are complied with and one or more of the following occurs—

(i)   the exercise of an option to purchase by that person,

(ii)   the doing of any other specified act by any party to the agreement,

(iii)   the happening of any other specified events; and

'motor vehicle' means a mechanically propelled vehicle intended or adapted for use on roads to which the public has access.

(2)   In this Part of this Act 'trade or finance purchaser' means a purchaser who, at the time of the disposition made to him, carries on a business which consists, wholly or partly—

(a)   of purchasing motor vehicles for the purpose of offering or exposing them for sale, or

(b)   of providing finance by purchasing motor vehicles for the purpose of bailing or (in Scotland) hiring them under hire-purchase agreements or agreeing to sell them under conditional sale agreements,

and 'private purchaser' means a purchaser who, at the time of the disposition made to him, does not carry on any such business.

(3)   For the purposes of this Part of this Act a person becomes a purchaser of a motor vehicle if, and at the time when, a disposition of the vehicle is made to him; and a person shall be taken to be a purchaser of a motor vehicle without notice of a hire-purchase agreement or conditional sale agreement if, at the time of the disposition made to him, he has no actual notice that the vehicle is or was the subject of any such agreement.

(4)   In this Part of this Act the 'debtor' in relation to a motor vehicle which has been bailed or hired under a hire-purchase agreement, or, as the case may be, agreed to be sold under a conditional sale agreement, means the person who at the material time (whether the agreement has before that time been terminated or not) either—

(a)   is the person to whom the vehicle is bailed or hired under that agreement, or

(b)   is, in relation to the agreement, the buyer,

including a person who at that time is, by virtue of section 130(4) of the Consumer Credit Act 1974 treated as a bailee or (in Scotland) a custodier of the vehicle.

(5)   In this Part of this Act any reference to the title of the creditor to a motor vehicle which has been bailed or (in Scotland) hired under a hire-purchase agreement or agreed to be sold under a conditional sale agreement, and is disposed of by the debtor, is a reference to such title (if any) to the vehicle as, immediately before that disposition, was vested in the person who then was the creditor in relation to the agreement.]

EMPLOYERS' LIABILITY (DEFECTIVE EQUIPMENT) ACT 1969
(1969, c 37)

1 Extension of employer's liability for defective equipment

(1)   Where after the commencement of this Act—

(a)   an employee suffers personal injury in the course of his employment in consequence of a defect in equipment provided by his employer for the purposes of the employer's business; and

(b)   the defect is attributable wholly or partly to the fault of a third party (whether identified or not), the injury shall be deemed to be also attributable to negligence on the part of the employer (whether or not he is liable in respect of the injury apart from this subsection), but without prejudice to the law relating to contributory negligence and to any remedy by way of contribution or in contract or otherwise which is available to the employer in respect of the injury.

(2) In so far as any agreement purports to exclude or limit any liability of an employer arising under subsection (1) of this section, the agreement shall be void.

(3) In this section—

'business' includes the activities carried on by any public body;

'employee' means a person who is employed by another person under a contract of service or apprenticeship and is so employed for the purposes of a business carried on by that other person, and 'employer' shall be construed accordingly;

'equipment' includes any plant and machinery, vehicle, aircraft and clothing;

'fault' means negligence, breach of statutory duty or other act or omission which gives rise to liability in tort in England and Wales or which is wrongful and gives rise to liability in damages in Scotland; and

'personal injury' includes loss of life, any impairment of a person's physical or mental condition and any disease.

(4) This section binds the Crown, and persons in the service of the Crown shall accordingly be treated for the purposes of this section as employees of the Crown if they would not be so treated apart from this subsection.

EMPLOYERS' LIABILITY (COMPULSORY INSURANCE) ACT 1969
(1969, c 57)

1 Insurance against liability for employees

(1) Except as otherwise provided by this Act, every employer [. . .] shall insure, and maintain insurance, under one or more approved policies with an authorised insurer or insurers against liability for bodily injury or disease sustained by [those of his relevant employees who are employed by him for work on or from an off-shore installation, or on or from an associated structure in the course of an activity undertaken on or in connection with an offshore installation, and arising out of and in the course of their employment for that work.]

(2) Regulations may provide that the amount for which an employer is required by this Act to insure and maintain insurance shall, either generally or in such cases or classes of case as may be prescribed by the regulations, be limited in such manner as may be so prescribed.

2 Employees to be covered

(1) For the purposes of this Act the term 'employee' means an individual who has entered into or works under a contract of service or apprenticeship with an employer whether by way of manual labour, clerical work or otherwise, whether such contract is expressed or implied, oral or in writing.

(2) This Act shall not require an employer to insure—

(a) in respect of an employee of whom the employer is the husband, wife, [civil partner,] father, mother, grandfather, grandmother, step-father, step-mother, son, daughter, grandson, granddaughter, stepson, stepdaughter, brother, sister, half-brother, half-sister.

SUPPLY OF GOODS (IMPLIED TERMS) ACT 1973
(1973, c 13)

8 Implied terms as to title

[(1) In every hire-purchase agreement, other than one to which subsection (2) below applies, there is—

(a)   an implied term on the part of the creditor that he will have a right to sell the goods at the time when the property is to pass; and

(b)   an implied term that—

(i) the goods are free, and will remain free until the time when the property is to pass, from any charge or encumbrance not disclosed or known to the person to whom the goods are bailed or (in Scotland) hired before the agreement is made, and

(ii) that person will enjoy quiet possession of the goods except so far as it may be disturbed by any person entitled to the benefit of any charge or encumbrance so disclosed or known.

(2)   In a hire-purchase agreement, in the case of which there appears from the agreement or is to be inferred from the circumstances of the agreement an intention that the creditor should transfer only such title as he or a third person may have, there is—

(a)   an implied term that all charges or encumbrances known to the creditor and not known to the person to whom the goods are bailed or hired have been disclosed to that person before the agreement is made; and

(b)   an implied term that neither—

(i) the creditor; nor

(ii) in a case where the parties to the agreement intend that any title which may be transferred shall be only such title as a third person may have, that person; nor

(iii) anyone claiming through or under the creditor or that third person not otherwise than under a charge or encumbrance disclosed or known to the person to whom the goods are bailed or hired, before the agreement is made;

will disturb the quiet possession of the person to whom the goods are bailed or hired.

(3)   As regards England and Wales and Northern Ireland, the term implied by subsection (1)(a) above is a condition and the terms implied by subsections (1)(b), (2)(a) and (2)(b) above are warranties.]

9 Bailing or hiring by description

[(1)   Where under a hire-purchase agreement goods are bailed or (in Scotland) hired by description, there is an implied term that the goods will correspond with the description, and if under the agreement the goods are bailed or hired by reference to a sample as well as a description, it is not sufficient that the bulk of the goods corresponds with the sample if the goods do not also correspond with the description.

(1A)   As regards England and Wales and Northern Ireland, the term implied by subsection (1) above is a condition.

(2)   Goods shall not be prevented from being bailed or hired by description by reason only that, being exposed for sale, bailment or hire, they are selected by the person to whom they are bailed or hired.]

10 Implied undertakings as to quality or fitness

[(1)   Except as provided by this section and section 11 below and subject to the provisions of any other enactment, including any enactment of the Parliament of Northern Ireland or the Northern Ireland Assembly, there is no implied term as to the quality or fitness for any particular purpose of goods bailed or (in Scotland) hired under a hire-purchase agreement.

(2)   Where the creditor bails or hires goods under a hire-purchase agreement in the course of a business, there is an implied term that the goods supplied under the agreement are of satisfactory quality.

(2A)   For the purposes of this Act, goods are of satisfactory quality if they meet the standard that a reasonable person would regard as satisfactory, taking account of any description of the goods, the price (if relevant) and all the other relevant circumstances.

(2B)   For the purposes of this Act, the quality of goods includes their state and condition and the following (among others) are in appropriate cases aspects of the quality of goods—

(a)   fitness for all the purposes for which goods of the kind in question are commonly supplied,

(b)   appearance and finish,

(c)   freedom from minor defects,

(d)   safety, and

(e)   durability.

(2C)   The term implied by subsection (2) above does not extend to any matter making the quality of goods unsatisfactory—

(a)   which is specifically drawn to the attention of the person to whom the goods are bailed or hired before the agreement is made,

(b)   where that person examines the goods before the agreement is made, which that examination ought to reveal, or

(c)   where the goods are bailed or hired by reference to a sample, which would have been apparent on a reasonable examination of the sample.

[(2D)   If the person to whom the goods are bailed or hired deals as consumer or, in Scotland, if the goods are hired to a person under a consumer contract, the relevant circumstances mentioned in subsection (2A) above include any public statements on the specific characteristics of the goods made about them by the creditor, the producer or his representative, particularly in advertising or on labelling.

(2E)   A public statement is not by virtue of subsection (2D) above a relevant circumstance for the purposes of subsection (2A) above in the case of a contract of hire-purchase, if the creditor shows that—

(a)   at the time the contract was made, he was not, and could not reasonably have been, aware of the statement,

(b)   before the contract was made, the statement had been withdrawn in public or, to the extent that it contained anything which was incorrect or misleading, it had been corrected in public, or

(c)   the decision to acquire the goods could not have been influenced by the statement.

(2F)   Subsections (2D) and (2E) above do not prevent any public statement from being a relevant circumstance for the purposes of subsection (2A) above (whether or not the person to whom the goods are bailed or hired deals as consumer or, in Scotland, whether or not the goods are hired to a person under a consumer contract) if the statement would have been such a circumstance apart from those subsections.]

(3)   Where the creditor bails or hires goods under a hire-purchase agreement in the course of a business and the person to whom the goods are bailed or hired, expressly or by implication, makes known—

(a)   to the creditor in the course of negotiations conducted by the creditor in relation to the making of the hire-purchase agreement, or

(b)   to a credit-broker in the course of negotiations conducted by that broker in relation to goods sold by him to the creditor before forming the subject matter of the hire-purchase agreement,

any particular purpose for which the goods are being bailed or hired, there is an implied term that the goods supplied under the agreement are reasonably fit for that purpose, whether or not that is a purpose for which such goods are commonly supplied, except where the circumstances show that the person to whom the goods are bailed or hired does not rely, or that it is unreasonable for him to rely, on the skill or judgment of the creditor or credit-broker.

(4)   An implied term as to quality or fitness for a particular purpose may be annexed to a hire-purchase agreement by usage.

(5)   The preceding provisions of this section apply to a hire-purchase agreement made by a person who in the course of a business is acting as agent for the

creditor as they apply to an agreement made by the creditor in the course of a business, except where the creditor is not bailing or hiring in the course of a business and either the person to whom the goods are bailed or hired knows that fact or reasonable steps are taken to bring it to the notice of that person before the agreement is made.

(6) In subsection (3) above and this subsection—

(a) 'credit-broker' means a person acting in the course of a business of credit brokerage;

(b) 'credit brokerage' means the effecting of introductions of individuals desiring to obtain credit—

(i) to persons carrying on any business so far as it relates to the provision of credit, or

(ii) to other persons engaged in credit brokerage.

(7) As regards England and Wales and Northern Ireland, the terms implied by subsections (2) and (3) above are conditions.

[(8) In Scotland, 'consumer contract' in this section has the same meaning as in section 12A(3) below.]

11 Samples

[(1) Where under a hire-purchase agreement goods are bailed or (in Scotland) hired by reference to a sample, there is an implied term—

(a) that the bulk will correspond with the sample in quality; and

(b) that the person to whom the goods are bailed or hired will have a reasonable opportunity of comparing the bulk with the sample; and

(c) that the goods will be free from any defect, making their quality unsatisfactory, which would not be apparent on reasonable examination of the sample.

(2) As regards England and Wales and Northern Ireland, the term implied by subsection (1) above is a condition.]

[12 Exclusion of implied terms

An express term does not negative a term implied by this Act unless inconsistent with it.]

[12A Remedies for breach of hire-purchase agreement as respects Scotland

(1) Where in a hire-purchase agreement the creditor is in breach of any term of the agreement (express or implied), the person to whom the goods are hired shall be entitled—

(a) to claim damages, and

(b) if the breach is material, to reject any goods delivered under the agreement and treat it as repudiated.

(2) Where a hire-purchase agreement is a consumer contract, then, for the purposes of subsection (1) above, breach by the creditor of any term (express or implied)—

(a) as to the quality of the goods or their fitness for a purpose,

(b) if the goods are, or are to be, hired by description, that the goods will correspond with the description,

(c) if the goods are, or are to be, hired by reference to a sample, that the bulk will correspond with the sample in quality,

shall be deemed to be a material breach.

(3) In subsection (2) above 'consumer contract' has the same meaning as in section 25(1) of the Unfair Contract Terms Act 1977; and for the purposes of that subsection the onus of proving that a hire-purchase agreement is not to be regarded as a consumer contract shall lie on the creditor.

(4) This section applies to Scotland only.]

[. . .]

14　Special provisions as to conditional sale agreements

[(1)　Section 11(4) of the Sale of Goods Act 1979 (whereby in certain circumstances a breach of a condition in a contract of sale is treated only as a breach of warranty) shall not apply to [a conditional sale agreement] where the buyer deals as consumer within Part I of the Unfair Contract Terms Act 1977 or, in Scotland, the agreement is a consumer contract within Part II of that Act.]

15　Supplementary

[(1)　In sections 8 to 14 above and this section—

'business' includes a profession and the activities of any government department (including a Northern Ireland department), [or local or public authority];

'buyer' and 'seller' includes a person to whom rights and duties under a conditional sale agreement have passed by assignment or operation of law;

'conditional sale agreement' means an agreement for the sale of goods under which the purchase price or part of it is payable by instalments, and the property in the goods is to remain in the seller (notwithstanding that the buyer is to be in possession of the goods) until such conditions as to the payment of instalments or otherwise as may be specified in the agreement are fulfilled;

['consumer sale' has the same meaning as in section 55 of the Sale of Goods Act 1979 (as set out in paragraph 11 of Schedule 1 to that Act)];

'creditor' means the person by whom the goods are bailed or (in Scotland) hired under a hire-purchase agreement or the person to whom his rights and duties under the agreement have passed by assignment or operation of law; and

'hire-purchase agreement' means an agreement, other than conditional sale agreement, under which—

(a)　goods are bailed or (in Scotland) hired in return for periodical payments by the person to whom they are bailed or hired, and

(b)　the property in the goods will pass to that person if the terms of the agreement are complied with and one or more of the following occurs—

(i)　the exercise of an option to purchase by that person,

(ii)　the doing of any other specified act by any party to the agreement,

(iii)　the happening of any other specified event.

['producer' means the manufacturer of goods, the importer of goods into the European Economic Area or any person purporting to be a producer by placing his name, trade mark or other distinctive sign on the goods;]

(3)　In section 14(2) above 'corresponding hire-purchase agreement' means, in relation to a conditional sale agreement, a hire-purchase agreement relating to the same goods as the conditional sale agreement and made between the same parties and at the same time and in the same circumstances and, as nearly as may be, in the same terms as the conditional sale agreement.

(4)　Nothing in sections 8 to 13 above shall prejudice the operation of any other enactment including any enactment of the Parliament of Northern Ireland or the Northern Ireland Assembly or any rule of law whereby any term, other than one relating to quality or fitness, is to be implied in any hire-purchase agreement.]

PRESCRIPTION AND LIMITATION (SCOTLAND) ACT 1973
(1973 c 52)

PART I
PRESCRIPTION

Positive prescription

[1　Validity of right

(1)　If land has been possessed by any person, or by any person and his successors, for a continuous period of ten years openly, peaceably and without any judicial interruption and the possession was founded on, and followed—

    (a)   the recording of a deed which is sufficient in respect of its terms to constitute in favour of that person a real right in—

        (i)   that land; or

        (ii) land of a description *habile* to include that land; or

    (b)   registration of a real right in that land, in favour of that person, in the Land Register of Scotland, subject to an exclusion of indemnity under section 12(2) of the Land Registration (Scotland) Act 1979 (c 33),

then, as from the expiry of that period, the real right so far as relating to that land shall be exempt from challenge.

    (2)   Subsection (1) above shall not apply where—

    (a)   possession was founded on the recording of a deed which is invalid *ex facie* or was forged; or

    (b)   possession was founded on registration in the Land Register of Scotland proceeding on a forged deed and the person appearing from the Register to have the real right in question was aware of the forgery at the time of registration in his favour.

    (3)   In subsection (1) above, the reference to a real right is to a real right which is registrable in the Land Register of Scotland or a deed relating to which can competently be recorded; but this section does not apply to [real burdens,] servitudes or public rights of way.

    (4)   In the computation of a prescriptive period for the purposes of this section in a case where the deed in question is a decree of adjudication for debt, any period before the expiry of the legal shall be disregarded.

    (5)   Where, in any question involving any foreshore or any salmon fishings, this section is pled against the Crown as owner of the regalia, subsection (1) above shall have effect as if for the words 'ten years' there were substituted 'twenty years'.

    (6)   This section is without prejudice to section 2 of this Act.]

[2 Special cases

    (1)   If—

    (a)   land has been possessed by any person, or by any person and his successors, for a continuous period of twenty years openly, peaceably and without any judicial interruption; and

    (b)   the possession was founded on, and followed the execution of, a deed (whether recorded or not) which is sufficient in respect of its terms to constitute in favour of that person a real right in that land, or in land of a description *habile* to include that land, then, as from the expiry of that period, the real right so far as relating to that land shall be exempt from challenge except on the ground that the deed is invalid *ex facie* or was forged.

    (2)   This section applies—

    (a)   to the real right of the lessee under a lease; and

    (b)   to any other real right in land, being a real right of a kind which, under the law in force immediately before the commencement of this Part of this Act, was sufficient to form a foundation for positive prescription without the deed constituting the title to the real right having been recorded,

but does not apply to servitudes or public rights of way.

    (3)   This section is without prejudice to section 1 of this Act or to section 3(3) of the Land Registration (Scotland) Act 1979 (c 33).]

3 Positive servitudes and public rights of way

    (1)   If in the case of a positive servitude over land—

    (a)   the servitude has been possessed for a continuous period of twenty years openly, peaceably and without any judicial interruption, and

    (b)   the possession was founded on, and followed the execution of, a deed

which is sufficient in respect of its terms (whether expressly or by implication)
to constitute the servitude,

then, as from the expiration of the said period, the validity of the servitude as so
constituted shall be exempt from challenge except on the ground that the deed is
invalid *ex facie* or was forged.

(2) If a positive servitude over land has been possessed for a continuous period
of twenty years openly, peaceably and without judicial interruption, then, as from
the expiration of that period, the existence of the servitude as so possessed shall be
exempt from challenge.

(3) If a public right of way over land has been possessed by the public for a
continuous period of twenty years openly, peaceably and without judicial interruption, then, as from the expiration of that period, the existence of the right of
way as so possessed shall be exempt from challenge.

(4) References in subsections (1) and (2) of this section to possession of a servitude are references to possession of the servitude by any person in possession of
the relative dominant tenement.

(5) This section is without prejudice to the operation of section 7 of this Act.

4 Judicial interruption of periods of possession for purposes of sections 1, 2 and 3

(1) In sections 1, 2 and 3 of this Act references to a judicial interruption, in relation to possession, are references to the making in appropriate proceedings, by
any person having a proper interest to do so, of a claim which challenges the
possession in question.

(2) In this section 'appropriate proceedings' means—

(a) any proceedings in a court of competent jurisdiction in Scotland or elsewhere, except proceedings in the Court of Session initiated by a summons which
is not subsequently called;

(b) any arbitration in Scotland;

(c) any arbitration in a country other than Scotland, being an arbitration an
award in which would be enforceable in Scotland.

(3) The date of a judicial interruption shall be taken to be—

(a) where the claim has been made in an arbitration and the nature of the
claim has been stated in a preliminary notice relating to that arbitration, the date
when the preliminary notice was served;

(b) in any other case, the date when the claim was made.

(4) In the foregoing subsection 'preliminary notice' in relation to an arbitration
means a notice served by one party to the arbitration on the other party or parties
requiring him or them to appoint an arbiter or to agree to the appointment of an
arbiter, or, where the arbitration agreement or any relevant enactment provides
that the reference shall be to a person therein named or designated, a notice requiring him or them to submit the dispute to the person so named or designated.

5 Further provisions supplementary to sections 1, 2 and 3

(1) In sections 1, 2 and 3 of this Act 'deed' includes a judicial decree; and for
the purposes of the said sections any of the following, namely an instrument of
sasine, a notarial instrument and a notice of title, which narrates or declares that a
person has a [right in land shall be treated as a deed sufficient to constitute that
right].

[. . .]

Negative prescription

6 Extinction of obligations by prescriptive periods of five years

(1) If, after the appropriate date, an obligation to which this section applies has
subsisted for a continuous period of five years—

(a)   without any relevant claim having been made in relation to the obligation, and

(b)   without the subsistence of the obligation having been relevantly acknowledged,

then as from the expiration of that period the obligation shall be extinguished:

Provided that in its application to an obligation under a bill of exchange or a promissory note this subsection shall have effect as if paragraph (b) thereof were omitted.

(2)   Schedule 1 to this Act shall have effect for defining the obligations to which this section applies.

(3)   In subsection (1) above the reference to the appropriate date, in relation to an obligation of any kind specified in Schedule 2 to this Act is a reference to the date specified in that Schedule in relation to obligations of that kind, and in relation to an obligation of any other kind is a reference to the date when the obligation became enforceable.

(4)   In the computation of a prescriptive period in relation to any obligation for the purposes of this section—

(a)   any period during which by reason of—

(i)   fraud on the part of the debtor or any person acting on his behalf, or

(ii)   error induced by words or conduct of the debtor or any person acting on his behalf,

the creditor was induced to refrain from making a relevant claim in relation to the obligation, and

(b)   any period during which the original creditor (while he is the creditor) was under legal disability,

shall not be reckoned as, or as part of, the prescriptive period:

Provided that any period such as is mentioned in paragraph (a) of this subsection shall not include any time occurring after the creditor could with reasonable diligence have discovered the fraud or error, as the case may be, referred to in that paragraph.

(5)   Any period such as is mentioned in paragraph (a) or (b) of subsection (4) of this section shall not be regarded as separating the time immediately before it from the time immediately after it.

7   Extinction of obligations by prescriptive periods of twenty years

(1)   If, after the date when any obligation to which this section applies has become enforceable, the obligation has subsisted for a continuous period of twenty years—

(a)   without any relevant claim having been made in relation to the obligation, and

(b)   without the subsistence of the obligation having been relevantly acknowledged,

then as from the expiration of that period the obligation shall be extinguished:

Provided that in its application to an obligation under a bill of exchange or a promissory note this subsection shall have effect as if paragraph (b) thereof were omitted.

(2)   This section applies to an obligation of any kind (including an obligation to which section 6 of this Act applies), not being an obligation [to which section 22A of this Act applies or an obligation] specified in Schedule 3 to this Act as an imprescriptible obligation [or an obligation to make reparation in respect of personal injuries within the meaning of Part II of this Act or in respect of the death of any person as a result of such injuries.]

8   Extinction of other rights relating to property by prescriptive periods of twenty years

(1)   If, after the date when any right to which this section applies has become exercisable or enforceable, the right has subsisted for a continuous period of

twenty years unexercised by or unenforced, and without any relevant claim in relation to it having been made, then as from the expiration of that period the right shall be extinguished.

(2)   This section applies to any right relating to property, whether heritable or moveable, not being a right specified in Schedule 3 to this Act as an imprescriptible right or falling within section 6 or 7 of this Act as being a right correlative to an obligation to which either of those sections applies.

[8A   Extinction of obligations to make contribution between wrongdoers

(1)   If any obligation to make a contribution by virtue of section 3(2) of the Law Reform (Miscellaneous Provisions) (Scotland) Act 1940 in respect of any damages or expenses has subsisted for a continuous period of 2 years after the date on which the right to recover the contribution became enforceable by the creditor in the obligation—

(a)   without any relevant claim having been made in relation to the obligation; and

(b)   without the subsistence of the obligation having been relevantly acknowledged;

then as from the expiration of that period the obligation shall be extinguished.

(2)   Subsections (4) and (5) of section 6 of this Act shall apply for the purposes of this section as they apply for the purposes of that section.]

9   Definition of 'relevant claim' for purposes of sections 6, 7 and 8

(1)   In sections 6 [, 7 and 8A] of this Act the expression 'relevant claim', in relation to an obligation, means a claim made by or on behalf of the creditor for implement or part-implement of the obligation, being a claim made—

(a)   in appropriate proceedings, or

[(b)   by the presentation of, or the concurring in, a petition for sequestration or by the submission of a claim under section 22 or 48 of the Bankruptcy (Scotland) Act 1985 [. . .]; or

(c)   by a creditor to the trustee acting under a trust deed as defined in section 5(2)(c) of the Bankruptcy (Scotland) Act 1985; or

(d)   by the presentation of, or the concurring in, a petition for the winding up of a company or by the submission of a claim in a liquidation in accordance with rules made under section 411 of the Insolvency Act 1986;]

and for the purposes of the said sections 6 [, 7 and 8A] the execution by or on behalf of the creditor in an obligation of any form of diligence directed to the enforcement of the obligation shall be deemed to be a relevant claim in relation to the obligation.

(2)   In section 8 of this Act the expression 'relevant claim', in relation to a right, means a claim made in appropriate proceedings by or on behalf of the creditor to establish the right or to contest any claim to a right inconsistent therewith.

(3)   Where a claim which, in accordance with the foregoing provisions of this section, is a relevant claim for the purposes of section 6, 7[, 8 or 8A] of this Act is made in an arbitration, and the nature of the claim has been stated in a preliminary notice relating to that arbitration, the date when the notice was served shall be taken for those purposes to be the date of the making of the claim.

(4)   In this section the expression 'appropriate proceedings' and, in relation to an arbitration, the expression 'preliminary notice' have the same meanings as in section 4 of this Act.

10   Relevant acknowledgement for purposes of sections 6 and 7

(1)   The subsistence of an obligation shall be regarded for the purposes of sections 6 [, 7 and 8A] of this Act as having been relevantly acknowledged if, and only if, either of the following conditions is satisfied, namely—

(a)   that there has been such performance by or on behalf of the debtor towards implement of the obligation as clearly indicates that the obligation still subsists;

(b)   that there has been made by or on behalf of the debtor to the creditor or his agent an unequivocal written admission clearly acknowledging that the obligation still subsists.

(2)   Subject to subsection (3) below, where two or more persons are bound jointly by an obligation so that each is liable for the whole, and the subsistence of the obligation has been relevantly acknowledged by or on behalf of one of those persons then—

(a)   if the acknowledgment is made in the manner specified in paragraph (a) of the foregoing subsection it shall have effect for the purposes of the said sections 6 [, 7 and 8A] as respects the liability of each of those persons, and

(b)   if it is made in the manner specified in paragraph (b) of that subsection it shall have effect for those purposes only as respects the liability of the person who makes it.

(3)   Where the subsistence of an obligation affecting a trust has been relevantly acknowledged by or on behalf of one two or more co-trustees in the manner specified in paragraph (a) or (b) of subsection (1) of this section, the acknowledgment shall have effect for the purposes of the said sections 6 [, 7 and 8A] as respects the liability of the trust estate and any liability of each of the trustees.

(4)   In this section references to performance in relation to an obligation include, where the nature of the obligation so requires, references to refraining from doing something and to permitting or suffering something to be done or maintained.

11   Obligations to make reparation

(1)   Subject to subsections (2) and (3) below, any obligation (whether arising from any enactment, or from any rule of law or from, or by reason of any breach of, a contract or promise) to make reparation for loss, injury or damage caused by an act, neglect or default shall be regarded for the purposes of section 6 of this Act as having become enforceable on the date when the loss, injury or damage occurred.

(2)   Where as a result of a continuing act, neglect or default loss, injury or damage has occurred before the cessation of the act, neglect or default the loss, injury or damage shall be deemed for the purposes of subsection (1) above to have occurred on the date when the act, neglect or default ceased.

(3)   In relation to a case where on the date referred to in subsection (1) above (or, as the case may be, that subsection as modified by subsection (2) above) the creditor was not aware, and could not with reasonable diligence have been aware, that loss, injury or damage caused as aforesaid had occurred, the said subsection (1) shall have effect as if for the reference therein to that date there were substituted a reference to the date when the creditor first became, or could with reasonable diligence have become, so aware.

(4)   Subsections (1) and (2) above (with the omission of any reference therein to subsection (3) above) shall have effect for the purposes of section 7 of this Act as they have effect for the purposes of section 6 of this Act.

12   Savings

(1)   Where by virtue of any enactment passed or made before the passing of this Act a claim to establish a right or enforce implement of an obligation may be made only within a period of limitation specified in or determined under the enactment, and, by the expiration of a prescriptive period determined under section 6, 7 or 8 of this Act the right or obligation would, apart from this subsection, be extinguished before the expiration of the period of limitation, the said section shall have effect as if the relevant prescriptive period were extended so that it expires—

(a)   on the date when the period of limitation expires, or

(b) if on that date any such claim made within that period has not been finally disposed of, on the date when the claim is so disposed of.

(2) Nothing in section 6, 7 or 8 of this Act shall be construed so as to exempt any deed from challenge at any time on the ground that it is invalid *ex facie* or was forged.

13 Prohibition of contracting out

Any provision in any agreement purporting to provide in relation to any right or obligation that section 6, 7 [, 8 or 8A] of this Act shall not have effect shall be null.

General

14 Computation of prescriptive periods

(1) In the computation of a prescriptive period for the purposes of any provision of this Part of this Act—

(a) time occurring before the commencement of this Part of this Act shall be reckonable towards the prescriptive period in like manner as time occurring thereafter, but subject to the restriction that any time reckoned under this paragraph shall be less than the prescriptive period;

(b) any time during which any person against whom the provision is pled was under legal disability shall (except so far as otherwise provided by [subsection (4) of section 6 of this Act including that subsection as applied by section 8A of this Act] be reckoned as if the person were free from that disability;

(c) if the commencement of the prescriptive period would, apart from this paragraph, fall at a time in any day other than the beginning of the day, the period shall be deemed to have commenced at the beginning of the next following day;

(d) if the last day of the prescriptive period would, apart from this paragraph, be a holiday, the period shall, notwithstanding anything in the said provision, be extended to include any immediately succeeding day which is a holiday, any further immediately succeeding days which are holidays, and the next succeeding day which is not a holiday;

(e) save as otherwise provided in this Part of this Act regard shall be had to the like principles as immediately before the commencement of this Part of this Act were applicable to the computation of periods of prescription for the purposes of the Prescription Act 1617.

(2) In this section 'holiday' means a day of any of the following descriptions, namely, a Saturday, a Sunday and a day which, in Scotland, is a bank holiday under the Banking and Financial Dealings Act 1971.

15 Interpretation of Part I

(1) In this Part of this Act, unless the context otherwise requires, the following expressions have the meanings hereby assigned to them, namely—

'bill of exchange' has the same meaning as it has for the purposes of the Bills of Exchange Act 1882;

'date of execution', in relation to a deed executed on several dates, means the last of those dates;

'enactment' includes an order, regulation, rule or other instrument having effect by virtue of an Act;

'holiday' has the meaning assigned to it by section 14 of this Act;

'land' includes heritable property of any description;

'lease' includes a sub-lease;

'legal disability' means legal disability by reason of nonage or unsoundness of mind;

'possession' includes civil possession, and 'possessed' shall be construed accordingly;

'prescriptive period' means a period required for the operation of section 1, 2, 3, 6, 7 [, 8 or 8A] of this Act;

'promissory note' has the same meaning as it has for the purposes of the Bills of Exchange Act 1882;

'trustee' includes any person holding property in fiduciary capacity for another and, without prejudice to that generality, includes a trustee within the meaning of the Trusts (Scotland) Act 1921; and 'trust' shall be construed accordingly;

and references to the recording of a deed are references to the recording thereof in the General Register of Sasines.

(2)   In this Part of this Act, unless the context otherwise requires, any reference to an obligation or to a right includes a reference to the right or, as the case may be, to the obligation (if any), correlative thereto.

(3)   In this Part of this Act any reference to an enactment shall, unless the context otherwise requires, be construed as a reference to that enactment as amended or extended, and as including a reference thereto as applied, by or under any other enactment.

16   Amendments and repeals related to Part I

(1)   The enactment specified in Part I of Schedule 4 to this Act shall have effect subject to the amendment there specified, being an amendment related to this Part of this Act.

(2)   Subject to the next following subsection, the enactments specified in Part I of Schedule 5 to this Act (which includes certain enactments relating to the limitation of proof) are hereby repealed to the extent specified in column 3 of that Schedule.

(3)   Where by virtue of any Act repealed by this section the subsistence of an obligation in force at the date of the commencement of this Part of this Act was immediately before that date, by reason of the passage of time, provable only by the writ or oath of the debtor the subsistence of the obligation shall [(notwithstanding anything in sections 16(1) and 17(2)(a) of the Interpretation Act 1978, which relates to the effect of repeals)] as from that date be provable as if the said repealed Act had not passed.

PART II
LIMITATION OF ACTIONS

[17   Actions in respect of personal injuries not resulting in death

(1)   This section applies to an action of damages where the damages claimed consist of or include damages in respect of personal injuries, being an action (other than an action to which section 18 of this Act applies) brought by the person who sustained the injuries or any other person.

(2)   Subject to subsection (3) below and section 19A of this Act, no action to which this section applies shall be brought unless it is commenced within a period of 3 years after—

(a)   the date on which the injuries were sustained or, where the act or omission to which the injuries were attributable was a continuing one, that date or the date on which the act or omission ceased, whichever is the later; or

(b)   the date (if later than any date mentioned in paragraph (a) above) on which the pursuer in the action became, or on which, in the opinion of the court, it would have been reasonably practicable for him in all the circumstances to become, aware of all the following facts—

(i)   that the injuries in question were sufficiently serious to justify his bringing an action of damages on the assumption that the person against whom the action was brought did not dispute liability and was able to satisfy a decree;

(ii)   that the injuries were attributable in whole or in part to an act or omission; and

(iii)   that the defender was a person to whose act or omission the injuries were attributable in whole or in part or the employer or principal of such a person.

(3)   In the computation of the period specified in subsection (2) above there shall be disregarded any time during which the person who sustained the injuries was under legal disability by reason of nonage or unsoundness of mind.

18   Actions where death has resulted from personal injuries

(1)   This section applies to any action in which, following the death of any person from personal injuries, damages are claimed in respect of the injuries or the death.

(2)   Subject to subsections (3) and (4) below and section 19A of this Act, no action to which this section applies shall be brought unless it is commenced within a period of 3 years after—

(a)   the date of death of the deceased; or

(b)   the date (if later than the date of death) on which the pursuer in the action became, or on which, in the opinion of the court, it would have been reasonably practicable for him in all the circumstances to become, aware of both of the following facts—

(i)   that the injuries of the deceased were attributable in whole or in part to an act or omission; and

(ii)   that the defender was a person to whose act or omission the injuries were attributable in whole or in part or the employer or principal of such a person.

(3)   Where the pursuer is a relative of the deceased, there shall be disregarded in the computation of the period specified in subsection (2) above any time during which the relative was under legal disability by reason of nonage or unsoundness of mind.

(4)   Subject to section 19A of this Act, where an action of damages has not been brought by or on behalf of a person who has sustained personal injuries within the period specified in section 17(2) of this Act and that person subsequently dies in consequence of those injuries, no action to which this section applies shall be brought in respect of those injuries or the death from those injuries.

(5)   In this section 'relative' has the same meaning as in Schedule 1 to the Damages (Scotland) Act 1976.

[18A   Limitation of defamation and other actions

(1)   Subject to subsections (2) and (3) below and section 19A of this Act, no action for defamation shall be brought unless it is commenced within a period of 3 years after the date when the right of action accrued.

(2)   In the computation of the period specified in subsection (1) above there shall be disregarded any time during which the person alleged to have been defamed was under legal disability by reason of nonage or unsoundness of mind.

(3)   Nothing in this section shall affect any right of action which accrued before the commencement of this section.

(4)   In this section—

(a)   'defamation' includes *convicium* and malicious falsehood, and 'defamed' shall be construed accordingly; and

(b)   references to the date when a right of action accrued shall be construed as references to the date when the publication or communication in respect of which the action for defamation is to be brought first came to the notice of the pursuer.

18B   Actions of harassment

(1)   This section applies to actions of harassment (within the meaning of section 8 of the Protection from Harassment Act 1997) which include a claim for damages.

(2)   Subject to subsection (3) below and to section 19A of this Act, no action to

which this section applies shall be brought unless it is commenced within a period of 3 years after—

(a)   the date on which the alleged harassment ceased; or

(b)   the date (if later than the date mentioned in paragraph (a) above) on which the pursuer in the action became, or on which, in the opinion of the court, it would have been reasonably practicable for him in all the circumstances to have become, aware, that the defender was a person responsible for the alleged harassment or the employer or principal of such a person.

(3)   In the computation of the period specified in subsection (2) above there shall be disregarded any time during which the person who is alleged to have suffered the harassment was under legal disability by reason of nonage or unsoundness of mind.]

[. . .]

[19A   Power of court to override time-limits etc

(1)   Where a person would be entitled, but for any of the provisions of sections 17, [18, 18A or 18B] of this Act, to bring an action, the court may, if it seems to it equitable to do so, allow him to bring the action notwithstanding that provision.

(2)   The provisions of subsection (1) above shall have effect not only as regards rights of action accruing after the commencement of this section but also as regards those, in respect of which a final judgment has not been pronounced, accruing before such commencement.

(3)   In subsection (2) above, the expression 'final judgment' means an interlocutor of a court of first instance which, by itself, or taken along with previous interlocutors, disposes of the subject matter of a cause notwithstanding that judgment may not have been pronounced on every question raised or that the expenses found due may not have been modified, taxed or decerned for; but the expression does not include an interlocutor dismissing a cause by reason only of a provision mentioned in subsection (1) above.

(4)   An action which would not be entertained but for this section shall not be tried by jury.]

[. . .]

[22   Interpretation of Part II and supplementary provisions

(1)   In this Part of this Act—

'the court' means the Court of Session or the sheriff court; and

'personal injuries' includes any disease and any impairment of a person's physical or mental condition.

(2)   Where the pursuer in an action to which section 17, 18 [or 18A] of this Act applies is pursuing the action by virtue of the assignation of a right of action, the reference in subsection (2)(b) of the said section 17 or, [of the said section, or, as the case may be, subsection (4)(b) of the said section 18A] to the pursuer in the action shall be construed as a reference to the assignor of the right of action.

(3)   For the purposes of the said subsection (2)(b) knowledge that any act or omission was or was not, as a matter of law, actionable, is irrelevant.

(4)   An action which would not be entertained but for the said subsection (2)(b) shall not be tried by jury.]

[PART IIA

PRESCRIPTION OF OBLIGATIONS AND LIMITATION OF ACTIONS UNDER PART I OF THE CONSUMER PROTECTION ACT 1987

Prescription of obligations

[22A   Ten years' prescription of obligations

(1)   An obligation arising from liability under section 2 of the 1987 Act (to make

reparation for damage caused wholly or partly by a defect in a product) shall be extinguished if a period of 10 years has expired from the relevant time, unless a relevant claim was made within that period and has not been finally disposed of, and no such obligation shall come into existence after the expiration of the said period.

(2) If, at the expiration of the period of 10 years mentioned in subsection (1) above, a relevant claim has been made but has not been finally disposed of, the obligation to which the claim relates shall be extinguished when the claim is finally disposed of.

(3) In this section a claim is finally disposed of when—

(a) a decision disposing of the claim has been made against which no appeal is competent;

(b) an appeal against such a decision is competent with leave, and the time limit for leave has expired and no application has been made or leave has been refused;

(c) leave to appeal against such a decision is granted or is not required, and no appeal is made within the time limit for appeal; or

(d) the claim is abandoned;

'relevant claim' in relation to an obligation means a claim made by or on behalf of the creditor for implement or part implement of the obligation, being a claim made—

(a) in appropriate proceedings within the meaning of section 4(2) of this Act; or

(b) by the presentation of, or the concurring in, a petition for sequestration or by the submission of a claim under section 22 or 48 of the Bankruptcy (Scotland) Act 1985; or

(c) by the presentation of, or the concurring in, a petition for the winding up of a company or by the submission of a claim in a liquidation in accordance with the rules made under section 411 of the Insolvency Act 1986;

'relevant time' has the meaning given in section 4(2) of the 1987 Act.

(4) Where a relevant claim is made in an arbitration, and the nature of the claim has been stated in a preliminary notice (within the meaning of section 4(4) of this Act) relating to that arbitration, the date when the notice is served shall be taken for those purposes to be the date of the making of the claim.]

Limitation of actions

[22B   3 year limitation of actions

(1) This section shall apply to an action to enforce an obligation arising from liability under section 2 of the 1987 Act (to make reparation for damage caused wholly or partly by a defect in a product), except where section 22C of this Act applies.

(2) Subject to subsection (4) below, an action to which this section applies shall not be competent unless it is commenced within the period of 3 years after the earliest date on which the person seeking to bring (or a person who could at an earlier date have brought) the action was aware, or on which, in the opinion of the court, it was reasonably practicable for him in all the circumstances to become aware, of all the facts mentioned in subsection (3) below.

(3) The facts referred to in subsection (2) above are—

(a) that there was a defect in a product;

(b) that the damage was caused or partly caused by the defect;

(c) that the damage was sufficiently serious to justify the pursuer (or other person referred to in subsection (2) above) in bringing an action to which this section applies on the assumption that the defender did not dispute liability and was able to satisfy a decree;

(d) that the defender was a person liable for the damage under the said section 2.

(4) In the computation of the period of 3 years mentioned in subsection (2) above, there shall be disregarded any period during which the person seeking to bring the action was under legal disability by reason of nonage or unsoundness of mind.

(5) The facts mentioned in subsection (3) above do not include knowledge of whether particular facts and circumstances would or would not, as a matter of law, result in liability for damage under the said section 2.

(6) Where a person would be entitled, but for this section, to bring an action for reparation other than one in which the damages claimed are confined to damages for loss of or damage to property, the court may, if it seems to it equitable to do so, allow him to bring the action notwithstanding this section.

22C Actions under the 1987 Act where death has resulted from personal injuries

(1) This section shall apply to an action to enforce an obligation arising from liability under section 2 of the 1987 Act (to make reparation for damage caused wholly or partly by a defect in a product) where a person has died from personal injuries and the damages claimed include damages for those personal injuries or that death.

(2) Subject to subsection (4) below, an action to which this section applies shall not be competent unless it is commenced within the period of 3 years after the later of—

(a)   the date of death of the injured person;

(b)   the earliest date on which the person seeking to make (or a person who could at an earlier date have made) the claim was aware, or on which, in the opinion of the court, it was reasonably practicable for him in all the circumstances to become aware—

(i) that there was a defect in the product;

(ii) that the injuries of the deceased were caused (or partly caused) by the defect; and

(iii) that the defender was a person liable for the damage under the said section 2.

(3) Where the person seeking to make the claim is a relative of the deceased, there shall be disregarded in the computation of the period mentioned in subsection (2) above any period during which that relative was under legal disability by reason of nonage or unsoundness of mind.

(4) Where an action to which section 22B of this Act applies has not been brought within the period mentioned in subsection (2) of that section and the person subsequently dies in consequence of his injuries, an action to which this section applies shall not be competent in respect of those injuries or that death.

(5) Where a person would be entitled, but for this section, to bring an action for reparation other than one in which the damages claimed are confined to damages for loss of or damage to property, the court may, if it seems to it equitable to do so, allow him to bring the action notwithstanding this section.

(6) In this section 'relative' has the same meaning as in the Damages (Scotland) Act 1976.

(7) For the purposes of subsection (2)(b) above there shall be disregarded knowledge of whether particular facts and circumstances would or would not, as a matter of law, result in liability for damage under the said section 2.]

Supplementary

[22D Interpretation of this Part

(1) Expressions used in this Part and in Part I of the 1987 Act shall have the same meanings in this Part as in the said Part I.

(2) For the purposes of section 1(1) of the 1987 Act, this Part shall have effect and be construed as if it were contained in Part I of that Act.

(3) In this Part, 'the 1987 Act' means the Consumer Protection Act 1987.]

[. . .]

23A Private international law application

(1) Where the substantive law of a country other than Scotland falls to be applied by a Scottish court as the law governing an obligation, the court shall apply the relevant rules of law of that country relating to the extinction of the obligations or the limitation of time within which proceedings may be brought to enforce the obligation to the exclusion of any corresponding rule of Scots law.

(2) This section shall not apply where it appears to the court that the application of the relevant foreign rule of law would be incompatible with the principles of public policy applied by the court.

(3) This section shall not apply in any case where the application of the corresponding rule of Scots law has extinguished the obligation, or barred the bringing of proceedings prior to the coming into force of the Prescription and Limitation (Scotland) Act 1984.

24 The Crown
This Act binds the Crown.

25 Short title, commencement and extent

(1) This Act may be cited as the Prescription and Limitation (Scotland) Act 1973.

(2) This Act shall come into operation as follows—

(a) Parts II and III of this Act, Part II of Schedule 4 to this Act and Part II of Schedule 5 to this Act shall come into operation on the date on which this Act is passed;

(b) except as aforesaid this Act shall come into operation on the expiration of three years from the said date.

[. . .]

(4) This Act extends to Scotland only.

SCHEDULES

Section 6   SCHEDULE 1
OBLIGATIONS AFFECTED BY PRESCRIPTIVE PERIODS OF FIVE YEARS
UNDER SECTION 6

1. Subject to paragraph 2 below, section 6 of this Act applies—

(a) to any obligation to pay a sum of money due in respect of a particular period—

(i) by way of interest;

(ii) by way of an instalment of an annuity;

[. . .]

(v) by way of rent or other periodical payment under a lease;

(vi) by way of a periodical payment in respect of the occupancy or use of land, not being an obligation falling within any other provision of this sub-paragraph;

(vii) by way of a periodical payment under a [title condition], not being an obligation falling within any other provision of this sub-paragraph;

[(aa) to any obligation to make a compensatory payment ('compensatory payment' being construed in accordance with section 8(1) of the Abolition of Feudal

Tenure etc (Scotland) Act 2000 (asp 5), including that section as read with section 56 of that Act);

(aa)   to any obligation to pay compensation by virtue of section 2 of the Leasehold Casualties (Scotland) Act 2001 (asp 5);

(ab)   to any obligation arising by virtue of a right—

(i)   of reversion under the third proviso to section 2 of the School Sites Act 1841 (4 & 5 Vict c 38) (or of reversion under that proviso as applied by virtue of any other enactment);

(ii)   to petition for a declaration of forfeiture under section 7 of the Entail Sites Act 1840 (3 & 4 Vict c 48);]

[(ac)   to any obligation to pay a sum of money by way of costs to which section 12 of the Tenements (Scotland) Act 2004 (asp 11) applies;]

(b)   to any obligation based on redress of unjustified enrichment, including without prejudice to that generality any obligation of restitution, repetition or recompense;

(c)   to any obligation arising from *negotiorum gestio*;

(d)   to any obligation arising from liability (whether arising from any enactment or from any rule of law) to make reparation;

(e)   to any obligation under a bill of exchange or a promissory note;

(f)   to any obligation of accounting, other than accounting for trust funds;

(g)   to any obligation arising from, or by reason of any breach of, a contract or promise, not being an obligation falling within any other provision of this paragraph.

2.   Notwithstanding anything in the foregoing paragraph, section 6 of this Act does not apply—

(a)   to any obligation to recognise or obtemper a decree of court, an arbitration award or an order of a tribunal or authority exercising jurisdiction under any enactment;

(b)   to any obligation arising from the issue of a bank note;

[. . .]

(d)   to any obligation under a contract of partnership or of agency, not being an obligation remaining, or becoming prestable on or after the termination of the relationship between the parties under the contract;

(e)   except as provided in paragraph 1(a)[, (aa) or (ac)] of this Schedule, to any obligation relating to land (including an obligation to recognise a servitude);

[(ee)   so as to extinguish, before the expiry of the continuous period of five years which immediately follows the coming into force of section 88 of the Title Conditions (Scotland) Act 2003 (asp 9) (prescriptive period for obligations arising by virtue of 1841 Act or 1840 Act), an obligation mentioned in sub-paragraph (ab) of paragraph 1 of this Schedule;]

(f)   to any obligation to satisfy any claim to [. . .] legitim, jus relicti or jus relictae, or to any prior right of a surviving spouse under section 8 or 9 of the Succession (Scotland) Act 1964;

(g)   to any obligation to make reparation in respect of personal injuries within the meaning of Part II of this Act or in respect of the death of any person as a result of such injuries;

[(gg)   to any obligation to make reparation or otherwise make good in respect of defamation within the meaning of section 18A of this Act;

(ggg)   to any obligation arising from liability under section 2 of the Consumer Protection Act 1987 (to make reparation for damage caused wholly or partly by a defect in a product);]

(h)   to any obligation specified in Schedule 3 to this Act as an imprescriptible obligation.

[. . .]

[4.   In this Schedule, 'title condition' shall be construed in accordance with section 122(1) of the Title Conditions (Scotland) Act 2003 (asp 9).]

SCHEDULE 2   Section 6
APPROPRIATE DATES FOR CERTAIN OBLIGATIONS FOR PURPOSES OF
SECTION 6

1—(1)   This paragraph applies to any obligation, not being part of a banking transaction, to pay money in respect of—
   (a)   goods supplied on sale or hire, or
   (b)   services rendered,
in a series of transactions between the same parties (whether under a single contract or under several contracts) and charged on continuing account.
   (2)   In the foregoing sub-paragraph—
   (a)   any reference to the supply of goods on sale includes a reference to the supply of goods under a hire-purchase agreement, a credit-sale agreement or a conditional sale agreement as defined (in each case) by section 1 of the Hire-Purchase (Scotland) Act 1965; and
   (b)   any reference to services rendered does not include the work of keeping the account in question.
   (3)   Where there is a series of transactions between a partnership and another party, the series shall be regarded for the purposes of this paragraph as terminated (without prejudice to any other mode of termination) if the partnership (in the further provisions of this sub-paragraph referred to as 'the old partnership') is dissolved and is replaced by a single new partnership having among its partners any person who was a partner in the old partnership, then, for the purposes of this paragraph, the new partnership shall be regarded as if it were identical with the old partnership.
   (4)   The appropriate date in relation to an obligation to which this paragraph applies is the date on which payment for the goods last supplied, or, as the case may be, the services last rendered, became due.
   2—(1)   This paragraph applies to any obligation to repay the whole, or any part of, a sum of money lent to, or deposited with, the debtor under a contract of loan or, as the case may be, deposit.
   (2)   The appropriate date in relation to an obligation to which this paragraph applies is—
   (a)   if the contract contains a stipulation which makes provision with respect to the date on or before which repayment of the sum or, as the case may be, the part thereof is to be made, the date on or before which, in terms of that stipulation, the sum or part thereof is to be repaid; and
   (b)   if the contract contains no such stipulation, but a written demand for repayment of the sum, or, as the case may be, the part thereof, is made by or on behalf of the creditor to the debtor, the date when such demand is made or first made.
   3—(1)   This paragraph applies to any obligation under a contract of partnership or of agency, being an obligation remaining, or becoming, prestable on or after the termination of the relationship between the parties under the contract.
   (2)   The appropriate date in relation to an obligation to which this paragraph applies is—
   (a)   if the contract contains a stipulation which makes provision with respect to the date on or before which performance on the obligation is to be due, the date on or before which, in terms of that stipulation, the obligation is to be performed; and
   (b)   in any other case the date when the said relationship terminated.
   4—(1)   This paragraph applies to any obligation—
   (a)   to pay an instalment of a sum of money payable by instalments,
   (b)   to execute any instalment of work due to be executed by instalments, not being an obligation to which any of the foregoing paragraphs applies.
   (2)   The appropriate date in relation to an obligation to which this paragraph

applies is the date on which the last of the instalments is due to be paid or, as the case may be, to be executed.

Sections 7 & 8: Schedule 1   SCHEDULE 3
RIGHTS AND OBLIGATIONS WHICH ARE IMPRESCRIPTIBLE FOR THE
PURPOSES OF SECTIONS 7 AND 8 AND SCHEDULE 1

The following are imprescriptible rights and obligations for the purposes of sections 7(2) and 8(2) of, and paragraph 2(h) of Schedule 1 to, this Act, namely—
  (a) any real right of ownership in land;
  (b) the right in land of the lessee under a recorded lease;
  (c) any right exercisable as a *res merae facultatis*;
  (d) any right to recover property *extra commercium*;
  (e) any obligation of a trustee—
    (i) to produce accounts of the trustee's intromissions with any property of the trust;
    (ii) to make reparation or restitution in respect of any fraudulent breach of trust to which the trustee was a party or was privy;
    (iii) to make furthcoming to any person entitled thereto any trust property, or the proceeds of any such property, in the possession of the trustee, or to make good the value of any such property previously received by the trustee and appropriated to his own use;
  (f) any obligation of a third party to make furthcoming to any person entitled thereto any trust property received by the third party otherwise then in good faith and in his possession;
  (g) any right to recover stolen property from the person by whom it was stolen or from any person privy to the stealing thereof;
  (h) any right to be served as heir to an ancestor or to take any steps necessary for making up or completing title to any [real right] in land.

GUARD DOGS ACT 1975
(1975, c 50)

1 Control of guard dogs
(1) A person shall not use or permit the use of a guard dog at any premises unless a person ('the handler') who is capable of controlling the dog is present on the premises and the dog is under the control of the handler at all times while it is being so used except while it is secured so that it is not at liberty to go freely about the premises.
(2) The handler of a guard dog shall keep the dog under his control at all times while it is being used as a guard dog at any premises except—
  (a) while another handler has control over the dog; or
  (b) while the dog is secured so that it is not at liberty to go freely about the premises.
(3) A person shall not use or permit the use of a guard dog at any premises unless a notice containing a warning that a guard dog is present is clearly exhibited at each entrance to the premises.

DANGEROUS WILD ANIMALS ACT 1976
(1976, c 38)

7 Interpretation
(1) Subject to subsection (2) of this section, for the purposes of this Act a person is a keeper of an animal if he has it in his possession; and if at any time an animal ceases to be in the possession of a person, any person who immediately

before that time was a keeper thereof by virtue of the preceding provisions of this subsection continues to be a keeper of the animal until another person becomes a keeper thereof by virtue of those provisions.

(2)   Where an animal is in the possession of any person for the purpose of—

(a)   preventing it from causing damage,

(b)   restoring it to its owner,

(c)   undergoing veterinary treatment, or

(d)   being transported on behalf of another person,

the person having such possession shall not by virtue only of that possession be treated for the purposes of this Act as a keeper of the animal.

(3)   In this Act expressions cognate with 'keeper' shall be construed in accordance with subsections (1) and (2) of this section.

(4)   In this Act, unless the context otherwise requires, the following expressions have the meanings hereby respectively assigned to them, that is to say—

'circus' includes any place where animals are kept or introduced wholly or mainly for the purpose of performing tricks or manoeuvres;

'damage' includes the death of, or injury to, any person;

'dangerous wild animal' means any animal of a kind for the time being specified in the first column of the Schedule to this Act;

'local authority' means in relation to England [. . .] a district council, a London borough council or the Common Council of the City of London [, in relation to Wales, a county council or county borough council] and, in relation to Scotland, [a council constituted under section 2 of the Local Government etc (Scotland) Act 1994];

'premises' includes any place;

'veterinary practitioner' means a person who is for the time being registered in the supplementary veterinary register;

'veterinary surgeon' means a person who is for the time being registered in the register of veterinary surgeons;

[. . .]

(5)   The second column of the Schedule to this Act is included by way of explanation only; in the event of any dispute or proceedings, only the first column is to be taken into account.

[SCHEDULE
KINDS OF DANGEROUS WILD ANIMALS

NOTE: See section 7(5) of this Act for the effect of the second column of this schedule.

Scientific name	Common name or names
Antilocapridae	Pronghorn
Bovidae except the species Cephalophus, Sylvicapra grimmia, Oreotragus oreotragus, Ourebia, Raphicerus, Nesotragus moschatus, Neotragus pygmeaus, Madoqua, any domestic form of Capra hircus, Dorcatragus megalotis, Ovis aries and all species of the genera Bos and Bubalus.	These include cattle, antelopes, gazelles, goats and sheep except that duikers, grey duiker, klipspringer, oribi, grysbok, suni, royal antelope, dik-dik, domestic goat, Beira antelope, domestic sheep and domestic cattle are specifically excluded
Camelidae except the species Lama glama and Lama pacos.	This kind includes the bactrian camel and Arabian camel except that llama and alpaca are specifically excluded

Scientific name	Common name or names
Canidae except the species Canis familiaris, all species of the genera Vulpes, Alopex, Dusicyon and Otocyon	This kind includes the wild dog, wolf, jackal, coyote except that the domestic dog and all foxes are specifically excluded
Casuariidae	Cassowary
Cercopithecidae	Old world monkeys, including langur, colobus, macaque, guenon, patas, mangabey, baboon and mandrill
Crocodylia	Ths kind includes the alligator, crocodile, gharial, false gharial and caiman
Dromaiidae	Emu
Elapidae (including Hydrophiidae)	This kind includes the cobra, krait, mamba, coral snake and sea snake, and all Australian poisonous snakes including the death adder
Equidae except the species Equus caballus, Equus asinus and Equus caballus x Equus asinus	Horses except that the domestic horse, domestic donkey, mules and hinny are specifically excluded
Felidae, except the species Felis catus	This kind includes the lynx, caracal, serval, bobcat, cheetah, lion, tiger, leopard, panther, jaguar, puma, cougar and ocelot, except that the domestic cat is specifically excluded
Giraffidae	This kind includes the giraffe and okapi
Helodermatidae	Gila monster and Mexican beaded lizard
Hippopotamidae	This kind includes the hippopotamus and pygmy hippopotamus
Hyaenidae except the species Proteles cristatus	Hyaenas except that the aardwolf is specifically excluded
Hylobatidae	Gibbon
Pongidae	Anthropoid apes including orang utan, gorilla and chimpanzee
Proboscidae	Elephants including the African and Indian elephant
Rhinocerotidae	Rhinoceros
Struthionidae	Ostrich
Suidae except any domestic form of Sus scrofa	Old world pigs except that the domestic pig is specifically excluded
Tapiridae	Tapirs

Scientific name	Common name or names
Tayassuidae	New world pigs including the collared peccary and white lipped peccary
Ursidae	This kind includes the polar bear, brown bear and grizzly bear
Viperidae (including Crotalidae)	This kind includes— (a) most snakes known as vipers and adders, and (b) the rattlesnake, bushmaster, fer-de-lance, water moccasin and copperhead.]

DAMAGES (SCOTLAND) ACT 1976
(1976, c 13)

1 Rights of relatives of a deceased person

(1)   Where a person dies in consequence of personal injuries sustained by him as a result of an act or omission of another person, being an act or omission giving rise to liability to pay damages to the injured person or his executor, then, subject to the following provisions of this Act, the person liable to pay those damages (in this section referred to as 'the responsible person') shall also be liable to pay damages in accordance with this section to any relative of the deceased, being a relative within the meaning of Schedule 1 to this Act.

(2)   No liability shall arise under this section if the liability to the deceased or his executor in respect of the act or omission has been excluded or discharged (whether by antecedent agreement or otherwise) by the deceased before his death, or is excluded by virtue of any enactment.

(3)   The damages which the responsible person shall be liable to pay to a relative of a deceased under this section shall (subject to the provisions of this Act) be such as will compensate the relative for any loss of support suffered by him since the date of the deceased's death or likely to be suffered by him as a result of the act or omission in question, together with any reasonable expense incurred by him in connection with the deceased's funeral.

(4)   If the relative is a member of the deceased's immediate family (within the meaning of section 10(2) of this Act) there shall be awarded, without prejudice to any claim under subsection (3) above, such sum of damages, if any, as the court thinks just by way of compensation for the loss of [all or any of the following—

(a)   distress and anxiety endured by the relative in contemplation of the suffering of the deceased before his death;

(b)   grief and sorrow of the relative caused by the deceased's death;

(c)   the loss of such non-patrimonial benefit as the relative might have been expected to derive from the deceased's society and guidance if the deceased had not died,

and the court in making an award under this subsection shall not be required to ascribe specifically any part of the award to any of paragraphs (a), (b) and (c) above.]

(5)   [Subject to subsection (5A) below] in assessing for the purposes of this section the amount of any loss of support suffered by a relative of a deceased no account shall be taken of—

(a)   any patrimonial gain or advantage which has accrued or will or may accrue to the relative from the deceased or from any other person by way of succession or settlement;

(b)   any insurance money, benefit, pension or gratuity which has been, or will be or may be, paid as a result of the deceased's death;

and in this subsection—

'benefit' means benefit under the Social Security Act 1975 or the Social Security (Northern Ireland) Act 1975, and any payment by a friendly society or trade union for the relief or maintenance of a member's dependants;

'insurance money' includes a return of premiums; and

'pension' includes a return of contributions and any payment of a lump sum in respect of a person's employment.

[(5A)   Where a deceased has been awarded a provisional award of damages under section 12(2) of the Administration of Justice Act 1982, the making of that award does not prevent liability from arising under this section but in assessing for the purposes of this section the amount of any loss of support suffered by a relative of the deceased the court shall take into account such part of the provisional award relating to future patrimonial loss as was intended to compensate the deceased for a period beyond the date on which he died.]

(6)   In order to establish loss of support for the purposes of this section it shall not be essential for a claimant to show that the deceased was, or might have become, subject to a duty in law to provide or contribute to the support of the claimant; but if any such fact is established it may be taken into account in determining whether, and if so to what extent, the deceased, if he had not died, would have been likely to provide or contribute to such support.

(7)   Except as provided in this section [or in Part II of the Administration of Justice Act 1982 or under section 1 of the International Transport Conventions Act 1983] no person shall be entitled by reason of relationship to damages (including damages by way of solatium) in respect of the death of another person.

[1A   Transmissibility to executor of rights of deceased relative

Any right to damages under any provision of section 1 of this Act which is vested in the relative concerned immediately before his death shall be transmitted to the relative's executor; but, in determining the amount of damages payable to an executor by virtue of this section, the court shall have regard only to the period ending immediately before the relative's death.]

[2   Rights transmitted to executor in respect of deceased person's injuries

(1)   Subject to the following provisions of this section, there shall be transmitted to the executor of a deceased person the like rights to damages in respect of personal injuries (including a right to damages by way of solatium) sustained by the deceased as were vested in him immediately before his death.

(2)   There shall not be transmitted to the executor under this section a right to damages by way of compensation for patrimonial loss attributable to any period after the deceased's death.

(3)   In determining the amount of damages by way of solatium payable to an executor by virtue of this section, the court shall have regard only to the period ending immediately before the deceased's death.

(4)   In so far as a right to damages vested in the deceased comprised a right to damages (other than for patrimonial loss) in respect of injury resulting from defamation or any other verbal injury or other injury to reputation sustained by the deceased, that right shall be transmitted to the deceased's executor only if an action to enforce that right had been brought by the deceased before his death and had not been concluded by then within the meaning of section 2A(2) of this Act.]

[2A   Enforcement by executor of rights transmitted to him

(1)   For the purpose of enforcing any right transmitted to an executor under section 1A or 2 of this Act the executor shall be entitled—

(a)   to bring an action; or

(b)   if an action for that purpose had been brought by the deceased but had not been concluded before his death, to be sisted as pursuer in that action.

(2)   For the purpose of subsection (1) above, an action shall not be taken to be concluded while any appeal is competent or before any appeal taken has been disposed of.]

[4   Executor's claim not to be excluded by relatives' claim: and vice versa

A claim by the executor of a deceased person for damages under section 2 of this Act is not excluded by the making of a claim by a relative of the deceased for damages under section 1 of this Act [or by a deceased relative's executor under section 1A of this Act; nor is a claim by a relative of a deceased person or by a deceased relative's executor for damages under the said section 1 or (as the case may be) the said section 1A].

[. . .]

6   Limitation of total amount of liability

(1)   Where in any action to which [this] section applies, so far as directed against any defender, it is shown that by antecedent agreement, compromise or otherwise, the liability arising in relation to that defender from the personal injuries in question had, before the deceased's death, been limited to damages of a specified or ascertainable amount, or where that liability is so limited by virtue of any enactment, nothing in this Act shall make the defender liable to pay damages exceeding that amount; and accordingly where in such an action there are two or more pursuers any damages to which they would respectively be entitled under this Act apart from the said limitation shall, if necessary, be reduced *pro rata*.

(2)   Where two or more such actions are conjoined, the conjoined actions shall be treated for the purposes of this section as if they were a single action.

[(3)   This section applies to any action in which, following the death of any person from personal injuries, damages are claimed—

(a)   by the executor of the deceased, in respect of the injuries from which the deceased died;

(b)   in respect of the death of the deceased, by any relative of his [or, if the relative has died, by the relative's executor].]

7   Amendment of references in other Acts

In any Act passed before this Act, unless the context otherwise requires, any reference to solatium in respect of the death of any person (however expressed) shall be construed as a reference to a loss of society award within the meaning of section 1 of this Act; and any reference to a dependant of a deceased person, in relation to an action claiming damages in respect of the deceased person's death, shall be construed as including a reference to a relative of the deceased person within the meaning of this Act.

8   Abolition of right of assythment

After the commencement of this Act no person shall in any circumstances have a right to assythment, and accordingly any action claiming that remedy shall (to the extent that it does so) be incompetent.

9   Damages due to injured person for patrimonial loss caused by personal injuries whereby expectation of life is diminished

(1)   This section applies to any action for damages in respect of personal injuries sustained by the pursuer where his expected date of death is earlier than it would have been if he had not sustained the injuries.

(2)   In assessing, in any action to which this section applies, the amount of any patrimonial loss in respect of the period after the date of decree—

(a)   it shall be assumed that the pursuer will live until the date when he would have been expected to die if he had not sustained the injuries (hereinafter referred to as the 'notional date of death');

(b) the court may have regard to any amount, whether or not it is an amount related to earnings by the pursuer's own labour or other gainful activity, which in its opinion the pursuer, if he had not sustained the injuries in question, would have received in the period up to his notional date of death by way of benefits in money or money's worth, being benefits derived from sources other than the pursuer's own estate;

(c) the court shall have regard to any diminution of any such amount as aforesaid by virtue of expenses which in the opinion of the court the pursuer, if he had not sustained the injuries in question, would reasonably have incurred in the said period by way of living expenses.

[9A Solatium for loss of expectation of life

(1) In assessing, in an action for damages in respect of personal injuries, the amount of damages by way of solatium, the court shall, if—

(a) the injured person's expectation of life has been reduced by the injuries; and

(b) the injured person is, was at any time or is likely to become, aware of that reduction,

have regard to the extent that, in consequence of that awareness, he has suffered or is likely to suffer.

(2) Subject to subsection (1) above, no damages by way of solatium shall be recoverable in respect of loss of expectation of life.

(3) The court in making an award of damages by way of solatium shall not be required to ascribe specifically any part of the award to loss of expectation of life.]

10 Interpretation

(1) In this Act, unless the context otherwise requires—

[. . .]

'personal injuries' includes any disease or any impairment of a person's physical or mental condition [and injury resulting from defamation or any other verbal injury or other injury to reputation or injury resulting from harassment actionable under section 8 of the Protection from Harassment Act 1997;]

'relative', in relation to a deceased person, has the meaning assigned to it by Schedule 1 to this Act.

(2) References in this Act to a member of a deceased person's immediate family are references to any relative of his who falls within subparagraph (a), [(aa)], (b) or (c) of paragraph 1 of Schedule 1 to this Act.

(3) References in this Act to any other Act are references to that Act as amended, extended or applied by any other enactment, including this Act.

[. . .]

12 Citation, application to Crown, commencement and extent

(1) This Act may be cited as the Damages (Scotland) Act 1976.

(2) This Act binds the Crown.

(5) This Act extends to Scotland only.

SCHEDULE 1
DEFINITION OF 'RELATIVE'

(1) In this Act 'relative' in relation to a deceased person includes—

(a) any person who immediately before the deceased's death was the spouse [or civil partner] of the deceased;

[(aa) any person, not being the spouse of the deceased, who was, immediately before the deceased's death, living with the deceased as husband or wife;]

(b) any person who was a parent or child of the deceased;

(c) any person not falling within paragraph (b) above who was accepted by the deceased as a child of his family;

(d)   any person who was an ascendant or descendant (other than a parent or child) of the deceased;

(e)   any person who was, or was the issue of, a brother, sister, uncle or aunt of the deceased;

(f)   any person who, having been a spouse of the deceased, had ceased to be so by virtue of a divorce; [and

(g)   any person who, having been a civil partner of the deceased, had ceased to be so by virtue of the dissolution of the civil partnership;]

but does not include any other person.

(2)   In deducing any relationship for the purposes of the foregoing paragraph—

(a)   any relationship by affinity shall be treated as a relationship by consanguinity; any relationship of the half blood shall be treated as a relationship of the whole blood; and the stepchild of any person shall be treated as his child; and

(b)   section 1(1) of the Law Reform (Parent and Child) (Scotland) Act 1986 shall apply; and any reference (however expressed) in this Act to a relative shall be construed accordingly.

UNFAIR CONTRACT TERMS ACT 1977
(1977, c 50)

PART II
AMENDMENT OF LAW FOR SCOTLAND

15   Scope of Part II

(1)   This Part of this Act [. . .] is subject to Part III of this Act and does not affect the validity of any discharge or indemnity given by a person in consideration of the receipt by him of compensation in settlement of any claim which he has.

(2)   Subject to subsection (3) below, sections 16 to 18 of this Act apply to any contract only to the extent that the contract—

(a)   relates to the transfer of the ownership or possession of goods from one person to another (with or without work having been done on them);

(b)   constitutes a contract of service or apprenticeship;

(c)   relates to services of whatever kind, including (without prejudice to the foregoing generality) carriage, deposit and pledge, care and custody, mandate, agency, loan and services relating to the use of land;

(d)   relates to the liability of an occupier of land to persons entering upon or using that land;

(e)   relates to a grant of any right or permission to enter upon or use land not amounting to an estate or interest in the land.

(3)   Notwithstanding anything in subsection (2) above, sections 16 to 18—

(a)   do not apply to any contract to the extent that the contract—

(i)   is a contract of insurance (including a contract to pay an annuity on human life);

(ii)   relates to the formation, constitution or dissolution of any body corporate or unincorporated association or partnership;

(b)   apply to—

a contract of marine salvage or towage;

a charter party of a ship or hovercraft;

a contract for the carriage of goods by ship or hovercraft; or

a contract to which subsection (4) below relates,

only to the extent that—

(i)   both parties deal or hold themselves out as dealing in the course of a business (and then only in so far as the contract purports to exclude or restrict liability for breach of duty in respect of death or personal injury); or

(ii) the contract is a consumer contract (and then only in favour of the consumer).

(4) This subsection relates to a contract in pursuance of which goods are carried by ship or hovercraft and which either—

(a) specifies ship or hovercraft as the means of carriage over part of the journey to be covered; or

(b) makes no provision as to the means of carriage and does not exclude ship or hovercraft as that means,

in so far as the contract operates for and in relation to the carriage of the goods by that means.

16 Liability for breach of duty

(1) [Subject to subsection (1A) below,] where a term of a contract [, or a provision of a notice given to persons generally or to particular persons,] purports to exclude or restrict liability for breach of duty arising in the course of any business or from the occupation of any premises used for business purposes of the occupier, that term [or provision]—

(a) shall be void in any case where such exclusion or restriction is in respect of death or personal injury;

(b) shall, in any other case, have no effect if it was not fair and reasonable to incorporate the term in the contract [or, as the case may be, if it is not fair and reasonable to allow reliance on the provision].

[(1A) Nothing in paragraph (b) of subsection (1) above shall be taken as implying that a provision of a notice has effect in circumstances where, apart from that paragraph, it would not have effect.]

(2) Subsection (1)(a) above does not affect the validity of any discharge and indemnity given by a person, on or in connection with an award to him of compensation for pneumoconiosis attributable to employment in the coal industry, in respect of any further claim arising from his contracting that disease.

(3) Where under subsection (1) above a term of a contract [or a provision of a notice] is void or has no effect, the fact that a person agreed to, or was aware of, the term [or provision] shall not of itself be sufficient evidence that he knowingly and voluntarily assumed any risk.

17 Control of unreasonable exemptions in consumer or standard form contracts

(1) Any term of a contract which is a consumer contract or a standard form contract shall have no effect for the purpose of enabling a party to the contract—

(a) who is in breach of a contractual obligation, to exclude or restrict any liability of his to the consumer or customer in respect of the breach;

(b) in respect of a contractual obligation, to render no performance, or to render a performance substantially different from that which the consumer or customer reasonably expected from the contract;

if it was not fair and reasonable to incorporate the term in the contract.

(2) In this section 'customer' means a party to a standard form contract who deals on the basis of written standard terms of business of the other party to the contract who himself deals in the course of a business.

18 Unreasonable indemnity clauses in consumer contracts

(1) Any term of a contract which is a consumer contract shall have no effect for the purpose of making the consumer indemnify another person (whether a party to the contract or not) in respect of liability which that other person may incur as a result of breach of duty or breach of contract, if it was not fair and reasonable to incorporate the term in the contract.

(2) In this section 'liability' means liability arising in the course of any business or from the occupation of any premises used for business purposes of the occupier.

19 'Guarantee' of consumer goods

(1) This section applies to a guarantee—

(a)   in relation to goods which are of a type ordinarily supplied for private use or consumption; and

(b)   which is not a guarantee given by one party to the other party to a contract under or in pursuance of which the ownership or possession of the goods to which the guarantee relates is transferred.

(2) A term of a guarantee to which this section applies shall be void in so far as it purports to exclude or restrict liability for loss or damage (including death or personal injury)—

(a)   arising from the goods proving defective while—

(i) in use otherwise than exclusively for the purposes of a business; or

(ii) in the possession of a person for such use; and

(b)   resulting from the breach of duty of a person concerned in the manufacture or distribution of the goods.

(3) For the purposes of this section, any document is a guarantee if it contains or purports to contain some promise or assurance (however worded or presented) that defects will be made good by complete or partial replacement, or by repair, monetary compensation or otherwise.

20 Obligations implied by law in sale and hire-purchase contracts

(1) Any term of a contract which purports to exclude or restrict liability for breach of the obligations arising from—

(a)   section 12 of the Sale of Goods Act [1979] (seller's implied undertakings as to title etc);

(b)   section 8 of the Supply of Goods (Implied Terms) Act 1973 (implied terms as to title in hire-purchase agreements),

shall be void.

(2) Any term of a contract which purports to exclude or restrict liability for breach of the obligations arising from—

(a)   section 13, 14 or 15 of the said Act of [1979] (seller's implied undertakings as to conformity of goods with description or sample, or as to their quality or fitness for a particular purpose);

(b)   section 9, 10 or 11 of the said Act of 1973 (the corresponding provisions in relation to hire-purchase),

shall—

(i) in the case of a consumer contract, be void against the consumer;

(ii) in any other case, have no effect if it was not fair and reasonable to incorporate the term in the contract.

21 Obligations implied by law in other contracts for the supply of goods

(1) Any term of a contract to which this section applies purporting to exclude or restrict liability for breach of an obligation—

(a)   such as is referred to in subsection (3)(a) below—

(i) in the case of a consumer contract, shall be void against the consumer, and

(ii) in any other case, shall have no effect if it was not fair and reasonable to incorporate the term in the contract;

(b)   such as is referred to in subsection (3)(b) below, shall have no effect if it was not fair and reasonable to incorporate the term in the contract.

(2) This section applies to any contract to the extent that it relates to any such matter as is referred to in section 15(2)(a) of this Act, but does not apply to—

(a)   a contract of sale of goods or a hire-purchase agreement; or

(b)   a charterparty of a ship or hovercraft unless it is a consumer contract (and then only in favour of the consumer).

(3) An obligation referred to in this subsection is an obligation incurred under

a contract in the course of a business and arising by implication of law from the nature of the contract which relates—

(a)   to the correspondence of goods with description or sample, or to the quality or fitness of goods for any particular purpose; or

(b)   to any right to transfer ownership or possession of goods, or to the enjoyment of quiet possession of goods.

[(3A)   Notwithstanding anything in the foregoing provisions of this section, any term of a contract which purports to exclude or restrict liability for breach of the obligations arising under section 11B of the Supply of Goods and Services Act 1982 (implied terms about title, freedom from encumbrances and quiet possession in certain contracts for the transfer of property in goods) shall be void.]

(4)   Nothing in this section applies to the supply of goods on a redemption of trading stamps within the Trading Stamps Act 1964.

22   Consequence of breach

For the avoidance of doubt, where any provision of this Part of this Act requires that the incorporation of a term in a contract must be fair and reasonable for that term to have effect—

(a)   if that requirement is satisfied, the term may be given effect to notwithstanding that the contract has been terminated in consequence of breach of that contract;

(b)   for the term to be given effect to, that requirement must be satisfied even where a party who is entitled to rescind the contract elects not to rescind it.

23   Evasion by means of secondary contract

Any term of any contract shall be void which purports to exclude or restrict, or has the effect of excluding or restricting—

(a)   the exercise, by a party to any other contract, of any right or remedy which arises in respect of that other contract in consequence of breach of duty, or of obligation, liability for which could not by virtue of the provisions of this Part of this Act be excluded or restricted by a term of that other contract;

(b)   the application of the provisions of this Part of this Act in respect of that or any other contract.

24   The 'reasonableness' test

(1)   In determining for the purposes of this Part of this Act whether it was fair and reasonable to incorporate a term in a contract, regard shall be had only to the circumstances which were, or ought reasonably to have been, known to or in the contemplation of the parties to the contract at the time the contract was made.

(2)   In determining for the purposes of section 20 or 21 of this Act whether it was fair and reasonable to incorporate a term in a contract, regard shall be had in particular to the matters specified in Schedule 2 to this Act; but this sub-section shall not prevent a court or arbiter from holding in accordance with any rule of law, that a term which purports to exclude or restrict any relevant liability is not a term of the contract.

[(2A)   In determining for the purposes of this Part of this Act whether it is fair and reasonable to allow reliance on a provision of a notice (not being a notice having contractual effect), regard shall be had to all the circumstances obtaining when the liability arose or (but for the provision) would have arisen.]

(3)   Where a term in a contract [or a provision of a notice] purports to restrict liability to a specified sum of money, and the question arises for the purposes of this Part of this Act whether it was fair and reasonable to incorporate the term in the contract [or whether it is fair and reasonable to allow reliance on the provision], then, without prejudice to subsection (2) above [in the case of a term in a contract], regard shall be had in particular to—

(a)   the resources which the party seeking to rely on that term [or provision] could expect to be available to him for the purpose of meeting the liability should it arise;

(b) how far it was open to that party to cover himself by insurance.

(4) The onus of proving that it was fair and reasonable to incorporate a term in a contract [or that it is fair and reasonable to allow reliance on a provision of a notice] shall lie on the party so contending.

25 Interpretation of Part II

(1) In this Part of this Act—

'breach of duty' means the breach—

(a) of any obligation, arising from the express or implied terms of a contract, to take reasonable care or exercise reasonable skill in the performance of the contract;

(b) of any common law duty to take reasonable care or exercise reasonable skill;

(c) of the duty of reasonable care imposed by section 2(1) of the Occupiers' Liability (Scotland) Act 1960;

'business' includes a profession and the activities of any government department or local or public authority;

'consumer' has the meaning assigned to that expression in the definition in this section of 'consumer contract';

'consumer contract' means [subject to subsections (1A) and (1B) below] a contract [. . .] in which—

(a) one party to the contract deals, and the other party to the contract ('the consumer') does not deal or hold himself out as dealing, in the course of a business, and

(b) in the case of a contract such as is mentioned in section 15(2)(a) of this Act, the goods are of a type ordinarily supplied for private use or consumption; and for the purposes of this Part of this Act the onus of proving that a contract is not to be regarded as a consumer contract shall lie on the party so contending;

'goods' has the same meaning as in the Sale of Goods Act [1979];

'hire-purchase agreement' has the same meaning as in section 189(1) of the Consumer Credit Act 1974;

['notice' includes an announcement, whether or not in writing, and any other communication or pretended communication;]

'personal injury' includes any disease and any impairment of physical or mental condition.

[(1A) Where the consumer is an individual, paragraph (b) in the definition of 'consumer contract' in subsection (1) must be disregarded.

(1B) The expression of 'consumer contract' does not include a contract in which—

(a) the buyer is an individual and the goods are second hand goods sold by public auction at which individuals have the opportunity of attending in person; or

(b) the buyer is not an individual and the goods are sold by auction or competitive tender.]

(2) In relation to any breach of duty or obligation, it is immaterial for any purpose of this Part of this Act whether the act or omission giving rise to that breach was inadvertent or intentional or whether liability for it arises directly or vicariously.

(3) In this Part of this Act, any reference to excluding or restricting any liability includes—

(a) making the liability or its enforcement subject to any restrictive or onerous conditions;

(b) excluding or restricting any right or remedy in respect of the liability, or subjecting a person to any prejudice in consequence of his pursuing any such right or remedy;

(c)   excluding or restricting any rule of evidence or procedure;

[. . .]

(5)   In section 15 and 16 and 19 to 21 of this Act, any reference to excluding or restricting liability for breach of any obligation or duty shall include a reference to excluding or restricting the obligation or duty itself.

PART III
PROVISIONS APPLYING TO WHOLE OF UNITED KINGDOM

26   International supply contracts

(1)   The limits imposed by this Act on the extent to which a person may exclude or restrict liability by reference to a contract term do not apply to liability arising under such a contract as is described in subsection (3) below.

(2)   The terms of such a contract are not subject to any requirement of reasonableness under section 3 or 4: and nothing in Part II of this Act should require the incorporation of the terms of such a contract to be fair and reasonable for them to have effect.

(3)   Subject to subsection (4), that description of contract is one whose characteristics are the following—

(a)   either it is a contract of sale of goods or it is one under or in pursuance of which the possession of ownership of goods passes, and

(b)   it is made by parties whose places of business (or, if they have none, habitual residences) are in the territories of different States (the Channel Islands and the Isle of Man being treated for this purpose as different States from the United Kingdom).

(4)   A contract falls within subsection (3) above only if either—

(a)   the goods in question are, at the time of the conclusion of the contract, in the course of carriage, or will be carried, from the territory of one State to the territory of another; or

(b)   the acts constituting the offer and acceptance have been done in the territories of different States; or

(c)   the contract provides for the goods to be delivered to the territory of a state other than that within whose territory those acts were done.

27   Choice of law clauses

(1)   Where the [law applicable to] a contract is the law of any part of the United Kingdom only by choice of the parties (and apart from that choice would be the law of some country outside the United Kingdom) sections 2 to 7 and 16 to 21 of this Act do not operate as part [of the law applicable to the contract].

(2)   This Act has effect notwithstanding any contract term which applies or purports to apply the law of some country outside the United Kingdom, where (either or both)—

(a)   the term appears to the court, or arbitrator or arbiter to have been imposed wholly or mainly for the purpose of enabling the party imposing it to evade the operation of this Act; or

(b)   in the making of the contract one of the parties dealt as consumer, and he was then habitually resident in the United Kingdom, and the essential steps necessary for the making of the contract were taken there, whether by him or by others on his behalf.

29   Saving for other relevant legislation

(1)   Nothing in this Act removes or restricts the effect of, or prevents reliance upon, any contractual provision which—

(a)   is authorised or required by the express terms or necessary implication of an enactment; or

(b)   being made with a view to compliance with an international agreement to which the United Kingdom is a party, does not operate more restrictively than is contemplated by the agreement.

(2)   A contract term is to be taken—

(a)   for the purposes of Part I of this Act, as satisfying the requirement of reasonableness . . .

if it is incorporated or approved by, or incorporated pursuant to a decision or ruling of, a competent authority acting in the exercise of any statutory jurisdiction or function and is not a term in a contract to which the competent authority is itself a party.

(3)   In this section—

'competent authority' means any court, arbitrator or arbiter, government department or public authority;

'enactment' means any legislation (including subordinate legislation) of the United Kingdom or Northern Ireland and any instrument having effect by virtue of such legislation; and

'statutory' means conferred by an enactment.

. . .

SCHEDULE 2
'GUIDELINES' FOR APPLICATION OF REASONABLENESS TEST

Sections 11(2) and 24(2)

The matters to which regard is to be had in particular for the purposes of sections 6(3), 7(3) and (4), 20 and 21 are any of the following which appear to be relevant—

(a)   the strength of the bargaining positions of the parties relative to each other, taking into account (among other things) alternative means by which the customer's requirements could have been met;

(b)   whether the customer received an inducement to agree to the terms, or in accepting it had an opportunity of entering into a similar contract with other persons, but without having to accept similar terms;

(c)   whether the customer knew or ought reasonably to have known of the existence and extent of the term (having regard, among other things, to any customs of the trade and any previous course of dealing between the parties);

(d)   where the term excludes or restricts any relevant liability if some condition is not complied with, whether it was reasonable at the time of the contract to expect that compliance with that condition would be practicable;

(e)   whether the goods were manufactured, processed or adapted to the special order of the customer.

SALE OF GOODS ACT 1979
(1979, c 54)

PART I
CONTRACTS TO WHICH ACT APPLIES

1   Contracts to which Act applies

(1)   This Act applies to contracts of sale of goods made on or after (but not to those made before) 1 January 1894.

(2)   In relation to contracts made on certain dates, this Act applies subject to the modification of certain of its sections as mentioned in Schedule 1 below.

(3)   Any such modification is indicated in the section concerned by a reference to Schedule 1 below.

(4)   Accordingly, where a section does not contain such a reference, this Act

applies in relation to the contract concerned without such modification of the section.

PART II
FORMATION OF THE CONTRACT

Contract of sale

2   Contract of sale

(1)   A contract of sale of goods is a contract by which the seller transfers or agrees to transfer the property in goods to the buyer for a money consideration, called the price.

(2)   There may be a contract of sale between one part owner and another.

(3)   A contract of sale may be absolute or conditional.

(4)   Where under a contract of sale the property in the goods is transferred from the seller to the buyer the contract is called a sale.

(5)   Where under a contract of sale the transfer of the property in the goods is to take place at a future time or subject to some condition later to be fulfilled the contract is called an agreement to sell.

(6)   An agreement to sell becomes a sale when the time elapses or the conditions are fulfilled subject to which the property in the goods is to be transferred.

3   Capacity to buy and sell

(1)   Capacity to buy and sell is regulated by the general law concerning capacity to contract and to transfer and acquire property.

(2)   Where necessaries are sold and delivered [. . .] to a person who by reason of mental incapacity or drunkenness is incompetent to contract, he must pay a reasonable price for them.

(3)   In subsection (2) above 'necessaries' means goods suitable to the condition in life of the [. . .] person concerned and to his actual requirements at the time of the sale and delivery.

Formalities of contract

4   How contract of sale is made

(1)   Subject to this and any other Act, a contract of sale may be made in writing (either with or without seal), or by word of mouth, or partly in writing and partly by word of mouth, or may be implied from the conduct of the parties.

(2)   Nothing in this section affects the law relating to corporations.

Subject matter of contract

5   Existing or future goods

(1)   The goods which form the subject of a contract of sale may be either existing goods, owned or possessed by the seller, or goods to be manufactured or acquired by him after the making of the contract of sale, in this Act called future goods.

(2)   There may be a contract for the sale of goods the acquisition of which by the seller depends on a contingency which may or may not happen.

(3)   Where by a contract of sale the seller purports to effect a present sale of future goods, the contract operates as an agreement to sell the goods.

6   Goods which have perished

Where there is a contract for the sale of specific goods, and the goods without the knowledge of the seller have perished at the time when a contract is made, the contract is void.

7   Goods perishing before sale but after agreement to sell

Where there is an agreement to sell specific goods and subsequently the goods, without any fault on the part of the seller or buyer, perish before the risk passes to the buyer, the agreement is avoided.

The price

8   Ascertainment of price
  (1)   The price in a contract of sale may be fixed by the contract, or may be left to be fixed in a manner agreed by the contract, or may be determined by the course of dealing between the parties.
  (2)   Where the price is not determined as mentioned in subsection (1) above the buyer must pay a reasonable price.
  (3)   What is a reasonable price is a question of fact dependent on the circumstances of each particular case.

9   Agreement to sell at valuation
  (1)   Where there is an agreement to sell goods on the terms that the price is to be fixed by the valuation of a third party, and he cannot or does not make the valuation, the agreement is avoided; but if the goods or any part of them have been delivered to and appropriated by the buyer he must pay a reasonable price for them.
  (2)   Where the third party is prevented from making the valuation by the fault of the seller or buyer, the party not at fault may maintain an action for damages against the party at fault.

[Implied terms etc]

10   Stipulations about time
  (1)   Unless a different intention appears from the terms of the contract, stipulations as to time of payment are not of the essence of a contract of sale.
  (2)   Whether any other stipulation as to time is or is not of the essence of the contract depends on the terms of the contract.
  (3)   In a contract of sale 'month' prima facie means calendar month.

11   [*Does not apply to Scotland.*]

12   Implied terms about title, etc
  (1)   In a contract of sale, other than one to which subsection (3) below applies, there is an implied [term] on the part of the seller that in the case of a sale he has a right to sell the goods, and in the case of an agreement to sell he will have such a right at the time when the property is to pass.
  (2)   In a contract of sale, other than one to which subsection (3) below applies, there is also an implied [term] that—
    (a)   the goods are free, and will remain free until the time when the property is to pass, from any charge or encumbrance not disclosed or known to the buyer before the contract is made, and
    (b)   the buyer will enjoy quiet possession of the goods except so far as it may be disturbed by the owner or other person entitled to the benefit of any charge or encumbrance so disclosed or known.
  (3)   This subsection applies to a contract of sale in the case of which there appears from the contract or is to be inferred from its circumstances an intention that the seller should transfer only such title as he or a third person may have.
  (4)   In a contract to which subsection (3) above applies there is an implied [term] that all charges or encumbrances known to the seller and not known to the buyer have been disclosed to the buyer before the contract is made.
  (5)   In a contract to which subsection (3) above applies there is also an implied [term] that none of the following will disturb the buyer's quiet possession of the goods, namely—
    (a)   the seller;

(b)   in a case where the parties to the contract intend that the seller should transfer only such title as a third person may have, that person;

(c)   anyone claiming through or under the seller or that third person otherwise than under a charge or encumbrance disclosed or known to the buyer before the contract is made.

[(5A)   As regards England and Wales and Northern Ireland, the term implied by subsection (1) above is a condition and the terms implied by subsections (2), (4) and (5) above are warranties.]

(6)   Paragraph 3 of Schedule 1 below applies in relation to a contract made before 18 May 1973.

13   Sale by description

(1)   Where there is a contract for the sale of goods by description, there is an implied [term] that the goods will correspond with the description.

[(1A)   As regards England and Wales and Northern Ireland, the term implied by subsection (1) above is a condition.]

(2)   If the sale is by sample as well as by description it is not sufficient that the bulk of the goods corresponds with the sample if the goods do not also correspond with the description.

(3)   A sale of goods is not prevented from being a sale by description by reason only that, being exposed for sale or hire, they are selected by the buyer.

(4)   Paragraph 4 of Schedule 1 below applies in relation to a contract made before 18 May 1973.

14   Implied terms about quality or fitness

(1)   Except as provided by this section and section 15 below and subject to any other enactment, there is no implied [term] about the quality or fitness for any particular purpose of goods supplied under a contract of sale.

[(2) Where the seller sells goods in the course of a business, there is an implied term that the goods supplied under the contract are of satisfactory quality.

(2A)   For the purposes of this Act, goods are of satisfactory quality if they meet the standard that a reasonable person would regard as satisfactory, taking account of any description of the goods, the price (if relevant) and all the other relevant circumstances.

(2B)   For the purposes of this Act, the quality of goods includes their state and condition and the following (among others) are in appropriate cases aspects of the quality of goods—

(a)   fitness for all the purposes for which goods of the kind in question are commonly supplied,

(b)   appearance and finish,

(c)   freedom from minor defects,

(d)   safety, and

(c)   durability.

(2C)   The term implied by subsection (2) above does not extend to any matter making the quality of goods unsatisfactory—

(a)   which is specifically drawn to the buyer's attention before the contract is made,

(b)   where the buyer examines the goods before the contract is made, which that examination ought to reveal, or

(c)   in the case of a contract for sale by sample, which would have been apparent on a reasonable examination of the sample.]

[(2D)   If the buyer deals as consumer or, in Scotland, if a contract of sale is a consumer contract, the relevant circumstances mentioned in subsection (2A) above include any public statements on the specific characteristics of the goods made about them by the seller, the producer or his representative, particularly in advertising or on labelling.

(2E)   A public statement is not by virtue of subsection (2D) above a relevant circumstance for the purposes of subsection (2A) above in the case of a contract of sale, if the seller shows that—

    (a)   at the time the contract was made, he was not, and could not reasonably have been, aware of the statement,

    (b)   before the contract was made, the statement had been withdrawn in public or, to the extent that it contained anything which was incorrect or misleading, it had been corrected in public, or

    (c)   the decision to buy the goods could not have been influenced by the statement.

(2F)   Subsections (2D) and (2E) above do not prevent any public statement from being a relevant circumstance for the purposes of subsection (2A) above (whether or not the buyer deals as consumer or, in Scotland, whether or not the contract of sale is a consumer contract) if the statement would have been such a circumstance apart from those subsections.]

(3)   Where the seller sells goods in the course of a business and the buyer, expressly or by implication, makes known—

    (a)   to the seller, or

    (b)   where the purchase price or part of it is payable by instalments and the goods were previously sold by a credit-broker to the seller, to that credit-broker,

    any particular purpose for which the goods are being bought,

there is an implied [term] that the goods supplied under the contract are reasonably fit for that purpose, whether or not that is a purpose for which such goods are commonly supplied, except where the circumstances show that the buyer does not rely, or that it is unreasonable for him to rely, on the skill or judgment of the seller or credit-broker.

(4)   An implied [term] about quality or fitness for a particular purpose may be annexed to a contract of sale by usage.

(5)   The preceding provisions of this section apply to a sale by a person who in the course of a business is acting as agent for another as they apply to a sale by a principal in the course of a business, except where that other is not selling in the course of a business and either the buyer knows that fact or reasonable steps are taken to bring it to the notice of the buyer before the contract is made.

[(6)   As regards England and Wales and Northern Ireland, the terms implied by subsections (2) and (3) above are conditions.]

(7)   Paragraph 5 of Schedule 1 below applies in relation to a contract made on or after 18 May 1973 and before the appointed day, and paragraph 6 in relation to one made before 18 May 1973.

(8)   In subsection (7) above and paragraph 5 of Schedule 1 below references to the appointed day are to the day appointed for the purposes of those provisions by an order of the Secretary of State made by statutory instrument.

Sale by sample

15 Sale by sample

(1)   A contract of sale is a contract for sale by sample where there is an express or implied term to that effect in the contract.

(2)   In the case of a contract for sale by sample there is an implied [term]—

    (a)   that the bulk will correspond with the sample in quality;

    [. . .]

    (c)   that the goods will be free from any defect, making their quality unsatisfactory, which would not be apparent on reasonable examination of the sample.

[(3)   As regards England and Wales and Northern Ireland, the term implied by subsection (2) above is a condition.]

(4)   Paragraph 7 of Schedule 1 below applies in relation to a contract made before 18 May 1973.

Miscellaneous

15A   [*Does not apply to Scotland.*]

[15B   Remedies for breach of contract as respects Scotland
   (1)   Where in a contract of sale the seller is in breach of any term of the contract (express or implied), the buyer shall be entitled—
      (a)   to claim damages, and
      (b)   if the breach is material, to reject any goods delivered under the contract and treat it as repudiated.
   (2)   Where a contract of sale is a consumer contract, then, for the purposes of subsection (1)(b) above, breach by the seller of any term (express or implied)—
      (a)   as to the quality of the goods or their fitness for a purpose,
      (b)   if the goods are, or are to be, sold by description, that the goods will correspond with the description,
      (c)   if the goods are, or are to be, sold by reference to a sample, that the bulk will correspond with the sample in quality,
shall be deemed to be a material breach.
   (3)   This section applies to Scotland only.]

PART III
EFFECTS OF THE CONTRACT

Transfer of property as between seller and buyer

16   Goods must be ascertained
[Subject to section 20A below] where there is a contract for the sale of unascertained goods no property in the goods is transferred to the buyer unless and until the goods are ascertained.

17   Property passes when intended to pass
   (1)   Where there is a contract for the sale of specific or ascertained goods the property in them is transferred to the buyer at such time as the parties to the contract intend it to be transferred.
   (2)   For the purpose of ascertaining the intention of the parties regard shall be had to the terms of the contract, the conduct of the parties and the circumstances of the case.

18   Rules for ascertaining intention
Unless a different intention appears, the following are rules for ascertaining the intention of the parties as to the time at which the property in the goods is to pass to the buyer.
   Rule 1.—Where there is an unconditional contract for the sale of specific goods in a deliverable state the property in the goods passes to the buyer when the contract is made, and it is immaterial whether the time of payment or the time of delivery, or both, be postponed.
   Rule 2.—Where there is a contract for the sale of specific goods and the seller is bound to do something to the goods for the purpose of putting them into a deliverable state, the property does not pass until the thing is done and the buyer has notice that it has been done.
   Rule 3.—Where there is a contract for the sale of specific goods in a deliverable state but the seller is bound to weigh, measure, test, or do some other act or thing with reference to the goods for the purpose of ascertaining the price, the property does not pass until the act or thing is done and the buyer has notice that it has been done.
   Rule 4.—When goods are delivered to the buyer on approval or on sale or return or other similar terms the property in the goods passes to the buyer:—

(a)   when he signifies his approval or acceptance to the seller or does any other act adopting the transaction;

(b)   if he does not signify his approval or acceptance to the seller but retains the goods without giving notice of rejection, then, if a time has been fixed for the return of the goods, on the expiration of that time, and, if no time has been fixed, on the expiration of a reasonable time.

Rule 5.—(1)   Where there is a contract for the sale of unascertained or future goods by description, and goods of that description and in a deliverable state are unconditionally appropriated to the contract, either by the seller with the assent of the buyer or by the buyer with the assent of the seller, the property in the goods then passes to the buyer; and the assent may be express or implied, and may be given either before or after the appropriation is made.

(2)   Where, in pursuance of the contract, the seller delivers the goods to the buyer or to a carrier or other bailee or custodier (whether named by the buyer or not) for the purpose of transmission to the buyer, and does not reserve the right of disposal, he is to be taken to have unconditionally appropriated the goods to the contract.

[(3)   Where there is a contract for the sale of a specified quantity of unascertained goods in a deliverable state forming part of a bulk which is identified either in the contract or by subsequent agreement between the parties and the bulk is reduced to (or to less than) that quantity, then, if the buyer under that contract is the only buyer to whom goods are then due out of the bulk—

(a)   the remaining goods are to be taken as appropriated to that contract at the time when the bulk is so reduced; and

(b)   the property in those goods then passes to that buyer.

(4)   Paragraph (3) above applies also (with the necessary modifications) where a bulk is reduced to (or to less than) the aggregate of the quantities due to a single buyer under separate contracts relating to that bulk and he is the only buyer to whom goods are then due out of that bulk.]

19   Reservation of right of disposal

(1)   Where there is a contract for the sale of specific goods or where goods are subsequently appropriated to the contract, the seller may, by the terms of the contract or appropriation, reserve the right of disposal of the goods until certain conditions are fulfilled; and in such a case, notwithstanding the delivery of the goods to the buyer, or to a carrier or other bailee or custodier for the purpose of transmission to the buyer, the property in the goods does not pass to the buyer until the conditions imposed by the seller are fulfilled.

(2)   Where goods are shipped, and by the bill of lading the goods are deliverable to the order of the seller or his agent, the seller is prima facie to be taken to reserve the right of disposal.

(3)   Where the seller of goods draws on the buyer for the price, and transmits the bill of exchange and bill of lading to the buyer together to secure acceptance or payment of the bill of exchange, the buyer is bound to return the bill of lading if he does not honour the bill of exchange, and if he wrongfully retains the bill of lading the property in the goods does not pass to him.

20   [Passing of risk]

(1)   Unless otherwise agreed, the goods remain at the seller's risk until the property in them is transferred to the buyer, but when the property in them is transferred to the buyer the goods are at the buyer's risk whether delivery has been made or not.

(2)   But where delivery has been delayed through the fault of either buyer or seller the goods are at the risk of the party at fault as regards any loss which might not have occurred but for such fault.

(3)   Nothing in this section affects the duties or liabilities of either seller or buyer as a bailee or custodier of the goods of the other party.

[(4)   In a case where the buyer deals as consumer or, in Scotland, where there is a consumer contract in which the buyer is a consumer, subsections (1) to (3) above must be ignored and the goods remain at the seller's risk until they are delivered to the consumer.]

[20A   Undivided shares in goods forming part of a bulk

(1)   This section applies to a contract for the sale of a specified quantity of unascertained goods if the following conditions are met—

(a)   the goods or some of them form part of a bulk which is identified either in the contract or by subsequent agreement between the parties; and

(b)   the buyer has paid the price for some or all of the goods which are the subject of the contract and which form part of the bulk.

(2)   Where this section applies, then (unless the parties agree otherwise), as soon as the conditions specified in paragraphs (a) and (b) of subsection (1) above are met or at such later time as the parties may agree—

(a)   property in an undivided share in the bulk is transferred to the buyer; and

(b)   the buyer becomes an owner in common of the bulk.

(3)   Subject to subsection (4) below, for the purposes of this section, the undivided share of a buyer in a bulk at any time shall be such share as the quantity of goods paid for and due to the buyer out of the bulk bears to the quantity of goods in the bulk at that time.

(4)   Where the aggregate of the undivided shares of buyers in a bulk determined under subsection (3) above would at any time exceed the whole of the bulk at that time, the undivided share in the bulk of each buyer shall be reduced proportionately so that the aggregate of the undivided shares is equal to the whole bulk.

(5)   Where a buyer has paid the price for only some of the goods due to him out of a bulk, any delivery to the buyer out of the bulk shall, for the purposes of this section, be ascribed in the first place to the goods in respect of which payment has been made.

(6)   For the purpose of this section payment of part of the price for any goods shall be treated as payment for a corresponding part of the goods.]

[20B   Deemed consent by co-owner to dealings in bulk goods

(1)   A person who has become an owner in common of a bulk by virtue of section 20A above shall be deemed to have consented to—

(a)   any delivery of goods out of the bulk to any other owner in common of the bulk, being goods which are due to him under his contract;

(b)   any removal, dealing with, delivery or disposal of goods in the bulk by any other person who is an owner in common of the bulk in so far as the goods fall within that co-owner's undivided share in the bulk at the time of the removal, dealing, delivery or disposal.

(2)   No cause of action shall accrue to anyone against a person by reason of that person having acted in accordance with paragraph (a) or (b) of subsection (1) above in reliance on any consent deemed to have been given under that subsection.

(3)   Nothing in this section or section 20A above shall—

(a)   impose an obligation on a buyer of goods out of a bulk to compensate any other buyer of goods out of that bulk for any shortfall in the goods received by that other buyer;

(b)   affects any contractual arrangement between buyers of goods out of a bulk for adjustments between themselves; or

(c)   affect the rights of any buyer under his contract.]

Transfer of title

21 Sale by person not the owner
(1) Subject to this Act, where goods are sold by a person who is not their owner, and who does not sell them under the authority or with the consent of the owner, the buyer acquires no better title to the goods than the seller had, unless the owner of the goods is by his conduct precluded from denying the seller's authority to sell.

(2) Nothing in this Act affects—

(a) the provisions of the Factors Acts or any enactment enabling the apparent owner of goods to dispose of them as if he were their true owner;

(b) the validity of any contract of sale under any special common law or statutory power of sale or under the order of a court of competent jurisdiction.

22 [*Does not apply to Scotland.*]

23 Sale under voidable title
When the seller of goods has a voidable title to them, but his title has not been avoided at the time of the sale, the buyer acquires a good title to the goods, provided he buys them in good faith and without notice of the seller's defect of title.

24 Seller in possession after sale
Where a person having sold goods continues or is in possession of the goods, or of the documents of title to the goods, the delivery or transfer by that person, or by a mercantile agent acting for him, of the goods or documents of title under any sale, pledge, or other disposition thereof, to any person receiving the same in good faith and without notice of the previous sale, has the same effect as if the person making the delivery or transfer were expressly authorised by the owner of the goods to make the same.

25 Buyer in possession after sale
(1) Where a person having bought or agreed to buy goods obtains, with the consent of the seller, possession of the goods or the documents of title to the goods, the delivery or transfer by that person, or by a mercantile agent acting for him, of the goods or documents of title, under any sale, pledge, or other disposition thereof, to any person receiving the same in good faith and without notice of any lien or other right of the original seller in respect of the goods, has the same effect as if the person making the delivery or transfer were a mercantile agent in possession of the goods or documents of title with the consent of the owner.

(2) For the purposes of subsection (1) above—

(a) the buyer under a conditional sale agreement is to be taken not to be a person who has bought or agreed to buy goods, and

(b) 'conditional sale agreement' means an agreement for the sale of goods which is a consumer credit agreement within the meaning of the Consumer Credit Act 1974 under which the purchase price or part of it is payable by instalments, and the property in the goods is to remain in the seller (notwithstanding that the buyer is to be in possession of the goods) until such conditions as to the payment of instalments or otherwise as may be specified in the agreement are fulfilled.

(3) Paragraph 9 of Schedule 1 below applies in relation to a contract under which a person buys or agrees to buy goods and which is made before the appointed day.

(4) In subsection (3) above and paragraph 9 of Schedule 1 below references to the appointed day are to the day appointed for the purposes of those provisions by an order of the Secretary of State made by statutory instrument.

26 Supplementary to sections 24 and 25
In sections 24 and 25 above 'mercantile agent' means a mercantile agent having in the customary course of his business as such agent authority either—

(a)   to sell goods, or
(b)   to consign goods for the purpose of sale, or
(c)   to buy goods, or
(d)   to raise money on the security of goods.

PART IV
PERFORMANCE OF THE CONTRACT

27   Duties of seller and buyer
It is the duty of the seller to deliver the goods, and of the buyer to accept and pay for them, in accordance with the terms of the contract of sale.

28   Payment and delivery are concurrent conditions
Unless otherwise agreed, delivery of the goods and payment of the price are concurrent conditions, that is to say, the seller must be ready and willing to give possession of the goods to the buyer in exchange for the price and the buyer must be ready and willing to pay the price in exchange for possession of the goods.

29   Rules about delivery
(1)   Whether it is for the buyer to take possession of the goods or for the seller to send them to the buyer is a question depending in each case on the contract, express or implied, between the parties.

(2)   Apart from any such contract, express or implied, the place of delivery is the seller's place of business if he has one, and if not, his residence; except that, if the contract is for the sale of specific goods, which to the knowledge of the parties when the contract is made are in some other place, then that place is the place of delivery.

(3)   Where under the contract of sale the seller is bound to send the goods to the buyer, but no time for sending them is fixed, the seller is bound to send them within a reasonable time.

(4)   Where the goods at the time of sale are in the possession of a third person, there is no delivery by seller to buyer unless and until the third person acknowledges to the buyer that he holds the goods on his behalf; but nothing in this section affects the operation of the issue or transfer of any document of title to goods.

(5)   Demand or tender of delivery may be treated as ineffectual unless made at a reasonable hour, and what is a reasonable hour is a question of fact.

(6)   Unless otherwise agreed, the expenses of and incidental to putting the goods into a deliverable state must be borne by the seller.

30   Delivery of wrong quantity
(1)   Where the seller delivers to the buyer a quantity of goods less than he contracted to sell, the buyer may reject them, but if the buyer accepts the goods so delivered he must pay for them at the contract rate.

(2)   Where the seller delivers to the buyer a quantity of goods larger than he contracted to sell, the buyer may accept the goods included in the contract and reject the rest, or he may reject the whole.

. . .

(2C)   Subsections (2A) and (2B) above do not apply to Scotland.

(2D)   Where the seller delivers a quantity of goods—
(a)   less than he contracted to sell, the buyer shall not be entitled to reject the goods under subsection (1) above,
(b)   larger than he contracted to sell, the buyer shall not be entitled to reject the whole under subsection (2) above,
unless the shortfall or excess is material.

(2E)   Subsection (2D) above applies to Scotland only.]

(3)   Where the seller delivers to the buyer a quantity of goods larger than he

contracted to sell and the buyer accepts the whole of the goods so delivered he must pay for them at the contract rate.

[. . .]

(5)   This section is subject to any usage of trade, special agreement, or course of dealing between the parties.

31   Instalment deliveries

(1)   Unless otherwise agreed, the buyer of goods is not bound to accept delivery of them by instalments.

(2)   Where there is a contract for the sale of goods to be delivered by stated instalments, which are to be separately paid for, and the seller makes defective deliveries in respect of one or more instalments, or the buyer neglects or refuses to take delivery of or pay for one or more instalments, it is a question in each case depending on the terms of the contract and the circumstances of the case whether the breach of contract is a repudiation of the whole contract or whether it is a severable breach giving rise to a claim for compensation but not to a right to treat the whole contract as repudiated.

32   Delivery to carrier

(1)   Where, in pursuance of a contract of sale, the seller is authorised or required to send the goods to the buyer, delivery of the goods to a carrier (whether named by the buyer or not) for the purpose of transmission to the buyer is prima facie deemed to be delivery of the goods to the buyer.

(2)   Unless otherwise authorised by the buyer, the seller must make such contact with the carrier on behalf of the buyer as may be reasonable having regard to the nature of the goods and the other circumstances of the case; and if the seller omits to do so, and the goods are lost or damaged in course of transit, the buyer may decline to treat the delivery to the carrier as a delivery to himself or may hold the seller responsible in damages.

(3)   Unless otherwise agreed, where goods are sent by the seller to the buyer by a route involving sea transit, under circumstances in which it is usual to insure, the seller must give such notice to the buyer as may enable him to insure them during their sea transit, and if the seller fails to do so, the goods are at his risk during such sea transit.

[(4)   In a case where the buyer deals as consumer or, in Scotland, where there is a consumer contract in which the buyer is a consumer, subsections (1) to (3) above must be ignored, but if in pursuance of a contract of sale the seller is authorised or required to send the goods to the buyer, delivery of the goods to the carrier is not delivery of the goods to the buyer.]

33   Risk where goods are delivered at distant place

Where the seller of goods agrees to deliver them at his own risk at a place other than that where they are when sold, the buyer must nevertheless (unless otherwise agreed) take any risk of deterioration in the goods necessarily incident to the course of transit.

34   Buyer's right of examining the goods

[Unless otherwise agreed, when the seller tenders delivery of goods to the buyer, he is bound on request to afford the buyer a reasonable opportunity of examining the goods for the purpose of ascertaining whether they are in conformity with the contract and, in the case of a contract for sale by sample, of comparing the bulk with the sample.]

35   Acceptance

(1)   The buyer is deemed to have accepted the goods [subject to subsection (2) below—

   (a)   when he intimates to the seller that he has accepted them, or

(b)   when the goods have been delivered to him and he does any act in relation to them which is inconsistent with the ownership of the seller.

(2)   Where goods are delivered to the buyer, and he has not previously examined them, he is not deemed to have accepted them under subsection (1) above until he has had a reasonable opportunity of examining them for the purpose—

(a)   of ascertaining whether they are in conformity with the contract, and

(b)   in the case of a contract for sale by sample, of comparing the bulk with the sample.

(3)   Where the buyer deals as consumer or (in Scotland) the contract of sale is a consumer contract, the buyer cannot lose his right to rely on subsection (2) above by agreement, waiver or otherwise.

(4)   The buyer is also deemed to have accepted the goods when after the lapse of a reasonable time he retains the goods without intimating to the seller that he has rejected them.

(5)   The questions that are material in determining for the purposes of subsection (4) above whether a reasonable time has elapsed include whether the buyer has had a reasonable opportunity of examining the goods for the purpose mentioned in subsection (2) above.

(6)   The buyer is not by virtue of this section deemed to have accepted the goods merely because—

(a)   he asks for, or agrees to, their repair by or under an arrangement with the seller, or

(b)   the goods are delivered to another under a sub-sale or other disposition.

(7)   Where the contract is for the sale of goods making one or more commercial units, a buyer accepting any goods included in a unit is deemed to have accepted all the goods making the unit; and in this subsection 'commercial unit' means a unit division of which would materially impair the value of the goods or the character of the unit.

(8)]   Paragraph 10 of Schedule 1 below applies in relation to a contract made before 22 April 1967 or (in the application of this Act to Northern Ireland) 28 July 1967.

[35A   Right of partial rejection

(1)   If the buyer—

(a)   has the right to reject the goods by reason of a breach on the part of the seller that affects some or all of them, but

(b)   accepts some of the goods, including, where there are any goods unaffected by the breach, all such goods,

he does not by accepting them lose his right to reject the rest.

(2)   In the case of a buyer having the right to reject an instalment of goods, subsection (1) above applies as if references to the goods were references to the goods comprised in the instalment.

(3)   For the purposes of subsection (1) above, goods are affected by a breach if by reason of the breach they are not in conformity with the contract.

(4)   This section applies unless a contrary intention appears in, or is to be implied from, the contract.]

36   Buyer not bound to return rejected goods

Unless otherwise agreed, where goods are delivered to the buyer, and he refuses to accept them, having the right to do so, he is not bound to return them to the seller, but it is sufficient if he intimates to the seller that he refuses to accept them.

37   Buyer's liability for not taking delivery of goods

(1)   When the seller is ready and willing to deliver the goods, and requests the buyer to take delivery, and the buyer does not within a reasonable time after such request take delivery of the goods, he is liable to the seller for any loss occasioned

by his neglect or refusal to take delivery, and also for a reasonable charge for the care and custody of the goods.

(2)   Nothing in this section affects the rights of the seller where the neglect or refusal of the buyer to take delivery amounts to a repudiation of the contract.

PART V
RIGHTS OF UNPAID SELLER AGAINST THE GOODS

Preliminary

38   Unpaid seller defined

(1)   The seller of goods is an unpaid seller within the meaning of this Act—

(a)   when the whole of the price has not been paid or tendered;

(b)   when a bill of exchange or other negotiable instrument has been received as conditional payment, and the condition on which it was received has not been fulfilled by reason of the dishonour of the instrument or otherwise.

(2)   In this Part of this Act 'seller' includes any person who is in the position of a seller, as, for instance, an agent of the seller to whom the bill of lading has been indorsed, or a consignor or agent who has himself paid (or is directly responsible for) the price.

39   Unpaid seller's rights

(1)   Subject to this and any other Act, notwithstanding that the property in the goods may have passed to the buyer, the unpaid seller of goods, as such, has by implication of law—

(a)   a lien on the goods or right to retain them for the price while he is in possession of them;

(b)   in the case of the insolvency of the buyer, a right of stopping the goods in transit after he has parted with the possession of them;

(c)   a right of re-sale as limited by this Act.

(2)   Where the property in goods has not passed to the buyer, the unpaid seller has (in addition to his other remedies) a right of withholding delivery similar to and coextensive with his rights of lien or retention and stoppage in transit where the property has passed to the buyer.

[. . .]

Unpaid seller's lien

41   Seller's lien

(1)   Subject to this Act, the unpaid seller of goods who is in possession of them is entitled to retain possession of them until payment or tender of the price in the following cases:—

(a)   where the goods have been sold without any stipulation as to credit;

(b)   where the goods have been sold on credit but the term of credit has expired;

(c)   where the buyer becomes insolvent.

(2)   The seller may exercise his lien or right of retention notwithstanding that he is in possession of the goods as agent or bailee or custodier for the buyer.

42   Part delivery

Where an unpaid seller has made part delivery of the goods, he may exercise his lien or right of retention on the remainder, unless such part delivery has been made under such circumstances as to show an agreement to waive the lien or right of retention.

43   Termination of lien

(1)   The unpaid seller of goods loses his lien or right of retention in respect of them—

(a)   when he delivers the goods to a carrier or other bailee or custodier for the purpose of transmission to the buyer without reserving the right of disposal of the goods;

(b)   when the buyer or his agent lawfully obtains possession of the goods;

(c)   by waiver of the lien or right of retention.

(2)   An unpaid seller of goods who has a lien or right of retention in respect of them does not lose his lien or right of retention by reason only that he has obtained judgment or decree for the price of the goods.

Stoppage in transit

44   Right of stoppage in transit

Subject to this Act, when the buyer of goods becomes insolvent the unpaid seller who has parted with the possession of the goods has the right of stopping them in transit, that is to say, he may resume possession of the goods as long as they are in course of transit, and may retain them until payment or tender of the price.

45   Duration of transit

(1)   Goods are deemed to be in course of transit from the time when they are delivered to a carrier or other bailee or custodier for the purpose of transmission to the buyer, until the buyer or his agent in that behalf takes delivery of them from the carrier or other bailee or custodier.

(2)   If the buyer or his agent in that behalf obtains delivery of the goods before their arrival at the appointed destination, the transit is at an end.

(3)   If, after the arrival of the goods at the appointed destination, the carrier or other bailee or custodier acknowledges to the buyer or his agent that he holds the goods on his behalf and continues in possession of them as bailee or custodier for the buyer or his agent, the transit is at an end, and it is immaterial that a further destination for the goods may have been indicated by the buyer.

(4)   If the goods are rejected by the buyer, and the carrier or other bailee or custodier continues in possession of them, the transit is not deemed to be at an end, even if the seller has refused to receive them back.

(5)   When goods are delivered to a ship chartered by the buyer it is a question depending on the circumstances of the particular case whether they are in the possession of the master as a carrier or as agent to the buyer.

(6)   Where the carrier or other bailee or custodier wrongfully refuses to deliver the goods to the buyer or his agent in that behalf, the transit is deemed to be at an end.

(7)   Where part delivery of the goods has been made to the buyer or his agent in that behalf, the remainder of the goods may be stopped in transit, unless such part delivery has been made under such circumstances as to show an agreement to give up possession of the whole of the goods.

46   How stoppage in transit is effected

(1)   The unpaid seller may exercise his right of stoppage in transit either by taking actual possession of the goods or by giving notice of his claim to the carrier or other bailee or custodier in whose possession the goods are.

(2)   The notice may be given either to the person in actual possession of the goods or to his principal.

(3)   If given to the principal, the notice is ineffective unless given at such time and under such circumstances that the principal, by the exercise of reasonable diligence, may communicate it to his servant or agent in time to prevent a delivery to the buyer.

(4)   When notice of stoppage in transit is given by the seller to the carrier or other bailee or custodier in possession of the goods, he must re-deliver the goods to, or according to the directions of, the seller; and the expenses of the re-delivery must be borne by the seller.

Re-sale etc by buyer

47   Effect of sub-sale etc by buyer

(1)   Subject to this Act, the unpaid seller's right of lien or retention or stoppage in transit is not affected by any sale or other disposition of the goods which the buyer may have made, unless the seller has assented to it.

(2)   Where a document of title to goods has been lawfully transferred to any person as buyer or owner of the goods, and that person transfers the document to a person who takes it in good faith and for valuable consideration, then—

(a)   if the last-mentioned transfer was by way of sale the unpaid seller's right of lien or retention or stoppage in transit is defeated; and

(b)   if the last-mentioned transfer was made by way of pledge or other disposition for value, the unpaid seller's right of lien or retention of stoppage in transit can only be exercised subject to the rights of the transferee.

Rescission: and re-sale by seller

48   Rescission: and re-sale by seller

(1)   Subject to this section, a contract of sale is not rescinded by the mere exercise by an unpaid seller of his right of lien or retention or stoppage in transit.

(2)   Where an unpaid seller who has exercised his right of lien or retention or stoppage in transit re-sells the goods, the buyer acquires a good title to them as against the original buyer.

(3)   Where the goods are of a perishable nature, or where the unpaid seller gives notice to the buyer of his intention to re-sell, and the buyer does not within a reasonable time pay or tender the price, the unpaid seller may re-sell the goods and recover from the original buyer damages for any loss occasioned by his breach of contract.

(4)   Where the seller expressly reserves the right of re-sale in case the buyer should make default, and on the buyer making default re-sells the goods, the original contract of sale is rescinded but without prejudice to any claim the seller may have for damages.

[PART VA
ADDITIONAL RIGHTS OF BUYER IN CONSUMER CASES

48A   Introductory

(1)   This section applies if—

(a)   the buyer deals as consumer or, in Scotland, there is a consumer contract in which the buyer is a consumer, and

(b)   the goods do not conform to the contract of sale at the time of delivery.

(2)   If this section applies, the buyer has the right—

(a)   under and in accordance with section 48B below, to require the seller to repair or replace the goods, or

(b)   under and in accordance with section 48C below—

(i)   to require the seller to reduce the purchase price of the goods to the buyer by an appropriate amount, or

(ii)   to rescind the contract with regard to the goods in question.

(3)   For the purposes of subsection (1)(b) above goods which do not conform to the contract of sale at any time within the period of six months starting with the date on which the goods were delivered to the buyer must be taken not to have so conformed at that date.

(4)   Subsection (3) above does not apply if—

(a)   it is established that the goods did so conform at that date;

(b)   its application is incompatible with the nature of the goods or the nature of the lack of conformity.

48B   Repair or replacement of the goods

(1)   If section 48A above applies, the buyer may require the seller—

(a)   to repair the goods, or

(b)   to replace the goods.

(2)   If the buyer requires the seller to repair or replace the goods, the seller must—

(a)   repair or, as the case may be, replace the goods within a reasonable time but without causing significant inconvenience to the buyer;

(b)   bear any necessary costs incurred in doing so (including in particular the cost of any labour, materials or postage).

(3)   The buyer must not require the seller to repair or, as the case may be, replace the goods if that remedy is—

(a)   impossible, or

(b)   disproportionate in comparison to the other of those remedies, or

(c)   disproportionate in comparison to an appropriate reduction in the purchase price under paragraph (a), or rescission under paragraph (b), of section 48C(1) below.

(4)   One remedy is disproportionate in comparison to the other if the one imposes costs on the seller which, in comparison to those imposed on him by the other, are unreasonable, taking into account—

(a)   the value which the goods would have if they conformed to the contract of sale,

(b)   the significance of the lack of conformity, and

(c)   whether the other remedy could be effected without significant inconvenience to the buyer.

(5)   Any question as to what is a reasonable time or significant inconvenience is to be determined by reference to—

(a)   the nature of the goods, and

(b)   the purpose for which the goods were acquired.

48C   Reduction of purchase price or rescission of contract

(1)   If section 48A above applies, the buyer may—

(a)   require the seller to reduce the purchase price of the goods in question to the buyer by an appropriate amount, or

(b)   rescind the contract with regard to those goods,

if the condition in subsection (2) below is satisfied.

(2)   The condition is that—

(a)   by virtue of section 48B(3) above the buyer may require neither repair nor replacement of the goods; or

(b)   the buyer has required the seller to repair or replace the goods, but the seller is in breach of the requirement of section 48B(2)(a) above to do so within a reasonable time and without significant inconvenience to the buyer.

(3)   For the purposes of this Part, if the buyer rescinds the contract, any reimbursement to the buyer may be reduced to take account of the use he has had of the goods since they were delivered to him.

48D   Relation to other remedies etc

(1)   If the buyer requires the seller to repair or replace the goods the buyer must not act under subsection (2) until he has given the seller a reasonable time in which to repair or replace (as the case may be) the goods.

(2)   The buyer acts under this subsection if—

(a)   in England and Wales or Northern Ireland he rejects the goods and terminates the contract for breach of condition;

(b)   in Scotland he rejects any goods delivered under the contract and treats it as repudiated;

(c)   he requires the goods to be replaced or repaired (as the case may be).

48E   Powers of the court

(1)   In any proceedings in which a remedy is sought by virtue of this Part the court, in addition to any other power it has, may act under this section.

(2)   On the application of the buyer the court may make an order requiring specific performance or, in Scotland, specific implement by the seller of any obligation imposed on him by virtue of section 48B above.

(3)   Subsection (4) applies if—

(a)   the buyer requires the seller to give effect to a remedy under section 48B or 48C above or has claims to rescind under section 48C, but

(b)   the court decides that another remedy under section 48B or 48C is appropriate.

(4)   The court may proceed—

(a)   as if the buyer had required the seller to give effect to the other remedy, or if the other remedy is rescission under section 48C; or

(b)   as if the buyer had claimed to rescind the contract under that section.

(5)   If the buyer has claimed to rescind the contract the court may order that any reimbursement to the buyer is reduced to take account of the use he has had of the goods since they were delivered to him.

(6)   The court may make an order under this section unconditionally or on such terms and conditions as to damages, payment of the price and otherwise as it thinks just.

48F   Conformity with the contract

For the purposes of this Part, goods do not conform to a contract of sale if there is, in relation to the goods, a breach of an express term of the contract or a term implied by section 13, 14 or 15 above.]

PART VI

ACTIONS FOR BREACH OF THE CONTRACT

Seller's remedies

49   Action for price

(1)   Where, under a contract of sale, the property in the goods has passed to the buyer and he wrongfully neglects or refuses to pay for the goods according to the terms of the contract, the seller may maintain an action against him for the price of the goods.

(2)   Where, under a contract of sale, the price is payable on a day certain irrespective of delivery and the buyer wrongfully neglects or refuses to pay such price, the seller may maintain an action for the price, although the property in goods has not passed and the goods have not been appropriated to the contract.

(3)   Nothing in this section prejudices the right of the seller in Scotland to recover interest on the price from the date of tender of the goods, or from the date on which the price was payable, as the case may be.

50   Damages for non-acceptance

(1)   Where the buyer wrongfully neglects or refuses to accept and pay for the goods, the seller may maintain an action against him for damages for non-acceptance.

(2)   The measure of damages is the estimated loss directly and naturally resulting in the ordinary course of events, from the buyer's breach of contract.

(3)   Where there is an available market for the goods in question the measure of damages is prima facie to be ascertained by the difference between the contract price and the market or current price at the time or times when the goods ought to have been accepted or (if no time was fixed for acceptance) at the time of the refusal to accept.

Buyer's remedies

51 Damages for non-delivery

(1)   Where the seller wrongfully neglects or refuses to deliver the goods to the buyer, the buyer may maintain an action against the seller for damages for non-delivery.

(2)   The measure of damages is the estimated loss directly and naturally resulting, in the ordinary course of events, from the seller's breach of contract.

(3)   Where there is an available market for the goods in question the measure of damages is prima facie to be ascertained by the difference between the contract price and the market or current price of the goods at the time or times when they ought to have been delivered or (if no time was fixed) at the time of the refusal to deliver.

52 Specific performance

(1)   If any action for breach of contract to deliver specific or ascertained goods the court may, if it thinks fit, on the plaintiff's application, by its judgment or decree direct that the contract shall be performed specifically, without giving the defendant the option of retaining the goods on payment of damages.

(2)   The plaintiff's application may be made at any time before judgment or decree.

(3)   The judgment or decree may be unconditional, or on such terms and conditions as to damages, payment of the price and otherwise as seem just to the court.

(4)   The provisions of this section shall be deemed to be supplementary to, and not in derogation of, the right of specific implement in Scotland.

53 [*Does not apply to Scotland.*]

[53A Measure of damages as respects Scotland

(1)   The measure of damages for the seller's breach of contract is the estimated loss directly and naturally resulting, in the ordinary course of events, from the breach.

(2)   Where the seller's breach consists of the delivery of goods which are not of the quality required by the contract and the buyer retains the goods, such loss as aforesaid is prima facie the difference between the value of the goods at the time of delivery to the buyer and the value they would have had if they had fulfilled the contract.

(3)   This section applies to Scotland only.]

Interest, etc

54 Interest, etc

Nothing in this Act affects the right of the buyer or the seller to recover interest or special damages in any case where by law interest or special damages may be recoverable, or to recover money paid where the consideration for the payment of it has failed.

PART VII
SUPPLEMENTARY

55 Exclusion of implied terms

(1)   Where a right, duty or liability would arise under a contract of sale of goods by implication of law, it may (subject to the Unfair Contract Terms Act 1977) be negatived or varied by express agreement, or by the course of dealing between the parties, or by such usage as binds both parties to the contract.

(2)   An express [term] does not negative a [term] implied by this Act unless inconsistent with it.

(3)   Paragraph 11 of Schedule 1 below applies in relation to a contract made on

or after 18 May 1973 and before 1 February 1978, and paragraph 12 in relation to one made before 18 May 1973.

56 Conflict of laws

Paragraph 13 of Schedule 1 below applies in relation to a contract made on or after 18 May 1973 and before 1 February 1978, so as to make provision about conflict of laws in relation to such a contract.

57 Auction sales

(1)   Where goods are put up for sale by auction in lots, each lot is prima facie deemed to be the subject of a separate contract of sale.

(2)   A sale by auction is complete when the auctioneer announces its completion by the fall of the hammer, or in other customary manner; and until the announcement is made any bidder may retract his bid.

(3)   A sale by auction may be notified to be subject to a reserve or upset price, and a right to bid may also be reserved expressly by or on behalf of the seller.

(4)   Where a sale by auction is not notified to be subject to a right to bid by or on behalf of the seller, it is not lawful for the seller to bid himself or to employ any person to bid at the sale, or for the auctioneer knowingly to take any bid from the seller or any such person.

(5)   A sale contravening subsection (4) above may be treated as fraudulent by the buyer.

(6)   Where, in respect of a sale by auction, a right to bid is expressly reserved (but not otherwise) the seller or any one person on his behalf may bid at the auction.

58 Payment into court in Scotland

In Scotland where a buyer has elected to accept goods which he might have rejected, and to treat a breach of contract as only giving rise to a claim for damages, he may, in an action by the seller for the price, be required, in the discretion of the court before which the action depends, to consign or pay into court the price of the goods, or part of the price, or to give other reasonable security for its due payment.

59 Reasonable time a question of fact

Where a reference is made in this Act to a reasonable time the question what is a reasonable time is a question of fact.

60 Rights etc enforceable by action

Where a right, duty or liability is declared by this Act, it may (unless otherwise provided by this Act) be enforced by action.

61 Interpretation

(1)   In this Act, unless the context or subject matter otherwise requires,—

'action' includes counterclaim and set-off, and in Scotland condescendence and claim and compensation;

['bulk' means a mass or collection of goods of the same kind which—

(a)   is contained in a defined space or area; and

(b)   is such that any goods in the bulk are interchangeable with any other goods therein of the same number or quantity;]

'business' includes a profession and the activities of any government department (including a Northern Ireland department) or local or public authority;

'buyer' means a person who buys or agrees to buy goods;

['consumer contract' has the same meaning as in section 25(1) of the Unfair Contract Terms Act 1977; and for the purposes of this Act the onus of proving that a contract is not to be regarded as a consumer contract shall lie on the seller;]

'contract of sale' includes an agreement to sell as well as a sale;

'credit-broker' means a person acting in the course of a business of credit brokerage carried on by him, that is a business of effecting introductions of individuals desiring to obtain credit—

(a)   to persons carrying on any business so far as it relates to the provision of credit, or

(b)   to other persons engaged in credit brokerage;

'defendant' includes in Scotland defender, respondent, and claimant in a multiplepoinding;

'delivery' means voluntary transfer of possession from one person to another; [except that in relation to sections 20A and 20B above it includes such appropriation of goods to the contract as results in property in the goods being transferred to the buyer;]

'document of title to goods' has the same meaning as it has in the Factors Acts;

'Factors Acts' means the Factors Act 1889, the Factors (Scotland) Act 1890, and any enactment amending or substituted for the same;

'fault' means wrongful act or default;

'future goods' means goods to be manufactured or acquired by the seller after the making of the contract of sale;

'goods' includes all personal chattels other than things in action and money, and in Scotland all corporeal moveables except money; and in particular 'goods' includes emblements, industrial growing crops, and things attached to or forming part of the land which are agreed to be severed before sale or under the contract of sale; [and includes an undivided share in goods;]

'plaintiff' includes pursuer, complainer, claimant in a multiplepoinding and defendant or defender counter-claiming;

['producer' means the manufacturer of goods, the importer of goods into the European Economic Area or any person purporting to be a producer by placing his name, trade mark or other distinctive sign on the goods;]

'property' means the general property in goods, and not merely a special property;

['repair' means, in cases where there is a lack of conformity in goods for the purposes of section 48F of this Act, to bring the goods into conformity with the contract;]

'sale' includes a bargain and sale as well as a sale and delivery;

'seller' means a person who sells or agrees to sell goods;

'specific goods' means goods identified and agreed on at the time a contract of sale is made; [and includes an undivided share, specified as a fraction or percentage, of goods identified and agreed on as aforesaid;]

'warranty' (as regards England and Wales and Northern Ireland) means an agreement with reference to goods which are the subject of a contract of sale, but collateral to the main purpose of such contract, the breach of which gives rise to a claim for damages, but not to a right to reject the goods and treat the contract as repudiated.

[. . .]

(3)   A thing is deemed to be done in good faith within the meaning of this Act when it is in fact done honestly, whether it is done negligently or not.

(4)   A person is deemed to be insolvent within the meaning of this Act if he has either ceased to pay his debts in the ordinary course of business or he cannot pay his debts as they become due, [. . .]

(5)   Goods are in a deliverable state within the meaning of this Act when they are in such a state that the buyer would under the contract be bound to take delivery of them.

[(5A)   References in this Act to dealing as consumer are to be construed in accordance with Part I of the Unfair Contract Terms Act 1977; and, for the purposes of this Act, it is for a seller claiming that the buyer does not deal as consumer to show that he does not.]

(6)   As regards the definition of 'business' in subsection (1) above, paragraph 14

of Schedule 1 below applies in relation to a contract made on or after 18 May 1973 and before 1 February 1978, and paragraph 15 in relation to one made before 18 May 1973,

62   Savings: rules of law etc

(1)   The rules in bankruptcy relating to contracts of sale apply to those contracts, notwithstanding anything in this Act.

(2)   The rules of the common law, including the law merchant, except in so far as they are inconsistent with the provisions of this Act, and in particular the rules relating to the law of principal and agent and the effect of fraud, misrepresentation, duress or coercion, mistake, or other invalidating cause, apply to contracts for the sale of goods.

(3)   Nothing in this Act or the Sale of Goods Act 1893 affects the enactments relating to bills of sale, or any enactment relating to the sale of goods which is not expressly repealed or amended by this Act or that.

(4)   The provisions of this Act about contracts of sale do not apply to a transaction in the form of a contract of sale which is intended to operate by way of mortgage, pledge, charge, or other security.

(5)   Nothing in this Act prejudices or affects the landlord's right of hypothec or sequestration for rent in Scotland.

64   Short title and commencement

(1)   This Act may be cited as the Sale of Goods Act 1979.

(2)   This Act comes into force on 1 January 1980.

CIVIL AVIATION ACT 1982
(1982, c 16)

Trespass by aircraft and aircraft nuisance, noise, etc

76   Liability of aircraft in respect of trespass, nuisance and surface damage

(1)   No action shall lie in respect of trespass or in respect of nuisance, by reason only of the flight of an aircraft over any property at a height above the ground which, having regard to wind, weather and all the circumstances of the case is reasonable, or the ordinary incidents of such flight, so long as the provisions of any Air Navigation Order and of any orders under section 62 above have been duly complied with and there has been no breach of section 81 below.

(2)   Subject to subsection (3) below, where material loss or damage is caused to any person or property on land or water by, or by a person in, or an article, animal or person falling from, an aircraft while in flight, taking off or landing, then unless the loss or damage was caused or contributed to by the negligence of the person by whom it was suffered, damages in respect of the loss or damage shall be recoverable without proof of negligence or intention or other cause of action, as if the loss or damage had been caused by the wilful act, neglect, or default of the owner of the aircraft.

(3)   Where material loss or damage is caused as aforesaid in circumstances in which—

(a)   damages are recoverable in respect of the said loss or damage by virtue only of subsection (2) above, and

(b)   a legal liability is created in some person other than the owner to pay damages in respect of the said loss or damage,

the owner shall be entitled to be indemnified by that other person against any claim in respect of the said loss or damage.

Rights etc in relation to aircraft

86 Power to provide for the mortgaging of aircraft

(1) Her Majesty may by Order in Council make provision for the mortgaging of aircraft registered in the United Kingdom or capable of being so registered.

(2) Without prejudice to the generality of the powers conferred by subsection (1) above, an Order in Council under this section may, in particular—

(a) include provisions which correspond (subject to such modifications as appear to Her Majesty in Council to be necessary or expedient) to any of the provisions of the Merchant Shipping Act [1995] relating to the mortgaging of ships;

(b) make provision as respects the rights and liabilities of mortgagors and mortgagees of such aircraft as are mentioned in subsection (1) above, and as respects the priority inter se of such rights and the relationship of such rights to other rights in or over such aircraft, including possessory liens for work done to such aircraft and rights under section 88 below or under regulations made by virtue of [section 83 of the Transport Act 2000 (detention and sale of aircraft)];

(c) make provision as respects the operation, in relation to such aircraft as aforesaid, of any of the enactments in force in any part of the United Kingdom relating to bills of sale or the registration of charges on the property or undertaking of companies;

(d) provide for the rights of mortgagees of such aircraft to be exercisable, in such circumstances as may be specified in the Order, in relation to payments for the use of the aircraft;

(e) confer on courts in the United Kingdom powers in respect of any register maintained in pursuance of the Order and in respect of transactions affecting aircraft registered therein;

(f) make provision for enabling the mortgage of an aircraft to extend to any store of spare parts for that aircraft and for applying, for that purpose, to any such spare parts provisions such as are mentioned in the preceding paragraphs of this subsection;

(g) make provision specifying, subject to the consent of the Treasury, the fees to be paid in respect of the making or deletion of entries in any such register as aforesaid and in respect of any other matters in respect of which it appears to Her Majesty in Council to be expedient for the purposes of the Order to charge fees;

(h) provide for the imposition of penalties in respect of the making of false statements in connection with matters dealt with in the Order and in respect of the forgery of documents relating to such matters.

SUPPLY OF GOODS AND SERVICES ACT 1982
(1982, c 29)

[PART IA
SUPPLY OF GOODS AS RESPECTS SCOTLAND

Contracts for the transfer of property in goods

11A The contracts concerned

(1) In this Act in its application to Scotland a 'contract for the transfer of goods' means a contract under which one person transfers or agrees to transfer to another the property in goods, other than an excepted contract.

(2) For the purposes of this section an excepted contract means any of the following—

(a) a contract of sale of goods;

(b) a hire-purchase agreement;

(c)   a contract under which the property in goods is (or is to be) transferred in exchange for trading stamps on their redemption;

(d)   a transfer or agreement to transfer for which there is no consideration;

(e)   a contract intended to operate by way of mortgage, pledge, charge or other security.

(3)   For the purposes of this Act in its application to Scotland a contract is a contract for the transfer of goods whether or not services are also provided or to be provided under the contract, and (subject to subsection (2) above) whatever is the nature of the consideration for the transfer or agreement to transfer.

11B   Implied terms about title, etc

(1)   In a contract for the transfer of goods, other than one to which subsection (3) below applies, there is an implied term on the part of the transferor that in the case of a transfer of the property in the goods he has a right to transfer the property and in the case of an agreement to transfer the property in the goods he will have such a right at the time when the property is to be transferred.

(2)   In a contract for the transfer of goods, other than one to which subsection (3) below applies, there is also an implied term that—

(a)   the goods are free, and will remain free until the time when the property is to be transferred, from any charge or encumbrance not disclosed or known to the transferee before the contract is made, and

(b)   the transferee will enjoy quiet possession of the goods except so far as it may be disturbed by the owner or other person entitled to the benefit of any charge or encumbrance so disclosed or known.

(3)   This subsection applies to a contract for the transfer of goods in the case of which there appears from the contract or is to be inferred from its circumstances an intention that the transferor should transfer only such title as he or a third person may have.

(4)   In a contract to which subsection (3) above applies there is an implied term that all charges or encumbrances known to the transferor and not known to the transferee have been disclosed to the transferee before the contract is made.

(5)   In a contract to which subsection (3) above applies there is also an implied term that none of the following will disturb the transferee's quiet possession of the goods, namely—

(a)   the transferor;

(b)   in a case where the parties to the contract intend that the transferor should transfer only such title as a third person may have, that person;

(c)   anyone claiming through or under the transferor or that third person otherwise than under a charge or encumbrance disclosed or known to the transferee before the contract is made.

(6)   [*amends Unfair Contract Terms Act 1977*]

11C   Implied terms where transfer is by description

(1)   This section applies where, under a contract for the transfer of goods, the transferor transfers or agrees to transfer the property in the goods by description.

(2)   In such a case there is an implied term that the goods will correspond with the description.

(3)   If the transferor transfers or agrees to transfer the property in the goods by reference to a sample as well as by description it is not sufficient that the bulk of the goods corresponds with the sample if the goods do not also correspond with the description.

(4)   A contract is not prevented from falling within subsection (1) above by reason only that, being exposed for supply, the goods are selected by the transferee.

11D   Implied terms about quality or fitness

(1)   Except as provided by this section and section 11E below and subject to the

provisions of any other enactment, there is no implied term about the quality or fitness for any particular purpose of goods supplied under a contract for the transfer of goods.

(2)   Where, under such a contract, the transferor transfers the property in goods in the course of a business, there is an implied term that the goods supplied under the contract are of satisfactory quality.

(3)   For the purposes of this section and section 11E below, goods are of satisfactory quality if they meet the standard that a reasonable person would regard as satisfactory, taking account of any description of the goods, the price (if relevant) and all the other relevant circumstances.

[(3A)   If the contract for the transfer of goods is a consumer contract, the relevant circumstances mentioned in subsection (3) above include any public statements on the specific characteristics of the goods made about them by the transferor, the producer or his representative, particularly in advertising or on labelling.

(3B)   A public statement is not by virtue of subsection (3A) above a relevant circumstance for the purposes of subsection (3) above in the case of a contract for the transfer of goods, if the transferor shows that—

(a)   at the time the contract was made, he was not, and could not reasonably have been, aware of the statement,

(b)   before the contract was made, the statement had been withdrawn in public or, to the extent that it contained anything which was incorrect or misleading, it had been corrected in public, or

(c)   the decision to acquire the goods could not have been influenced by the statement.

(3C)   Subsections (3A) and (3B) above do not prevent any public statement from being a relevant circumstance for the purposes of subsection (3) above (whether or not the contract for the transfer of goods is a consumer contract) if the statement would have been such a circumstance apart from those subsections.]

(4)   The term implied by subsection (2) above does not extend to any matter making the quality of goods unsatisfactory—

(a)   which is specifically drawn to the transferee's attention before the contract is made,

(b)   where the transferee examines the goods before the contract is made, which that examination ought to reveal, or

(c)   where the property in the goods is, or is to be, transferred by reference to a sample, which would have been apparent on a reasonable examination of the sample.

(5)   Subsection (6) below applies where, under a contract for the transfer of goods, the transferor transfers the property in goods in the course of a business and the transferee, expressly or by implication, makes known—

(a)   to the transferor, or

(b)   where the consideration or part of the consideration for the transfer is a sum payable by instalments and the goods were previously sold by a credit-broker to the transferor, to that credit-broker,

any particular purpose for which the goods are being acquired.

(6)   In that case there is (subject to subsection (7) below) an implied term that the goods supplied under the contract are reasonably fit for the purpose, whether or not that is a purpose for which such goods are commonly supplied.

(7)   Subsection (6) above does not apply where the circumstances show that the transferee does not rely, or that it is unreasonable for him to rely, on the skill or judgment of the transferor or credit-broker.

(8)   An implied term about quality or fitness for a particular purpose may be annexed by usage to a contract for the transfer of goods.

(9)   The preceding provisions of this section apply to a transfer by a person

who in the course of a business is acting as agent for another as they apply to a transfer by a principal in the course of a business, except where that other is not transferring in the course of a business and either the transferee knows that fact or reasonable steps are taken to bring it to the transferee's notice before the contract concerned is made.

[(10)   For the purposes of this section, 'consumer contract' has the same meaning as in section 11F(3) below.]

11E   Implied terms where transfer is by sample
(1)   This section applies where, under a contract for the transfer of goods, the transferor transfers or agrees to transfer the property in the goods by reference to a sample.
(2)   In such a case there is an implied term—
    (a)   that the bulk will correspond with the sample in quality;
    (b)   that the transferee will have a reasonable opportunity of comparing the bulk with the sample; and
    (c)   that the goods will be free from any defect, making their quality unsatisfactory, which would not be apparent on reasonable examination of the sample.
(3)   For the purposes of this section a transferor transfers or agrees to transfer the property in goods by reference to a sample where there is an express or implied term to that effect in the contract concerned.

11F   Remedies for breach of contract
(1)   Where in a contract for the transfer of goods a transferor is in breach of any term of the contract (express or implied), the other party to the contract (in this section referred to as 'the transferee') shall be entitled—
    (a)   to claim damages; and
    (b)   if the breach is material, to reject any goods delivered under the contract and treat it as repudiated.
(2)   Where a contract for the transfer of goods is a consumer contract and the transferee is the consumer, then, for the purposes of subsection (1)(b) above, breach by the transferor of any term (express or implied)—
    (a)   as to the quality of the goods or their fitness for a purpose;
    (b)   if the goods are, or are to be, transferred by description, that the goods will correspond with the description;
    (c)   if the goods are, or are to be, transferred by reference to a sample, that the bulk will correspond with the sample in quality,
shall be deemed to be a material breach.
(3)   In subsection (2) above, 'consumer contract' has the same meaning as in section 25(1) of the 1977 Act; and for the purposes of that subsection the onus of proving that a contract is not to be regarded as a consumer contract shall lie on the transferor.

Contracts for the hire of goods

11G   The contracts concerned
(1)   In this Act in its application to Scotland a 'contract for the hire of goods' means a contract under which one person ('the supplier') hires or agrees to hire goods to another, other than an excepted contract.
(2)   For the purposes of this section, an excepted contract means any of the following—
    (a)   a hire-purchase agreement;
    (b)   a contract under which goods are (or are to be) hired in exchange for trading stamps on their redemption.
(3)   For the purposes of this Act in its application to Scotland a contract is a contract for the hire of goods whether or not services are also provided or to be

provided under the contract, and (subject to subsection (2) above) whatever is the nature of the consideration for the hire or agreement to hire.

11H Implied terms about right to transfer possession etc

(1) In a contract for the hire of goods there is an implied term on the part of the supplier that—

(a) in the case of a hire, he has a right to transfer possession of the goods by way of hire for the period of the hire; and

(b) in the case of an agreement to hire, he will have such a right at the time of commencement of the period of the hire.

(2) In a contract for the hire of goods there is also an implied term that the person to whom the goods are hired will enjoy quiet possession of the goods for the period of the hire except so far as the possession may be disturbed by the owner or other person entitled to the benefit of any charge or encumbrance disclosed or known to the person to whom the goods are hired before the contract is made.

(3) The preceding provisions of this section do not affect the right of the supplier to repossess the goods under an express or implied term of the contract.

11I Implied terms where hire is by description

(1) This section applies where, under a contract for the hire of goods, the supplier hires or agrees to hire the goods by description.

(2) In such a case there is an implied term that the goods will correspond with the description.

(3) If under the contract the supplier hires or agrees to hire the goods by reference to a sample as well as by description it is not sufficient that the bulk of the goods corresponds with the sample if the goods do not also correspond with the description.

(4) A contract is not prevented from falling within subsection (1) above by reason only that, being exposed for supply, the goods are selected by the person to whom the goods are hired.

11J Implied terms about quality or fitness

(1) Except as provided by this section and section 11K below and subject to the provisions of any other enactment, there is no implied term about the quality or fitness for any particular purpose of goods hired under a contract for the hire of goods.

(2) Where, under such a contract, the supplier hires goods in the course of a business, there is an implied term that the goods supplied under the contract are of satisfactory quality.

(3) For the purposes of this section and section 11K below, goods are of satisfactory quality if they meet the standard that a reasonable person would regard as satisfactory, taking account of any description of the goods, the consideration for the hire (if relevant) and all the other relevant circumstances.

[(3A) If the contract for the transfer of goods is a consumer contract, the relevant circumstances mentioned in subsection (3) above include any public statements on the specific characteristics of the goods made about them by the transferor, the producer or his representative, particularly in advertising or on labelling.

(3B) A public statement is not by virtue of subsection (3A) above a relevant circumstance for the purposes of subsection (3) above in the case of a contract for the transfer of goods, if the transferor shows that—

(a) at the time the contract was made, he was not, and could not reasonably have been, aware of the statement,

(b) before the contract was made, the statement had been withdrawn in public or, to the extent that it contained anything which was incorrect or misleading, it had been corrected in public, or

(c) the decision to acquire the goods could not have been influenced by the statement.

(3C)   Subsections (3A) and (3B) above do not prevent any public statement from being a relevant circumstance for the purposes of subsection (3) above (whether or not the contract for the transfer of goods is a consumer contract) if the statement would have been such a circumstance apart from those subsections.]

(4)   The term implied by subsection (2) above does not extend to any matter making the quality of goods unsatisfactory—

(a)   which is specifically drawn to the attention of the person to whom the goods are hired before the contract is made, or

(b)   where that person examines the goods before the contract is made, which that examination ought to reveal; or

(c)   where the goods are hired by reference to a sample, which would have been apparent on reasonable examination of the sample.

(5)   Subsection (6) below applies where, under a contract for the hire of goods, the supplier hires goods in the course of a business and the person to whom the goods are hired, expressly or by implication, makes known—

(a)   to the supplier in the course of negotiations conducted by him in relation to the making of the contract; or

(b)   to a credit-broker in the course of negotiations conducted by that broker in relation to goods sold by him to the supplier before forming the subject matter of the contract,

any particular purpose for which the goods are being hired.

(6)   In that case there is (subject to subsection (7) below) an implied term that the goods supplied under the contract are reasonably fit for that purpose, whether or not that is a purpose for which such goods are commonly supplied.

(7)   Subsection (6) above does not apply where the circumstances show that the person to whom the goods are hired does not rely, or that it is unreasonable for him to rely, on the skill or judgment of the hirer or credit-broker.

(8)   An implied term about quality or fitness for a particular purpose may be annexed by usage to a contract for the hire of goods.

(9)   The preceding provisions of this section apply to a hire by a person who in the course of a business is acting as agent for another as they apply to a hire by a principal in the course of a business, except where that other is not hiring in the course of a business and either the person to whom the goods are hired knows that fact or reasonable steps are taken to bring it to that person's notice before the contract concerned is made.

[(10)   For the purposes of this section, 'consumer contract' has the same meaning as in section 11F(3) above.]

11K   Implied terms where hire is by sample

(1)   This section applies where, under a contract for the hire of goods, the supplier hires or agrees to hire the goods by reference to a sample.

(2)   In such a case there is an implied term—

(a)   that the bulk will correspond with the sample in quality; and

(b)   that the person to whom the goods are hired will have a reasonable opportunity of comparing the bulk with the sample; and

(c)   that the goods will be free from any defect, making their quality unsatisfactory, which would not be apparent on reasonable examination of the sample.

(3)   For the purposes of this section a supplier hires or agrees to hire goods by reference to a sample where there is an express or implied term to that effect in the contract concerned.

Exclusion of implied terms, etc

11L   Exclusion of implied terms etc

(1)   Where a right, duty or liability would arise under a contract for the transfer of goods or a contract for the hire of goods by implication of law, it may (subject to

subsection (2) below and the 1977 Act) be negatived or varied by express agreement, or by the course of dealing between the parties, or by such usage as binds both parties to the contract.

(2)   An express term does not negative a term implied by the preceding provisions of this Part of this Act unless inconsistent with it.

(3)   Nothing in the preceding provisions of this Part of this Act prejudices the operation of any other enactment or any rule of law whereby any term (other than one relating to quality or fitness) is to be implied in a contract for the transfer of goods or a contract for the hire of goods.]

[PART IB
ADDITIONAL RIGHTS OF TRANSFEREE IN CONSUMER CASES

11M   Introductory

(1)   This section applies if—

(a)   the transferee deals as consumer or, in Scotland, there is a consumer contract in which the transferee is a consumer, and

(b)   the goods do not conform to the contract for the transfer of goods at the time of delivery.

(2)   If this section applies, the transferee has the right—

(a)   under and in accordance with section 11N below, to require the transferor to repair or replace the goods, or

(b)   under and in accordance with section 11P below—

(i)   to require the transferor to reduce the amount to be paid for the transfer by the transferee by an appropriate amount, or

(ii)   to rescind the contract with regard to the goods in question.

(3)   For the purposes of subsection (1)(b) above, goods which do not conform to the contract for the transfer of goods at any time within the period of six months starting with the date on which the goods were delivered to the transferee must be taken not to have so conformed at that date.

(4)   Subsection (3) above does not apply if—

(a)   it is established that the goods did so conform at that date;

(b)   its application is incompatible with the nature of the goods or the nature of the lack of conformity.

(5)   For the purposes of this section, 'consumer contract' has the same meaning as in section 11F(3) above.

11N   Repair or replacement of the goods

(1)   If section 11M above applies, the transferee may require the transferor—

(a)   to repair the goods, or

(b)   to replace the goods.

(2)   If the transferee requires the transferor to repair or replace the goods, the transferor must—

(a)   repair or, as the case may be, replace the goods within a reasonable time but without causing significant inconvenience to the transferee;

(b)   bear any necessary costs incurred in doing so (including in particular the cost of any labour, materials or postage).

(3)   The transferee must not require the transferor to repair or, as the case may be, replace the goods if that remedy is—

(a)   impossible,

(b)   disproportionate in comparison to the other of those remedies, or

(c)   disproportionate in comparison to an appropriate reduction in the purchase price under paragraph (a), or rescission under paragraph (b), of section 11P(1) below.

(4)   One remedy is disproportionate in comparison to the other if the one imposes costs on the transferor which, in comparison to those imposed on him by the other, are unreasonable, taking into account—

(a)   the value which the goods would have if they conformed to the contract for the transfer of goods,

(b)   the significance of the lack of conformity to the contract for the transfer of goods, and

(c)   whether the other remedy could be effected without significant inconvenience to the transferee.

(5)   Any question as to what is a reasonable time or significant inconvenience is to be determined by reference to—

(a)   the nature of the goods, and

(b)   the purpose for which the goods were acquired.

11P   Reduction of purchase price or rescission of contract

(1)   If section 11M above applies, the transferee may—

(a)   require the transferor to reduce the purchase price of the goods in question to the transferee by an appropriate amount, or

(b)   rescind the contract with regard to those goods,

if the condition in subsection (2) below is satisfied.

(2)   The condition is that—

(a)   by virtue of section 11N(3) above the transferee may require neither repair nor replacement of the goods, or

(b)   the transferee has required the transferor to repair or replace the goods, but the transferor is in breach of the requirement of section 11N(2)(a) above to do so within a reasonable time and without significant inconvenience to the transferee.

(3)   If the transferee rescinds the contract, any reimbursement to the transferee may be reduced to take account of the use he has had of the goods since they were delivered to him.

11Q   Relation to other remedies etc

(1)   If the transferee requires the transferor to repair or replace the goods the transferee must not act under subsection (2) until he has given the transferor a reasonable time in which to repair or replace (as the case may be) the goods.

(2)   The transferee acts under this subsection if—

(a)   in England and Wales or Northern Ireland he rejects the goods and terminates the contract for breach of condition;

(b)   in Scotland he rejects any goods delivered under the contract and treats it as repudiated; or

(c)   he requires the goods to be replaced or repaired (as the case may be).

11R   Powers of the court

(1)   In any proceedings in which a remedy is sought by virtue of this Part the court, in addition to any other power it has, may act under this section.

(2)   On the application of the transferee the court may make an order requiring specific performance or, in Scotland, specific implement by the transferor of any obligation imposed on him by virtue of section 11N above.

(3)   Subsection (4) applies if—

(a)   the transferee requires the transferor to give effect to a remedy under section 11N or 11P above or has claims to rescind under section 11P, but

(b)   the court decides that another remedy under section 11N or 11P is appropriate.

(4)   The court may proceed—

(a)   as if the transferee had required the transferor to give effect to the other remedy, or if the other remedy is rescission under section 11P,

(b)   as if the transferee had claimed to rescind the contract under that section.

(5)   If the transferee has claimed to rescind the contract the court may order that any reimbursement to the transferee is reduced to take account of the use he has had of the goods since they were delivered to him.

(6) The court may make an order under this section unconditionally or on such terms and conditions as to damages, payment of the price and otherwise as it thinks just.

11S Conformity with the contract
(1) Goods do not conform to a contract for the supply or transfer of goods if—
(a) there is, in relation to the goods, a breach of an express term of the contract or a term implied by section 3, 4 or 5 above or, in Scotland, by section 11C, 11D or 11E above, or
(b) installation of the goods forms part of the contract for the transfer of goods, and the goods were installed by the transferor, or under his responsibility, in breach of the term implied by section 13 below or (in Scotland) in breach of any term implied by any rule of law as to the manner in which the installation is carried out.]

ADMINISTRATION OF JUSTICE ACT 1982
(1982, c 53)

8 Services rendered to injured person
(1) Where necessary services have been rendered to the injured person by a relative in consequence of the injuries in question, then, unless the relative has expressly agreed in the knowledge that an action for damages has been raised or is in contemplation that no payment should be made in respect of those services, the responsible person shall be liable to pay to the injured person by way of damages such sum as represents reasonable remuneration for those services and repayment of reasonable expenses incurred in connection therewith.
[(2) The injured person shall be under an obligation to account to the relative for any damages recovered from the responsible person under subsection (1) above.
(3) Where, at the date of an award of damages in favour of the injured person, it is likely that necessary services will, after that date, be rendered to him by a relative in consequence of the injuries in question, then, unless the relative has expressly agreed that no payment shall be made in respect of those services, the responsible person shall be liable to pay to the injured person by way of damages such sum as represents—
(a) reasonable remuneration for those services; and
(b) reasonable expenses which are likely to be incurred in connection therewith.
(4) The relative shall have no direct right of action in delict against the responsible person in respect of any services or expenses referred to in this section.]

9 Services to injured person's relative
(1) The responsible person shall be liable to pay to the injured person a reasonable sum by way of damages in respect of the inability of the injured person to render the personal services referred to in subsection (3) below.
(2) Where the injured person has died, any relative of his entitled to damages in respect of loss of support under section 1(3) of the Damages (Scotland) Act 1976 shall be entitled to include as a head of damage under that section a reasonable sum in respect of the loss to him of the personal services mentioned in subsection (3) below.
(3) The personal services referred to in subsections (1) and (2) above are personal services—
(a) which were or might have been expected to have been rendered by the injured person before the occurrence of the act or omission giving rise to liability,
(b) of a kind which, when rendered by a person other than a relative, would ordinarily be obtainable on payment, and

(c) which the injured person but for the injuries in question might have been expected to render gratuitously to a relative.

(4) Subject to subsection (2) above, the relative shall have no direct right of action in delict against the responsible person in respect of the personal services mentioned in subsection (3) above.

10 Assessment of damages for personal injuries

Subject to any agreement to the contrary, in assessing the amount of damages payable to the injured person in respect of personal injuries there shall not be taken into account so as to reduce that amount—

(a) any contractual pension or benefit (including any payment by a friendly society or trade union);

(b) any pension or retirement benefit payable from public funds other than any pension or benefit to which section 2(1) of the Law Reform (Personal Injuries) Act 1948 applies;

(c) any benefit payable from public funds, in respect of any period after the date of the award of damages, designed to secure to the injured person or any relative of his a minimum level of subsistence;

(d) any redundancy payment under the [Employment Rights Act 1996], or any payment made in circumstances corresponding to those in which a right to a redundancy payment would have accrued if section 135 of that Act had applied;

(e) any payment made to the injured person or to any relative of his by the injured person's employer following upon the injuries in question where the recipient is under an obligation to reimburse the employer in the event of damages being recovered in respect of those injuries;

(f) subject to paragraph (iv) below, any payment of a benevolent character made to the injured person or to any relative of his by any person following upon the injuries in question;
but there shall be taken into account—

(i) any remuneration or earnings from employment;

(ii) any [contribution-based jobseeker's allowance (payable under the Jobseekers Act 1995)];

(iii) any benefit referred to in paragraph (c) above payable in respect of any period prior to the date of the award of damages;

(iv) any payment of a benevolent character made to the injured person or to any relative of his by the responsible person following on the injuries in question, where such a payment is made directly and not through a trust or other fund from which the injured person or his relatives have benefited or may benefit.

11 Maintenance at public expense to be taken into account in assessment of damages: Scotland

In an action for damages for personal injuries (including any such action arising out of a contract) any saving to the injured person which is attributable to his maintenance wholly or partly at public expense in—

(a) a hospital [. . .] or other institution

[(b) accommodation provided by a care home service (as defined by section 2(3) of the Regulation of Care (Scotland) Act 2001 (asp 8)).]
shall be set off against any income lost by him as a result of the injuries.

12 Award of provisional damages for personal injuries: Scotland

(1) This section applies to an action for damages for personal injuries in which—

(a) there is proved or admitted to be a risk that at some definite or indefinite time in the future the injured person will, as a result of the act or omission which gave rise to the cause of the action, develop some serious disease or suffer some serious deterioration in his physical or mental condition; and

(b)   the responsible person was, at the time of the act or omission giving rise to the cause of the action,
    (i)   a public authority or public corporation; or
    (ii)   insured or otherwise indemnified in respect of the claim.
(2)   In any case to which this section applies, the court may, on the application of the injured person, order—
    (a)   that the damages referred to in subsection (4)(a) below be awarded to the injured person; and
    (b)   that the injured person may apply for the further award of damages referred to in subsection (4)(b) below,
and the court may, if it considers it appropriate, order that an application under paragraph (b) above may be made only within a specified period.
(3)   Where an injured person in respect of whom an award has been made under subsection (2)(a) above applies to the court for an award under subsection (2)(b) above, the court may award to the injured person the further damages referred to in subsection (4)(b) below.
(4)   The damages referred to in subsections (2) and (3) above are—
    (a)   damages assessed on the assumption that the injured person will not develop the disease or suffer the deterioration in his condition; and
    (b)   further damages if he develops the disease or suffers the deterioration.
(5)   Nothing in this section shall be construed—
    (a)   as affecting the exercise of any power relating to expenses including a power to make rules of court relating to expenses; or
    (b)   as prejudicing any duty of the court under any enactment or rule of law to reduce or limit the total damages which would have been recoverable apart from any such duty.
(6)   The Secretary of State may, by order, provide that categories of defenders shall, for the purposes of paragraph (b) of subsection (1) above, become or cease to be responsible persons, and may make such modifications of that paragraph as appear to him to be necessary for the purpose.
And an order under this subsection shall be made by statutory instrument subject to annulment in pursuance of a resolution of either House of Parliament.

13   Supplementary

(1)   In this Part of this Act, unless the context otherwise requires—
'personal injuries' includes any disease or any impairment of a person's physical or mental condition [and injury resulting from defamation or any other verbal injury or other injury to reputation].
'relative', in relation to the injured person, means—
    (a)   the spouse or divorced spouse;
    [(aa)   the civil partner or former civil partner,]
    (b)   any person, not being the spouse of the injured person, who was, at the time of the act or omission giving rise to liability in the responsible person, living with the injured person as husband or wife;
    (c)   any ascendant or descendant;
    (d)   any brother, sister, uncle or aunt; or any issue of any such person;
    (e)   any person accepted by the injured person as a child of his family.
In deducing any relationship for the purposes of the foregoing definition—
    (a)   any relationship by affinity shall be treated as a relationship by consanguinity; any relationship of the half blood shall be treated as a relationship of the whole blood; and the stepchild of any person shall be treated as his child; and
    (b)   [section 1(1) of the Law Reform (Parent and Child) (Scotland) Act 1986 shall apply; and any reference (however expressed) in this Part of this Act to a relative shall be construed accordingly.]
(2)   Any reference in this Part of this Act to a payment, benefit or pension shall

be construed as a reference to any such payment, benefit or pension whether in cash or in kind.

(3)   This Part of this Act binds the Crown.

LAW REFORM (HUSBAND AND WIFE) (SCOTLAND) ACT 1984
(1984, c 15)

Abolition of actions of breach of promise of marriage, adherence and enticement

1 Promise of marriage not an enforceable obligation

(1)   No promise of marriage or agreement between two persons to marry one another shall have effect under the law of Scotland to create any rights or obligations; and no action for breach of any such promise or agreement may be brought in any court in Scotland, whatever the law applicable to the promise or agreement.

(2)   This section shall have effect in relation to any promise made or agreement entered into before it comes into force, but shall not affect any action commenced before it comes into force.

2 Actions of adherence and enticement abolished

(1)   No spouse shall be entitled to apply for a decree from any court in Scotland ordaining the other spouse to adhere.

(2)   No person shall be liable in delict to any person by reason only of having induced the spouse of that person to leave or remain apart from that person.

(3)   This section shall not affect any action commenced before this Act comes into force.

LAW REFORM (MISCELLANEOUS PROVISIONS) (SCOTLAND) ACT 1985
(1985, c 73)

Provisions relating to leases

. . .

4 Irritancy clauses etc relating to monetary breaches of lease

(1)   A landlord shall not, for the purpose of treating a lease as terminated or terminating it, be entitled to rely—

(a)   on a provision in the lease which purports to terminate it, or to enable him to terminate it, in the event of a failure of the tenant to pay rent, or to make any other payment, on or before the due date therefor or such later date or within such period as may be provided for in the lease; or

(b)   on the fact that such a failure is, or is deemed by a provision of the lease to be, a material breach of contract,

unless subsection (2) or (5) below applies.

(2)   This subsection applies if—

(a)   the landlord has, at any time after the payment of rent or other payment mentioned in subsection (1) above has become due, served a notice on the tenant—

(i)   requiring the tenant to make payment of the sum which he has failed to pay together with any interest thereon in terms of the lease within the period specified in the notice; and

(ii)   stating that, if the tenant does not comply with the requirement mentioned in sub-paragraph (i) above, the lease may be terminated; and

(b)   the tenant has not complied with that requirement.

(3)   The period to be specified in any such notice shall be not less than—

(a)   a period of 14 days immediately following the service of the notice; or

(b)   if any period remaining between the service of the notice and the expiry of any time provided for in the lease or otherwise for the late payment of the sum which the tenant has failed to pay is greater than 14 days, that greater period.

(4)   Any notice served under subsection (2) above shall be sent by recorded delivery and shall be sufficiently served if it is sent to the tenant's last business or residential address in the United Kingdom known to the landlord or to the last address in the United Kingdom provided to the landlord by the tenant for the purpose of such service.

(5)   This subsection applies if the tenant does not have an address in the United Kingdom known to the landlord and has not provided an address in the United Kingdom to the landlord for the purpose of service.

5   Irritancy clauses etc not relating to monetary breaches of leases

(1)   Subject to subsection (2) below, a landlord shall not, for the purpose of treating a lease as terminated or terminating it, be entitled to rely—

(a)   on a provision in the lease which purports to terminate it, or to enable the landlord to terminate it, in the event of an act or omission by the tenant (other than such a failure as is mentioned in section 4(1)(a) of this Act) or of a change in the tenant's circumstances; or

(b)   on the fact that such act or omission or change is, or is deemed by a provision of the lease to be, a material breach of contract,

if in all the circumstances of the case a fair and reasonable landlord would not seek so to rely.

(2)   No provision of a lease shall of itself, irrespective of the particular circumstances of the case, be held to be unenforceable by virtue of subsection (1) above.

(3)   In the consideration, for the purposes of subsection (1)(a) or (b) above, of the circumstances of a case where—

(a)   an act, omission or change is alleged to constitute a breach of a provision of the lease or a breach of contract; and

(b)   the breach is capable of being remedied in reasonable time,

regard shall be had to whether a reasonable opportunity has been afforded to the tenant to enable the breach to be remedied.

6   Supplementary and transitional provisions relating to sections 4 and 5

(1)   The parties to a lease shall not be entitled to disapply any provision of section 4 or 5 of this Act from it.

(2)   Where circumstances have occurred before the commencement of sections 4 and 5 of this Act which would have entitled a landlord to terminate a lease in reliance on a provision in the lease or on the ground that the circumstances constituted a material breach of contract, but the landlord has not before such commencement given written notice to the tenant of his intention to terminate the lease in respect of those circumstances, he shall, after such commencement, be entitled to terminate the lease in respect of those circumstances only in accordance with the provisions of section 4 or 5 (as the case may be) of this Act.

(3)   Nothing in section 4 or 5 of this Act shall apply in relation to any payment which has to be made, or any other condition which has to be fulfilled, before a tenant is entitled to entry under a lease.

7   Interpretation of sections 4 to 6

(1)   In sections 4 to 6 of this Act 'lease' means a lease of land, whether entered into before or after the commencement of those sections, but does not include a lease of land—

(a)   used wholly or mainly for residential purposes;

(b)   comprising [. . .] a croft, the subject of a cottar or the holding of a landholder or a statutory small tenant [; or

(c)   where the lease is an agricultural lease.]

(2)   In subsection (1) above—

['agricultural lease' means a lease constituting a 1991 Act tenancy within the meaning of the Agricultural Holdings (Scotland) Act 2003 (asp 11) or a lease constituting a short limited duration tenancy or a limited duration tenancy (within the meaning of that Act);]

'cottar' has the same meaning as in section 28(4) of the Crofters (Scotland) Act 1955;

'croft' has the same meaning as in section 3 of the Crofters (Scotland) Act 1955; and

'holding' (in relation to a landholder or statutory small tenant), 'landholder' and 'statutory small tenant' have the same meanings as in the Small Landholders (Scotland) Acts 1886 to 1931.

Provisions relating to other contracts and obligations

8 Rectification of defectively expressed documents

(1) Subject to section 9 of this Act, where the court is satisfied, on an application made to it, that—

(a) a document intended to express or to give effect to an agreement fails to express accurately the common intention of the parties to the agreement at the date when it was made; or

(b) a document intended to create, transfer, vary or renounce a right, not being a document falling within paragraph (a) above, fails to express accurately the intention of the grantor of the document at the date when it was executed,

it may order the document to be rectified in any manner that it may specify in order to give effect to that intention.

(2) For the purposes of subsection (1) above, the court shall be entitled to have regard to all relevant evidence, whether written or oral.

(3) Subject to section 9 of this Act, in ordering the rectification of a document under subsection (1) above (in this subsection referred to as 'the original document'), the court may, at its own instance or on an application made to it, order the rectification of any other document intended for any of the purposes mentioned in paragraph (a) or (b) of subsection (1) above which is defectively expressed by reason of the defect in the original document.

(4) Subject to section 9(4) of this Act, a document ordered to be rectified under this section shall have effect as if it had always been so rectified.

(5) Subject to section 9(5) of this Act, where a document recorded in the Register of Sasines is ordered to be rectified under this section and the order is likewise recorded, the document shall be treated as having been always so recorded as rectified.

(6) Nothing in this section shall apply to a document of a testamentary nature.

(7) It shall be competent to register in the Register of Inhibitions and Adjudications a notice of an application under this section for the rectification of a deed relating to land, being an application in respect of which authority for service or citation has been granted; and the land to which the application relates shall be rendered litigious as from the date of registration of such a notice.

(8) A notice under subsection (7) above shall specify the names and designations of the parties to the application and the date when authority for service or citation was granted and contain a description of the land to which the application relates.

(9) In this section and section 9 of this Act 'the court' means the Court of Session or the sheriff.

9 Provisions supplementary to section 8: protection of other interest

(1) The court shall order a document to be rectified under section 8 of this Act only where it is satisfied—

(a) that the interests of a person to whom this section applies would not be adversely affected to a material extent by the rectification; or

(b) that that person has consented to the proposed rectification.

(2)   Subject to subsection (3) below, this section applies to a person (other than a party to the agreement or the grantor of the document) who has acted or refrained from acting in reliance on the terms of the document or on the title sheet of an interest in land registered in the Land Register of Scotland being an interest to which the document relates, with the result that his position has been affected to a material extent.

(3)   This section does not apply to a person—

(a)   who, at the time when he acted or refrained from acting as mentioned in subsection (2) above, knew, or ought in the circumstances known to him at that time to have been aware, that the document or (as the case may be) the title sheet failed accurately to express the common intention of the parties to the agreement or, as the case may be, the intention of the grantor of the document; or

(b)   whose reliance on the terms of the document or on the title sheet was otherwise unreasonable.

(4)   Notwithstanding subsection (4) of section 8 of this Act and without prejudice to subsection (5) below, the court may, for the purpose of protecting the interests of a person to whom this section applies, order that the rectification of a document shall have effect as at such date as it may specify, being a date later than that as at which it would have effect by virtue of the said subsection (4).

(5)   Notwithstanding subsection (5) of section 8 of this Act and without prejudice to subsection (4) above, the court may, for the purpose of protecting the interests of a person to whom this section applies, order that a document as rectified shall be treated as having been recorded as mentioned in the said subsection (5) at such date as it may specify, being a date later than that as at which it would be treated by virtue of that subsection as having been so recorded.

(6)   For the purposes of subsection (1) above, the court may require the Keeper of the Registers of Scotland to produce such information as he has in his possession relating to any persons who have asked him to supply details with regard to a title sheet mentioned in subsection (2) above; and any expense incurred by the Keeper under this subsection shall be borne by the applicant for the order.

(7)   Where a person to whom this section applies was unaware, before a document was ordered to be rectified under section 8 of this Act, that an application had been made under that section for the rectification of the document, the Court of Session, on an application made by that person within the time specified in subsection (8) below, may—

(a)   reduce the rectifying order; or

(b)   order the applicant for the rectifying order to pay such compensation to that person as it thinks fit in respect of his reliance on the terms of the document or on the title sheet.

(8)   The time referred to in subsection (7) above is whichever is the earlier of the following—

(a)   the expiry of 5 years after the making of the rectifying order;

(b)   the expiry of 2 years after the making of that order first came to the notice of the person referred to in that subsection.

10   Negligent misrepresentation

(1)   A party to a contract who has been induced to enter into it by negligent misrepresentation made by or on behalf of another party to the contract shall not be disentitled, by reason only that the misrepresentation is not fraudulent, from recovering damages from the other party in respect of any loss or damage he has suffered as a result of the misrepresentation; and any rule of law that such damages cannot be recovered unless fraud is proved shall cease to have effect.

(2)   Subsection (1) applies to any proceedings commenced on or after the date on which it comes into force, whether or not the negligent misrepresentation was made before or after that date, but does not apply to any proceedings commenced before that date.

ANIMALS (SCOTLAND) ACT 1987
(1987, c 9)

1   New provisions as to strict liability for injury or damage caused by animals

(1)   Subject to subsection (4) and (5) below and section 2 of this Act, a person shall be liable for any injury or damage caused by an animal if—

(a)   at the time of the injury or damage complained of, he was a keeper of the animal;

(b)   the animal belongs to a species whose members generally are by virtue of their physical attributes or habits likely (unless controlled or restrained) to injure severely or kill persons or animals, or damage property to a material extent; and

(c)   the injury or damage complained of is directly referable to such physical attributes or habits.

(2)   In this section 'species' includes—

(a)   a form or variety of the species or a sub-division of the species, or the form or variety, identifiable by age, sex or such other criteria as are relevant to the behaviour of animals; and

(b)   a kind which is the product of hybridisation.

(3)   For the purposes of subsection (1)(b) above—

(a)   dogs, and dangerous wild animals within the meaning of section 7(4) of the Dangerous Wild Animals Act 1976, shall be deemed to be likely (unless controlled or restrained) to injure severely or kill persons or animals by biting or otherwise savaging, attacking or harrying; and

(b)   any of the following animals in the course of foraging, namely—

cattle, horses, asses, mules, hinnies, sheep, pigs, goats and deer,

shall be deemed to be likely (unless controlled or restrained) to damage to a material extent land or the produce of land, whether harvested or not.

(4)   Subsection (1) above shall not apply to any injury caused by an animal where the injury consists of disease transmitted by means which are unlikely to cause severe injury other than disease.

(5)   Subsection (1) above shall not apply to injury or damage caused by the mere fact that an animal is present on a road or in any other place.

(6)   For the purposes of the Law Reform (Contributory Negligence) Act 1945, any injury or damage for which a person is liable under this section shall be treated as due to his fault as defined in that Act.

(7)   Subsections (1) and (2) of section 3 of the Law Reform (Miscellaneous Provisions) (Scotland) Act 1940 (contribution among joint wrongdoers) shall, subject to any necessary modifications, apply in relation to an action of damages in respect of injury or damage which is brought in pursuance of this section as they apply in relation to an action of damages in respect of loss or damage arising from any wrongful acts or omissions; but nothing in this subsection shall affect any contractual, or (except as aforesaid) any other, right of relief or indemnity.

(8)   The foregoing provisions of this section and section 2 of this Act replace—

(a)   any rule of law which imposes liability, without proof of a negligent act or omission, on the owner or possessor of an animal for injury or damage caused by that animal on the ground that the animal is *ferae naturae* or is otherwise known to be dangerous or harmful;

(b)   the Winter Herding Act 1686;

(c)   section 1(1) and (2) of the Dogs Act 1906 (injury to cattle or poultry).

2   Exceptions from liability under section 1

(1)   A person shall not be liable under section 1(1) of this Act if—

(a)   the injury or damage was due wholly to the fault of—

(i)   the person sustaining it; or

(ii)   in the case of injury sustained by an animal, a keeper of the animal;

(b)   the person sustaining the injury or damage or a keeper of the animal sustaining the injury willingly accepted the risk of it as his; or

(c)   subject to subsection (2) below, the injury or damage was sustained on, or in consequence of the person or animal sustaining the injury or damage coming on to, land which was occupied by a person who was a keeper, or by another person who authorised the presence on the land, of the animal which caused the injury or damage; and, either—

(i)   the person sustaining the injury or damage was not authorised or entitled to be on that land; or (as the case may be)

(ii)   no keeper of the animal sustaining the injury was authorised or entitled to have the animal present on that land.

(2)   A person shall not be exempt from liability by virtue of subsection (1)(c) above if the animal causing the injury or damage was kept on the land wholly or partly for the purpose of protecting persons or property, unless the keeping of the animal there, and the use made of the animal, for that purpose was reasonable, and, if the animal was a guard dog within the meaning of the Guard Dogs Act 1975, unless there was compliance with section 1 of that Act.

(3)   In subsection (1) above—

(a)   in paragraph (a) 'fault' has the same meaning as in the Law Reform (Contributory Negligence) Act 1945;

(b)   in paragraph (c) 'authorised' means expressly or impliedly authorised.

3   Detention of straying animals

(1)   Without prejudice to section 98 of the Roads (Scotland) Act 1984, where an animal strays on to any land and is not then under the control of any person, the occupier of the land may detain the animal for the purpose of preventing injury or damage by it.

(2)   Part VI of the Civic Government (Scotland) Act 1982 (lost and abandoned property) shall apply in relation to an animal, other than a stray dog, detained under subsection (1) above as it applies in relation to any property taken possession of under section 67 of that Act subject to the omission from section 74 of the words from 'or livestock' to '129 of this Act' and to any other necessary modifications; and section 4 of the Dogs Act 1906 shall, subject to any necessary modifications, apply to a stray dog detained under subsection (1) above as it applies to a stray dog taken possession of under that section.

4   Killing of, or injury to, animals attacking or harrying persons or livestock

(1)   Subject to subsection (2) below, in any civil proceedings against a person for killing or causing injury to an animal, it shall be a defence for him to prove—

(a)   that he acted—

(i)   in self-defence;

(ii)   for the protection of any other person; or

(iii)   for the protection of any livestock and was one of the persons mentioned in subsection (3) below; and

(b)   that within 48 hours after the killing or injury notice thereof was given by him or on his behalf at a police station or to a constable.

(2)   There shall be no defence available under subsection (1) above to a person killing or causing injury to an animal where the killing or injury—

(a)   occurred at or near a place where the person was present for the purpose of engaging in a criminal activity; and

(b)   was in furtherance of that activity.

(3)   The persons referred to in subsection (1)(a)(iii) above are—

(a)   a person who, at the time of the injury or killing complained of, was a keeper of the livestock concerned;

(b)   the owner or occupier of the land where the livestock was present; and

(c)   a person authorised (either expressly or impliedly) to act for the protection of the livestock by such a keeper of the livestock or by the owner or occupier of the land where the livestock was present.

(4)   A person killing or causing injury to an animal ('the defender') shall be regarded, for the purposes of this section, as acting in self defence or for the protection of another person or any livestock if, and only if—

(a)   the animal is attacking him or that other person or that livestock and (whether or not the animal is under the control of anyone) the defender has reasonable grounds for believing that there are no other practicable means of ending the attack; or

(b)   the defender has reasonable grounds for believing—

(i)   that the animal is about to attack him, such person or livestock and that (whether or not the animal is under the control of anyone) there are no other practicable means of preventing the attack; or

(ii)   that the animal has been attacking a person or livestock, is not under the control of anyone and has not left the vicinity where the attack took place, and that there are no other practicable means of preventing a further attack by the animal while it is still in that vicinity.

(5)   In subsection (4) above 'attack' or 'attacking' includes 'harry' or 'harrying'.

(6)   In this section—

'livestock' means any animal of a domestic variety (including in particular sheep, cattle and horses) and, while they are in captivity, any other animals.

5   Meaning of a keeper of an animal

(1)   Subject to subsection (2) below, for the purposes of this Act a person is a keeper of an animal if—

(a)   he owns the animal or has possession of it; or

(b)   he has actual care and control of a child under the age of 16 who owns the animal or has possession of it.

(2)   For the purposes of this section—

(a)   a person shall not be regarded as having possession of an animal by reason only that he is detaining it under section 3 of this Act or is otherwise temporarily detaining it for the purpose of protecting it or any person or other animal or of restoring it as soon as is reasonably practicable to its owner or a possessor of it;

(b)   if an animal has been abandoned or has escaped, a person who at the time of the abandonment or escape was the owner of it or had it in his possession shall remain its owner or shall be regarded as continuing to have possession of it until another person acquires its ownership or (as the case may be) comes into possession of it; and

(c)   the Crown shall not acquire ownership of an animal on its abandonment.

6   Application to Crown

This Act binds the Crown, but this section shall not authorise proceedings to be brought against Her Majesty in her private capacity.

7   Interpretation

In this Act, unless the context otherwise requires—

'animal' does not include viruses, bacteria, algae, fungi or protozoa;

'harry' includes chase in such a way as may be likely to cause injury or suffering; and 'harrying' shall be construed accordingly;

'injury' includes death, any abortion or other impairment of physical or mental condition and any loss of or diminution in the produce of an animal and, subject to section 1(4) of this Act, disease.

8   Transitional provision and repeals

(1)   This Act shall apply only in relation to injury or damage caused after the commencement of the Act.

(2)   The enactments mentioned in the Schedule to this Act are hereby repealed to the extent specified in the third column of that Schedule.

9   Short title, commencement and extent

(1)   This Act may be cited as the Animals (Scotland) Act 1987.

(2)   This Act shall come into force at the end of a period of 2 months beginning with the date on which it is passed.

(3)   This Act extends to Scotland only.

CONSUMER PROTECTION ACT 1987
(1987, c 43)

PART I
PRODUCT LIABILITY

1   Purpose and construction of Part I

(1)   This Part shall have effect for the purpose of making such provision as is necessary in order to comply with the product liability Directive and shall be construed accordingly.

(2)   In this Part, except in so far as the context otherwise requires—

[. . .]

'dependant' and 'relative' have the same meaning as they have in, respectively, the Fatal Accidents Act 1976 and the Damages (Scotland) Act 1976;

'producer', in relation to a product, means—

(a)   the person who manufactured it;

(b)   in the case of a substance which has not been manufactured but has been won or abstracted, the person who won or abstracted it;

(c)   in the case of a product which has not been manufactured, won or abstracted but essential characteristics of which are attributable to an industrial or other process having been carried out (for example, in relation to agricultural produce), the person who carried out that process;

'product' means any goods or electricity and (subject to subsection (3) below) includes a product which is comprised in another product, whether by virtue of being a component part or raw material or otherwise; and

'the product liability Directive' means the Directive of the Council of the European Communities, dated 25th July 1985, (No 85/374/EEC) on the approximation of the laws, regulations and administrative provisions of the member States concerning liability for defective products.

(3)   For the purposes of this Part a person who supplies any product in which products are comprised, whether by virtue of being component parts or raw materials or otherwise, shall not be treated by reason only of his supply of that product as supplying any of the products so comprised.

2   Liability for defective products

(1)   Subject to the following provisions of this Part, where any damage is caused wholly or partly by a defect in a product, every person to whom subsection (2) below applies shall be liable for the damage.

(2)   This subsection applies to—

(a)   the producer of the product;

(b)   any person who, by putting his name on the product or using a trade mark or other distinguishing mark in relation to the product, has held himself out to be the producer of the product;

(c)   any person who has imported the product into a member State from a place outside the member States in order, in the course of any business of his, to supply it to another.

(3)   Subject as aforesaid, where any damage is caused wholly or partly by a defect in a product, any person who supplied the product (whether to the person

who suffered the damage, to the producer of any product in which the product in question is comprised or to any other person) shall be liable for the damage if—

(a)   the person who suffered the damage requests the supplier to identify one or more of the persons (whether still in existence or not) to whom subsection (2) above applies in relation to the product;

(b)   that request is made within a reasonable period after the damage occurs and at a time when it is not reasonably practicable for the person making the request to identify all those persons; and

(c)   the supplier fails, within a reasonable period after receiving the request, either to comply with the request or to identify the person who supplied the product to him.

[. . .]

(5)   Where two or more persons are liable by virtue of this Part for the same damage, their liability shall be joint and several.

(6)   This section shall be without prejudice to any liability arising otherwise than by virtue of this Part.

3   Meaning of 'defect'

(1)   Subject to the following provisions of the section, there is a defect in a product for the purposes of this Part if the safety of the product is not such as persons generally are entitled to expect; and for those purposes 'safety', in relation to a product, shall include safety with respect to products comprised in that product and safety in the context of risks of damage to property, as well as in the context of risks of death or personal injury.

(2)   In determining for the purposes of subsection (1) above what persons generally are entitled to expect in relation to a product all the circumstances shall be taken into account, including—

(a)   the manner in which, and purposes for which, the product has been marketed, its get-up, the use of any mark in relation to the product and any instructions for, or warnings with respect to, doing or refraining from doing anything with or in relation to the product;

(b)   what might reasonably be expected to be done with or in relation to the product; and

(c)   the time when the product was supplied by its producer to another;

and nothing in this section shall require a defect to be inferred from the fact alone that the safety of a product which is supplied after that time is greater than the safety of the product in question.

4   Defences

(1)   In any civil proceedings by virtue of this Part against any person ('the person proceeded against') in respect of a defect in a product it shall be a defence for him to show—

(a)   that the defect is attributable to compliance with any requirement imposed by or under any enactment or with any Community obligation; or

(b)   that the person proceeded against did not at any time supply the product to another; or

(c)   that the following conditions are satisfied, that is to say—

(i)   that the only supply of the product to another by the person proceeded against was otherwise than in the course of a business of that person's; and

(ii)   that section 2(2) above does not apply to that person or applies to him by virtue only of things done otherwise than with a view to profit; or

(d)   that the defect did not exist in the product at the relevant time; or

(e)   that the state of scientific and technical knowledge at the relevant time was not such that a producer of products of the same description as the product in question might be expected to have discovered the defect if it had existed in his products while they were under his control; or

(f)   that the defect—
(i)   constituted a defect in a product ('the subsequent product') in which the product in question had been comprised; and
(ii)   was wholly attributable to the design of the subsequent product or to compliance by the producer of the product in question with instructions given by the producer of the subsequent product.
(2)   In this section 'the relevant time', in relation to electricity, means the time at which it was generated, being a time before it was transmitted or distributed, and in relation to any other product, means—
(a)   if the person proceeded against is a person to whom subsection (2) of section 2 above applies in relation to the product, the time when he supplied the product to another;
(b)   if that subsection does not apply to that person in relation to the product, the time when the product was last supplied by a person to whom that subsection does apply in relation to the product.

5   Damage giving rise to liability

(1)   Subject to the following provisions of this section, in this Part 'damages' means death or personal injury or any loss of or damage to any property (including land).
(2)   A person shall not be liable under section 2 above in respect of any defect in a product for the loss of or any damage to the product itself or for the loss of or any damage to the whole or any part of any product which has been supplied with the product in question comprised in it.
(3)   A person shall not be liable under section 2 above for any loss of or damage to any property which, at the time it is lost or damaged, is not—
(a)   of a description of property ordinarily intended for private use, occupation or consumption; and
(b)   intended by the person suffering the loss or damage mainly for his own private use, occupation or consumption.
(4)   No damages shall be awarded to any person by virtue of this Part in respect of any loss of or damage to any property if the amount which would fall to be so awarded to that person, apart from this subsection and any liability for interest, does not exceed £275.
(8)   Subsections (5) to (7) above shall not extend to Scotland.

6   Application of certain enactments etc

(1)   Any damage for which a person is liable under section 2 above shall be deemed to have been caused—
(a)   for the purposes of the Fatal Accidents Act 1976, by that person's wrongful act, neglect or default;
(b)   for the purposes of section 3 of the Law Reform (Miscellaneous Provisions) (Scotland) Act 1940 (contribution among joint wrongdoers), by that person's wrongful act or negligent act or omission;
(c)   for the purposes of section 1 of the Damages (Scotland) Act 1976 (rights of relatives of a deceased), by that person's act or omission, and
(d)   for the purposes of Part II of the Administration of Justice Act 1982 (damages for personal injuries, etc—Scotland), by an act or omission giving rise to liability in that person to pay damages.
(2)   Where—
(a)   a person's death is caused wholly or partly by a defect in a product, or a person dies after suffering damage which has been so caused;
(b)   a request such as mentioned in paragraph (a) of subsection (3) of section 2 above is made to a supplier of the product by that person's personal representatives or, in the case of a person whose death is caused wholly or partly by the defect, by any dependant or relative of that person; and

(c)   the conditions specified in paragraphs (b) and (c) of that subsection are satisfied in relation to that request,
this Part shall have effect for the purposes of the Law Reform (Miscellaneous Provisions) Act 1934, the Fatal Accidents Acts 1976 and the Damages (Scotland) Act 1976 as if liability of the supplier to that person under that subsection did not depend on that person having requested the supplier to identify certain persons or on the said conditions having been satisfied in relation to a request made by that person.

(3)   Section 1 of the Congenital Disabilities (Civil Liability) Act 1976 shall have effect for the purposes of this Part as if—

(a)   a person were answerable to a child in respect of an occurrence caused wholly or partly by a defect in a product if he is or has been liable under section 2 above in respect of any effect of the occurrence on a parent of the child, or would be so liable if the occurrence caused a parent of the child to suffer damage;

(b)   the provisions of this Part relating to liability under section 2 above applied in relation to liability by virtue of paragraph (a) above under the said section 1; and

(c)   subsection (6) of the said section 1 (exclusion of liability) were omitted.

(4)   Where any damage is caused partly by a defect in a product and partly by the fault of the person suffering the damage, the Law Reform (Contributory Negligence) Act 1945 and section 5 of the Fatal Accidents Act 1976 (contributory negligence) shall have effect as if the defect were the fault of every person liable by virtue of this Part for the damage caused by the defect.

(5)   In subsection (4) above 'fault' has the same meaning as in the said Act of 1945.

(6)   Schedule 1 to this Act shall have effect for the purpose of amending the Limitation Act 1980 and the Prescription and Limitation (Scotland) Act 1973 in their application in relation to the bringing of actions by virtue of this Part.

(7)   It is hereby declared that liability by virtue of this Part is to be treated as liability in tort for the purposes of any enactment conferring jurisdiction on any court with respect to any matter.

(8)   Nothing in this Part shall prejudice the operation of section 12 of the Nuclear Installations Act 1965 (rights to compensation for certain breaches of duties confined to rights under that Act).

7   Prohibition on exclusions from liability
The liability of a person by virtue of this Part to person who has suffered damage caused wholly or partly by a defect in a product, or to a dependant or relative of such a person, shall not be limited or excluded by any contract term, by any notice or by any other provision.

8   Power to modify Part I
(1)   Her Majesty may by Order in Council make such modifications of this Part and of any other enactment (including an enactment contained in the following Parts of this Act, or in an Act passed after this Act) as appear to Her Majesty in Council to be necessary or expedient in consequence of any modification of the product liability Directive which is made at any time after the passing of this Act.

(2)   An Order in Council under subsection (1) above shall not be submitted to Her Majesty in Council unless a draft of the Order has been laid before, and approved by a resolution of, each House of Parliament.

9   Application of Part I to Crown
(1)   Subject to subsection (2) below, this Part shall bind the Crown.

(2)   The Crown shall not, as regards the Crown's liability by virtue of this Part, be bound by this Part further than the Crown is made liable in tort or in reparation under the Crown Proceedings Act 1947, as that Act has effect from time to time.

45 Interpretation

(1) In this Act, except in so far as the context otherwise requires—

'aircraft' includes gliders, balloons and hovercraft;

'business' includes a trade or profession and the activities of a professional or trade association or of a local authority or other public authority;

'conditional sale agreement', 'credit-sale agreement' and 'hire-purchase agreement' have the same meanings as in the Consumer Credit Act 1974 but as if in the definitions in that Act 'goods' had the same meaning as in this Act;

'contravention' includes a failure to comply and cognate expressions shall be construed accordingly;

'enforcement authority' means the Secretary of State, any other Minister of the Crown in charge of a Government department, any such department and any authority, council or other person on whom functions under this Act are conferred by or under section 27 above;

'gas' has the same meaning as in Part I of the Gas Act 1986;

'goods' includes substances, growing crops and things comprised in land by virtue of being attached to it and any ship, aircraft or vehicle;

'information' includes accounts, estimates and returns;

'magistrates' court', in relation to Northern Ireland, means a court of summary jurisdiction;

'modifications' includes additions, alterations and omissions, and cognate expressions shall be construed accordingly;

'motor vehicle' has the same meaning as in the Road Traffic Act 1972;

'notice' means a notice in writing;

'notice to warn' means a notice under section 13(1)(b) above;

'officer', in relation to an enforcement authority, means a person authorised in writing to assist the authority in carrying out its functions under or for the purposes of the enforcement of any of the safety provisions or of any of the provisions made by or under Part III of this Act;

'personal injury' includes any disease and any other impairment of a person's physical or mental condition;

'premises' includes any place and any ship, aircraft or vehicle;

'prohibition notice' means a notice under section 13(1)(a) above;

'records' includes any books or documents and any records in non-documentary form;

'safety provision' means the general safety requirement in section 10 above or any provision of safety regulations, a prohibition notice or a suspension notice;

'safety regulations' means regulations under section 11 above;

'ship' includes any boat and any other description of vessel used in navigation;

'subordinate legislation' has the same meaning as in the Interpretation Act 1978;

'substance' means any natural or artificial substance, whether in solid, liquid or gaseous form or in the form of a vapour, and includes substances that are comprised in or mixed with other goods;

'supply' and cognate expressions shall be construed in accordance with section 46 below;

'suspension notice' means a notice under section 14 above.

(2) Except in so far as the context otherwise requires, references in this Act to a contravention of a safety provision shall, in relation to any goods, include references to anything which would constitute such a contravention if the goods were supplied to any person.

(3) References in this Act to any goods in relation to which any safety provision has been or may have been contravened shall include references to any goods which it is not reasonably practicable to separate from any such goods.

(4) Section 68(2) of the Trade Marks Act 1938 (construction of references to use of a mark) shall apply for the purposes of this Act as it applies for the purposes of that Act.

(5) In Scotland, any reference in this Act to things comprised in land by virtue of being attached to it is a reference to moveables which have become heritable by accession to heritable property.

COURT OF SESSION ACT 1988
(1988, c 36)

46 Specific relief may be granted in interdict proceedings
Where a respondent in any application or proceedings in the Court, whether before or after the institution of such proceedings or application, has done any act which the Court might have prohibited by interdict, the Court may ordain the respondent to perform any act which may be necessary for reinstating the petitioner in his possessory right, or for granting specific relief against the illegal act complained of.

47 Interim interdict and other interim orders
(1) In any cause containing a conclusion or a crave for interdict or liberation, the Division of the Inner House or the Lord Ordinary (as the case may be) may, on the motion of any party to the cause, grant interim interdict or liberation; and it shall be competent for the Division of the Inner House or the Lord Ordinary before whom any cause in which interim interdict has been granted is pending to deal with any breach of the interim interdict without the presentation of a petition and complaint.

(2) In any cause in dependence before the Court, the Court may, on the motion of any party to the cause, make such order regarding the interim possession of any property to which the cause relates, or regarding the subject matter of the cause, as the Court may think fit.

(3) Every interim act, warrant and decree granted during the dependence of a cause in the Court shall, unless the Court otherwise directs, be extractible *ad interim*.

CONTRACTS (APPLICABLE LAW) ACT 1990
(1990, c 36)

1 Meaning of 'the Conventions'
In this Act—

(a) 'the Rome Convention' means the Convention on the law applicable to contractual obligations opened for signature in Rome on 19th June 1980 and signed by the United Kingdom on 7th December 1981;

(b) 'the Luxembourg Convention' means the Convention on the accession of the Hellenic Republic to the Rome Convention signed by the United Kingdom in Luxembourg on 10th April 1984; and

(c) 'the Brussels Protocol' means the first Protocol on the interpretation of the Rome Convention by the European Court signed by the United Kingdom in Brussels on 19th December 1988;

[(d) 'the Funchal Convention' means the Convention on the accession of the Kingdom of Spain and the Portuguese Republic to the Rome Convention and the Brussels Protocol, with adjustments made to the Rome Convention by the Luxembourg Convention, signed by the United Kingdom in Funchal on 18th May 1992;

(e) 'the 1996 Accession Convention' means the Convention on the accession of the Republic of Austria, the Republic of Finland and the Kingdom of Sweden to the Rome Convention and the Brussels Protocol, with the adjustments made to the Rome Convention by the Luxembourg Convention and the Funchal Convention, signed by the United Kingdom in Brussels on 29th November 1996;

and these Conventions and this Protocol are together referred to as 'the Conventions'.]

2 Conventions to have force of law

(1) Subject to subsections (2) and (3) below, the Conventions shall have the force of law in the United Kingdom.

[(1A) The internal law for the purposes of Article 1(3) of the Rome Convention is the provisions of the regulations for the time being in force under section 424(3) of the Financial Services and Markets Act 2000.]

(2) Articles 7(1) and 10(1)(e) of the Rome Convention shall not have the force of law in the United Kingdom.

(3) Notwithstanding Article 19(2) of the Rome Convention the Conventions shall apply in the case of conflicts between the laws of different parts of the United Kingdom.

(4) For ease of reference there are set out in Schedules [1, 2, 3, 3A and 3B to this Act respectively the English texts of—

    (a)   the Rome Convention;

    (b)   the Luxembourg Convention; [. . .]

    (c)   the Brussels Protocol;

    (d)   the Funchal Convention; and

    [(e)   the 1996 Accession Convention.]

3 Interpretation of Conventions

(1) Any question as to the meaning or effect of any provision of the Conventions shall, if not referred to the European Court in accordance with the Brussels Protocol, be determined in accordance with the principles laid down by and any relevant decision of, the European Court.

(2) Judicial notice shall be taken of any decision of, or expression of opinion by, the European Court on any such question.

(3) Without prejudice to any practice of the courts as to the matters which may be considered apart from this subsection—

    (a)   the report on the Rome Convention by Professor Mario Giuliano and Professor Paul Lagarde which is reproduced in the Official Journal of the Communities of 31st October 1980 may be considered in ascertaining the meaning or effect of any provision of that Convention; and

    (b)   any report on the Brussels Protocol which is reproduced in the Official Journal of the Communities may be considered in ascertaining the meaning or effect of any provision of that Protocol.

4 Revision of Conventions etc

(1) If at any time it appears to Her Majesty in Council that Her Majesty's Government in the United Kingdom—

    (a)   have agreed to a revision of any of the Conventions (including, in particular, any revision connected with the accession to the Rome Convention of any state), or

    (b)   have given notification in accordance with Article 22(3) of the Rome Convention that either or both of the provisions mentioned in section 2(2) above shall have the force of law in the United Kingdom,

Her Majesty may by Order in Council make such consequential modifications of this Act or any other statutory provision, whenever passed or made, as Her Majesty considers appropriate.

(2) An Order in Council under subsection (1) above shall not be made unless a draft of the Order has been laid before Parliament and approved by a resolution of each House.

(3) In subsection (1) above—

'modifications' includes additions, omissions and alterations;

'revision' means an omission from, addition to or alteration of any of the Conventions and includes replacement of any of the Conventions to any extent by another convention, protocol or other description of international agreement; and 'statutory provision' means any provision contained in an Act, or in any Northern Ireland legislation, or in—

(a)   subordinate legislation (as defined in section 21(1) of the Interpretation Act 1978); or

(b)   any instrument of a legislative character made under any Northern Ireland legislation.

5   Consequential amendments

The enactments specified in Schedule 4 to this Act shall have effect subject to the amendments specified in that Schedule.

6   Application to Crown

This Act binds the Crown.

7   Commencement

This Act shall come into force on such day as the Lord Chancellor and the Lord Advocate may by order made by statutory instrument appoint; and different days may be appointed for different provisions or different purposes.

8   Extent

(1)   This Act extends to Northern Ireland.

(2)   Her Majesty may by Order in Council direct that all or any of the provisions of this Act shall extend to any of the following territories, namely—

(a)   the Isle of Man;

(b)   any of the Channel Islands;

(c)   Gibraltar;

(d)   the Sovereign Base Areas of Akrotiri and Dhekelia (that is to say, the areas mentioned in section 2(1) of the Cyprus Act 1960).

(3)   An Order in Council under subsection (2) above may modify this Act in its application to any of the territories mentioned in that subsection and may contain such supplementary provisions as Her Majesty considers appropriate; and in this subsection 'modify' shall be construed in accordance with section 4 above.

9   Short title

This Act may be cited as the Contracts (Applicable Law) Act 1990.

SCHEDULES

SCHEDULE 1
THE ROME CONVENTION

The High Contracting Parties to the Treaty establishing the European Economic Community,

Anxious to continue in the field of private international law the work of unification of law which has already been done within the Community, in particular in the field of jurisdiction and enforcement of judgments,

Wishing to establish uniform rules concerning the law applicable to contractual obligations,

Have agreed as follows:

TITLE I
SCOPE OF THE CONVENTION

Article 1. Scope of the Convention

1.   The rules of this Convention shall apply to contractual obligations in any situation involving a choice between the laws of different countries.

2. They shall not apply to:

(a) questions involving the status or legal capacity of natural persons, without prejudice to Article 11;

(b) contractual obligations relating to:

—wills and succession,

—rights in property arising out of a matrimonial relationship,

—rights and duties arising out of a family relationship, parentage, marriage or affinity, including maintenance obligations in respect of children who are not legitimate;

(c) obligations arising under bills of exchange, cheques and promissory notes and other negotiable instruments to the extent that the obligations under such other negotiable instruments arise out of their negotiable character;

(d) arbitration agreements and agreements on the choice of court;

(e) questions governed by the law of companies and other bodies corporate or unincorporate such as the creation, by registration or otherwise, legal capacity, internal organisation or winding up of companies and other bodies corporate or unincorporate and the personal liability of officers and members as such for the obligations of the company or body;

(f) the question whether an agent is able to bind a principal or an organ to bind a company or body corporate or unincorporate, to a third party;

(g) the constitution of trusts and the relationship between settlors, trustees and beneficiaries;

(h) evidence and procedure, without prejudice to Article 14.

3. The rules of this Convention do not apply to contracts of insurance which cover risks situated in the territories of the Member States of the European Economic Community. In order to determine whether a risk is situated in these territories the court shall apply its internal law.

4. The preceding paragraph does not apply to contracts of re-insurance.

Article 2. Application of law of non-contracting States

Any law specified by this Convention shall be applied whether or not it is the law of a Contracting State.

TITLE II

UNIFORM RULES

Article 3. Freedom of choice

1. A contract shall be governed by the law chosen by the parties. The choice must be express or demonstrated with reasonable certainty by the terms of the contract or the circumstances of the case. By their choice the parties can select the law applicable to the whole or a part only of the contract.

2. The parties may at any time agree to subject the contract to a law other than that which previously governed it, whether as a result of an earlier choice under this Article or of other provisions of this Convention. Any variation by the parties of the law to be applied made after the conclusion of the contract shall not prejudice its formal validity under Article 9 or adversely affect the rights of third parties.

3. The fact that the parties have chosen a foreign law, whether or not accompanied by the choice of a foreign tribunal, shall not, where all the other elements relevant to the situation at the time of the choice are connected with one country only, prejudice the application of rules of the law of that country which cannot be derogated from by contract, hereinafter called 'mandatory rules'.

4. The existence and validity of the consent of the parties as to the choice of the applicable law shall be determined in accordance with the provisions of Articles 8, 9 and 11.

Article 4. Applicable law in the absence of choice

1.   To the extent that the law applicable to the contract has not been chosen in accordance with Article 3, the contract shall be governed by the law of the country with which it is most closely connected. Nevertheless, a severable part of the contract which has a closer connection with another country may by way of exception be governed by the law of that other country.

2.   Subject to the provisions of paragraph 5 of this Article, it shall be presumed that the contract is most closely connected with the country where the party who is to effect the performance which is characteristic of the contract has, at the time of conclusion of the contract, his habitual residence, or, in the case of a body corporate or unincorporate, its central administration. However, if the contract is entered into in the course of that party's trade or profession, that country shall be the country in which the principal place of business is situated or, where under the terms of the contract the performance is to be effected through a place of business other than the principal place of business, the country in which that other place of business is situated.

3.   Notwithstanding the provisions of paragraph 2 of this Article, to the extent that the subject matter of the contract is a right in immovable property or a right to use immovable property it shall be presumed that the contract is most closely connected with the country where the immovable property is situated.

4.   A contract for the carriage of goods shall not be subject to the presumption in paragraph 2. In such a contract if the country in which, at the time the contract is concluded, the carrier has his principal place of business is also the country in which the place of loading or the place of discharge or the principal place of business of the consignor is situated, it shall be presumed that the contract is most closely connected with that country. In applying this paragraph single voyage charter-parties and other contracts the main purpose of which is the carriage of goods shall be treated as contracts for the carriage of goods.

5.   Paragraph 2 shall not apply if the characteristic performance cannot be determined, and the presumptions in paragraphs 2, 3 and 4 shall be disregarded if it appears from the circumstances as a whole that the contract is more closely connected with another country.

Article 5. Certain consumer contracts

1.   This Article applies to a contract the object of which is the supply of goods or services to a person ('the consumer') for a purpose which can be regarded as being outside his trade or profession, or a contract for the provision of credit for that object.

2.   Notwithstanding the provisions of Article 3, a choice of law made by the parties shall not have the result of depriving the consumer of the protection afforded to him by the mandatory rules of the law of the country in which he has his habitual residence:

—if in that country the conclusion of the contract was preceded by a specific invitation addressed to him or by advertising, and he had taken in that country all the steps necessary on his part for the conclusion of the contract, or

—if the other party or his agent received the consumer's order in that country, or

—if the contract is for the sale of goods and the consumer travelled from that country to another country and there gave his order, provided that the consumer's journey was arranged by the seller for the purpose of inducing the consumer to buy.

3.   Notwithstanding the provisions of Article 4, a contract to which this Article applies shall, in the absence of choice in accordance with Article 3, be governed by the law of the country in which the consumer has his habitual residence if it is entered into in the circumstances described in paragraph 2 of this Article.

4.   This Article shall not apply to:

(a)   a contract of carriage;

(b)   a contract for the supply of services where the services are to be supplied to the consumer exclusively in a country other than that in which he has his habitual residence.

5.   Notwithstanding the provisions of paragraph 4, this Article shall apply to a contract which, for an inclusive price, provides for a combination of travel and accommodation.

Article 6. Individual employment contracts

1.   Notwithstanding the provisions of Article 3, in a contract of employment a choice of law made by the parties shall not have the result of depriving the employee of the protection afforded to him by the mandatory rules of the law which would be applicable under paragraph 2 in the absence of choice.

2.   Notwithstanding the provisions of Article 4, a contract of employment shall, in the absence of choice in accordance with Article 3, be governed:

(a)   by the law of the country in which the employee habitually carries out his work in performance of the contract, even if he is temporarily employed in another country; or

(b)   if the employee does not habitually carry out his work in any one country, by the law of the country in which the place of business through which he was engaged is situated;

unless it appears from the circumstances as a whole that the contract is more closely connected with another country, in which case the contract shall be governed by the law of that country.

Article 7. Mandatory rules

1.   When applying under this Convention the law of a country, effect may be given to the mandatory rules of the law of another country with which the situation has a close connection, if and in so far as, under the law of the latter country, those rules must be applied whatever the law applicable to the contract. In considering whether to give effect to these mandatory rules, regard shall be had to their nature and purpose and to the consequences of their application or nonapplication.

2.   Nothing in this Convention shall restrict the application of the rules of the law of the forum in a situation where they are mandatory irrespective of the law otherwise applicable to the contract.

Article 8. Material validity

1.   The existence and validity of a contract, or of any term of a contract, shall be determined by the law which would govern it under this Convention if the contract or term were valid.

2.   Nevertheless a party may rely upon the law of the country in which he has his habitual residence to establish that he did not consent if it appears from the circumstances that it would not be reasonable to determine the effect of his conduct in accordance with the law specified in the preceding paragraph.

Article 9. Formal validity

1.   A contract concluded between persons who are in the same country is formally valid if it satisfies the formal requirements of the law which governs it under this Convention or of the law of the country where it is concluded.

2.   A contract concluded between persons who are in different countries is formally valid if it satisfies the formal requirements of the law which governs it under this Convention or of the law of one of those countries.

3.   Where a contract is concluded by an agent, the country in which the agent acts is the relevant country for the purposes of paragraphs 1 and 2.

4.   An act intended to have legal effect relating to an existing or contemplated contract is formally valid if it satisfies the formal requirements of the law which

under this Convention governs or would govern the contract or of the law of the country where the act was done.

5. The provisions of the preceding paragraphs shall not apply to a contract to which Article 5 applies, concluded in the circumstances described in paragraph 2 of Article 5. The formal validity of such a contract is governed by the law of the country in which the consumer has his habitual residence.

6. Notwithstanding paragraphs 1 to 4 of this Article, a contract the subject matter of which is a right in immovable property or a right to use immovable property shall be subject to the mandatory requirements of form of the law of the country where the property is situated if by that law those requirements are imposed irrespective of the country where the contract is concluded and irrespective of the law governing the contract.

Article 10. Scope of the applicable law

1. The law applicable to a contract by virtue of Articles 3 to 6 and 12 of this Convention shall govern in particular:

   (a) interpretation;
   (b) performance;
   (c) within the limits of the powers conferred on the court by its procedural law, the consequences of breach, including the assessment of damages in so far as it is governed by rules of law;
   (d) the various ways of extinguishing obligations, and prescription and limitation of actions;
   (e) the consequences of nullity of the contract.

2. In relation to the manner of performance and the steps to be taken in the event of defective performance regard shall be had to the law of the country in which performance takes place.

Article 11. Incapacity

In a contract concluded between persons who are in the same country, a natural person who would have capacity under the law of that country may invoke his incapacity resulting from another law only if the other party to the contract was aware of this incapacity at the time of the conclusion of the contract or was not aware thereof as a result of negligence.

Article 12. Voluntary assignment

1. The mutual obligations of assignor and assignee under a voluntary assignment of a right against another person ('the debtor') shall be governed by the law which under this Convention applies to the contract between the assignor and assignee.

2. The law governing the right to which the assignment relates shall determine its assignability, the relationship between the assignee and the debtor, the conditions under which the assignment can be invoked against the debtor and any question whether the debtor's obligations have been discharged.

Article 13. Subrogation

1. Where a person ('the creditor') has a contractual claim upon another ('the debtor'), and a third person has a duty to satisfy the creditor, or has in fact satisfied the creditor in discharge of that duty, the law which governs the third person's duty to satisfy the creditor shall determine whether the third person is entitled to exercise against the debtor the rights which the creditor had against the debtor under the law governing their relationship and, if so, whether he may do so in full or only to a limited extent.

2. The same rule applies where several persons are subject to the same contractual claim and one of them has satisfied the creditor.

Article 14. Burden of proof, etc

1. The law governing the contract under this Convention applies to the extent

that it contains, in the law of contract, rules which raise presumptions of law or determine the burden of proof.

2.   A contract or an act intended to have legal effect may be proved by any mode of proof recognised by the law of the forum or by any of the laws referred to in Article 9 under which that contract or act is formally valid, provided that such mode of proof can be administered by the forum.

Article 15. Exclusion of renvoi
The application of the law of any country specified by this Convention means the application of the rules of law in force in that country other than its rules of private international law.

Article 16. 'Ordre public'
The application of a rule of the law of any country specified by this Convention may be refused only if such application is manifestly incompatible with the public policy ('ordre public') of the forum.

Article 17. No retrospective effect
This Convention shall apply in a Contracting State to contracts made after the date on which this Convention has entered into force with respect to that State.

Article 18. Uniform interpretation
In the interpretation and application of the preceding uniform rules regard shall be had to their international character and to the desirability of achieving uniformity in their interpretation and application.

Article 19. States with more than one legal system
1.   Where a State comprises several territorial units each of which has its own rules of law in respect of contractual obligations, each territorial unit shall be considered as a country for the purposes of identifying the law applicable under this Convention.

2.   A State within which different territorial units have their own rules of law in respect of contractual obligations shall not be bound to apply this Convention to conflicts solely between the laws of such units.

Article 20. Precedence of Community law
This Convention shall not affect the application of provisions which, in relation to particular matters, lay down choice of law rules relating to contractual obligations and which are or will be contained in acts of the institutions of the European Communities or in national laws harmonised in implementation of such acts.

Article 21. Relationship with other conventions
This Convention shall not prejudice the application of international conventions to which a Contracting State is, or becomes, a party.

Article 22. Reservations
1.   Any Contracting State may, at the time of signature, ratification, acceptance or approval, reserve the right not to apply:
    (a)   the provisions of Article 7(1);
    (b)   the provisions of Article 10(1)(e).
    [. . .]
3.   Any Contracting State may at any time withdraw a reservation which it has made; the reservation shall cease to have effect on the first day of the third calendar month after notification of the withdrawal.

TITLE III
FINAL PROVISIONS

Article 23
1.   If, after the date on which this Convention has entered into force for a Con-

tracting State, that State wishes to adopt any new choice of law rule in regard to any particular category of contract within the scope of this Convention, it shall communicate its intention to the other signatory States through the Secretary-General of the Council of the European Communities.

2.   Any signatory State may, within six months from the date of the communication made to the Secretary-General, request him to arrange consultations between signatory States in order to reach agreement.

3.   If no signatory State has requested consultations within this period or if within two years following the communication made to the Secretary-General no agreement is reached in the course of consultations, the Contracting State concerned may amend its law in the manner indicated. The measures taken by that State shall be brought to the knowledge of the other signatory States through the Secretary-General of the Council of the European Communities.

Article 24

1.   If, after the date on which this Convention has entered into force with respect to a Contracting State, that State wishes to become a party to a multilateral convention whose principal aim or one of whose principal aims is to lay down rules of private international law concerning any of the matters governed by this Convention, the procedure set out in Article 23 shall apply. However, the period of two years, referred to in paragraph 3 of that Article, shall be reduced to one year.

2.   The procedure referred to in the preceding paragraph need not be followed if a Contracting State or one of the European Communities is already a party to the multilateral convention, or if its object is to revise a convention to which the State concerned is already a party, or if it is a convention concluded within the framework of the Treaties establishing the European Communities.

Article 25

If a Contracting State considers that the unification achieved by this Convention is prejudiced by the conclusion of agreements not covered by Article 24(1), that State may request the Secretary-General of the Council of the European Communities to arrange consultations between the signatory States of this Convention.

Article 26

Any Contracting State may request the revision of this Convention. In this event a revision conference shall be convened by the President of the Council of the European Communities.

Article 28

1.   This Convention shall be open from 19 June 1980 for signature by the States party to the Treaty establishing the European Economic Community.

2.   This Convention shall be subject to ratification, acceptance or approval by the signatory States. The instruments of ratification, acceptance or approval shall be deposited with the Secretary-General of the Council of the European Communities.

Article 29

1.   This Convention shall enter into force on the first day of the third month following the deposit of the seventh instrument of ratification, acceptance or approval.

2.   This Convention shall enter into force for each signatory State ratifying, accepting or approving at a later date on the first day of the third month following the deposit of its instrument of ratification, acceptance or approval.

Article 30

1.   This Convention shall remain in force for 10 years from the date of its entry into force in accordance with Article 29(1), even for States for which it enters into force at a later date.

2.   If there has been no denunciation it shall be renewed tacitly every five years.

3. A Contracting State which wishes to denounce shall, not less than six months before the expiration of the period of 10 or five years, as the case may be, give notice to the Secretary-General of the Council of the European Communities. [. . .]

4. The denunciation shall have effect only in relation to the State which has notified it. The Convention will remain in force as between all other Contracting States.

Article 31
The Secretary-General of the Council of the European Communities shall notify the States party to the Treaty establishing the European Economic Community of:
   (a)   the signatures;
   (b)   the deposit of each instrument of ratification, acceptance or approval;
   (c)   the date of entry into force of this Convention;
   (d)   communications made in pursuance of Articles 23, 24, 25, 26 and 30;
   (e)   the reservations and withdrawals of reservations referred to in Article 22.

Article 32
The Protocol annexed to this Convention shall form an integral part thereof.

Article 33
This Convention, drawn up in a single original in the Danish, Dutch, English, French, German, Irish and Italian languages, these texts being equally authentic, shall be deposited in the archives of the Secretariat of the Council of the European Communities. The Secretary-General shall transmit a certified copy thereof to the Government of each signatory State.

[PROTOCOL

The High Contracting Parties have agreed upon the following provision which shall be annexed to the Convention:

Notwithstanding the provisions of the Convention, Denmark, Sweden and Finland may retain national provisions concerning the law applicable to questions relating to the carriage of goods by sea and may amend such provisions without following the procedure provided for in Article 23 of the Convention of Rome. The national provisions applicable in this respect are the following:
   – in Denmark, paragraphs 252 and 321(3) and (4) of the 'Sølov' (maritime law);
   – in Sweden, Chapter 13, Article 2(1) and (2), and Chapter 14, Article 1(3), of 'sjölagen' (maritime law);
   – in Finland, Chapter 13, Article 2(1) and (2), and Chapter 14, Article 1(3) of 'merilaki'/'sjölagen' (maritime law).]

SCHEDULE 2
THE LUXEMBOURG CONVENTION

The High Contracting Parties to the Treaty establishing the European Economic Community,

Considering that the Hellenic Republic, in becoming a Member of the Community, undertook to accede to the Convention on the law applicable to contractual obligations, opened for signature in Rome on 19 June 1980,

Have decided to conclude this Convention, and to this end have designated as their plenipotentiaries:

(Designation of plenipotentiaries)

Who, meeting within the Council, having exchanged their full powers, found in good and due form,

Have agreed as follows:

Article 1
The Hellenic Republic hereby accedes to the Convention on the law applicable to contractual obligations, opened for signature in Rome on 19 June 1980.

Article 2
The Secretary-General of the Council of the European Communities shall transmit a certified copy of the Convention on the law applicable to contractual obligations in the Danish, Dutch, English, French, German, Irish and Italian languages to the Government of the Hellenic Republic.

The text of the Convention on the law applicable to contractual obligations in the Greek language is annexed hereto. The text in the Greek language shall be authentic under the same conditions as the other texts of the Convention on the law applicable to contractual obligations.

Article 3
This Convention shall be ratified by the Signatory States. The instruments of ratification shall be deposited with the Secretary-General of the Council of the European Communities.

Article 4
This Convention shall enter into force, as between the States which have ratified it, on the first day of the third month following the deposit of the last instrument of ratification by the Hellenic Republic and seven States which have ratified the Convention on the law applicable to contractual obligations.

This Convention shall enter into force for each Contracting State which subsequently ratifies it on the first day of the third month following the deposit of its instrument of ratification.

Article 5
The Secretary-General of the Council of the European Communities shall notify the Signatory States of:
(a)   the deposit of each instrument of ratification;
(b)   the dates of entry into force of this Convention for the Contracting States.

Article 6
This Convention, drawn up in a single original in the Danish, Dutch, English, French, German, Greek, Irish and Italian languages, all eight texts being equally authentic, shall be deposited in the archives of the General Secretariat of the Council of the European Communities. The Secretary-General shall transmit a certified copy to the Government of each Signatory State.

SCHEDULE 3
THE BRUSSELS PROTOCOL

The High Contracting Parties to the Treaty establishing the European Economic Community,

Having regard to the Joint Declaration annexed to the Convention on the law applicable to contractual obligations, opened for signature in Rome on 19 June 1980,

Have decided to conclude a Protocol conferring jurisdiction on the Court of Justice of the European Communities to interpret that Convention and to this end have designated as their Plenipotentiaries:

(Designation of plenipotentiaries)

Who, meeting within the Council of the European Communities, having exchanged their full powers, found in good and due form,

Have agreed as follows:

Article 1

The Court of Justice of the European Communities shall have jurisdiction to give rulings on the interpretation of—

(a)   the Convention on the law applicable to contractual obligations, opened for signature in Rome on 19 June 1980, hereinafter referred to as 'the Rome Convention';

(b)   the Convention on accession to the Rome Convention by the States which have become Members of the European Communities since the date on which it was opened for signature;

(c)   this Protocol.

Article 2

Any of the courts referred to below may request the Court of Justice to give a preliminary ruling on a question raised in a case pending before it and concerning interpretation of the provisions contained in the instruments referred to in Article 1 if that court considers that a decision on the question is necessary to enable it to give judgment:

(a)   —in Belgium:
    la Cour de cassation (het Hof van Cassatie) and le Conseil d'Etat (de Raad van State),
  —in Denmark:
    Højesteret,
  —in the Federal Republic of Germany:
    die obersten Gerichtschöfe des Bundes,
  —in Greece:
    τα ανώτατα Αικαστήρια,
  —in Spain:
    el Tribunal Supremo,
  —in France:
    la Cour de cassation and le Conseil d'Etat,
  —in Ireland:
    the Supreme Court,
  —in Italy:
    la Corte suprema di cassazione and il Consiglio di Stato,
  —in Luxembourg:
    la Cour Supérieure de Justice, when sitting as Cour de cassation,
  [—in Austria:
    the Oberste Gerichtshof, the Verwaltungsgerichtshof and the Verfassungsgerichtshof,]
  —in the Netherlands:
    de Hoge Raad,
  —in Portugal:
    o Supremo Tribunal de Justiça and o Supremo Tribunal Administrativo,
  [—in Finland:
    korkein oikeus/högsta domstolen, korkein hallinto-oikeus/högsta förvaltningsdomstolen, markkinatuomioistuin/marknadsdomstolen and työtuomioistuin/arbetsdomstolen,
  —in Sweden:
    Högsta domstolen, Regeringsrätten, Arbetsdomstolen and Marknadsdomstolen]
  —in the United Kingdom:
    the House of Lords and other courts from which no further appeal is possible;

(b)   the courts of the Contracting States when acting as appeal courts.

Article 3

1.   The competent authority of a Contracting State may request the Court of Justice to give a ruling on a question of interpretation of the provisions contained in the instruments referred to in Article 1 if judgments given by courts of that State conflict with the interpretation given either by the Court of Justice or in a judgment of one of the courts of another Contracting State referred to in Article 2. The provisions of this paragraph shall apply only to judgments which have become *res judicata*.

2.   The interpretation given by the Court of Justice in response to such a request shall not affect the judgments which gave rise to the request for interpretation.

3.   The Procurators-General of the Supreme Courts of Appeal of the Contracting States, or any other authority designated by a Contracting State, shall be entitled to request the Court of Justice for a ruling on interpretation in accordance with paragraph 1.

4.   The Registrar of the Court of Justice shall give notice of the request to the Contracting States, to the Commission and to the Council of the European Communities; they shall then be entitled within two months of the notification to submit statements of case or written observations to the Court.

5.   No fees shall be levied or any costs or expenses awarded in respect of the proceedings provided for in this Article.

Article 4

1.   Except where this Protocol otherwise provides, the provisions of the Treaty establishing the European Economic Community and those of the Protocol on the Statute of the Court of Justice annexed thereto, which are applicable when the Court is requested to give a preliminary ruling, shall also apply to any proceedings for the interpretation of the instruments referred to in Article 1.

2.   The Rules of Procedure of the Court of Justice shall, if necessary, be adjusted and supplemented in accordance with Article 188 of the Treaty establishing the European Economic Community.

Article 5

This Protocol shall be subject to ratification by the Signatory States. The instruments of ratification shall be deposited with the Secretary-General of the Council of the European Communities.

Article 6

1.   To enter into force, this Protocol must be ratified by seven States in respect of which the Rome Convention is in force. This Protocol shall enter into force on the first day of the third month following the deposit of the instrument of ratification by the last such State to take this step. If, however, the Second Protocol conferring on the Court of Justice of the European Communities certain powers to interpret the Convention on the law applicable to contractual obligations, opened for signature in Rome on 19 June 1980, concluded in Brussels on 19 December 1988, enters into force on a later date, this Protocol shall enter into force on the date of entry into force of the Second Protocol.

2.   Any ratification subsequent to the entry into force of this Protocol shall take effect on the first day of the third month following the deposit of the instrument of ratification provided that the ratification, acceptance or approval of the Rome Convention by the State in question has become effective.

Article 7

The Secretary-General of the Council of the European Communities shall notify the Signatory States of:

(a)   the deposit of each instrument of ratification;
(b)   the date of entry into force of this Protocol;
(c)   any designation communicated pursuant to Article 3(3);
(d)   any communication made pursuant to Article 8.

Article 8

The Contracting States shall communicate to the Secretary-General of the Council of the European Communities the texts of any provisions of their laws which necessitate an amendment to the list of courts in Article 2(a).

Article 9

This Protocol shall have effect for as long as the Rome Convention remains in force under the conditions laid down in Article 30 of that Convention.

Article 10

Any Contracting State may request the revision of this Protocol. In this event, a revision conference shall be convened by the President of the Council of the European Communities.

Article 11

This Protocol, drawn up in a single original in the Danish, Dutch, English, French, German, Greek, Irish, Italian, Portuguese and Spanish languages, all 10 texts being equally authentic, shall be deposited in the archives of the General Secretariat of the Council of the European Communities. The Secretary-General shall transmit a certified copy to the Government of each Signatory State.

[SCHEDULE 3A
THE FUNCHAL CONVENTION

The High Contracting Parties to the Treaty establishing the European Economic Community.

Considering that the Kingdom of Spain and the Portuguese Republic, in becoming Members of the Community, undertook to accede to the Convention on the law applicable to contractual obligations, opened for signature in Rome on 19th June 1980.

Have decided to conclude this Convention, and to this end have designated as their plenipotentiaries:
(Designation of plenipotentiaries)

Who, meeting within the Council, having exchanged their full powers, found in good and due form.

Have agreed as follows:

Article 1

The Kingdom of Spain and the Portuguese Republic hereby accede to the Convention on the law applicable to contractual obligations, opened for signature in Rome on 19th June 1980.

Article 2

The Convention on the law applicable to contractual obligations is hereby amended as follows:

(1) Article 22(2), Article 27 and the second sentence of Article 30(3) shall be deleted.

(2) The reference to Article 27 in Article 31(d) shall be deleted.

Article 3

The Secretary-General of the Council of the European Communities shall transmit a certified copy of the Convention on the law applicable to contractual obligations in the Danish, Dutch, English, French, German, Greek, Irish and Italian languages to the Governments of the Kingdom of Spain and the Portuguese Republic.

Article 4

This Convention shall be ratified by the Signatory States. The instruments of ratification shall be deposited with the Secretary-General of the Council of the European Communities.

Article 5
This Convention shall enter into force, as between the States which have ratified it, on the first day of the third month following deposit of the last instrument of ratification by the Kingdom of Spain or the Portuguese Republic and by one State which has ratified the Convention on the law applicable to contractual obligations.

This Convention shall enter into force for each Contracting State which subsequently ratifies it on the first day of the third month following that of deposit of its instrument of ratification.

Article 6
The Secretary-General of the Council of the European Communities shall notify the Signatory States of:
(a)   the deposit of each instrument of ratification;
(b)   the dates of entry into force of this Convention for the Contracting States.

Article 7
This Convention, drawn up in a single original in the Danish, Dutch, English, French, German, Greek, Irish, Italian, Portuguese and Spanish languages, all ten texts being equally authentic, shall be deposited in the archives of the General Secretariat of the Council of the European Communities. The Secretary-General shall transmit a certified copy to the Government of each Signatory State.]

[SCHEDULE 3B
THE 1996 ACCESSION CONVENTION

Section 2

The High Contracting Parties to the Treaty establishing the European Community.

Considering that the Republic of Austria, the Republic of Finland and the Kingdom of Sweden, in becoming Members of the European Union, undertook to accede to the Convention on the Law applicable to Contractual Obligations, opened for signature in Rome on 19th June 1980, and to the First and Second Protocols on its interpretation by the Court of Justice,

Have agreed as follows:

TITLE I
GENERAL PROVISIONS

Article 1
The Republic of Austria, the Republic of Finland and the Kingdom of Sweden hereby accede to:
(a)   the Convention on the Law applicable to Contractual Obligations, opened for signature in Rome on 19th June 1980, hereinafter referred to as 'the Convention of 1980', as it stands following incorporation of all the adjustments and amendments made thereto by:
—the Convention signed in Luxembourg on 10th April 1984, hereinafter referred to as 'the Convention of 1984', on the accession of the Hellenic Republic to the Convention on the Law applicable to Contractual Obligations;
—the Convention signed in Funchal on 18th May 1992, hereinafter referred to as 'the Convention of 1992', on the accession of the Kingdom of Spain and the Portuguese Republic to the Convention on the Law applicable to Contractual Obligations;
(b)   the First Protocol, signed on 19th December 1988, hereinafter referred to as 'the First Protocol of 1988', on the interpretation by the Court of Justice of the European Communities of the Convention on the Law applicable to Contractual Obligations;
(c)   the Second Protocol, signed on 19th December 1988, hereinafter referred to as 'the Second Protocol of 1988', conferring on the Court of Justice of the European

Communities certain powers to interpret the Convention on the Law applicable to Contractual Obligations.

TITLE II
ADJUSTMENTS TO THE PROTOCOL ANNEXED TO THE CONVENTION OF 1980

Article 2

The Protocol annexed to the Convention of 1980 is hereby replaced by the following:

'Notwithstanding the provisions of the Convention, Denmark, Sweden and Finland may retain national provisions concerning the law applicable to questions relating to the carriage of goods by sea and may amend such provisions without following the procedure provided for in Article 23 of the Convention of Rome. The national provisions applicable in this respect are the following:
—in Denmark, paragraphs 252 and 321(3) and (4) of the "Sølov" (maritime law);
—in Sweden, Chapter 13, Article 2(1) and (2), and Chapter 14, Article 1(3), of "sjölagen" (maritime law);
—in Finland, Chapter 13, Article 2(1) and (2), and Chapter 14, Article 1(3), of "merilaki"/"sjölagen" (maritime law).'

TITLE III
ADJUSTMENTS TO THE FIRST PROTOCOL OF 1988

Article 3

The following indents shall be inserted in Article 2(a) of the First Protocol of 1988:
(a)   between the tenth and eleventh indents:
'—in Austria:
the Oberste Gerìchtshof, the Verwaltungsgerichtshof and the Verfassungsgerichtshof,'
(b)   between the eleventh and twelfth indents:
'—in Finland:
Korkein oikeus/högsta domstolen, korkein hallinto-oikeus/högsta förvaltningsdomstolen, markkinatuomioistuin/marknadsdomstolen and työtuomioistuin/arbetsdomstolen,
—in Sweden:
Högsta domstolen, Regeringsrätten, Arbetsdomstolen and Marknadsdomstolen,'.

TITLE IV
FINAL PROVISIONS

Article 4

1.   The Secretary-General of the Council of the European Union shall transmit a certified copy of the Convention of 1980, the Convention of 1984, the First Protocol of 1988, the Second Protocol of 1988 and the Convention of 1992 in the Danish, Dutch, English, French, German, Greek, Irish, Italian, Spanish and Portuguese languages to the Governments of the Republic of Austria, the Republic of Finland and the Kingdom of Sweden.

2.   The text of the Convention of 1980, the Convention of 1984, the First Protocol of 1988, the Second Protocol of 1988 and the Convention of 1992 in the Finnish and Swedish languages shall be authentic under the same conditions as the other texts of the Convention of 1980, the Convention of 1984, the First Protocol of 1988, the Second Protocol of 1988 and the Convention of 1992.

Article 5
This Convention shall be ratified by the Signatory States. The instruments of ratification shall be deposited with the Secretary-General of the Council of the European Union.

Article 6
1.   This Convention shall enter into force, as between the States which have ratified it, on the first day of the third month following the deposit of the last instrument of ratification by the Republic of Austria, the Republic of Finland or the Kingdom of Sweden and by one Contracting State which has ratified the Convention on the Law applicable to Contractual Obligations.
2.   This Convention shall enter into force for each Contracting State which subsequently ratifies it on the first day of the third month following the deposit of its instrument of ratification.

Article 7
The Secretary-General of the Council of the European Union shall notify the Signatory States of:
(a)   the deposit of each instrument of ratification;
(b)   the dates of entry into force of this Convention for the Contracting States.

Article 8
This Convention, drawn up in a single original in the Danish, Dutch, English, Finnish, French, German, Greek, Irish, Italian, Portuguese, Spanish and Swedish languages, all twelve texts being equally authentic, shall be deposited in the archives of the General Secretariat of the Council of the European Union. The Secretary-General shall transmit a certified copy to the Government of each Signatory State.]

AGE OF LEGAL CAPACITY (SCOTLAND) ACT 1991
(1991, c 50)

1   Age of legal capacity
(1)   As from the commencement of this Act—
(a)   a person under the age of 16 years shall, subject to section 2 below, have no legal capacity to enter into any transaction;
(b)   a person of or over the age of 16 years shall have legal capacity to enter into any transaction.
(2)   Subject to section 8 below, any reference in any enactment to a pupil (other than in the context of education or training) or to a person under legal disability or incapacity by reason of nonage shall, insofar as it relates to any time after the commencement of this Act, be construed as a reference to a person under the age of 16 years.
(3)   Nothing in this Act shall—
(a)   apply to any transaction entered into before the commencement of this Act;
(b)   confer any legal capacity on any person who is under legal disability or incapacity other than by reason of nonage;
(c)   affect the delictual or criminal responsibility of any person;
(d)   affect any enactment which lays down an age limit expressed in years for any particular purpose;
(e)   prevent any person under the age of 16 years from receiving or holding any right, title or interest;
(f)   affect any existing rule of law or practice whereby—
(i)   any civil proceedings may be brought or defended, or any step in civil proceedings may be taken, in the name of a person under the age of 16 years [in relation to whom there is no person entitled to act as his legal representa-

tive (within the meaning of Part I of the Children (Scotland) Act 1995), or where there is such a person,] is unable (whether by reason of conflict of interest or otherwise) or refuses to bring or defend such proceedings or take such step;

(ii) the court may, in any civil proceedings, appoint a curator ad litem to a person under the age of 16 years;

(iii) the court may, in relation to the approval of an arrangement under section 1 of the Trusts (Scotland) Act 1961, appoint a curator ad litem to a person of or over the age of 16 years but under the age of 18 years;

(iv) the court may appoint a curator bonis to any person;

(g) prevent any person under the age of 16 years from [exercising parental responsibilities and parental rights (within the meaning of sections 1(3) and 2(4) respectively of the Children (Scotland) Act 1995) in relation to any child of his.]

(4) Any existing rule of law relating to the legal capacity of minors and pupils which is inconsistent with the provisions of this Act shall cease to have effect.

(5) Any existing rule of law relating to reduction of a transaction on the ground of minority and lesion shall cease to have effect.

2 Exceptions to general rule

(1) A person under the age of 16 years shall have legal capacity to enter into a transaction—

(a) of a kind commonly entered into by persons of his age and circumstances, and

(b) on terms which are not unreasonable.

(2) A person of or over the age of 12 years shall have testamentary capacity, including legal capacity to exercise by testamentary writing any power of appointment.

(3) A person of or over the age of 12 years shall have legal capacity to consent to the making of an adoption order in relation to him; and accordingly—

(a) for section 12(8) (adoption orders) of the Adoption (Scotland) Act 1978 there shall be substituted the following subsection—

'(8) An adoption order shall not be made in relation to a child of or over the age of 12 years unless with the child's consent; except that, where the court is satisfied that the child is incapable of giving his consent to the making of the order, it may dispense with that consent.'; and

(b) for section 18(8) (freeing child for adoption) of that Act there shall be substituted the following subsection—

'(8) An order under this section shall not be made in relation to a child of or over the age of 12 years unless with the child's consent; except that where the court is satisfied that the child is incapable of giving his consent to the making of the order, it may dispense with that consent.'

(4) A person under the age of 16 years shall have legal capacity to consent on his own behalf to any surgical, medical or dental procedure or treatment where, in the opinion of a qualified medical practitioner attending him, he is capable of understanding the nature and possible consequences of the procedure or treatment.

[(4A) A person under the age of sixteen years shall have legal capacity to instruct a solicitor, in connection with any civil matter, where that person has a general understanding of what it means to do so; and without prejudice to the generality of this subsection a person twelve years of age or more shall be presumed to be of sufficient age and maturity to have such understanding.

(4B) A person who by virtue of subsection (4A) above has legal capacity to instruct a solicitor shall also have legal capacity to sue, or to defend, in any civil proceedings.

(4C)   Subsections (4A) and (4B) above are without prejudice to any question of legal capacity arising in connection with any criminal matter.]
(5)   Any transaction—
(a)   which a person under the age of 16 years purports to enter into after the commencement of this Act, and
(b)   in relation to which that person does not have legal capacity by virtue of this section,
shall be void.

3   Setting aside of transactions

(1)   A person under the age of 21 years ('the applicant') may make application to the court to set aside a transaction which he entered into while he was of or over the age of 16 years but under the age of 18 years and which is a prejudicial transaction.
(2)   In this section 'prejudicial transaction' means a transaction which—
(a)   an adult, exercising reasonable prudence, would not have entered into in the circumstances of the applicant at the time of entering into the transaction, and
(b)   has caused or is likely to cause substantial prejudice to the applicant.
(3)   Subsection (1) above shall not apply to—
(a)   the exercise of testamentary capacity;
(b)   the exercise by testamentary writing of any power of appointment;
(c)   the giving of consent to the making of an adoption order;
(d)   the bringing or defending of, or the taking of any step in, civil proceedings;
(e)   the giving of consent to any surgical, medical or dental procedure or treatment;
(f)   a transaction in the course of the applicant's trade, business or profession;
(g)   a transaction into which any other party was induced to enter by virtue of any fraudulent misrepresentation by the applicant as to age or other material fact;
(h)   a transaction ratified by the applicant after he attained the age of 18 years and in the knowledge that it could be the subject of an application to the court under this section to set it aside; or
(j)   a transaction ratified by the court under section 4 below.
(4)   Where an application to set aside a transaction can be made or could have been made under this section by the person referred to in subsection (1) above, such application may instead be made by that person's executor, trustee in bankruptcy, trustee acting under a trust deed for creditors or curator bonis at any time prior to the date on which that person attains or would have attained the age of 21 years.
(5)   An application under this section to set aside a transaction may be made—
(a)   by an action in the Court of Session or the sheriff court, or
(b)   by an incidental application in other proceedings in such court,
and the court may make an order setting aside the transaction and such further order, if any, as seems appropriate to the court in order to give effect to the rights of the parties.

4   Ratification by court of proposed transaction

(1)   Where a person of or over the age of 16 years but under the age of 18 years proposes to enter into a transaction which, if completed, could be the subject of an application to the court under section 3 above to set aside, all parties to the proposed transaction may make a joint application to have it ratified by the court.
(2)   The court shall not grant an application under this section if it appears to the court that an adult, exercising reasonable prudence and in the circumstances of the person referred to in subsection (1) above, would not enter into the transaction.

(3)   An application under this section shall be made by means of a summary application—

(a)   to the sheriff of the sheriffdom in which any of the parties to the proposed transaction resides, or

(b)   where none of the said parties resides in Scotland, to the sheriff at Edinburgh,

and the decision of the sheriff on such application shall be final.

5   Guardians of persons under 16

(1)   Except insofar as otherwise provided in Schedule 1 to this Act, as from the commencement of this Act any reference in any rule of law, enactment or document to the tutor [. . .] of a pupil child shall be construed as a reference to [a person entitled to act as a child's legal representative (within the meaning of Part I of the Children (Scotland) Act 1995) and any reference to the tutory of such a child shall be construed as a reference to the entitlement to act as a child's legal representative enjoyed by a person, by, under or by virtue of the said Part I.]

(2)   Subject to section 1(3)(f) above, as from the commencement of this Act no guardian of a person under the age of 16 years shall be appointed as such except under [section 7 of the Children (Scotland) Act 1995.]

(3)   As from the commencement of this Act, no person shall, by reason of age alone, be subject to the curatory of another person.

(4)   As from the commencement of this Act, no person shall be appointed as factor loco tutoris.

6   Attainment of age

(1)   The time at which a person attains a particular age expressed in years shall be taken to be the beginning of the relevant anniversary of the date of his birth.

(2)   Where a person has been born on 29th February in a leap year, the relevant anniversary in any year other than a leap year shall be taken to be 1st March.

(3)   The provisions of this section shall apply only to a relevant anniversary which occurs after the commencement of this Act.

7   Acquisition of domicile

The time at which a person first becomes capable of having an independent domicile shall be the date at which he attains the age of 16 years.

8   Transitional provision

Where any person referred to in section 6(4)(b), 17(3), 18(3) or 18A(2) of the Prescription and Limitation (Scotland) Act 1973 as having been under legal disability by reason of nonage was of or over the age of 16 years but under the age of 18 years immediately before the commencement of this Act, any period prior to such commencement shall not be reckoned as, or as part of, the period of 5 years, or (as the case may be) 3 years, specified respectively in section 6, 17, 18 or 18A of that Act.

9   Interpretation

In this Act, unless the context otherwise requires—

'existing' means existing immediately before the commencement of this Act;

[. . .]

'transaction' means a transaction having legal effect, and includes—

(a)   any unilateral transaction;

(b)   the exercise of testamentary capacity;

(c)   the exercise of any power of appointment;

(d)   the giving by a person of any consent having legal effect;

(e)   the bringing or defending of, or the taking of any step in, civil proceedings;

(f)   acting as arbiter or trustee;

(g)   acting as an instrumentary witness.

10   Amendments and repeals

(1)   The enactments mentioned in Schedule 1 to this Act shall have effect subject to the amendments therein specified.

(2)   The enactments specified in Schedule 2 to this Act are repealed to the extent specified in the third column of that Schedule.

11   Short title, commencement and extent

(1)   This Act may be cited as the Age of Legal Capacity (Scotland) Act 1991.

(2)   This Act shall come into force at the end of the period of two months beginning with the date on which it is passed.

(3)   This Act shall extend to Scotland only.

CARRIAGE OF GOODS BY SEA ACT 1992
(1992, c 50)

1   Shipping documents etc to which Act applies

(1)   This Act applies to the following documents, that is to say—

   (a)   any bill of lading;

   (b)   any sea waybill; and

   (c)   any ship's delivery order.

(2)   References in this Act to a bill of lading—

   (a)   do not include references to a document which is incapable of transfer either by indorsement or, as a bearer bill, by delivery without indorsement; but

   (b)   subject to that, do include references to a received for shipment bill of lading.

(3)   References in this Act to a sea waybill are references to any document which is not a bill of lading but—

   (a)   is such a receipt for goods as contains or evidences a contract for the carriage of goods by sea; and

   (b)   identifies the person to whom delivery of the goods is to be made by the carrier in accordance with that contract.

(4)   References in this Act to a ship's delivery order are references to any document which is neither a bill of lading nor a sea waybill but contains an undertaking which—

   (a)   is given under or for the purposes of a contract for the carriage by sea of the goods to which the document relates, or of goods which include those goods; and

   (b)   is an undertaking by the carrier to a person identified in the document to deliver the goods to which the document relates to that person.

(5)   The Secretary of State may by regulations make provision for the application of this Act to cases where a telecommunication system or any other information technology is used for effecting transactions corresponding to—

   (a)   the issue of a document to which this Act applies;

   (b)   the indorsement, delivery or other transfer of such a document; or

   (c)   the doing of anything else in relation to such a document.

(6)   Regulations under subsection (5) above may—

   (a)   make such modifications of the following provisions of this Act as the Secretary of State considers appropriate in connection with the application of this Act to any case mentioned in that subsection; and

   (b)   contain supplemental, incidental, consequential and transitional provision;

and the power to make regulations under that subsection shall be exercisable by statutory instrument subject to annulment in pursuance of a resolution of either House of Parliament.

2   Rights under shipping documents

(1)   Subject to the following provisions of this section, a person who becomes—

(a)   the lawful holder of a bill of lading;

(b)   the person who (without being an original party to the contract of carriage) is the person to whom delivery of the goods to which a sea waybill relates is to be made by the carrier in accordance with that contract; or

(c)   the person to whom delivery of the goods to which a ship's delivery order relates is to be made in accordance with the undertaking contained in the order,

shall (by virtue of becoming the holder of the bill or, as the case may be, the person to whom delivery is to be made) have transferred to and vested in him all rights of suit under the contract of carriage as if he had been a party to that contract.

(2)   Where, when a person becomes the lawful holder of a bill of lading, possession of the bill no longer gives a right (as against the carrier) to possession of the goods to which the bill relates, that person shall not have any rights transferred to him by virtue of subsection (1) above unless he becomes the holder of the bill—

(a)   by virtue of a transaction effected in pursuance of any contractual or other arrangements made before the time when such a right to possession ceased to attach to possession of the bill; or

(b)   as a result of the rejection to that person by another person of goods or documents delivered to the other person in pursuance of any such arrangements.

(3)   The rights vested in any person by virtue of the operation of subsection (1) above in relation to a ship's delivery order—

(a)   shall be so vested subject to the terms of the order; and

(b)   where the goods to which the order relates form a part only of the goods to which the contract of carriage relates, shall be confined to rights in respect of the goods to which the order relates.

(4)   Where, in the case of any document to which this Act applies—

(a)   a person with any interest or right in or in relation to goods to which the document relates sustains loss or damage in consequence of a breach of the contract of carriage; but

(b)   subsection (1) above operates in relation to that document so that rights of suit in respect of that breach are vested in another person,

the other person shall be entitled to exercise those rights for the benefit of the person who sustained the loss or damage to the same extent as they could have been exercised if they had been vested in the person for whose benefit they are exercised.

(5)   Where rights are transferred by virtue of the operation of subsection (1) above in relation to any document, the transfer for which that subsection provides shall extinguish any entitlement to those rights which derives—

(a)   where that document is a bill of lading, from a person's having been an original party to the contract of carriage; or

(b)   in the case of any document to which this Act applies, from the previous operation of that subsection in relation to that document;

but the operation of that subsection shall be without prejudice to any rights which derive from a person's having been an original party to the contract contained in, or evidenced by, a sea waybill and, in relation to a ship's delivery order, shall be without prejudice to any rights deriving otherwise than from the previous operation of that subsection in relation to that order.

3   Liabilities under shipping documents

(1)   Where subsection (1) of section 2 of this Act operates in relation to any document to which this Act applies and the person in whom rights are vested by virtue of that subsection—

(a)   takes or demands delivery from the carrier of any of the goods to which the document relates;

(b)   makes a claim under the contract of carriage against the carrier in respect of any of those goods; or

(c)   is a person who, at a time before those rights were vested in him, took or demanded delivery from the carrier of any of those goods,

that person shall (by virtue of taking or demanding delivery or making the claim or, in a case falling within paragraph (c) above, of having the rights vested in him) become subject to the same liabilities under that contract as if he had been a party to that contract.

(2)   Where the goods to which a ship's delivery order relates form a part only of the goods to which the contract of carriage relates, the liabilities to which any person is subject by virtue of the operation of this section in relation to that order shall exclude liabilities in respect of any goods to which the order does not relate.

(3)   This section, so far as it imposes liabilities under any contract on any person, shall be without prejudice to the liabilities under the contract of any person as an original party to the contract.

4   Representations in bills of lading

A bill of lading which—

(a)   represents goods to have been shipped on board a vessel or to have been received for shipment on board a vessel; and

(b)   has been signed by the master of the vessel or by a person who was not the master but had the express, implied or apparent authority of the carrier to sign bills of lading,

shall, in favour of a person who has become the lawful holder of the bill, be conclusive evidence against the carrier of the shipment of the goods or, as the case may be, of their receipt for shipment.

5   Interpretation etc

(1)   In this Act—

'bill of lading', 'sea waybill' and 'ship's delivery order' shall be construed in accordance with section 1 above;

'the contract of carriage'—

(a)   in relation to a bill of lading or sea waybill, means the contract contained in or evidenced by that bill or waybill; and

(b)   in relation to a ship's delivery order, means the contract under or for the purposes of which the undertaking contained in the order is given;

'holder', in relation to a bill of lading, shall be construed in accordance with subsection (2) below;

'information technology' includes any computer or other technology by means of which information or other matter may be recorded or communicated without being reduced to documentary form; and

'telecommunication system' has the same meaning as in the Telecommunications Act 1984.

(2)   References in this Act to the holder of a bill of lading are references to any of the following persons, that is to say—

(a)   a person with possession of the bill who, by virtue of being the person identified in the bill, is the consignee of the goods to which the bill relates;

(b)   a person with possession of the bill as a result of the completion, by delivery of the bill, of any indorsement of the bill or, in the case of a bearer bill, of any other transfer of the bill;

(c)   a person with possession of the bill as a result of any transaction by virtue of which he would have become a holder falling within paragraph (a) or (b) above had not the transaction been effected at a time when possession of the bill no longer gave a right (as against the carrier) to possession of the goods to which the bill relates;

and a person shall be regarded for the purposes of this Act as having become the lawful holder of a bill of lading wherever he has become the holder of the bill in good faith.

(3) References in this Act to a person's being identified in a document include references to his being identified by a description which allows for the identity of the person in question to be varied, in accordance with the terms of the document, after its issue; and the reference in section 1(3)(b) of this Act to a document's identifying a person shall be construed accordingly.

(4) Without prejudice to sections 2(2) and 4 above, nothing in this Act shall preclude its operation in relation to a case where the goods to which a document relates—

(a) cease to exist after the issue of the document; or

(b) cannot be identified (whether because they are mixed with other goods or for any other reason);

and references in this Act to the goods to which a document relates shall be construed accordingly.

(5) The preceding provisions of this Act shall have effect without prejudice to the application, in relation to any case, of the rules (the Hague-Visby Rules) which for the time being have the force of law by virtue of section 1 of the Carriage of Goods by Sea Act 1971.

6 Short title, repeal, commencement and extent

(1) This Act may be cited as the Carriage of Goods by Sea Act 1992.

(2) The Bills of Lading Act 1855 is hereby repealed.

(3) This Act shall come into force at the end of the period of two months beginning with the day on which it is passed; but nothing in this Act shall have effect in relation to any document issued before the coming into force of this Act.

(4) This Act extends to Northern Ireland.

NATIONAL LOTTERY ACT 1993
(1993, c 39)

PART I
AUTHORISATION AND REGULATION OF THE NATIONAL LOTTERY

Preliminary

1 The National Lottery

(1) In this Act 'the National Lottery' means all the lotteries that form part of the National Lottery, taken as a whole.

(2) A lottery forms part of the National Lottery if the following conditions are satisfied.

(3) The lottery must be promoted or proposed to be promoted—

(a) by the body licensed to run the National Lottery under section 5, or

(b) in pursuance of an agreement that has been made between that body and the lottery's promoter or proposed promoter.

(4) The promotion of the lottery must be authorised by a licence that has been granted to its promoter or proposed promoter under section 6.

2 Legality of lotteries forming part of the National Lottery

(1) A lottery that forms part of the National Lottery shall not be unlawful.

(2) Schedule 1 contains amendments consequential on subsection (1).

REQUIREMENTS OF WRITING (SCOTLAND) ACT 1995
(1995, c 7)

1 Writing required for certain contracts, obligations, trusts, conveyances and wills

(1) Subject to subsection (2) below and any other enactment, writing shall not be required for the constitution of a contract, unilateral obligation or trust.

(2) Subject to subsection (3) below, a written document complying with section 2 of this Act shall be required for—

(a) the constitution of—

(i) a contract or unilateral obligation for the creation, transfer, variation or extinction of [a real right] in land;

(ii) a gratuitous unilateral obligation except an obligation undertaken in the course of business; and

(iii) a trust whereby a person declares himself to be sole trustee of his own property or any property which he may acquire;

(b) the creation, transfer, variation or extinction of [a real right] in land otherwise than by the operation of a court decree, enactment or rule of law; and

(c) the making of any will, testamentary trust disposition and settlement or codicil.

(3) Where a contract, obligation or trust mentioned in subsection (2)(a) above is not constituted in a written document complying with section 2 of this Act, but one of the parties to the contract, a creditor in the obligation or a beneficiary under the trust ('the first person') has acted or refrained from acting in reliance on the contract, obligation or trust with the knowledge and acquiescence of the other party to the contract, the debtor in the obligation or the truster ('the second person')—

(a) the second person shall not be entitled to withdraw from the contract, obligation or trust; and

(b) the contract, obligation or trust shall not be regarded as invalid, on the ground that it is not so constituted, if the condition set out in subsection (4) below is satisfied.

(4) The condition referred to in subsection (3) above is that the position of the first person—

(a) as a result of acting or refraining from acting as mentioned in that sub-section has been affected to a material extent; and

(b) as a result of such a withdrawal as is mentioned in that subsection would be adversely affected to a material extent.

(5) In relation to the constitution of any contract, obligation or trust mentioned in subsection (2)(a) above, subsections (3) and (4) above replace the rules of law known as *rei interventus* and homologation.

(6) This section shall apply to the variation of a contract, obligation or trust as it applies to the constitution thereof but as if in subsections (3) and (4) for the references to acting or refraining from acting in reliance on the contract, obligation or trust and withdrawing therefrom there were substituted respectively references to acting or refraining from acting in reliance on the variation of the contract, obligation or trust and withdrawing from the variation.

(7) In this section ['real right in land' means any real] right in or over land, including any right to occupy or to use land or to restrict the occupation or use of land, but does not include—

(a) a tenancy;

(b) a right to occupy or use land; or

(c) a right to restrict the occupation or use of land,

if the tenancy or right is not granted for more than one year, unless the tenancy or right is for a recurring period or recurring periods and there is a gap of more than one year between the beginning of the first, and the end of the last, such period.

(8) For the purposes of subsection (7) above 'land' does not include—
    (a) growing crops; or
    (b) a moveable building or other moveable structure.

2 Type of writing required for formal validity of certain documents

(1) No document required by section 1(2) of this Act shall be valid in respect of the formalities of execution unless it is subscribed by the granter of it or, if there is more than one granter, by each granter, but nothing apart from such subscription shall be required for the document to be valid as aforesaid.

(2) A contract mentioned in section 1(2)(a)(i) of this Act may be regarded as constituted or varied (as the case may be) if the offer is contained in one or more documents and the acceptance is contained in another document or other documents, and each document is subscribed by the granter or granters thereof.

(3) Nothing in this section shall prevent a document which has not been subscribed by the granter or granters of it from being used as evidence in relation to any right or obligation to which the document relates.

(4) This section is without prejudice to any other enactment which makes different provision in respect of the formalities of execution of a document to which this section applies.

3 Presumption as to granter's subscription or date or place of subscription

(1) Subject to subsections (2) to (7) below, where—
    (a) a document bears to have been subscribed by a granter of it;
    (b) the document bears to have been signed by a person as a witness of that granter's subscription and the document, or the testing clause or its equivalent, bears to state the name and address of the witness; and
    (c) nothing in the document, or in the testing clause or its equivalent, indicates—
        (i) that it was not subscribed by that granter as it bears to have been so subscribed; or
        (ii) that it was not validly witnessed for any reason specified in paragraphs (a) to (e) of subsection (4) below,
the document shall be presumed to have been subscribed by that granter.

(2) Where a testamentary document consists of more than one sheet, it shall not be presumed to have been subscribed by a granter as mentioned in subsection (1) above unless, in addition to it bearing to have been subscribed by him and otherwise complying with that subsection, it bears to have been signed by him on every sheet.

(3) For the purposes of subsection (1)(b) above—
    (a) the name and address of a witness may be added at any time before the document is—
        (i) founded on in legal proceedings; or
        (ii) registered for preservation in the Books of Council and Session or in sheriff court books; and
    (b) the name and address of a witness need not be written by the witness himself.

(4) Where, in any proceedings relating to a document in which a question arises as to a granter's subscription, it is established—
    (a) that a signature bearing to be the signature of the witness of that granter's subscription is not such a signature, whether by reason of forgery or otherwise;
    (b) that the person who signed the document as the witness of that granter's subscription is a person who is named in the document as a granter of it;
    (c) that the person who signed the document as the witness of that granter's subscription, at the time of signing—
        (i) did not know the granter;
        (ii) was under the age of 16 years; or

(iii)   was mentally incapable of acting as a witness;

(d)   that the person who signed the document, purporting to be the witness of that granter's subscription, did not witness such subscription;

(e)   that the person who signed the document as the witness of that granter's subscription did not sign the document after him or that the granter's subscription or, as the case may be, acknowledgement of his subscription and the person's signature as witness of that subscription were not one continuous process;

(f)   that the name or address of the witness of that granter's subscription was added after the document was founded on or registered as mentioned in subsection (3)(a) above or is erroneous in any material respect; or

(g)   in the case of a testamentary document consisting of more than one sheet, that a signature on any sheet bearing to be the signature of the granter is not such a signature, whether by reason of forgery or otherwise,

then, for the purposes of those proceedings, there shall be no presumption that the document has been subscribed by that granter.

(5)   For the purposes of subsection (4)(c)(i) above, the witness shall be regarded as having known the person whose subscription he has witnessed at the time of witnessing if he had credible information at that time of his identity.

(6)   For the purposes of subsection (4)(e) above, where—

(a)   a document is granted by more than one granter; and

(b)   a person is the witness to the subscription of more than one granter,

the subscription or acknowledgement of any such granter and the signature of the person witnessing that granter's subscription shall not be regarded as not being one continuous process by reason only that, between the time of that subscription or acknowledgement and that signature, another granter has subscribed the document or acknowledged his subscription.

(7)   For the purposes of the foregoing provisions of this section a person witnesses a granter's subscription of a document—

(a)   if he sees the granter subscribe it; or

(b)   if the granter acknowledges his subscription to that person.

(8)   Where—

(a)   by virtue of subsection (1) above a document to which this subsection applies is presumed to have been subscribed by a granter of it;

(b)   the document, or the testing clause or its equivalent, bears to state the date or place of subscription of the document by that granter; and

(c)   nothing in the document, or in the testing clause or its equivalent, indicates that that statement as to date or place is incorrect,

there shall be a presumption that the document was subscribed by that granter on the date or at the place as stated.

(9)   Subsection (8) above applies to any document other than a testamentary document.

(10)   Where—

(a)   a testamentary document bears to have been subscribed and the document, or the testing clause or its equivalent, bears to state the date or place of subscription (whether or not it is presumed under subsections (1) to (7) above to have been subscribed by a granter of it); and

(b)   nothing in the document, or in the testing clause or its equivalent, indicates that that statement as to date or place is incorrect,

there shall be a presumption that the statement as to date or place is correct.

4   Presumption as to granter's subscription or date or place of subscription when established in court proceedings

(1)   Where a document bears to have been subscribed by a granter of it, but there is no presumption under section 3 of this Act that the document has been subscribed by that granter, then, if the court, on an application being made to it by

any person who has an interest in the document, is satisfied that the document was subscribed by that granter, it shall—

   (a)   cause the document to be endorsed with a certificate to that effect; or

   (b)   where the document has already been registered in the Books of Council and Session or in sheriff court books, grant decree to that effect.

(2)   Where a document bears to have been subscribed by a granter of it, but there is no presumption under section 3 of this Act as to the date or place of subscription, then, if the court, on an application being made to it by any person who has an interest in the document, is satisfied as to the date or place of subscription, it shall—

   (a)   cause the document to be endorsed with a certificate to that effect; or

   (b)   where the document has already been registered in the Books of Council and Session or in sheriff court books, grant decree to that effect.

(3)   On an application under subsection (1) or (2) above evidence shall, unless the court otherwise directs, be given by affidavit.

(4)   An application under subsection (1) or (2) above may be made either as a summary application or as incidental to and in the course of other proceedings.

(5)   The effect of a certificate or decree—

   (a)   under subsection (1) above shall be to establish a presumption that the document has been subscribed by the granter concerned;

   (b)   under subsection (2) above shall be to establish a presumption that the statement in the certificate or decree as to date or place is correct.

(6)   In this section 'the court' means—

   (a)   in the case of a summary application—

      (i)   the sheriff in whose sheriffdom the applicant resides; or

      (ii)   if the applicant does not reside in Scotland, the sheriff at Edinburgh; and

   (b)   in the case of an application made in the course of other proceedings, the court before which those proceedings are pending.

5   Alterations to documents: formal validity and presumptions

(1)   An alteration made to a document required by section 1(2) of this Act—

   (a)   before the document is subscribed by the granter or, if there is more than one granter, by the granter first subscribing it, shall form part of the document as so subscribed;

   (b)   after the document is so subscribed shall, if the alteration has been signed by the granter or (as the case may be) by all the granters, have effect as a formally valid alteration of the document as so subscribed,

but an alteration made to such a document otherwise than as mentioned in paragraphs (a) and (b) above shall not be formally valid.

(2)   Subsection (1) above is without prejudice to—

   (a)   any rule of law enabling any provision in a testamentary document to be revoked by deletion or erasure without authentication of the deletion or erasure by the testator;

   (b)   the Erasures in Deeds (Scotland) Act 1836 and section 54 of the Conveyancing (Scotland) Act 1874.

(3)   The fact that an alteration to a document was made before the document was subscribed by the granter of it, or by the granter first subscribing it, may be established by all relevant evidence, whether written or oral.

(4)   Where a document bears to have been subscribed by the granter or, if there is more than one granter, by all the granters of it, then, if subsection (5) or (6) below applies, an alteration made to the document shall be presumed to have been made before the document was subscribed by the granter or, if there is more than one granter, by the granter first subscribing it, and to form part of the document as so subscribed.

(5)   This subsection applies where—

(a)   the document is presumed under section 3 of this Act to have been subscribed by the granter or granters (as the case may be);

(b)   it is stated in the document, or in the testing clause or its equivalent, that the alteration was made before the document was subscribed; and

(c)   nothing in the document, or in the testing clause or its equivalent, indicates that the alteration was made after the document was subscribed.

(6)   This subsection applies where subsection (5) above does not apply, but the court is satisfied, on an application being made to it, that the alteration was made before the document was subscribed by the granter or, if there is more than one granter, by the granter first subscribing it, and causes the document to be endorsed with a certificate to that effect or, where the document has already been registered in the Books of Council and Session or in sheriff court books, grants decree to that effect.

(7)   Subsections (3), (4) and (6) of section 4 of this Act shall apply in relation to an application under subsection (6) above as they apply in relation to an application under subsection (1) of that section.

(8)   Where an alteration is made to a document after the document has been subscribed by a granter, Schedule 1 to this Act (presumptions as to granter's signature and date and place of signing in relation to such alterations) shall have effect.

6   Registration of documents

(1)   Subject to subsection (3) below, it shall not be competent—

(a)   to record a document in the Register of Sasines; or

(b)   to register a document for execution or preservation in the Books of Council and Session or in sheriff court books,

unless subsection (2) below applies in relation to the document.

(2)   This subsection applies where—

(a)   the document is presumed under section 3 or 4 of this Act to have been subscribed by the granter; or

(b)   if there is more than one granter, the document is presumed under section 3 or 4 or partly under the one section and partly under the other to have been subscribed by at least one of the granters.

(3)   Subsection (1) above shall not apply in relation to—

(a)   the recording of a document in the Register of Sasines or the registration of a document in the Books of Council and Session or in sheriff court books, if such recording or registration is required or expressly permitted under any enactment;

(b)   the recording of a court decree in the Register of Sasines;

(c)   the registration in the Books of Council and Session or in sheriff court books of—

(i)   a testamentary document;

(ii)   a document which is directed by the Court of Session or (as the case may be) the sheriff to be so registered;

(iii)   a document whose formal validity is governed by a law other than Scots law, if the Keeper of the Registers of Scotland or (as the case may be) the sheriff clerk is satisfied that the document is formally valid according to the law governing such validity;

(iv)   a court decree granted under section 4 or 5 of this Act in relation to a document already registered in the Books of Council and Session or in sheriff court books (as the case may be); or

(d)   the registration of a court decree in a separate register maintained for that purpose.

(4)   A document may be registered for preservation in the Books of Council and Session or in sheriff court books without a clause of consent to registration.

7 Subscription and signing

(1) Except where an enactment expressly provides otherwise, a document is subscribed by a granter of it if it is signed by him at the end of the last page (excluding any annexation, whether or not incorporated in the document as provided for in section 8 of this Act).

(2) Subject to paragraph 2(2) of Schedule 2 to this Act, a document, or an alteration to a document, is signed by an individual natural person as a granter or on behalf of a granter of it if it is signed by him—

    (a) with the full name by which he is identified in the document or in any testing clause or its equivalent; or

    (b) with his surname, preceded by at least one forename (or an initial or abbreviation or familiar form of a forename); or

    (c) except for the purposes of section 3(1) to (7) of this Act, with a name (not in accordance with paragraph (a) or (b) above) or description or an initial or mark if it is established that the name, description, initial or mark—

        (i) was his usual method of signing, or his usual method of signing documents or alterations of the type in question; or

        (ii) was intended by him as his signature of the document or alteration.

(3) Where there is more than one granter, the requirement under subsection (1) above of signing at the end of the last page of a document shall be regarded as complied with if at least one granter signs at the end of the last page and any other granter signs on an additional page.

(4) Where a person grants a document in more than one capacity, one subscription of the document by him shall be sufficient to bind him in all such capacities.

(5) A document, or an alteration to a document, is signed by a witness if it is signed by him—

    (a) with the full name by which he is identified in the document or in any testing clause or its equivalent; or

    (b) with his surname, preceded by at least one forename (or an initial or abbreviation or familiar form of a forename),

and if the witness is witnessing the signature of more than one granter, it shall be unnecessary for him to sign the document or alteration more than once.

(6) This section is without prejudice to any rule of law relating to the subscription or signing of documents by members of the Royal Family, by peers or by the wives or the eldest sons of peers.

(7) Schedule 2 to this Act (special rules relating to subscription and signing of documents etc by partnerships, companies, [limited liability partnerships,] local authorities, other bodies corporate and Ministers) shall have effect.

8 Annexations to documents

(1) Subject to subsection (2) below and except where an enactment expressly otherwise provides, any annexation to a document shall be regarded as incorporated in the document if it is—

    (a) referred to in the document; and

    (b) identified on its face as being the annexation referred to in the document, without the annexation having to be signed or subscribed.

(2) Where a document relates to land and an annexation to it describes or shows all or any part of the land to which the document relates, the annexation shall be regarded as incorporated in the document if and only if—

    (a) it is referred to in the document; and

    (b) it is identified on its face as being the annexation referred to in the document; and

    (c) it is signed on—

        (i) each page, where it is a plan, drawing, photograph or other representation; or

(ii) the last page, where it is an inventory, appendix, schedule or other writing.

(3) Any annexation referred to in subsection (2) above which bears to have been signed by a granter of the document shall be presumed to have been signed by the person who subscribed the document as that granter.

(4) Section 7(2) of this Act shall apply in relation to any annexation referred to in subsection (2) above as it applies in relation to a document as if for any reference to a document (except the reference in paragraph (a)) there were substituted a reference to an annexation.

(5) It shall be competent to sign any annexation to a document at any time before the document is—

(a) founded on in legal proceedings;

(b) registered for preservation in the Books of Council and Session or in sheriff court books;

(c) recorded in the Register of Sasines;

(d) registered in the Land Register of Scotland.

(6) Where there is more than one granter, the requirement under subsection (2)(c)(ii) above of signing on the last page shall be regarded as complied with (provided that at least one granter signs at the end of the last page) if any other granter signs on an additional page.

9 Subscription on behalf of blind granter or granter unable to write

(1) Where a granter of a document makes a declaration to a relevant person that he is blind or unable to write, the relevant person—

(a) having read the document to that granter; or

(b) if the granter makes a declaration that he does not wish him to do so, without having read it to the granter,

shall, if authorised by the granter, be entitled to subscribe it and, if it is a testamentary document, sign it as mentioned in section 3(2) of this Act, on the granter's behalf.

(2) Subscription or signing by a relevant person under subsection (1) above shall take place in the presence of the granter.

(3) This Act shall have effect in relation to subscription or signing by a relevant person under subsection (1) above subject to the modifications set out in Schedule 3 to this Act.

(4) A document subscribed by a relevant person under subsection (1) above which confers on the relevant person or his spouse, son or daughter a benefit in money or money's worth (whether directly or indirectly) shall be invalid to the extent, but only to the extent, that it confers such benefit.

(5) This section and Schedule 3 to this Act apply in relation to the signing of—

(a) an annexation to a document as mentioned in section 8(2) of this Act;

(b) an alteration made to a document or to any such annexation to a document,

as they apply in relation to the subscription of a document; and for that purpose, any reference to reading a document includes a reference to describing a plan, drawing, photograph or other representation in such an annexation or in an alteration to such an annexation.

(6) In this Act 'relevant person' means a solicitor who has in force a practising certificate as defined in section 4(c) of the Solicitors (Scotland) Act 1980, an advocate, a justice of the peace or a sheriff clerk and, in relation to the execution of documents outwith Scotland, includes a notary public or any other person with official authority under the law of the place of execution to execute documents on behalf of persons who are blind or unable to write.

(7) Nothing in this section shall prevent the granter of a document who is blind from subscribing or signing the document as mentioned in section 7 of this Act.

10   Forms of testing clause

(1)   Without prejudice to the effectiveness of any other means of providing information relating to the execution of a document, this information may be provided in such form of testing clause as may be prescribed in regulations made by the Secretary of State.

(2)   Regulations under subsection (1) above shall be made by statutory instrument which shall be subject to annulment in pursuance of a resolution of either House of Parliament and may prescribe different forms for different cases or classes of case.

11   Abolition of proof by writ or oath, reference to oath and other common law rules

(1)   Any rule of law and any enactment whereby the proof of any matter is restricted to proof by writ or by reference to oath shall cease to have effect.

(2)   The procedure of proving any matter in any civil proceedings by reference to oath is hereby abolished.

(3)   The following rules of law shall cease to have effect—

(a)   any rule whereby certain contracts and obligations and any variations of those contracts and obligations, and assignations of incorporeal moveables, are required to be in writing; and

(b)   any rule which confers any privilege—

(i)   on a document which is holograph or adopted as holograph; or

(ii)   on a writ *in re mercatoria*.

(4)   Subsections (1) and (2) above shall not apply in relation to proceedings commenced before the commencement of this Act.

12   Interpretation

(1)   In this Act, except where the context otherwise requires—

'alteration' includes interlineation, marginal addition, deletion, substitution, erasure or anything written on erasure;

'annexation' includes any inventory, appendix, schedule, other writing, plan, drawing, photograph or other representation annexed to a document;

'authorised' means expressly or impliedly authorised and any reference to a person authorised to sign includes a reference to a person authorised to sign generally or in relation to a particular document;

'company' has the same meaning as in section 735(1) of the Companies Act 1985;

'decree' includes a judgment or order, or an official certified copy, abbreviate or extract of a decree;

'director' includes any person occupying the position of director, by whatever name he is called;

'document' includes any annexation which is incorporated in it under section 8 of this Act and any reference, however expressed, to the signing of a document includes a reference to the signing of an annexation;

'enactment' includes an enactment contained in a statutory instrument [and an enactment comprised in, or in an instrument made under, an Act of the Scottish Parliament];

'governing board', in relation to a body corporate to which paragraph 5 of Schedule 2 to this Act applies, means any governing body, however described;

'local authority' means a local authority within the meaning of section 235(1) of the Local Government (Scotland) Act 1973 and a council constituted under section 2 of the Local Government etc (Scotland) Act 1994;

'Minister' has the same meaning as 'Minister of the Crown' has in section 8 of the Ministers of the Crown Act 1975 [and also includes a Member of the Scottish Executive];

'office-holder' does not include a Minister but, subject to that, means—

(a)   the holder of an office created or continued in existence by a public general Act of Parliament;

(b)   the holder of an office the remuneration in respect of which is paid out of money provided by Parliament [or out of the Scottish Consolidated Fund];

(c)   the registrar of companies within the meaning of the Companies Act 1985;

'officer'—

(a)   in relation to a Minister, means any person in the civil service of the Crown who is serving in his Department [or as the case may be, as a member of the staff of the Scottish Ministers or the Lord Advocate];

(b)   in relation to an office-holder, means any member of his staff, or any person in the civil service of the Crown who has been assigned or appointed to assist him in the exercise of his functions;

'proper officer', in relation to a local authority, has the same meaning as in section 235(3) of the Local Government (Scotland) Act 1973; and

'secretary' means, if there are two or more joint secretaries, any one of them.

(2)   Any reference in this Act to subscription or signing by a granter of a document or an alteration made to a document, in a case where a person is subscribing or signing under a power of attorney on behalf of the granter, shall be construed as a reference to subscription or signing by that person of the document or alteration.

13   Application of Act to Crown
(1)   Nothing in this Act shall—

(a)   prevent Her Majesty from authenticating—

(i)   a document by superscription; or

(ii)   a document relating to her private estates situated or arising in Scotland in accordance with section 6 of the Crown Private Estates Act 1862;

(b)   prevent authentication under the Writs Act 1672 of a document passing the seal appointed by the Treaty of Union to be kept and used in Scotland in place of the Great Seal of Scotland formerly in use; or

(c)   prevent any document mentioned in paragraph (a) or (b) above authenticated as aforesaid from being recorded in the Register of Sasines or registered for execution or preservation in the Books of Council and Session or in sheriff court books.

[. . .]

(3)   Subject to subsections (1) and (2) above, this Act binds the Crown.

14   Minor and consequential amendments, repeals, transitional provisions and savings
(1)   The enactments mentioned in Schedule 4 to this Act shall have effect subject to the minor and consequential amendments specified in that Schedule.

(2)   The enactments mentioned in Schedule 5 to this Act are hereby repealed to the extent specified in the third column of that Schedule.

(3)   Subject to subsection (4) below and without prejudice to subsection (5) below and section 11(4) of this Act, nothing in this Act shall—

(a)   apply to any document executed or anything done before the commencement of this Act; or

(b)   affect the operation, in relation to any document executed before such commencement, of any procedure for establishing the authenticity of such a document.

(4)   In the repeal of the Blank Bonds and Trusts Act 1696 (provided for in Schedule 5 to this Act), the repeal of the words from 'And farder' to the end—

(a)   shall have effect in relation to a deed of trust, whether executed before or after the commencement of this Act; but

(b)   notwithstanding paragraph (a) above, shall not have effect in relation to proceedings commenced before the commencement of this Act in which a question arises as to the deed of trust.

(5)   The repeal of certain provisions of the Lyon King of Arms Act 1672 (pro-

vided for in Schedule 5 to this Act) shall not affect any right of a person to add a territorial designation to his signature or the jurisdiction of the Lord Lyon King of Arms in relation to any such designation.

(6) For the purposes of this Act, if it cannot be ascertained whether a document was executed before or after the commencement of this Act, there shall be a presumption that it was executed after such commencement.

15 Short title, commencement and extent

(1) This Act may be cited as the Requirements of Writing (Scotland) Act 1995.

(2) This Act shall come into force at the end of the period of three months beginning with the date on which it is passed.

(3) This Act extends to Scotland only.

SCHEDULES

SCHEDULE 1
ALTERATIONS MADE TO A DOCUMENT AFTER IT HAS BEEN SUBSCRIBED

Presumption as to granter's signature or date or place of signing

1.—(1) Subject to sub-paragraphs (2) to (7) below, where—

(a) an alteration to a document bears to have been signed by a granter of the document;

(b) the alteration bears to have been signed by a person as a witness of that granter's signature and the alteration, or the testing clause or its equivalent, bears to state the name and address of the witness; and

(c) nothing in the document or alteration, or in the testing clause or its equivalent, indicates—

(i) that the alteration was not signed by that granter as it bears to have been so signed; or

(ii) that it was not validly witnessed for any reason specified in paragraphs (a) to (e) of sub-paragraph (4) below,

the alteration shall be presumed to have been signed by that granter.

(2) Where an alteration to a testamentary document consists of more than one sheet, the alteration shall not be presumed to have been signed by a granter as mentioned in sub-paragraph (1) above unless, in addition to it bearing to have been signed by him on the last sheet and otherwise complying with that sub-paragraph, it bears to have been signed by him on every other sheet.

(3) For the purposes of sub-paragraph (1)(b) above—

(a) the name and address of a witness may be added at any time before the alteration is—

(i) founded on in legal proceedings; or

(ii) registered for preservation in the Books of Council and Session or in sheriff court books; and

(b) the name and address of a witness need not be written by the witness himself.

(4) Where, in any proceedings relating to an alteration to a document in which a question arises as to a granter's signature, it is established—

(a) that a signature bearing to be the signature of the witness of that granter's signature is not such a signature, whether by reason of forgery or otherwise;

(b) that the person who signed the alteration as the witness of that granter's signature is a person who is named in the document as a granter of the document;

(c) that the person who signed the alteration as the witness of that granter's signature, at the time of signing—
    (i) did not know the granter;
    (ii) was under the age of 16 years; or
    (iii) was mentally incapable of acting as a witness;
(d) that the person who signed the alteration, purporting to be the witness of that granter's signature, did not witness such signature;
(e) that the person who signed the alteration as the witness of that granter's signature did not sign the alteration after him or that the signing of the alteration by the granter or, as the case may be, the granter's acknowledgement of his signature and the signing by the person as witness were not one continuous process;
(f) that the name or address of the witness of that granter's signature was added after the alteration was founded on or registered as mentioned in sub-paragraph (3)(a) above or is erroneous in any material respect; or
(g) in the case of an alteration to a testamentary document consisting of more than one sheet, that a signature on any sheet of the alteration bearing to be the signature of the granter is not such a signature, whether by reason of forgery or otherwise,

then, for the purposes of those proceedings, there shall be no presumption that the alteration has been signed by that granter.

(5) For the purposes of sub-paragraph (4)(c)(i) above, the witness shall be regarded as having known the person whose signature he has witnessed at the time of witnessing if he had credible information at that time of his identity.

(6) For the purposes of sub-paragraph (4)(e) above, where—
(a) an alteration to a document is made by more than one granter; and
(b) a person is the witness to the signature of more than one granter,

the signing of the alteration by any such granter or the acknowledgement of his signature and the signing by the person witnessing that granter's signature shall not be regarded as not being one continuous process by reason only that, between the time of signing or acknowledgement by that granter and of signing by that witness, another granter has signed the alteration or acknowledged his signature.

(7) For the purposes of the foregoing provisions of this paragraph a person witnesses a granter's signature of an alteration—
(a) if he sees the granter sign it; or
(b) if the granter acknowledges his signature to that person.

(8) Where—
(a) by virtue of sub-paragraph (1) above an alteration to a document to which this sub-paragraph applies is presumed to have been signed by a granter of the document;
(b) the alteration, or the testing clause or its equivalent, bears to state the date or place of signing of the alteration by that granter; and
(c) nothing in the document or alteration, or in the testing clause or its equivalent, indicates that that statement as to date or place is incorrect,

there shall be a presumption that the alteration was signed by that granter on the date or at the place as stated.

(9) Sub-paragraph (8) above applies to any document other than a testamentary document.

(10) Where—
(a) an alteration to a testamentary document bears to have been signed and the alteration, or the testing clause or its equivalent, bears to state the date or place of signing (whether or not it is presumed under sub-paragraphs (1) to (7) above to have been signed by a granter of the document); and
(b) nothing in the document or alteration, or in the testing clause or its equivalent, indicates that that statement as to date or place is incorrect,

there shall be a presumption that the statement as to date or place is correct.

Presumption as to granter's signature or date or place of signing when established in court proceedings

2.—(1)   Where an alteration to a document bears to have been signed by a granter of the document, but there is no presumption under paragraph 1 above that the alteration has been signed by that granter, then, if the court, on an application being made to it by any person having an interest in the document, is satisfied that the alteration was signed by that granter, it shall—

    (a)   cause the document to be endorsed with a certificate to that effect; or

    (b)   where the document has already been registered in the Books of Council and Session or in sheriff court books, grant decree to that effect.

(2)   Where an alteration to a document bears to have been signed by a granter of the document, but there is no presumption under paragraph 1 above as to the date or place of signing, then, if the court, on an application being made to it by any person having an interest in the document, is satisfied as to the date or place of signing, it shall—

    (a)   cause the document to be endorsed with a certificate to that effect; or

    (b)   where the document has already been registered in the Books of Council and Session or in sheriff court books, grant decree to that effect.

(3)   In relation to an application under sub-paragraph (1) or (2) above evidence shall, unless the court otherwise directs, be given by affidavit.

(4)   An application under sub-paragraph (1) or (2) above may be made either as a summary application or as incidental to and in the course of other proceedings.

(5)   The effect of a certificate or decree—

    (a)   under sub-paragraph (1) above shall be to establish a presumption that the alteration has been signed by the granter concerned;

    (b)   under sub-paragraph (2) above shall be to establish a presumption that the statement in the certificate or decree as to date or place is correct.

(6)   In this paragraph 'the court' means—

    (a)   in the case of a summary application—

       (i)   the sheriff in whose sheriffdom the applicant resides; or

       (ii)   if the applicant does not reside in Scotland, the sheriff at Edinburgh; and

    (b)   in the case of an application made in the course of other proceedings, the court before which those proceedings are pending.

SCHEDULE 2
SUBSCRIPTION AND SIGNING: SPECIAL CASES

General

1.   Any reference in this Act to subscription or signing by a granter of a document or an alteration to a document, in a case where the granter is a person to whom any of paragraphs 2 to 6 of this Schedule applies shall, unless the context otherwise requires, be construed as a reference to subscription or, as the case may be, signing of the document or alteration by a person in accordance with that paragraph.

Partnerships

2.—(1)   Except where an enactment expressly provides otherwise, where a granter of a document is a partnership, the document is signed by the partnership if it is signed on its behalf by a partner or by a person authorised to sign the document on its behalf.

(2)   A person signing on behalf of a partnership under this paragraph may use his own name or the firm name.

(3)   Sub-paragraphs (1) and (2) of this paragraph apply in relation to the signing of an alteration made to a document as they apply in relation to the signing of a document.

(4)   In this paragraph 'partnership' has the same meaning as in section 1 of the Partnership Act 1890.

Companies

3.—(1)   Except where an enactment expressly provides otherwise, where a granter of a document is a company, the document is signed by the company if it is signed on its behalf by a director, or by the secretary, of the company or by a person authorised to sign the document on its behalf.

(2)   This Act is without prejudice to—

    (a)   section 283(3) of the Companies Act 1985; and

    (b)   paragraph 9 of Schedule 1, paragraph 9 of Schedule 2, and paragraph 7 of Schedule 4, to the Insolvency Act 1986.

(3)   Sub-paragraphs (1) and (2) of this paragraph apply in relation to the signing of an alteration made to a document as they apply in relation to the signing of a document.

(4)   Where a granter of a document is a company, section 3 of and Schedule 1 to this Act shall have effect subject to the modifications set out in sub-paragraphs (5) and (6) below.

(5)   In section 3—

    (a)   for subsection (1) there shall be substituted the following subsections—

        '(1)   Subject to subsections (1A) to (7) below, where—

           (a)   a document bears to have been subscribed on behalf of a company by a director, or by the secretary, of the company or by a person bearing to have been authorised to subscribe the document on its behalf;

           (b)   the document bears to have been signed by a person as a witness of the subscription of the director, secretary or other person subscribing on behalf of the company and to state the name and address of the witness; and

           (c)   nothing in the document, or in the testing clause or its equivalent, indicates—

              (i)   that it was not subscribed on behalf of the company as it bears to have been so subscribed; or

              (ii)   that it was not validly witnessed for any reason specified in paragraphs (a) to (e) of subsection (4) below,

the document shall be presumed to have been subscribed by the company.

(1A)   Where a document does not bear to have been signed by a person as a witness of the subscription of the director, secretary or other person subscribing on behalf of the company it shall be presumed to have been subscribed by the company if it bears to have been subscribed on behalf of the company by—

    (a)   two directors of the company; or

    (b)   a director and secretary of the company; or

    (c)   two persons bearing to have been authorised to subscribe the document on its behalf.

(1B)   For the purposes of subsection (1)(b) above, the name and address of the witness may bear to be stated in the document itself or in the testing clause or its equivalent.

(1C)   A presumption under subsection (1) or (1A) above as to subscription of a document does not include a presumption—

(a) that a person bearing to subscribe the document as a director or the secretary of the company was such director or secretary; or

(b) that a person subscribing the document on behalf of the company bearing to have been authorised to do so was authorised to do so.';

(b) in subsection (4) after paragraph (g) there shall be inserted the following paragraph—

'(h) if the document does not bear to have been witnessed, but bears to have been subscribed on behalf of the company by two of the directors of the company, or by a director and secretary of the company, or by two authorised persons, that a signature bearing to be the signature of a director, secretary or authorised person is not such a signature, whether by reason of forgery or otherwise;'.

(6) In paragraph 1 of Schedule 1—

(a) for sub-paragraph (1) there shall be substituted the following sub-paragraphs—

'(1) Subject to sub-paragraphs (1A) to (7) below, where—

(a) an alteration to a document bears to have been signed on behalf of a company by a director, or by the secretary, of the company or by a person bearing to have been authorised to sign the alteration on its behalf;

(b) the alteration bears to have been signed by a person as a witness of the signature of the director, secretary or other person signing on behalf of the company and to state the name and address of the witness; and

(c) nothing in the document or alteration, or in the testing clause or its equivalent, indicates—

(i) that the alteration was not signed on behalf of the company as it bears to have been so signed; or

(ii) that the alteration was not validly witnessed for any reason specified in paragraphs (a) to (e) of sub-paragraph (4) below,

the alteration shall be presumed to have been signed by the company.

(1A) Where an alteration does not bear to have been signed by a person as a witness of the signature of the director, secretary or other person signing on behalf of the company it shall be presumed to have been signed by the company if it bears to have been signed on behalf of the company by—

(a) two directors of the company; or

(b) a director and secretary of the company; or

(c) two persons bearing to have been authorised to sign the alteration on its behalf.

(1B) For the purposes of sub-paragraph (1)(b) above, the name and address of the witness may bear to be stated in the alteration itself or in the testing clause or its equivalent.

(1C) A presumption under sub-paragraph (1) or (1A) above as to signing of an alteration to a document does not include a presumption—

(a) that a person bearing to sign the alteration as a director or the secretary of the company was such director or secretary; or

(b) that a person signing the alteration on behalf of the company bearing to have been authorised to do so was authorised to do so.';

(b) in sub-paragraph (4) after paragraph (g) there shall be inserted the following paragraph—

'(h) if the alteration does not bear to have been witnessed, but bears to have been signed on behalf of the company by two of the directors of the company, or by a director and secretary of the company, or by two authorised persons, that a signature bearing to be the signature of a director, secretary or authorised person is not such a signature, whether by reason of forgery or otherwise;'.

[Limited liability partnerships

3A. (1) Except where an enactment expressly provides otherwise, where a granter of a document is a limited liability partnership, the document is signed by the limited liability partnership if it is signed on its behalf by a member of the limited liability partnership.

(2) This Act is without prejudice to paragraph 9 of Schedule 1, paragraph 9 of Schedule 2, and paragraph 7 of Schedule 4, to the Insolvency Act 1986.

(3) Sub-paragraphs (1) and (2) of this paragraph apply in relation to the signing of an alteration made to a document as they apply in relation to the signing of a document.

(4) Where a granter of a document is a limited liability partnership, section 3 of and Schedule 1 to this Act shall have effect subject to the modifications set out in sub-paragraphs (5) and (6) below.

(5) In section 3—

(a) for subsection (1) there shall be substituted the following subsections—

'(1) Subject to subsections (1A) to (7) below, where—

(a) a document bears to have been subscribed on behalf of a limited liability partnership by a member of the limited liability partnership;

(b) the document bears to have been signed by a person as a witness of the subscription of the member of the limited (c)#nothing in the document, or in the testing clause or its equivalent, indicates—

(i) that it was not subscribed on behalf of the limited liability partnership as it bears to have been so subscribed; or

(ii) that it was not validly witnessed for any reason specified in paragraphs (a) to (e) of subsection (4) below,

the document shall be presumed to have been subscribed by the limited liability partnership.

(1A) Where a document does not bear to have been signed by a person as a witness of the subscription of the member of the limited liability partnership it shall be presumed to have been subscribed by the limited liability partnership if it bears to have been subscribed on behalf of the limited liability partnership by two members of the limited liability partnership.

(1B) A presumption under subsection (1) or (1A) above as to subscription of a document does not include a presumption that a person bearing to subscribe the document as a member of the limited liability partnership was such member.'

(b) in subsection (4) after paragraph (g) there shall be inserted the following paragraph—

'(h) if the document does not bear to have been witnessed, but bears to have been subscribed on behalf of the limited liability partnership by two of the members of the limited liability partnership, that a signature bearing to be the signature of a member is not such a signature, whether by reason of forgery or otherwise;'

(6) In paragraph 1 of Schedule 1—

(a) for sub-paragraph (1) there shall be substituted the following sub-paragraphs—

'(1) Subject to sub-paragraphs (1A) to (7) below, where—

(a) an alteration to a document bears to have been signed on behalf of a limited liability partnership by a member of the limited liability partnership;

(b) the alteration bears to have been signed by a person as a witness of the signature of the member of the limited liability partnership and to state the name and address of the witness; and

(c)   nothing in the document or alteration, or in the testing clause or its equivalent, indicates—

(i)   that the alteration was not signed on behalf of the limited liability partnership as it bears to have been so signed; or

(ii)   that the alteration was not validly witnessed for any reason specified in paragraphs (a) to (e) of sub-paragraph (4) below,

the alteration shall be presumed to have been signed by the limited liability partnership.

(1A)   Where an alteration does not bear to have been signed by a person as a witness of the signature of the member of the limited liability partnership it shall be presumed to have been signed by the limited liability partnership if it bears to have been signed on behalf of the limited liability partnership by two members of the limited liability partnership.

(1B)   For the purposes of sub-paragraph (1)(b) above, the name and address of the witness may bear to be stated in the alteration itself or in the testing clause or its equivalent.

(1C)   A presumption under sub-paragraph (1) or (1A) above as to signing of an alteration to a document does not include a presumption that a person bearing to sign the alteration as a member of the limited liability partnership was such member';

(b)   in sub-paragraph (4) after paragraph (g) there shall be inserted the following—

'; or

(h)   if the alteration does not bear to have been witnessed, but bears to have been signed on behalf of the limited liability partnership by two of the members of the limited liability partnership, that a signature bearing to be the signature of a member is not such a signature, whether by reason of forgery or otherwise;']

Local authorities

4.—(1)   Except where an enactment expressly provides otherwise, where a granter of a document is a local authority, the document is signed by the authority if it is signed on their behalf by the proper officer of the authority.

(2)   For the purposes of the signing of a document under this paragraph, a person purporting to sign on behalf of a local authority as an officer of the authority shall be presumed to be the proper officer of the authority.

(3)   Sub-paragraphs (1) and (2) of this paragraph apply in relation to the signing of an alteration made to a document as they apply in relation to the signing of a document.

(4)   Where a granter of a document is a local authority, section 3 of and Schedule 1 to this Act shall have effect subject to the modifications set out in sub-paragraphs (5) to (8) below.

(5)   For section 3(1) there shall be substituted the following subsections—

'(1)   Subject to subsections (1A) to (7) below, where—

(a)   a document bears to have been subscribed on behalf of a local authority by the proper officer of the authority;

(b)   the document bears—

(i)   to have been signed by a person as a witness of the proper officer's subscription and to state the name and address of the witness; or

(ii)   (if the subscription is not so witnessed), to have been sealed with the common seal of the authority; and

(c) nothing in the document, or in the testing clause or its equivalent, indicates—

(i) that it was not subscribed on behalf of the authority as it bears to have been so subscribed; or

(ii) that it was not validly witnessed for any reason specified in paragraphs (a) to (e) of subsection (4) below or that it was not sealed as it bears to have been sealed or that it was not validly sealed for the reason specified in subsection (4)(h) below,

the document shall be presumed to have been subscribed by the proper officer and by the authority.

(1A) For the purposes of subsection (1)(b)(i) above, the name and address of the witness may bear to be stated in the document itself or in the testing clause or its equivalent.'.

(6) In section 3(4) after paragraph (g) there shall be inserted the following paragraph—

'(h) if the document does not bear to have been witnessed, but bears to have been sealed with the common seal of the authority, that it was sealed by a person without authority to do so or was not sealed on the date on which it was subscribed on behalf of the authority;'.

(7) For paragraph 1(1) of Schedule 1 there shall be substituted the following sub-paragraphs—

'(1) Subject to sub-paragraphs (1A) to (7) below, where—

(a) an alteration to a document bears to have been signed on behalf of a local authority by the proper officer of the authority;

(b) the alteration bears—

(i) to have been signed by a person as a witness of the proper officer's signature and to state the name and address of the witness; or

(ii) (if the signature is not so witnessed), to have been sealed with the common seal of the authority; and

(c) nothing in the document or alteration, or in the testing clause or its equivalent, indicates—

(i) that the alteration was not signed on behalf of the authority as it bears to have been so signed; or

(ii) that the alteration was not validly witnessed for any reason specified in paragraphs (a) to (e) of sub-paragraph (4) below or that it was not sealed as it bears to have been sealed or that it was not validly sealed for the reason specified in sub-paragraph (4)(h) below,

the alteration shall be presumed to have been signed by the proper officer and by the authority.

(1A) For the purposes of sub-paragraph (1)(b)(i) above, the name and address of the witness may bear to be stated in the alteration itself or in the testing clause or its equivalent.'.

(8) In paragraph 1(4) of Schedule 1 after paragraph (g) there shall be inserted the following paragraph—

'(h) if the alteration does not bear to have been witnessed, but bears to have been sealed with the common seal of the authority, that it was sealed by a person without authority to do so or was not sealed on the date on which it was signed on behalf of the authority;'.

Other bodies corporate

5.—(1) This paragraph applies to any body corporate other than a company or a local authority.

(2) Except where an enactment expressly provides otherwise, where a granter

of a document is a body corporate to which this paragraph applies, the document is signed by the body if it is signed on its behalf by—

(a)   a member of the body's governing board or, if there is no governing board, a member of the body;

(b)   the secretary of the body by whatever name he is called; or

(c)   a person authorised to sign the document on behalf of the body.

(3)   Sub-paragraphs (1) and (2) of this paragraph apply in relation to the signing of an alteration made to a document as they apply in relation to the signing of a document.

(4)   Where a granter of a document is a body corporate to which this paragraph applies, section 3 of and Schedule 1 to this Act shall have effect subject to the modifications set out in sub-paragraphs (5) to (8) below.

(5)   For section 3(1) there shall be substituted the following subsections—

'(1)   Subject to subsections (1A) to (7) below, where—

(a)   a document bears to have been subscribed on behalf of a body corporate to which paragraph 5 of Schedule 2 to this Act applies by—

(i)   a member of the body's governing board or, if there is no governing board, a member of the body;

(ii)   the secretary of the body; or

(iii)   a person bearing to have been authorised to subscribe the document on its behalf;

(b)   the document bears—

(i)   to have been signed by a person as a witness of the subscription of the member, secretary or other person signing on behalf of the body and to state the name and address of the witness; or

(ii)   (if the subscription is not so witnessed), to have been sealed with the common seal of the body; and

(c)   nothing in the document, or in the testing clause or its equivalent, indicates—

(i)   that it was not subscribed on behalf of the body as it bears to have been so subscribed; or

(ii)   that it was not validly witnessed for any reason specified in paragraphs (a) to (e) of subsection (4) below or that it was not sealed as it bears to have been sealed or that it was not validly sealed for the reason specified in subsection (4)(h) below,

the document shall be presumed to have been subscribed by the member, secretary or authorised person (as the case may be) and by the body.

(1A)   For the purposes of subsection (1)(b)(i) above, the name and address of the witness may bear to be stated in the document itself or in the testing clause or its equivalent.

(1B)   A presumption under subsection (1) above as to subscription of a document does not include a presumption—

(a)   that a person bearing to subscribe the document as a member of the body's governing board, a member of the body or the secretary of the body was such member or secretary; or

(b)   that a person subscribing the document on behalf of the body bearing to have been authorised to do so was authorised to do so.'.

(6)   In section 3(4) after paragraph (g) there shall be inserted the following paragraph—

'(h)   if the document does not bear to have been witnessed, but bears to have been sealed with the common seal of the body, that it was sealed by a person without authority to do so or was not sealed on the date on which it was subscribed on behalf of the body;'.

(7)   For paragraph 1(1) of Schedule 1 there shall be substituted the following sub-paragraphs—

'(1)   Subject to sub-paragraphs (1A) to (7) below, where—

(a)   an alteration to a document bears to have been signed on behalf of a body corporate to which paragraph 5 of Schedule 2 to this Act applies by—

    (i)   a member of the body's governing board or, if there is no governing board, a member of the body;

    (ii)   the secretary of the body; or

    (iii)   a person bearing to have been authorised to sign the alteration on its behalf,

(b)   the alteration bears—

    (i)   to have been signed by a person as a witness of the signature of the member, secretary or other person signing on behalf of the body and to state the name and address of the witness; or

    (ii)   (if the signature is not so witnessed), to have been sealed with the common seal of the body; and

(c)   nothing in the document or alteration, or in the testing clause or its equivalent, indicates—

    (i)   that the alteration was not signed on behalf of the body as it bears to have been so signed; or

    (ii)   that the alteration was not validly witnessed for any reason specified in paragraphs (a) to (e) of sub-paragraph (4) below or that it was not sealed as it bears to have been sealed or that it was not validly sealed for the reason specified in sub-paragraph (4)(h) below,

the alteration shall be presumed to have been signed by the member, secretary or authorised person (as the case may be) and by the body.

(1A)   For the purposes of sub-paragraph (1)(b)(i) above, the name and address of the witness may bear to be stated in the alteration itself or in the testing clause or its equivalent.

(1B)   A presumption under sub-paragraph (1) above as to signing of an alteration to a document does not include a presumption—

(a)   that a person bearing to sign the alteration as a member of the body's governing board, a member of the body or the secretary of the body was such member or secretary; or

(b)   that a person signing the alteration on behalf of the body bearing to have been authorised to do so was authorised to do so.'.

(8)   In paragraph 1(4) of Schedule 1 after paragraph (g) there shall be inserted the following paragraph—

'(h)   if the alteration does not bear to have been witnessed, but bears to have been sealed with the common seal of the body, that it was sealed by a person without authority to do so or was not sealed on the date on which it was signed on behalf of the body;'.

Ministers of the Crown and office-holders

6.—(1)   Except where an enactment expressly provides otherwise, where a granter of a document is a Minister or an office-holder, the document is signed by the Minister or office-holder if it is signed—

(a)   by him personally; or

(b)   in a case where by virtue of any enactment or rule of law a document by a Minister may be signed by an officer of his or by any other Minister, by that officer or by that other Minister as the case may be; or

(c)   in a case where by virtue of any enactment or rule of law a document by an office-holder may be signed by an officer of his, by that officer; or

(d)   by any other person authorised to sign the document on his behalf.

(2)   For the purposes of the signing of a document under this paragraph, a person purporting to sign—

(a)   as an officer as mentioned in sub-paragraph (1)(b) or (1)(c) above;

(b)   as another Minister as mentioned in sub-paragraph (1)(b) above;

(c)   as a person authorised as mentioned in sub-paragraph (1)(d) above,

shall be presumed to be the officer, other Minister or authorised person, as the case may be.

(3)   Sub-paragraphs (1) and (2) of this paragraph are without prejudice to section 3 of and Schedule 1 to the Ministers of the Crown Act 1975.

(4)   Sub-paragraphs (1) to (3) of this paragraph apply in relation to the signing of an alteration made to a document as they apply in relation to the signing of a document.

(5)   Where a granter of a document is a Minister or office-holder, section 3 of and Schedule 1 to this Act shall have effect subject to the modifications set out in sub-paragraphs (6) and (7) below.

(6)   For section 3(1) there shall be substituted the following subsections—

'(1)   Subject to subsections (1A) to (7) below, where—

(a)   a document bears to have been subscribed—

(i)   by a Minister or, in a case where by virtue of any enactment or rule of law a document by a Minister may be signed by an officer of his or by any other Minister, by that officer or by that other Minister; or

(ii)   by an office-holder or, in a case where by virtue of any enactment or rule of law a document by an office-holder may be signed by an officer of his, by that officer; or

(iii)   by any other person bearing to have been authorised to subscribe the document on behalf of the Minister or office-holder;

(b)   the document bears to have been signed by a person as a witness of the subscription mentioned in paragraph (a) above and to state the name and address of the witness; and

(c)   nothing in the document, or in the testing clause or its equivalent, indicates—

(i)   that it was not subscribed as it bears to have been subscribed; or

(ii)   that it was not validly witnessed for any reason specified in paragraphs (a) to (e) of subsection (4) below,

the document shall be presumed to have been subscribed by the officer, other Minister or authorised person and by the Minister or office-holder, as the case may be.

(1A)   For the purposes of subsection (1)(b) above, the name and address of the witness may bear to be stated in the document itself or in the testing clause or its equivalent.'.

(7)   For paragraph 1(1) of Schedule 1 there shall be substituted the following sub-paragraphs—

'(1)   Subject to sub-paragraphs (1A) to (7) below, where—

(a)   an alteration to a document bears to have been signed by—

(i)   a Minister or, in a case where by virtue of any enactment or rule of law a document by a Minister may be signed by an officer of his or by any other Minister, by that officer or by that other Minister; or

(ii)   an office-holder or, in a case where by virtue of any enactment or rule of law a document by an office-holder may be signed by an officer of his, by that officer; or

(iii)   any other person bearing to have been authorised to sign the alteration on behalf of the Minister or office-holder;

(b)   the alteration bears to have been signed by a person as a witness of the signature mentioned in paragraph (a) above and to state the name and address of the witness; and

(c)   nothing in the document or alteration, or in the testing clause or its equivalent, indicates—
   (i)   that the alteration was not signed as it bears to have been signed; or
   (ii)   that the alteration was not validly witnessed for any reason specified in paragraphs (a) to (e) of sub-paragraph (4) below,
the alteration shall be presumed to have been signed by the officer, other Minister or authorised person and by the Minister or office-holder, as the case may be.

(1A)   For the purposes of sub-paragraph (1)(b) above, the name and address of the witness may bear to be stated in the alteration itself or in the testing clause or its equivalent.'.

SCHEDULE 3
MODIFICATIONS OF THIS ACT IN RELATION TO SUBSCRIPTION OR SIGNING BY RELEVANT PERSON UNDER SECTION 9

1.   For any reference to the subscription or signing of a document by a granter there shall be substituted a reference to such subscription or signing by a relevant person under section 9(1).

2.   For section 3(1) there shall be substituted the following subsection—
   '(1)   Subject to subsections (2) to (6) below, where—
   (a)   a document bears to have been subscribed by a relevant person with the authority of a granter of it;
   (b)   the document, or the testing clause or its equivalent, states that the document was read to that granter by the relevant person before such subscription or states that it was not so read because the granter made a declaration that he did not wish him to do so;
   (c)   the document bears to have been signed by a person as a witness of the relevant person's subscription and the document, or the testing clause or its equivalent, bears to state the name and address of the witness; and
   (d)   nothing in the document, or in the testing clause or its equivalent, indicates—
      (i)   that it was not subscribed by the relevant person as it bears to have been so subscribed;
      (ii)   that the statement mentioned in paragraph (b) above is incorrect; or
      (iii)   that it was not validly witnessed for any reason specified in paragraphs (a) to (e) of subsection (4) below (as modified by paragraph 4 of Schedule 3 to this Act),
the document shall be presumed to have been subscribed by the relevant person and the statement so mentioned shall be presumed to be correct.'.

3.   In section 3(3) for the words 'subsection (1)(b)' there shall be substituted the words 'subsection (1)(c)'.

4.   For section 3(4) there shall be substituted the following subsection—
   '(4)   Where, in any proceedings relating to a document in which a question arises as to a relevant person's subscription on behalf of a granter under section 9(1) of this Act, it is established—
   (a)   that a signature bearing to be the signature of the witness of the relevant person's subscription is not such a signature, whether by reason of forgery or otherwise;
   (b)   that the person who signed the document as the witness of the

relevant person's subscription is a person who is named in the document as a granter of it;

(c) that the person who signed the document as the witness of the relevant person's subscription, at the time of signing—

(i) did not know the granter on whose behalf the relevant person had so subscribed;

(ii) was under the age of 16 years; or

(iii) was mentally incapable of acting as a witness;

(d) that the person who signed the document, purporting to be the witness of the relevant person's subscription, did not see him subscribe it;

(dd) that the person who signed the document as the witness of the relevant person's subscription did not witness the granting of authority by the granter concerned to the relevant person to subscribe the document on his behalf or did not witness the reading of the document to the granter by the relevant person or the declaration that the granter did not wish him to do so;

(e) that the person who signed the document as the witness of the relevant person's subscription did not sign the document after him or that such subscription and signature were not one continuous process;

(f) that the name or address of such a witness was added after the document was founded on or registered as mentioned in subsection (3)(a) above or is erroneous in any material respect; or

(g) in the case of a testamentary document consisting of more than one sheet, that a signature on any sheet bearing to be the signature of the relevant person is not such a signature, whether by reason of forgery or otherwise,

then, for the purposes of those proceedings, there shall be no presumption that the document has been subscribed by the relevant person on behalf of the granter concerned.'.

5. In section 3(6) the words 'or acknowledgement' in both places where they occur shall be omitted.

6. Section 3(7) shall be omitted.

7. For section 4(1) there shall be substituted the following subsection—

'(1) Where—

(a) a document bears to have been subscribed by a relevant person under section 9(1) of this Act on behalf of a granter of it; but

(b) there is no presumption under section 3 of this Act (as modified by paragraph 2 of Schedule 3 to this Act) that the document has been subscribed by that person or that the procedure referred to section 3(1)(b) of this Act as so modified was followed,

then, if the court, on an application being made to it by any person who has an interest in the document, is satisfied that the document was so subscribed by the relevant person with the authority of the granter and that the relevant person read the document to the granter before subscription or did not so read it because the granter declared that he did not wish him to do so, it shall—

(i) cause the document to be endorsed with a certificate to that effect; or

(ii) where the document has already been registered in the Books of Council and Session or in sheriff court books, grant decree to that effect.'.

8. At the end of section 4(5)(a) there shall be added the following words—
'and that the procedure referred to in section 3(1)(b) of this Act as modified by paragraph 2 of Schedule 3 to this Act was followed.'.

9. For paragraph 1(1) of Schedule 1 there shall be substituted the following sub-paragraph—

'(1) Subject to sub-paragraphs (2) to (6) below, where—

(a) an alteration to a document bears to have been signed by a relevant person with the authority of a granter of the document;

(b) the document or alteration, or the testing clause or its equivalent, states that the alteration was read to that granter by the relevant person before such signature or states that the alteration was not so read because the granter made a declaration that he did not wish him to do so;

(c) the alteration bears to have been signed by a person as a witness of the relevant person's signature and the alteration, or the testing clause or its equivalent, bears to state the name and address of the witness; and

(d) nothing in the document or alteration, or in the testing clause or its equivalent, indicates—

(i) that the alteration was not signed by the relevant person as it bears to have been so signed;

(ii) that the statement mentioned in paragraph (b) above is incorrect; or

(iii) that the alteration was not validly witnessed for any reason specified in paragraphs (a) to (e) of sub-paragraph (4) below (as modified by paragraph 11 of Schedule 3 to this Act),

the alteration shall be presumed to have been signed by the relevant person and the statement so mentioned shall be presumed to be correct.'.

10. In paragraph 1(3) of Schedule 1 for the words 'sub-paragraph (1)(b)' there shall be substituted the words 'sub-paragraph (1)(c)'.

11. For paragraph 1(4) of Schedule 1 there shall be substituted the following sub-paragraph—

'(4) Where, in any proceedings relating to an alteration to a document in which a question arises as to a relevant person's signature on behalf of a granter under section 9(1) of this Act, it is established—

(a) that a signature bearing to be the signature of the witness of the relevant person's signature is not such a signature, whether by reason of forgery or otherwise;

(b) that the person who signed the alteration as the witness of the relevant person's signature is a person who is named in the document as a granter of it;

(c) that the person who signed the alteration as the witness of the relevant person's signature, at the time of signing—

(i) did not know the granter on whose behalf the relevant person had so signed;

(ii) was under the age of 16 years; or

(iii) was mentally incapable of acting as a witness;

(d) that the person who signed the alteration, purporting to be the witness of the relevant person's signature, did not see him sign it;

(dd) that the person who signed the alteration as the witness of the relevant person's signature did not witness the granting of authority by the granter concerned to the relevant person to sign the alteration on his behalf or did not witness the reading of the alteration to the granter by the relevant person or the declaration that the granter did not wish him to do so;

(e) that the person who signed the alteration as the witness of the relevant person's signature did not sign the alteration after him or that the signing of the alteration by the granter and the witness was not one continuous process;

(f) that the name or address of such a witness was added after the alteration was founded on or registered as mentioned in sub-paragraph (3)(a) above or is erroneous in any material respect; or

(g)   in the case of an alteration to a testamentary document consisting of more than one sheet, that a signature on any sheet of the alteration bearing to be the signature of the relevant person is not such a signature, whether by reason of forgery or otherwise,

then, for the purposes of those proceedings, there shall be no presumption that the alteration has been signed by the relevant person on behalf of the granter concerned.'.

12.   In paragraph 1(6) of Schedule 1 the words 'or the acknowledgement of his signature' and the words 'or acknowledgement' shall be omitted.

13.   Paragraph 1(7) of Schedule 1 shall be omitted.

14.   For paragraph 2(1) of Schedule 1 there shall be substituted the following sub-paragraph—

'(1)   Where—

(a)   an alteration to a document bears to have been signed by a relevant person under section 9(1) of this Act on behalf of a granter of the document; but

(b)   there is no presumption under paragraph 1 of Schedule 1 to this Act (as modified by paragraph 9 of Schedule 3 to this Act) that the alteration has been signed by that person or that the procedure referred to in paragraph 1(1)(b) of Schedule 1 to this Act as so modified was followed,

then, if the court, on an application being made to it by any person who has an interest in the document, is satisfied that the alteration was so signed by the relevant person with the authority of the granter and that the relevant person read the alteration to the granter before signing or did not so read it because the granter declared that he did not wish him to do so, it shall—

(i)   cause the document to be endorsed with a certificate to that effect; or

(ii)   where the document has already been registered in the Books of Council and Session or in sheriff court books, grant decree to that effect.'.

15.   At the end of paragraph 2(5)(a) of Schedule 1 there shall be added the following words—

'and that the procedure referred to in paragraph 1(1)(b) of Schedule 1 to this Act as modified by paragraph 9 of Schedule 3 to this Act was followed.'.

CHILDREN (SCOTLAND) ACT 1995
(1995, c 36)

PART I
PARENTS, CHILDREN AND GUARDIANS

Parental responsibilities and parental rights

1   Parental responsibilities

(1)   Subject to section 3(1)(b) and (3) of this Act, a parent has in relation to his child the responsibility—

(a)   to safeguard and promote the child's health, development and welfare;

(b)   to provide, in a manner appropriate to the stage of development of the child—

(i)   direction;

(ii)   guidance,

to the child;

(c) if the child is not living with the parent, to maintain personal relations and direct contact with the child on a regular basis; and

(d) to act as the child's legal representative,

but only in so far as compliance with this section is practicable and in the interests of the child.

(2) 'Child' means for the purposes of—

(a) paragraphs (a), (b)(i), (c) and (d) of subsection (1) above, a person under the age of sixteen years;

(b) paragraph (b)(ii) of that subsection, a person under the age of eighteen years.

(3) The responsibilities mentioned in paragraphs (a) to (d) of subsection (1) above are in this Act referred to as 'parental responsibilities'; and the child, or any person acting on his behalf, shall have title to sue, or to defend, in any proceedings as respects those responsibilities.

(4) The parental responsibilities supersede any analogous duties imposed on a parent at common law; but this section is without prejudice to any other duty so imposed on him or to any duty imposed on him by, under or by virtue of any other provision of this Act or of any other enactment.

6 Views of children

(1) A person shall, in reaching any major decision which involves—

(a) his fulfilling a parental responsibility or the responsibility mentioned in section 5(1) of this Act; or

(b) his exercising a parental right or giving consent by virtue of that section, have regard so far as practicable to the views (if he wishes to express them) of the child concerned, taking account of the child's age and maturity, and to those of any other person who has parental responsibilities or parental rights in relation to the child (and wishes to express those views); and without prejudice to the generality of this subsection a child twelve years of age or more shall be presumed to be of sufficient age and maturity to form a view.

(2) A transaction entered into in good faith by a third party and a person acting as legal representative of a child shall not be challengeable on the ground only that the child, or a person with parental responsibilities or parental rights in relation to the child, was not consulted or that due regard was not given to his views before the transaction was entered into.

Guardianship

· · ·

10 Obligations and rights of person administering child's property

(1) A person acting as a child's legal representative in relation to the administration of the child's property—

(a) shall be required to act as a reasonable and prudent person would act on his own behalf; and

(b) subject to any order made under section 11 of this Act, shall be entitled to do anything which the child, if of full age and capacity, could do in relation to that property;

and subject to subsection (2) below, on ceasing to act as legal representative, shall be liable to account to the child for his intromissions with the child's property.

(2) No liability shall be incurred by virtue of subsection (1) above in respect of funds which have been used in the proper discharge of the person's responsibility to safeguard and promote the child's health, development and welfare.

PRIVATE INTERNATIONAL LAW (MISCELLANEOUS PROVISIONS) ACT 1995
(1995, c 42)

7   Validity and effect in Scots law of potentially polygamous marriages

(1)   A person domiciled in Scotland does not lack capacity to enter into a marriage by reason only that the marriage is entered into under a law which permits polygamy.

(2)   For the avoidance of doubt, a marriage valid by the law of Scotland and entered into—

(a)   under a law which permits polygamy; and

(b)   at a time when neither party to the marriage is already married,

has, so long as neither party marries a second spouse during the subsistence of the marriage, the same effects for all purposes of the law of Scotland as a marriage entered into under a law which does not permit polygamy.

8   Part II: supplemental

(1)   Nothing in this Part affects any law or custom relating to the marriage of members of the Royal Family.

(2)   The enactments specified in the Schedule to this Act (which contains consequential amendments and amendments removing unnecessary references to potentially polygamous marriages) are amended in accordance with that Schedule.

(3)   Nothing in that Schedule affects either the generality of any enactment empowering the making of subordinate legislation or any such legislation made before the commencement of this Part.

PART III
CHOICE OF LAW IN TORT AND DELICT

9   Purpose of Part III

(1)   The rules in this Part apply for choosing the law (in this Part referred to as 'the applicable law') to be used for determining issues relating to tort or (for the purposes of the law of Scotland) delict.

(2)   The characterisation for the purposes of private international law of issues arising in a claim as issues relating to tort or delict is a matter for the courts of the forum.

(3)   The rules in this Part do not apply in relation to issues arising in any claim excluded from the operation of this Part by section 13 below.

(4)   The applicable law shall be used for determining the issues arising in a claim, including in particular the question whether an actionable tort or delict has occurred.

(5)   The applicable law to be used for determining the issues arising in a claim shall exclude any choice of law rules forming part of the law of the country or countries concerned.

(6)   For the avoidance of doubt (and without prejudice to the operation of section 14 below) this Part applies in relation to events occurring in the forum as it applies in relation to events occurring in any other country.

(7)   In this Part as it extends to any country within the United Kingdom, 'the forum' means England and Wales, Scotland or Northern Ireland, as the case may be.

(8)   In this Part 'delict' includes quasi-delict.

10   Abolition of certain common law rules

The rules of the common law, in so far as they—

(a)   require actionability under both the law of the forum and the law of another country for the purpose of determining whether a tort or delict is actionable; or

(b)   allow (as an exception from the rules falling within paragraph (a) above)

for the law of a single country to be applied for the purpose of determining the issues, or any of the issues, arising in the case in question,
are hereby abolished so far as they apply to any claim in tort or delict which is not excluded from the operation of this Part by section 13 below.

11   Choice of applicable law: the general rule
(1)   The general rule is that the applicable law is the law of the country in which the events constituting the tort or delict in question occur.
(2)   Where elements of those events occur in different countries, the applicable law under the general rule is to be taken as being—
    (a)   for a cause of action in respect of personal injury caused to an individual or death resulting from personal injury, the law of the country where the individual was when he sustained the injury;
    (b)   for a cause of action in respect of damage to property, the law of the country where the property was when it was damaged; and
    (c)   in any other case, the law of the country in which the most significant element or elements of those events occurred.
(3)   In this section 'personal injury' includes disease or any impairment of physical or mental condition.

12   Choice of applicable law: displacement of general rule
(1)   If it appears, in all the circumstances, from a comparison of—
    (a)   the significance of the factors which connect a tort or delict with the country whose law would be the applicable law under the general rule; and
    (b)   the significance of any factors connecting the tort or delict with another country,
that it is substantially more appropriate for the applicable law for determining the issues arising in the case, or any of those issues, to be the law of the other country, the general rule is displaced and the applicable law for determining those issues or that issue (as the case may be) is the law of that other country.
(2)   The factors that may be taken into account as connecting a tort or delict with a country for the purposes of this section include, in particular, factors relating to the parties, to any of the events which constitute the tort or delict in question or to any of the circumstances or consequences of those events.

13   Exclusion of defamation claims from Part III
(1)   Nothing in this Part applies to affect the determination of issues arising in any defamation claim.
(2)   For the purposes of this section 'defamation claim' means—
    (a)   any claim under the law of any part of the United Kingdom for libel or slander or for slander of title, slander of goods or other malicious falsehood and any claim under the law of Scotland for verbal injury; and
    (b)   any claim under the law of any other country corresponding to or otherwise in the nature of a claim mentioned in paragraph (a) above.

14   Transitional provision and savings
(1)   Nothing in this Part applies to acts or omissions giving rise to a claim which occur before the commencement of this Part.
(2)   Nothing in this Part affects any rules of law (including rules of private international law) except those abolished by section 10 above.
(3)   Without prejudice to the generality of subsection (2) above, nothing in this Part—
    (a)   authorises the application of the law of a country outside the forum as the applicable law for determining issues arising in any claim in so far as to do so—
        (i)   would conflict with principles of public policy; or
        (ii)   would give effect to such a penal, revenue or other public law as would not otherwise be enforceable under the law of the forum; or

(b)   affects any rules of evidence, pleading or practice or authorises questions of procedure in any proceedings to be determined otherwise than in accordance with the law of the forum.

(4)   This Part has effect without prejudice to the operation of any rule of law which either has effect notwithstanding the rules of private international law applicable in the particular circumstances or modifies the rules of private international law that would otherwise be so applicable.

15   Crown application

(1)   This Part applies in relation to claims by or against the Crown as it applies in relation to claims to which the Crown is not a party.

(2)   In subsection (1) above a reference to the Crown does not include a reference to Her Majesty in Her private capacity or to Her Majesty in right of Her Duchy of Lancaster or to the Duke of Cornwall.

(3)   Without prejudice to the generality of section 14(2) above, nothing in this section affects any rule of law as to whether proceedings of any description may be brought against the Crown.

DEFAMATION ACT 1996
(1996, c 31)

1   Responsibility for publication

(1)   In defamation proceedings a person has a defence if he shows that—

(a)   he was not the author, editor or publisher of the statement complained of,

(b)   he took reasonable care in relation to its publication, and

(c)   he did not know, and had no reason to believe, that what he did caused or contributed to the publication of a defamatory statement.

(2)   For this purpose 'author', 'editor' and 'publisher' have the following meanings, which are further explained in subsection (3)—

'author' means the originator of the statement, but does not include a person who did not intend that his statement be published at all;

'editor' means a person having editorial or equivalent responsibility for the content of the statement or the decision to publish it; and

'publisher' means a commercial publisher, that is, a person whose business is issuing material to the public, or a section of the public, who issues material containing the statement in the course of that business.

(3)   A person shall not be considered the author, editor or publisher of a statement if he is only involved—

(a)   in printing, producing, distributing or selling printed material containing the statement;

(b)   in processing, making copies of, distributing, exhibiting or selling a film or sound recording (as defined in Part I of the Copyright, Designs and Patents Act 1988) containing the statement;

(c)   in processing, making copies of, distributing or selling any electronic medium in or on which the statement is recorded, or in operating or providing any equipment, system or service by means of which the statement is retrieved, copied, distributed or made available in electronic form;

(d)   as the broadcaster of a live programme containing the statement in circumstances in which he has no effective control over the maker of the statement;

(e)   as the operator of or provider of access to a communications system by means of which the statement is transmitted, or made available, by a person over whom he has no effective control.

In a case not within paragraphs (a) to (e) the court may have regard to those provisions by way of analogy in deciding whether a person is to be considered the author, editor or publisher of a statement.

(4)   Employees or agents of an author, editor or publisher are in the same position as their employer or principal to the extent that they are responsible for the
content of the statement or the decision to publish it.

(5)   In determining for the purposes of this section whether a person took
reasonable care, or had reason to believe that what he did caused or contributed to
the publication of a defamatory statement, regard shall be had to—

(a)   the extent of his responsibility for the content of the statement or the
decision to publish it,

(b)   the nature or circumstances of the publication, and

(c)   the previous conduct or character of the author, editor or publisher.

(6)   This section does not apply to any cause of action which arose before the
section came into force.

2   Offer to make amends

(1)   A person who has published a statement alleged to be defamatory of
another may offer to make amends under this section.

(2)   The offer may be in relation to the statement generally or in relation to a
specific defamatory meaning which the person making the offer accepts that the
statement conveys ('a qualified offer').

(3)   An offer to make amends—

(a)   must be in writing

(b)   must be expressed to be an offer to make amends under section 2 of the
Defamation Act 1996, and

(c)   must state whether it is a qualified offer and, if so, set out the defamatory meaning in relation to which it is made.

(4)   An offer to make amends under this section is an offer—

(a)   to make a suitable correction of the statement complained of and a sufficient apology to the aggrieved party;

(b)   to publish the correction and apology in a manner that is reasonable and
practicable in the circumstances, and

(c)   to pay to the aggrieved party such compensation (if any), and such costs,
as may be agreed or determined to be payable.

The fact that the offer is accompanied by an offer to take specific steps does not
affect the fact that an offer to make amends under this section is an offer to do all
the things mentioned in paragraphs (a) to (c).

(5)   An offer to make amends under this section may not be made by a person
after serving a defence in defamation proceedings brought against him by the
aggrieved party in respect of the publication in question.

(6)   An offer to make amends under this section may be withdrawn before it is
accepted; and a renewal of an offer which has been withdrawn shall be treated as
a new offer.

3   Accepting an offer to make amends

(1)   If an offer to make amends under section 2 is accepted by the aggrieved
party, the following provisions apply.

(2)   The party accepting the offer may not bring or continue defamation proceedings in respect of the publication concerned against the person making the offer,
but he is entitled to enforce the offer to make amends, as follows.

(3)   If the parties agree on the steps to be taken in fulfilment of the offer, the
aggrieved party may apply to the court for an order that the other party fulfil his
offer by taking the steps agreed.

(4)   If the parties do not agree on the steps to be taken by way of correction,
apology and publication, the party who made the offer may take such steps as he
thinks appropriate, and may in particular—

(a)   make the correction and apology by a statement in open court in terms
approved by the court, and

(b)   give an undertaking to the court as to the manner of their publication.

(5)   If the parties do not agree on the amount to be paid by way of compensation, it shall be determined by the court on the same principles as damages in defamation proceedings.

The court shall take account of any steps taken in fulfilment of the offer and (so far as not agreed between the parties) of the suitability of the correction, the sufficiency of the apology and whether the manner of their publication was reasonable in the circumstances, and may reduce or increase the amount of compensation accordingly.

(6)   If the parties do not agree on the amount to be paid by way of costs, it shall be determined by the court on the same principles as costs awarded in court proceedings.

(7)   The acceptance of an offer by one person to make amends does not affect any cause of action against another person in respect of the same publication, subject as follows.

(8)   [*applies to England and Wales only*]

(9)   In Scotland—

    (a)   subsection (2) of section 3 of the Law Reform (Miscellaneous Provisions) (Scotland) Act 1940 (right of one joint wrongdoer as respects another to recover contribution towards damages) applies in relation to compensation paid under an offer to make amends as it applies in relation to damages in an action to which that section applies; and

    (b)   where another person is liable in respect of the same damage (whether jointly or otherwise), the person whose offer to make amends was accepted is not required to pay by virtue of any contribution under section 3(2) of that Act a greater amount than the amount of compensation payable in pursuance of the offer.

(10)   Proceedings under this section shall be heard and determined without a jury.

4   Failure to accept offer to make amends

(1)   If an offer to make amends under section 2, duly made and not withdrawn, is not accepted by the aggrieved party, the following provisions apply.

(2)   The fact that the offer was made is a defence (subject to subsection (3)) to defamation proceedings in respect of the publication in question by that party against the person making the offer.

A qualified offer is only a defence in respect of the meaning to which the offer related.

(3)   There is no such defence if the person by whom the offer was made knew or had reason to believe that the statement complained of—

    (a)   referred to the aggrieved party or was likely to be understood as referring to him, and

    (b)   was both false and defamatory of that party;

but it shall be presumed until the contrary is shown that he did not know and had no reason to believe that was the case.

(4)   The person who made the offer need not rely on it by way of defence, but if he does he may not rely on any other defence.

If the offer was a qualified offer, this applies only in respect of the meaning to which the offer related.

(5)   The offer may be relied on in mitigation of damages whether or not it was relied on as a defence.

. . .

The meaning of a statement

7   Ruling on the meaning of a statement

In defamation proceedings the court shall not be asked to rule whether a statement is arguably capable, as opposed to capable, of bearing a particular meaning or meanings attributed to it.

. . .

Evidence of convictions

12   Evidence of convictions
(1)   [*applies to England and Wales only*]
(2)   In section 12 of the Law Reform (Miscellaneous Provisions) (Scotland) Act 1968 (conclusiveness of convictions for purposes of defamation actions), in subsections (1) and (2) for 'a person' substitute 'the pursuer' and for 'that person' substitute 'he'; and after subsection (2) insert—

'(2A) In the case of an action for defamation in which there is more than one pursuer—
(a)   the references in subsections (1) and (2) above to the pursuer shall be construed as references to any of the pursuers, and
(b)   proof that any of the pursuers stands convicted of an offence shall be conclusive evidence that he committed that offence so far as that fact is relevant to any issue arising in relation to his cause of action or that of any other pursuer.'.

The amendments made by this subsection apply only for the purposes of an action begun after this section comes into force, whenever the cause of action arose.
(3)   [*applies to Northern Ireland only*]

Evidence concerning proceedings in Parliament

13   Evidence concerning proceedings in Parliament
(1)   Where the conduct of a person in or in relation to proceedings in Parliament is in issue in defamation proceedings, he may waive for the purposes of those proceedings, so far as concerns him, the protection of any enactment or rule of law which prevents proceedings in Parliament being impeached or questioned in any court or place out of Parliament.
(2)   Where a person waives that protection—
(a)   any such enactment or rule of law shall not apply to prevent evidence being given, questions being asked or statements, submissions, comments or findings being made about his conduct, and
(b)   none of those things shall be regarded as infringing the privilege of either House of Parliament.
(3)   The waiver by one person of that protection does not affect its operation in relation to another person who has not waived it.
(4)   Nothing in this section affects any enactment or rule of law so far as it protects a person (including a person who has waived the protection referred to above) from legal liability for words spoken or things done in the course of, or for the purposes of or incidental to, any proceedings in Parliament.
(5)   Without prejudice to the generality of subsection (4), that subsection applies to—
(a)   the giving of evidence before either House or a committee;
(b)   the presentation or submission of a document to either House or a committee;
(c)   the preparation of a document for the purposes of or incidental to the transacting of any such business;
(d)   the formulation, making or publication of a document, including a report, by or pursuant to an order of either House or a committee; and
(e)   any communication with the Parliamentary Commissioner for Standards

or any person having functions in connection with the registration of members' interests.

In this subsection 'a committee' means a committee of either House or a joint committee of both Houses of Parliament.

Statutory privilege

14 Reports of court proceedings absolutely privileged

(1)   A fair and accurate report of proceedings in public before a court to which this section applies, if published contemporaneously with the proceedings, is absolutely privileged.

(2)   A report of proceedings which by an order of the court, or as a consequence of any statutory provision, is required to be postponed shall be treated as published contemporaneously if it is published as soon as practicable after publication is permitted.

(3)   This section applies to—

(a)   any court in the United Kingdom,

(b)   the European Court of Justice or any court attached to that court,

(c)   the European Court of Human Rights, and

(d)   any international criminal tribunal established by the Security Council of the United Nations or by an international agreement to which the United Kingdom is a party.

In paragraph (a) 'court' includes any tribunal or body exercising the judicial power of the State.

(4)   In section 8(6) of the Rehabilitation of Offenders Act 1974 and in Article 9(6) of the Rehabilitation of Offenders (Northern Ireland) Order 1978 (defamation actions: reports of court proceedings), for 'section 3 of the Law of Libel Amendment Act 1888' substitute 'section 14 of the Defamation Act 1996'.

15 Reports, etc protected by qualified privilege

(1)   The publication of any report or other statement mentioned in Schedule 1 to this Act is privileged unless the publication is shown to be made with malice, subject as follows.

(2)   In defamation proceedings in respect of the publication of a report or other statement mentioned in Part II of that Schedule, there is no defence under this section if the plaintiff shows that the defendant—

(a)   was requested by him to publish in a suitable manner a reasonable letter or statement by way of explanation or contradiction, and

(b)   refused or neglected to do so.

For this purpose 'in a suitable manner' means in the same manner as the publication complained of or in a manner that is adequate and reasonable in the circumstances.

(3)   This section does not apply to the publication to the public, or a section of the public, of matter which is not of public concern and the publication of which is not for the public benefit.

(4)   Nothing in this section shall be construed—

(a)   as protecting the publication of matter the publication of which is prohibited by law, or

(b)   as limiting or abridging any privilege subsisting apart from this section.

Supplementary provisions

. . .

17 Interpretation

(1)   In this Act—

'publication' and 'publish', in relation to a statement, have the meaning they have for the purposes of the law of defamation generally, but 'publisher' is specially defined for the purposes of section 1;

'statement' means words, pictures, visual images, gestures or any other method of signifying meaning; and

'statutory provision' means—

(a)   a provision contained in an Act or in subordinate legislation within the meaning of the Interpretation Act 1978, or

(b)   a statutory provision within the meaning given by section 1(f) of the Interpretation Act (Northern Ireland) 1954.

(2)   In this Act as it applies to proceedings in Scotland—

'costs' means expenses; and

'plaintiff' and 'defendant' mean pursuer and defender.

General provisions

18   Extent

. . .

(2)   The following provisions of this Act extend to Scotland—

section 1 (responsibility for publication),

sections 2 to 4 (offer to make amends), except section 3(8),

section 12(2) (evidence of convictions),

section 13 (evidence concerning proceedings in Parliament),

sections 14 and 15 and Schedule 1 (statutory privilege),

section 16 and Schedule 2 (repeals) so far as relating to enactments extending to Scotland,

section 17 (interpretation),

this subsection,

section 19 (commencement) so far as relating to provisions which extend to Scotland, and

section 20 (short title and saving).

. . .

20   Short title and saving

(1)   This Act may be cited as the Defamation Act 1996.

(2)   Nothing in this Act affects the law relating to criminal libel.

SCHEDULES

SCHEDULE 1
QUALIFIED PRIVILEGE

PART I
STATEMENTS HAVING QUALIFIED PRIVILEGE WITHOUT EXPLANATION OR CONTRADICTION

1.   A fair and accurate report of proceedings in public of a legislature anywhere in the world.

2.   A fair and accurate report of proceedings in public before a court anywhere in the world.

3.   A fair and accurate report of proceedings in public of a person appointed to hold a public inquiry by a government or legislature anywhere in the world.

4.   A fair and accurate report of proceedings in public anywhere in the world of an international organisation or an international conference.

5.   A fair and accurate copy of or extract from any register or other document required by law to be open to public inspection.

6.   A notice or advertisement published by or on the authority of a court, or of a judge or officer of a court, anywhere in the world.

7.   A fair and accurate copy of or extract from matter published by or on the authority of a government or legislature anywhere in the world.

8.   A fair and accurate copy of or extract from matter published anywhere in the world by an international organisation or an international conference.

PART II
STATEMENTS PRIVILEGED SUBJECT TO EXPLANATION OR CONTRADICTION

9.   (1)   A fair and accurate copy of or extract from a notice or other matter issued for the information of the public by or on behalf of—

(a)   a legislature in any member State or the European Parliament;

(b)   the government of any member State, or any authority performing governmental functions in any member State or part of a member State, or the European Commission;

(c)   an international organisation or international conference.

(2)   In this paragraph 'governmental functions' includes police functions.

10.   A fair and accurate copy of or extract from a document made available by a court in any member State or the European Court of Justice (or any court attached to that court), or by a judge or officer of any such court.

11.   (1)   A fair and accurate report of proceedings at any public meeting or sitting in the United Kingdom of—

(a)   a local authority or local authority committee;

(b)   a justice or justices of the peace acting otherwise than as a court exercising judicial authority;

(c)   a commission, tribunal, committee or person appointed for the purposes of any inquiry by any statutory provision, by Her Majesty or by a Minister of the Crown or a Northern Ireland Department;

(d)   a person appointed by a local authority to hold a local inquiry in pursuance of any statutory provision;

(e)   any other tribunal, board, committee or body constituted by or under, and exercising functions under, any statutory provision.

(2)   In sub-paragraph (1)(a)—

'local authority' means—

(a)   in relation to England and Wales, a principal council within the meaning of the Local Government Act 1972, any body falling within any paragraph of section 100J(1) of that Act or an authority or body to which the Public Bodies (Admission to Meetings) Act 1960 applies,

(b)   in relation to Scotland, a council constituted under section 2 of the Local Government etc (Scotland) Act 1994 or an authority or body to which the Public Bodies (Admission to Meetings) Act 1960 applies,

(c)   in relation to Northern Ireland, any authority or body to which sections 23 to 27 of the Local Government Act (Northern Ireland) 1972 apply; and

'local authority committee' means any committee of a local authority or of local authorities, and includes—

(a)   any committee or sub-committee in relation to which sections 100A to 100D of the Local Government Act 1972 apply by virtue of section 100E of that Act (whether or not also by virtue of section 100J of that Act), and

(b)   any committee or sub-committee in relation to which sections 50A to 50D of the Local Government (Scotland) Act 1973 apply by virtue of section 50E of that Act.

(3)   A fair and accurate report of any corresponding proceedings in any of the Channel Islands or the Isle of Man or in another member State.

12. (1) A fair and accurate report of proceedings at any public meeting held in a member State.

(2) In this paragraph a 'public meeting' means a meeting bona fide and lawfully held for a lawful purpose and for the furtherance or discussion of a matter of public concern, whether admission to the meeting is general or restricted.

13. (1) A fair and accurate report of proceedings at a general meeting of a UK public company.

(2) A fair and accurate copy of or extract from any document circulated to members of a UK public company—

(a) by or with the authority of the board of directors of the company,

(b) by the auditors of the company, or

(c) by any member of the company in pursuance of a right conferred by any statutory provision.

(3) A fair and accurate copy of or extract from any document circulated to members of a UK public company which relates to the appointment, resignation, retirement or dismissal of directors of the company.

(4) In this paragraph 'UK public company' means—

(a) a public company within the meaning of section 1(3) of the Companies Act 1985 or Article 12(3) of the Companies (Northern Ireland) Order 1986, or

(b) a body corporate incorporated by or registered under any other statutory provision, or by Royal Charter, or formed in pursuance of letters patent.

(5) A fair and accurate report of proceedings at any corresponding meeting of, or copy of or extract from any corresponding document circulated to members of, a public company formed under the law of any of the Channel Islands or the Isle of Man or of another member State.

14. A fair and accurate report of any finding or decision of any of the following descriptions of association, formed in the United Kingdom or another member State, or of any committee or governing body of such an association—

(a) an association formed for the purpose of promoting or encouraging the exercise of or interest in any art, science, religion or learning, and empowered by its constitution to exercise control over or adjudicate on matters of interest or concern to the association, or the actions or conduct of any person subject to such control or adjudication;

(b) an association formed for the purpose of promoting or safeguarding the interests of any trade, business, industry or profession, or of the persons carrying on or engaged in any trade, business, industry or profession, and empowered by its constitution to exercise control over or adjudicate upon matters connected with that trade, business, industry or profession, or the actions or conduct of those persons;

(c) an association formed for the purpose of promoting or safeguarding the interests of a game, sport or pastime to the playing or exercise of which members of the public are invited or admitted, and empowered by its constitution to exercise control over or adjudicate upon persons connected with or taking part in the game, sport or pastime;

(d) an association formed for the purpose of promoting charitable objects or other objects beneficial to the community and empowered by its constitution to exercise control over or to adjudicate on matters of interest or concern to the association, or the actions or conduct of any person subject to such control or adjudication.

15. (1) A fair and accurate report of, or copy of or extract from, any adjudication, report, statement or notice issued by a body, officer or other person designated for the purposes of this paragraph—

(a) for England and Wales or Northern Ireland, by order of the Lord Chancellor, and

(b) for Scotland, by order of the Secretary of State.

(2) An order under this paragraph shall be made by statutory instrument

which shall be subject to annulment in pursuance of a resolution of either House of Parliament.

PART III
SUPPLEMENTARY PROVISIONS

16. (1) In this Schedule—

'court' includes any tribunal or body exercising the judicial power of the State;

'international conference' means a conference attended by representatives of two or more governments;

'international organisation' means an organisation of which two or more governments are members, and includes any committee or other subordinate body of such an organisation; and

'legislature' includes a local legislature.

(2) References in this Schedule to a member State include any European dependent territory of a member State.

(3) In paragraphs 2 and 6 'court' includes—

(a) the European Court of Justice (or any court attached to that court) and the Court of Auditors of the European Communities,

(b) the European Court of Human Rights,

(c) any international criminal tribunal established by the Security Council of the United Nations or by an international agreement to which the United Kingdom is a party, and

(d) the International Court of Justice and any other judicial or arbitral tribunal deciding matters in dispute between States.

(4) In paragraphs 1, 3 and 7 'legislature' includes the European Parliament.

17. (1) Provision may be made by order identifying—

(a) for the purposes of paragraph 11, the corresponding proceedings referred to in sub-paragraph (3);

(b) for the purposes of paragraph 13, the corresponding meetings and documents referred to in sub-paragraph (5).

(2) An order under this paragraph may be made—

(a) for England and Wales or Northern Ireland, by the Lord Chancellor, and

(b) for Scotland, by the Secretary of State.

(3) An order under this paragraph shall be made by statutory instrument which shall be subject to annulment in pursuance of a resolution of either House of Parliament.

DAMAGES ACT 1996
(1996, c 48)

1 Assumed rate of return on investment of damages

(1) In determining the return to be expected from the investment of a sum awarded as damages for future pecuniary loss in an action for personal injury the court shall, subject to and in accordance with rules of court made for the purposes of this section, take into account such rate of return (if any) as may from time to time be prescribed by an order made by the Lord Chancellor.

(2) Subsection (1) above shall not however prevent the court taking a different rate of return into account if any party to the proceedings shows that it is more appropriate in the case in question.

(3) An order under subsection (1) above may prescribe different rates of return for different classes of case.

(4) Before making an order under subsection (1) above the Lord Chancellor shall consult the Government Actuary and the Treasury; and any order under that subsection shall be made by statutory instrument subject to annulment in pursuance of a resolution of either House of Parliament.

(5)   In the application of this section to Scotland—

(a)   for the reference to the Lord Chancellor in subsections (1) and (4) there is substituted a reference to the Scottish Ministers; and

(b)   in subsection (4)—

(i)   'and the Treasury' is omitted; and

(ii)   for 'either House of Parliament' there is substituted 'the Scottish Parliament'.

HOUSING GRANTS, CONSTRUCTION AND REGENERATION ACT 1996
(1996, c 53)

113   Prohibition of conditional payment provisions

(1)   A provision making payment under a construction contract conditional on the payer receiving payment from a third person is ineffective, unless that third person, or any other person payment by whom is under the contract (directly or indirectly) a condition of payment by that third person, is insolvent.

(2)   For the purposes of this section a company becomes insolvent—

[(a)   when it enters administration within the meaning of Schedule B1 to the Insolvency Act 1986,]

(b)   on the appointment of an administrative receiver or a receiver or manager of its property under Chapter I of Part III of that Act, or the appointment of a receiver under Chapter II of that Part,

(c)   on the passing of a resolution for voluntary winding-up without a declaration of solvency under section 89 of that Act, or

(d)   on the making of a winding-up order under Part IV or V of that Act.

(3)   For the purposes of this section a partnership becomes insolvent—

(a)   on the making of a winding-up order against it under any provision of the Insolvency Act 1986 as applied by an order under section 420 of that Act, or

(b)   when sequestration is awarded on the estate of the partnership under section 12 of the Bankruptcy (Scotland) Act 1985 or the partnership grants a trust deed for its creditors.

(4)   For the purposes of this section an individual becomes insolvent—

(a)   on the making of a bankruptcy order against him under Part IX of the Insolvency Act 1986, or

(b)   on the sequestration of his estate under the Bankruptcy (Scotland) Act 1985 or when he grants a trust deed for his creditors.

(5)   A company, partnership or individual shall also be treated as insolvent on the occurrence of any event corresponding to those specified in subsection (2), (3) or (4) under the law of Northern Ireland or of a country outside the United Kingdom.

(6)   Where a provision is rendered ineffective by subsection (1), the parties are free to agree other terms for payment.

In the absence of such agreement, the relevant provisions of the Scheme for Construction Contracts apply.

SOCIAL SECURITY (RECOVERY OF BENEFITS) ACT 1997
(1997, c 27)

3   'The relevant period'

(1)   In relation to a person ('the claimant') who has suffered any accident, injury or disease, 'the relevant period' has the meaning given by the following subsections.

(2)   Subject to subsection (4), if it is a case of accident or injury, the relevant period is the period of five years immediately following the day on which the accident or injury in question occurred.

(3)   Subject to subsection (4), if it is a case of disease, the relevant period is the

period of five years beginning with the date on which the claimant first claims a listed benefit in consequence of the disease.

(4) If at any time before the end of the period referred to in subsection (2) or (3)—

(a) a person makes a compensation payment in final discharge of any claim made by or in respect of the claimant and arising out of the accident, injury or disease, or

(b) an agreement is made under which an earlier compensation payment is treated as having been made in final discharge of any such claim,

the relevant period ends at that time.

6 Liability to pay Secretary of State amount of benefits

(1) A person who makes a compensation payment in any case is liable to pay to the Secretary of State an amount equal to the total amount of the recoverable benefits.

(2) The liability referred to in subsection (1) arises immediately before the compensation payment or, if there is more than one, the first of them is made.

(3) No amount becomes payable under this section before the end of the period of 14 days following the day on which the liability arises.

7 Recovery of payments due under section 6

(1) This section applies where a person has made a compensation payment but—

(a) has not applied for a certificate of recoverable benefits, or

(b) has not made a payment to the Secretary of State under section 6 before the end of the period allowed under that section.

(2) The Secretary of State may—

(a) issue the person who made the compensation payment with a certificate of recoverable benefits, if none has been issued, or

(b) issue him with a copy of the certificate of recoverable benefits or (if more than one has been issued) the most recent one,

and (in either case) issue him with a demand that payment of any amount due under section 6 be made immediately.

(3) The Secretary of State may, in accordance with subsections (4) and (5), recover the amount for which a demand for payment is made under subsection (2) from the person who made the compensation payment.

(4) If the person who made the compensation payment resides or carries on business in England and Wales and a county court so orders, any amount recoverable under subsection (3) is recoverable by execution issued from the county court or otherwise as if it were payable under an order of that court.

(5) If the person who made the payment resides or carries on business in Scotland, any amount recoverable under subsection (3) may be enforced in like manner as an extract registered decree arbitral bearing a warrant for execution issued by the sheriff court of any sheriffdom in Scotland.

(6) A document bearing a certificate which—

(a) is signed by a person authorised to do so by the Secretary of State, and

(b) states that the document, apart from the certificate, is a record of the amount recoverable under subsection (3),

is conclusive evidence that that amount is so recoverable.

(7) A certificate under subsection (6) purporting to be signed by a person authorised to do so by the Secretary of State is to be treated as so signed unless the contrary is proved.

SCHEDULES

SCHEDULE 1
COMPENSATION PAYMENTS

PART I
EXEMPTED PAYMENTS

1. Any small payment (defined in Part II of this Schedule).
2. Any payment made to or for the injured person under section [130 of the Powers of Criminal Courts (Sentencing) Act 2000] or section 249 of the Criminal Procedure (Scotland) Act 1995 (compensation orders against convicted persons).
3. Any payment made in the exercise of a discretion out of property held subject to a trust in a case where no more than 50 per cent. by value of the capital contributed to the trust was directly or indirectly provided by persons who are, or are alleged to be, liable in respect of—
    (a)   the accident, injury or disease suffered by the injured person, or
    (b)   the same or any connected accident, injury or disease suffered by another.
4. Any payment made out of property held for the purposes of any prescribed trust (whether the payment also falls within paragraph 3 or not).
5. (1) Any payment made to the injured person by an [insurer] under the terms of any contract of insurance entered into between the injured person and the [insurer] before—
    (a)   the date on which the injured person first claims a listed benefit in consequence of the disease in question, or
    (b)   the occurrence of the accident or injury in question.
    [(2) 'Insurer' means—
    (a)   a person who has permission under Part 4 of the Financial Services and Markets Act 2000 to effect or carry out contracts of insurance; or
    (b)   an EEA firm of the kind mentioned in paragraph 5(d) of Schedule 3 to that Act which has permission under paragraph 15 of that Schedule (as a result of qualifying for authorisation under paragraph 12 of that Schedule) to effect or carry out contracts of insurance.
    (3)   Sub-paragraph (2) must be read with—
    (a)   section 22 of the Financial Services and Markets Act 2000;
    (b)   any relevant order under that section; and
    (c)   Schedule 2 to that Act.]
6. Any redundancy payment falling to be taken into account in the assessment of damages in respect of an accident, injury or disease.
7. So much of any payment as is referable to costs.
8. Any prescribed payment.

PART II
POWER TO DISREGARD SMALL PAYMENTS

9.—(1) Regulations may make provision for compensation payments to be disregarded for the purposes of sections 6 and 8 in prescribed cases where the amount of the compensation payment, or the aggregate amount of two or more connected compensation payments, does not exceed the prescribed sum.
(2) A compensation payment disregarded by virtue of this paragraph is referred to in paragraph 1 as a 'small payment'.
(3) For the purposes of this paragraph—
    (a)   two or more compensation payments are 'connected' if each is made to or in respect of the same injured person and in respect of the same accident, injury or disease, and

(b)   any reference to a compensation payment is a reference to a payment which would be such a payment apart from paragraph 1.

SCHEDULE 2
CALCULATION OF COMPENSATION PAYMENT

(1) *Head of compensation*	(2) *Benefit*
1. Compensation for earnings lost during the relevant period	. . . Disablement pension payable under section 103 of the 1992 Act Incapacity benefit Income support Invalidity pension and allowance Jobseeker's allowance Reduced earnings allowance Severe disablement allowance Sickness benefit Statutory sick pay Unemployability supplement Unemployment benefit
2. Compensation for cost of care incurred during the relevant period	Attendance allowance Care component of disability living allowance Disablement pension increase payable under section 104 or 105 of the 1992 Act
3. Compensation for loss of mobility during the relevant period	Mobility allowance Mobility component of disability living allowance

CONTRACT (SCOTLAND) ACT 1997
(1997, c 34)

1   Extrinsic evidence of additional contract term etc

(1)   Where a document appears (or two or more documents appear) to comprise all the express terms of a contract or unilateral voluntary obligation, it shall be presumed, unless the contrary is proved, that the document does (or the documents do) comprise all the express terms of the contract or unilateral voluntary obligation.

(2)   Extrinsic oral or documentary evidence shall be admissible to prove, for the purposes of subsection (1) above, that the contract or unilateral voluntary obligation includes additional express terms (whether or not written terms).

(3)   Notwithstanding the foregoing provisions of this section, where one of the terms in the document (or in the documents) is to the effect that the document does (or the documents do) comprise all the express terms of the contract or unilateral voluntary obligation, that term shall be conclusive in the matter.

(4)   This section is without prejudice to any enactment which makes provision as respects the constitution, or formalities of execution, of a contract or unilateral voluntary obligation.

2   Supersession

(1)   Where a deed is executed in implement, or purportedly in implement, of a contract, an unimplemented, or otherwise unfulfilled, term of the contract shall not

be taken to be superseded by virtue only of that execution or of the delivery and acceptance of the deed.

(2) Subsection (1) above is without prejudice to any agreement which the parties to a contract may reach (whether or not an agreement incorporated into the contract) as to supersession of the contract.

3 Damages for breach of contract of sale

Any rule of law which precludes the buyer in a contract of sale of property from obtaining damages for breach of that contract by the seller unless the buyer rejects the property and rescinds the contract shall cease to have effect.

4 Short title, extent etc

(1) This Act may be cited as the Contract (Scotland) Act 1997.

(2) This Act shall come into force at the end of that period of three months which begins with the day on which the Act is passed.

(3) Section 1 of this Act applies only for the purposes of proceedings commenced on or after, and sections 2 and 3 only as respects contracts entered into on or after, the date on which this Act comes into force.

(4) This Act extends to Scotland only.

PROTECTION FROM HARASSMENT ACT 1997
(1997, c 40)

Scotland

8 Harassment

(1) Every individual has a right to be free from harassment and, accordingly, a person must not pursue a course of conduct which amounts to harassment of another and—

(a) is intended to amount to harassment of that person; or

(b) occurs in circumstances where it would appear to a reasonable person that it would amount to harassment of that person.

(2) An actual or apprehended breach of subsection (1) may be the subject of a claim in civil proceedings by the person who is or may be the victim of the course of conduct in question; and any such claim shall be known as an action of harassment.

(3) For the purposes of this section—

'conduct' includes speech;

'harassment' of a person includes causing the person alarm or distress; and

a course of conduct must involve conduct on at least two occasions.

(4) It shall be a defence to any action of harassment to show that the course of conduct complained of—

(a) was authorised by, under or by virtue of any enactment or rule of law;

(b) was pursued for the purpose of preventing or detecting crime; or

(c) was, in the particular circumstances, reasonable.

(5) In an action of harassment the court may, without prejudice to any other remedies which it may grant—

(a) award damages;

(b) grant—

(i) interdict or interim interdict;

(ii) if it is satisfied that it is appropriate for it to do so in order to protect the person from further harassment, an order, to be known as a 'non-harassment order', requiring the defender to refrain from such conduct in relation to the pursuer as may be specified in the order for such period (which includes an indeterminate period) as may be so specified,

but a person may not be subjected to the same prohibitions in an interdict or interim interdict and a non-harassment order at the same time.

(6) The damages which may be awarded in an action of harassment include damages for any anxiety caused by the harassment and any financial loss resulting from it.

(7) Without prejudice to any right to seek review of any interlocutor, a person against whom a non-harassment order has been made, or the person for whose protection the order was made, may apply to the court by which the order was made for revocation of or a variation of the order and, on any such application, the court may revoke the order or vary it in such manner as it considers appropriate.

(8) In section 10(1) of the Damages (Scotland) Act 1976 (interpretation), in the definition of 'personal injuries', after 'to reputation' there is inserted ', or injury resulting from harassment actionable under section 8 of the Protection from Harassment Act 1997'.

9 Breach of non-harassment order

(1) Any person who is [. . .] in breach of a non-harassment order made under section 8 is guilty of an offence and liable—

(a) on conviction on indictment, to imprisonment for a term not exceeding five years or to a fine, or to both such imprisonment and such fine; and

(b) on summary conviction, to imprisonment for a period not exceeding six months or to a fine not exceeding the statutory maximum, or to both such imprisonment and such fine.

(2) A breach of a non-harassment order shall not be punishable other than in accordance with subsection (1).

[(3) A constable may arrest without warrant any person he reasonably believes is committing or has committed an offence under subsection (1).

(4) Subsection (3) is without prejudice to any power of arrest conferred by law apart from that subsection.]

LATE PAYMENT OF COMMERCIAL DEBTS (INTEREST) ACT 1998
(1998, c 20)

PART I
STATUTORY INTEREST ON QUALIFYING DEBTS

1 Statutory interest

(1) It is an implied term in a contract to which this Act applies that any qualifying debt created by the contract carries simple interest subject to and in accordance with this Part.

(2) Interest carried under that implied term (in this Act referred to as 'statutory interest') shall be treated, for the purposes of any rule of law or enactment (other than this Act) relating to interest on debts, in the same way as interest carried under an express contract term.

(3) This Part has effect subject to Part II (which in certain circumstances permits contract terms to oust or vary the right to statutory interest that would otherwise be conferred by virtue of the term implied by subsection (1)).

2 Contracts to which Act applies

(1) This Act applies to a contract for the supply of goods or services where the purchaser and the supplier are each acting in the course of a business, other than an excepted contract.

(2) In this Act 'contract for the supply of goods or services' means—

(a) a contract of sale of goods; or

(b) a contract (other than a contract of sale of goods) by which a person does any, or any combination, of the things mentioned in subsection (3) for a consideration that is (or includes) a money consideration.

(3) Those things are—

(a) transferring or agreeing to transfer to another the property in goods;

(b)   bailing or agreeing to bail goods to another by way of hire or, in Scotland, hiring or agreeing to hire goods to another; and

(c)   agreeing to carry out a service.

(4)   For the avoidance of doubt a contract of service or apprenticeship is not a contract for the supply of goods or services.

(5)   The following are excepted contracts—

(a)   a consumer credit agreement;

(b)   a contract intended to operate by way of mortgage, pledge, charge or other security.

[. . .]

(7)   In this section—

'business' includes a profession and the activities of any government department or local or public authority;

'consumer credit agreement' has the same meaning as in the Consumer Credit Act 1974;

'contract of sale of goods' and 'goods' have the same meaning as in the Sale of Goods Act 1979;

['government department' includes any part of the Scottish Administration].

'property in goods' means the general property in them and not merely a special property.

[2A   Application of the Act to advocates
The provisions of this Act apply to a transaction in respect of which fees are paid for professional services to a member of the Faculty of Advocates as they apply to a contract for the supply of services for the purpose of this Act.]

3   Qualifying debts
(1)   A debt created by virtue of an obligation under a contract to which this Act applies to pay the whole or any part of the contract price is a 'qualifying debt' for the purposes of this Act, unless (when created) the whole of the debt is prevented from carrying statutory interest by this section.

(2)   A debt does not carry statutory interest if or to the extent that it consists of a sum to which a right to interest or to charge interest applies by virtue of any enactment (other than section 1 of this Act).

This subsection does not prevent a sum from carrying statutory interest by reason of the fact that a court, arbitrator or arbiter would, apart from this Act, have power to award interest on it.

(3)   A debt does not carry (and shall be treated as never having carried) statutory interest if or to the extent that a right to demand interest on it, which exists by virtue of any rule of law, is exercised.

[. . .]

4   Period for which statutory interest runs
(1)   Statutory interest runs in relation to a qualifying debt in accordance with this section (unless section 5 applies).

(2)   Statutory interest starts to run on the day after the relevant day for the debt, at the rate prevailing under section 6 at the end of the relevant day.

(3)   Where the supplier and the purchaser agree a date for payment of the debt (that is, the day on which the debt is to be created by the contract), that is the relevant day unless the debt relates to an obligation to make an advance payment.

A date so agreed may be a fixed one or may depend on the happening of an event or the failure of an event to happen.

(4)   Where the debt relates to an obligation to make an advance payment, the relevant day is the day on which the debt is treated by section 11 as having been created.

(5)   In any other case, the relevant day is the last day of the period of 30 days beginning with—

(a)   the day on which the obligation of the supplier to which the debt relates is performed; or

(b)   the day on which the purchaser has notice of the amount of the debt or (where that amount is unascertained) the sum which the supplier claims is the amount of the debt,

whichever is the later.

(6)   Where the debt is created by virtue of an obligation to pay a sum due in respect of a period of hire of goods, subsection (5)(a) has effect as if it referred to the last day of that period.

(7)   Statutory interest ceases to run when the interest would cease to run if it were carried under an express contract term.

(8)   In this section 'advance payment' has the same meaning as in section 11.

5   Remission of statutory interest

(1)   This section applies where, by reason of any conduct of the supplier, the interests of justice require that statutory interest should be remitted in whole or part in respect of a period for which it would otherwise run in relation to a qualifying debt.

(2)   If the interests of justice require that the supplier should receive no statutory interest for a period, statutory interest shall not run for that period.

(3)   If the interests of justice require that the supplier should receive statutory interest at a reduced rate for a period, statutory interest shall run at such rate as meets the justice of the case for that period.

(4)   Remission of statutory interest under this section may be required—

(a)   by reason of conduct at any time (whether before or after the time at which the debt is created); and

(b)   for the whole period for which statutory interest would otherwise run or for one or more parts of that period.

(5)   In this section 'conduct' includes any act or omission.

[5A   Compensation arising out of late payment

(1)   Once statutory interest begins to run in relation to a qualifying debt, the supplier shall be entitled to a fixed sum (in addition to the statutory interest on the debt).

(2)   That sum shall be—

(a)   for a debt less than £1,000, the sum of £40;

(b)   for a debt of £1,000 or more, but less than £10,000, the sum of £70;

(c)   for a debt of £10,000 or more, the sum of £100.

(3)   The obligation to pay an additional fixed sum under this section in respect of a qualifying debt shall be treated as part of the term implied by section 1(1) in the contract creating the debt.]

6   Rate of statutory interest

(1)   The Secretary of State shall by order made with the consent of the Treasury set the rate of statutory interest by prescribing—

(a)   a formula for calculating the rate of statutory interest; or

(b)   the rate of statutory interest.

(2)   Before making such an order the Secretary of State shall, among other things, consider the extent to which it may be desirable to set the rate so as to—

(a)   protect suppliers whose financial position makes them particularly vulnerable if their qualifying debts are paid late; and

(b)   deter generally the late payment of qualifying debts.

PART II
CONTRACT TERMS RELATING TO LATE PAYMENT OF QUALIFYING DEBTS

7   Purpose of Part II

(1)   This Part deals with the extent to which the parties to a contract to which

this Act applies may by reference to contract terms oust or vary the right to statutory interest that would otherwise apply when a qualifying debt created by the contract (in this Part referred to as 'the debt') is not paid.

(2)   This Part applies to contract terms agreed before the debt is created; after that time the parties are free to agree terms dealing with the debt.

(3)   This Part has effect without prejudice to any other ground which may affect the validity of a contract term.

8   Circumstances where statutory interest may be ousted or varied

(1)   Any contract terms are void to the extent that they purport to exclude the right to statutory interest in relation to the debt, unless there is a substantial contractual remedy for late payment of the debt.

(2)   Where the parties agree a contractual remedy for late payment of the debt that is a substantial remedy, statutory interest is not carried by the debt (unless they agree otherwise).

(3)   The parties may not agree to vary the right to statutory interest in relation to the debt unless either the right to statutory interest as varied or the overall remedy for late payment of the debt is a substantial remedy.

(4)   Any contract terms are void to the extent that they purport to—

(a)   confer a contractual right to interest that is not a substantial remedy for late payment of the debt, or

(b)   vary the right to statutory interest so as to provide for a right to statutory interest that is not a substantial remedy for late payment of the debt,

unless the overall remedy for late payment of the debt is a substantial remedy.

(5)   Subject to this section, the parties are free to agree contract terms which deal with the consequences of late payment of the debt.

9   Meaning of 'substantial remedy'

(1)   A remedy for the late payment of the debt shall be regarded as a substantial remedy unless—

(a)   the remedy is insufficient either for the purpose of compensating the supplier for late payment or for deterring late payment; and

(b)   it would not be fair or reasonable to allow the remedy to be relied on to oust or (as the case may be) to vary the right to statutory interest that would otherwise apply in relation to the debt.

(2)   In determining whether a remedy is not a substantial remedy, regard shall be had to all the relevant circumstances at the time the terms in question are agreed.

(3)   In determining whether subsection (1)(b) applies, regard shall be had (without prejudice to the generality of subsection (2)) to the following matters—

(a)   the benefits of commercial certainty;

(b)   the strength of the bargaining positions of the parties relative to each other;

(c)   whether the term was imposed by one party to the detriment of the other (whether by the use of standard terms or otherwise); and

(d)   whether the supplier received an inducement to agree to the term.

10   Interpretation of Part II

In this Part—

'contract term' means a term of the contract creating the debt or any other contract term binding the parties (or either of them);

'contractual remedy' means a contractual right to interest or any contractual remedy other than interest;

'contractual right to interest' includes a reference to a contractual right to charge interest;

'overall remedy', in relation to the late payment of the debt, means any combination of a contractual right to interest, a varied right to statutory interest or a contractual remedy other than interest;

'substantial remedy' shall be construed in accordance with section 9.

(2) In this Part a reference (however worded) to contract terms which vary the right to statutory interest is a reference to terms altering in any way the effect of Part I in relation to the debt (for example by postponing the time at which interest starts to run or by imposing conditions on the right to interest).

(3) In this Part a reference to late payment of the debt is a reference to late payment of the sum due when the debt is created (excluding any part of that sum which is prevented from carrying statutory interest by section 3).

PART III
GENERAL AND SUPPLEMENTARY

11 Treatment of advance payments of the contract price

(1) A qualifying debt created by virtue of an obligation to make an advance payment shall be treated for the purposes of this Act as if it was created on the day mentioned in subsection (3), (4) or (5) (as the case may be).

(2) In this section 'advance payment' means a payment falling due before the obligation of the supplier to which the whole contract price relates ('the supplier's obligation') is performed, other than a payment of a part of the contract price that is due in respect of any part performance of that obligation and payable on or after the day on which that part performance is completed.

(3) Where the advance payment is the whole contract price, the debt shall be treated as created on the day on which the supplier's obligation is performed.

(4) Where the advance payment is a part of the contract price, but the sum is not due in respect of any part performance of the supplier's obligation, the debt shall be treated as created on the day on which the supplier's obligation is performed.

(5) Where the advance payment is a part of the contract price due in respect of any part performance of the supplier's obligation, but is payable before that part performance is completed, the debt shall be treated as created on the day on which the relevant part performance is completed.

(6) Where the debt is created by virtue of an obligation to pay a sum due in respect of a period of hire of goods, this section has effect as if—

(a) references to the day on which the supplier's obligation is performed were references to the last day of that period; and

(b) references to part performance of that obligation were references to part of that period.

(7) For the purposes of this section an obligation to pay the whole outstanding balance of the contract price shall be regarded as an obligation to pay the whole contract price and not as an obligation to pay a part of the contract price.

12 Conflict of laws

(1) This Act does not have effect in relation to a contract governed by the law of a part of the United Kingdom by choice of the parties if—

(a) there is no significant connection between the contract and that part of the United Kingdom; and

(b) but for that choice, the applicable law would be a foreign law.

(2) This Act has effect in relation to a contract governed by a foreign law by choice of the parties if—

(a) but for that choice, the applicable law would be the law of a part of the United Kingdom; and

(b) there is no significant connection between the contract and any country other than that part of the United Kingdom.

(3) In this section—

'contract' means a contract falling within section 2(1); and

'foreign law' means the law of a country outside the United Kingdom.

13   Assignments, etc

(1)   The operation of this Act in relation to a qualifying debt is not affected by—

(a)   any change in the identity of the parties to the contract creating the debt; or

(b)   the passing of the right to be paid the debt, or the duty to pay it (in whole or in part) to a person other than the person who is the original creditor or the original debtor when the debt is created.

(2)   Any reference in this Act to the supplier or the purchaser is a reference to the person who is for the time being the supplier or the purchaser or, in relation to a time after the debt in question has been created, the person who is for the time being the creditor or the debtor, as the case may be.

(3)   Where the right to be paid part of a debt passes to a person other than the person who is the original creditor when the debt is created, any reference in this Act to a debt shall be construed as (or, if the context so requires, as including) a reference to part of a debt.

(4)   A reference in this section to the identity of the parties to a contract changing, or to a right or duty passing, is a reference to it changing or passing by assignment or assignation, by operation of law or otherwise.

14   Contract terms relating to the date for payment of the contract price

(1)   This section applies to any contract term which purports to have the effect of postponing the time at which a qualifying debt would otherwise be created by a contract to which this Act applies.

(2)   Sections 3(2)(b) and 17(1)(b) of the Unfair Contract Terms Act 1977 (no reliance to be placed on certain contract terms) shall apply in cases where such a contract term is not contained in written standard terms of the purchaser as well as in cases where the term is contained in such standard terms.

(3)   In this section 'contract term' has the same meaning as in section 10(1).

15   Orders and regulations

(1)   Any power to make an order or regulations under this Act is exercisable by statutory instrument.

(2)   Any statutory instrument containing an order or regulations under this Act, other than an order under section 17(2), shall be subject to annulment in pursuance of a resolution of either House of Parliament.

16   Interpretation

(1)   In this Act—

'contract for the supply of goods or services' has the meaning given in section 2(2);

'contract price' means the price in a contract of sale of goods or the money consideration referred to in section 2(2)(b) in any other contract for the supply of goods or services;

'purchaser' means (subject to section 13(2)) the buyer in a contract of sale or the person who contracts with the supplier in any other contract for the supply of goods or services;

'qualifying debt' means a debt falling within section 3(1);

'statutory interest' means interest carried by virtue of the term implied by section 1(1); and

'supplier' means (subject to section 13(2)) the seller in a contract of sale of goods or the person who does one or more of the things mentioned in section 2(3) in any other contract for the supply of goods or services.

(2)   In this Act any reference (however worded) to an agreement or to contract terms includes a reference to both express and implied terms (including terms established by a course of dealing or by such usage as binds the parties).

17 Short title, commencement and extent

(1) This Act may be cited as the Late Payment of Commercial Debts (Interest) Act 1998.

(2) This Act (apart from this section) shall come into force on such day as the Secretary of State may by order appoint; and different days may be appointed for different descriptions of contract or for other different purposes.

An order under this subsection may specify a description of contract by reference to any feature of the contract (including the parties).

(3) The Secretary of State may by regulations make such transitional, supplemental or incidental provision (including provision modifying any provision of this Act) as the Secretary of State may consider necessary or expedient in connection with the operation of this Act while it is not fully in force.

(4) This Act does not affect contracts of any description made before this Act comes into force for contracts of that description.

(5) This Act extends to Northern Ireland.

HUMAN RIGHTS ACT 1998
(1998, c 42)

Introduction

1 The Convention Rights

(1) In this Act 'the Convention rights' means the rights and fundamental freedoms set out in—

(a) Articles 2 to 12 and 14 of the Convention,

(b) Articles 1 to 3 of the First Protocol, and

(c) Articles 1 and 2 of the Sixth Protocol,

as read with Articles 16 to 18 of the Convention.

(2) Those Articles are to have effect for the purposes of this Act subject to any designated derogation or reservation (as to which see sections 14 and 15).

(3) The Articles are set out in Schedule 1.

(4) The [Secretary of State] may by order make such amendments to this Act as he considers appropriate to reflect the effect, in relation to the United Kingdom, of a protocol.

(5) In subsection (4) 'protocol' means a protocol to the Convention—

(a) which the United Kingdom has ratified; or

(b) which the United Kingdom has signed with a view to ratification.

(6) No amendment may be made by an order under subsection (4) so as to come into force before the protocol concerned is in force in relation to the United Kingdom.

2 Interpretation of Convention rights

(1) A court or tribunal determining a question which has arisen in connection with a Convention right must take into account any—

(a) judgment, decision, declaration or advisory opinion of the European Court of Human Rights,

(b) opinion of the Commission given in a report adopted under Article 31 of the Convention,

(c) decision of the Commission in connection with Article 26 or 27(2) of the Convention, or

(d) decision of the Committee of Ministers taken under Article 46 of the Convention,

whenever made or given, so far as, in the opinion of the court or tribunal, it is relevant to the proceedings in which that question has arisen.

(2) Evidence of any judgment, decision, declaration or opinion of which

account may have to be taken under this section is to be given in proceedings
before any court or tribunal in such manner as may be provided by rules.

(3)   In this section 'rules' means rules of court or, in the case of proceedings
before a tribunal, rules made for the purposes of this section—

(a)   by [. . .] the Secretary of State, in relation to any proceedings outside
Scotland;

(b)   by the Secretary of State, in relation to proceedings in Scotland; or

(c)   by a Northern Ireland department, in relation to proceedings before a
tribunal in Northern Ireland—

(i)   which deals with transferred matters; and

(ii)   for which no rules made under paragraph (a) are in force.

Legislation

3   Interpretation of legislation

(1)   So far as it is possible to do so, primary legislation and subordinate legislation must be read and given effect in a way which is compatible with the Convention rights.

(2)   This section—

(a)   applies to primary legislation and subordinate legislation whenever
enacted;

(b)   does not affect the validity, continuing operation or enforcement of any
incompatible primary legislation; and

(c)   does not affect the validity, continuing operation or enforcement of any
incompatible subordinate legislation if (disregarding any possibility of revocation) primary legislation prevents removal of the incompatibility.

4   Declaration of incompatibility

(1)   Subsection (2) applies in any proceedings in which a court determines
whether a provision of primary legislation is compatible with a Convention
right.

(2)   If the court is satisfied that the provision is incompatible with a Convention
right, it may make a declaration of that incompatibility.

(3)   Subsection (4) applies in any proceedings in which a court determines
whether a provision of subordinate legislation, made in the exercise of a power
conferred by primary legislation, is compatible with a Convention right.

(4)   If the court is satisfied—

(a)   that the provision is incompatible with a Convention right, and

(b)   that (disregarding any possibility of revocation) the primary legislation
concerned prevents removal of the incompatibility,
it may make a declaration of that incompatibility.

(5)   In this section 'court' means—

(a)   the House of Lords;

(b)   the Judicial Committee of the Privy Council;

(c)   the Courts-Martial Appeal Court;

(d)   in Scotland, the High Court of Justiciary sitting otherwise than as a trial
court or the Court of Session;

(e)   in England and Wales or Northern Ireland, the High Court or the Court
of Appeal.

(6)   A declaration under this section ('a declaration of incompatibility')—

(a)   does not affect the validity, continuing operation or enforcement of the
provision in respect of which it is given; and

(b)   is not binding on the parties to the proceedings in which it is made.

5   Right of Crown to intervene

(1)   Where a court is considering whether to make a declaration of incompatibility, the Crown is entitled to notice in accordance with rules of court.

(2)   In any case to which subsection (1) applies—
(a)   a Minister of the Crown (or a person nominated by him),
(b)   a member of the Scottish Executive,
(c)   a Northern Ireland Minister,
(d)   a Northern Ireland department,
is entitled, on giving notice in accordance with rules of court, to be joined as a party to the proceedings.

(3)   Notice under subsection (2) may be given at any time during the proceedings.

(4)   A person who has been made a party to criminal proceedings (other than in Scotland) as the result of a notice under subsection (2) may, with leave, appeal to the House of Lords against any declaration of incompatibility made in the proceedings.

(5)   In subsection (4)—
'criminal proceedings' includes all proceedings before the Courts-Martial Appeal Court; and
'leave' means leave granted by the court making the declaration of incompatibility or by the House of Lords.

Remedial action

10   Power to take remedial action

(1)   This section applies if—
(a)   a provision of legislation has been declared under section 4 to be incompatible with a Convention right and, if an appeal lies—
(i)   all persons who may appeal have stated in writing that they do not intend to do so;
(ii)   the time for bringing an appeal has expired and no appeal has been brought within that time; or
(iii)   an appeal brought within that time has been determined or abandoned; or
(b)   it appears to a Minister of the Crown or Her Majesty in Council that, having regard to a finding of the European Court of Human Rights made after the coming into force of this section in proceedings against the United Kingdom, a provision of legislation is incompatible with an obligation of the United Kingdom arising from the Convention.

(2)   If a Minister of the Crown considers that there are compelling reasons for proceeding under this section, he may by order make such amendments to the legislation as he considers necessary to remove the incompatibility.

(3)   If, in the case of subordinate legislation, a Minister of the Crown considers—
(a)   that it is necessary to amend the primary legislation under which the subordinate legislation in question was made, in order to enable the incompatibility to be removed, and
(b)   that there are compelling reasons for proceeding under this section,
he may by order make such amendments to the primary legislation as he considers necessary.

(4)   This section also applies where the provision in question is in subordinate legislation and has been quashed, or declared invalid, by reason of incompatibility with a Convention right and the Minister proposes to proceed under paragraph 2(b) of Schedule 2.

(5)   If the legislation is an Order in Council, the power conferred by subsection (2) or (3) is exercisable by Her Majesty in Council.

(6)   In this section 'legislation' does not include a Measure of the Church Assembly or of the General Synod of the Church of England.

(7)   Schedule 2 makes further provision about remedial orders.

21   Interpretation, etc

(1)   In this Act—

'amend' includes repeal and apply (with or without modifications);

'the appropriate Minister' means the Minister of the Crown having charge of the appropriate authorised government department (within the meaning of the Crown Proceedings Act 1947);

'the Commission' means the European Commission of Human Rights;

'the Convention' means the Convention for the Protection of Human Rights and Fundamental Freedoms, agreed by the Council of Europe at Rome on 4th November 1950 as it has effect for the time being in relation to the United Kingdom;

'declaration of incompatibility' means a declaration under section 4;

'Minister of the Crown' has the same meaning as in the Ministers of the Crown Act 1975;

'Northern Ireland Minister' includes the First Minister and the deputy First Minister in Northern Ireland;

'primary legislation' means any—

    (a)   public general Act;

    (b)   local and personal Act;

    (c)   private Act;

    (d)   Measure of the Church Assembly;

    (e)   Measure of the General Synod of the Church of England;

    (f)   Order in Council—

        (i)   made in exercise of Her Majesty's Royal Prerogative;

        (ii)   made under section 38(1)(a) of the Northern Ireland Constitution Act 1973 or the corresponding provision of the Northern Ireland Act 1998; or

        (iii)   amending an Act of a kind mentioned in paragraph (a), (b) or (c);

and includes an order or other instrument made under primary legislation (otherwise than by the National Assembly for Wales, a member of the Scottish Executive, a Northern Ireland Minister or a Northern Ireland department) to the extent to which it operates to bring one or more provisions of that legislation into force or amends any primary legislation;

'the First Protocol' means the protocol to the Convention agreed at Paris on 20th March 1952;

'the Sixth Protocol' means the protocol to the Convention agreed at Strasbourg on 28th April 1983;

'the Eleventh Protocol' means the protocol to the Convention (restructuring the control machinery established by the Convention) agreed at Strasbourg on 11th May 1994;

'remedial order' means an order under section 10;

'subordinate legislation' means any—

    (a)   Order in Council other than one—

        (i)   made in exercise of Her Majesty's Royal Prerogative;

        (ii)   made under section 38(1)(a) of the Northern Ireland Constitution Act 1973 or the corresponding provision of the Northern Ireland Act 1998; or

        (iii)   amending an Act of a kind mentioned in the definition of primary legislation;

    (b)   Act of the Scottish Parliament;

    (c)   Act of the Parliament of Northern Ireland;

    (d)   Measure of the Assembly established under section 1 of the Northern Ireland Assembly Act 1973;

    (e)   Act of the Northern Ireland Assembly;

    (f)   order, rules, regulations, scheme, warrant, byelaw or other instrument made under primary legislation (except to the extent to which it operates to bring one or more provisions of that legislation into force or amends any primary legislation);

(g)   order, rules, regulations, scheme, warrant, byelaw or other instrument made under legislation mentioned in paragraph (b), (c), (d) or (e) or made under an Order in Council applying only to Northern Ireland;

(h)   order, rules, regulations, scheme, warrant, byelaw or other instrument made by a member of the Scottish Executive, a Northern Ireland Minister or a Northern Ireland department in exercise of prerogative or other executive functions of Her Majesty which are exercisable by such a person on behalf of Her Majesty;

'transferred matters' has the same meaning as in the Northern Ireland Act 1998; and

'tribunal' means any tribunal in which legal proceedings may be brought.

(2)   The references in paragraphs (b) and (c) of section 2(1) to Articles are to Articles of the Convention as they had effect immediately before the coming into force of the Eleventh Protocol.

(3)   The reference in paragraph (d) of section 2(1) to Article 46 includes a reference to Articles 32 and 54 of the Convention as they had effect immediately before the coming into force of the Eleventh Protocol.

(4)   The references in section 2(1) to a report or decision of the Commission or a decision of the Committee of Ministers include references to a report or decision made as provided by paragraphs 3, 4 and 6 of Article 5 of the Eleventh Protocol (transitional provisions).

(5)   Any liability under the Army Act 1955, the Air Force Act 1955 or the Naval Discipline Act 1957 to suffer death for an offence is replaced by a liability to imprisonment for life or any less punishment authorised by those Acts; and those Acts shall accordingly have effect with the necessary modifications.

22   Short title, commencement, application and extent
(1)   This Act may be cited as the Human Rights Act 1998.
. . .

SCHEDULES

SCHEDULE 1
THE ARTICLES

PART I
THE CONVENTION

Rights and Freedoms

Article 2. Right to Life
1.   Everyone's right to life shall be protected by law. No one shall be deprived of his life intentionally save in the execution of a sentence of a court following his conviction of a crime for which this penalty is provided by law.

2.   Deprivation of life shall not be regarded as inflicted in contravention of this Article when it results from the use of force which is no more than absolutely necessary:
(a)   in defence of any person from unlawful violence;
(b)   in order to effect a lawful arrest or to prevent the escape of a person lawfully detained;
(c)   in action lawfully taken for the purpose of quelling a riot or insurrection.

Article 3. Prohibition of Torture
No one shall be subjected to torture or to inhuman or degrading treatment or punishment.

Article 4. Prohibition of Slavery and Forced Labour

1. No one shall be held in slavery or servitude.

2. No one shall be required to perform forced or compulsory labour.

3. For the purpose of this Article the term 'forced or compulsory labour' shall not include:

(a) any work required to be done in the ordinary course of detention imposed according to the provisions of Article 5 of this Convention or during conditional release from such detention;

(b) any service of a military character or, in case of conscientious objectors in countries where they are recognised, service exacted instead of compulsory military service;

(c) any service exacted in case of an emergency or calamity threatening the life or well-being of the community;

(d) any work or service which forms part of normal civic obligations.

Article 5. Right to Liberty and Security

1. Everyone has the right to liberty and security of person. No one shall be deprived of his liberty save in the following cases and in accordance with a procedure prescribed by law:

(a) the lawful detention of a person after conviction by a competent court;

(b) the lawful arrest or detention of a person for non-compliance with the lawful order of a court or in order to secure the fulfilment of any obligation prescribed by law;

(c) the lawful arrest or detention of a person effected for the purpose of bringing him before the competent legal authority on reasonable suspicion of having committed an offence or when it is reasonably considered necessary to prevent his committing an offence or fleeing after having done so;

(d) the detention of a minor by lawful order for the purpose of educational supervision or his lawful detention for the purpose of bringing him before the competent legal authority;

(e) the lawful detention of persons for the prevention of the spreading of infectious diseases, of persons of unsound mind, alcoholics or drug addicts or vagrants;

(f) the lawful arrest or detention of a person to prevent his effecting an unauthorised entry into the country or of a person against whom action is being taken with a view to deportation or extradition.

2. Everyone who is arrested shall be informed promptly, in a language which he understands, of the reasons for his arrest and of any charge against him.

3. Everyone arrested or detained in accordance with the provisions of paragraph 1(c) of this Article shall be brought promptly before a judge or other officer authorised by law to exercise judicial power and shall be entitled to trial within a reasonable time or to release pending trial. Release may be conditioned by guarantees to appear for trial.

4. Everyone who is deprived of his liberty by arrest or detention shall be entitled to take proceedings by which the lawfulness of his detention shall be decided speedily by a court and his release ordered if the detention is not lawful.

5. Everyone who has been the victim of arrest or detention in contravention of the provisions of this Article shall have an enforceable right to compensation.

Article 6. Right to a Fair Trial

1. In the determination of his civil rights and obligations or of any criminal charge against him, everyone is entitled to a fair and public hearing within a reasonable time by an independent and impartial tribunal established by law. Judgment shall be pronounced publicly but the press and public may be excluded from all or part of the trial in the interest of morals, public order or national security in a democratic society, where the interests of juveniles or the protection of the private life of the parties so require, or to the extent strictly necessary in the

opinion of the court in special circumstances where publicity would prejudice the interests of justice.

2.   Everyone charged with a criminal offence shall be presumed innocent until proved guilty according to law.

3.   Everyone charged with a criminal offence has the following minimum rights:

(a)   to be informed promptly, in a language which he understands and in detail, of the nature and cause of the accusation against him;

(b)   to have adequate time and facilities for the preparation of his defence;

(c)   to defend himself in person or through legal assistance of his own choosing or, if he has not sufficient means to pay for legal assistance, to be given it free when the interests of justice so require;

(d)   to examine or have examined witnesses against him and to obtain the attendance and examination of witnesses on his behalf under the same conditions as witnesses against him;

(e)   to have the free assistance of an interpreter if he cannot understand or speak the language used in court.

Article 7. No Punishment Without Law

1.   No one shall be held guilty of any criminal offence on account of any act or omission which did not constitute a criminal offence under national or international law at the time when it was committed. Nor shall a heavier penalty be imposed than the one that was applicable at the time the criminal offence was committed.

2.   This Article shall not prejudice the trial and punishment of any person for any act or omission which, at the time when it was committed, was criminal according to the general principles of law recognised by civilised nations.

Article 8. Right to Respect for Private and Family Life

1.   Everyone has the right to respect for his private and family life, his home and his correspondence.

2.   There shall be no interference by a public authority with the exercise of this right except such as is in accordance with the law and is necessary in a democratic society in the interests of national security, public safety or the economic well-being of the country, for the prevention of disorder or crime, for the protection of health or morals, or for the protection of the rights and freedoms of others.

Article 9. Freedom of Thought, Conscience and Religion

1.   Everyone has the right to freedom of thought, conscience and religion; this right includes freedom to change his religion or belief and freedom, either alone or in community with others and in public or private, to manifest his religion or belief, in worship, teaching, practice and observance.

2.   Freedom to manifest one's religion or beliefs shall be subject only to such limitations as are prescribed by law and are necessary in a democratic society in the interests of public safety, for the protection of public order, health or morals, or for the protection of the rights and freedoms of others.

Article 10. Freedom of Expression

1.   Everyone has the right to freedom of expression. This right shall include freedom to hold opinions and to receive and impart information and ideas without interference by public authority and regardless of frontiers. This Article shall not prevent States from requiring the licensing of broadcasting, television or cinema enterprises.

2.   The exercise of these freedoms, since it carries with it duties and responsibilities, may be subject to such formalities, conditions, restrictions or penalties as are prescribed by law and are necessary in a democratic society, in the interests of national security, territorial integrity or public safety, for the prevention of disorder or crime, for the protection of health or morals, for the protection of the

reputation or rights of others, for preventing the disclosure of information received in confidence, or for maintaining the authority and impartiality of the judiciary.

Article 11. Freedom of Assembly and Association

1.   Everyone has the right to freedom of peaceful assembly and to freedom of association with others, including the right to form and to join trade unions for the protection of his interests.

2.   No restrictions shall be placed on the exercise of these rights other than such as are prescribed by law and are necessary in a democratic society in the interests of national security or public safety, for the prevention of disorder or crime, for the protection of health or morals or for the protection of the rights and freedoms of others. This Article shall not prevent the imposition of lawful restrictions on the exercise of these rights by members of the armed forces, of the police or of the administration of the State.

Article 12. Right to Marry

Men and women of marriageable age have the right to marry and to found a family, according to the national laws governing the exercise of this right.

Article 14. Prohibition of Discrimination

The enjoyment of the rights and freedoms set forth in this Convention shall be secured without discrimination on any ground such as sex, race, colour, language, religion, political or other opinion, national or social origin, association with a national minority, property, birth or other status.

Article 16. Restrictions on Political Activity of Aliens

Nothing in Articles 10, 11 and 14 shall be regarded as preventing the High Contracting Parties from imposing restrictions on the political activity of aliens.

Article 17. Prohibition of Abuse of Rights

Nothing in this Convention may be interpreted as implying for any State, group or person any right to engage in any activity or perform any act aimed at the destruction of any of the rights and freedoms set forth herein or at their limitation to a greater extent than is provided for in the Convention.

Article 18. Limitation on Use of Restrictions on Rights

The restrictions permitted under this Convention to the said rights and freedoms shall not be applied for any purpose other than those for which they have been prescribed.

PART II
THE FIRST PROTOCOL

Article 1. Protection of Property

Every natural or legal person is entitled to the peaceful enjoyment of his possessions. No one shall be deprived of his possessions except in the public interest and subject to the conditions provided for by law and by the general principles of international law.

The preceding provisions shall not, however, in any way impair the right of a State to enforce such laws as it deems necessary to control the use of property in accordance with the general interest or to secure the payment of taxes or other contributions or penalties.

Article 2. Right to Education

No person shall be denied the right to education. In the exercise of any functions which it assumes in relation to education and to teaching, the State shall respect the right of parents to ensure such education and teaching in conformity with their own religious and philosophical convictions.

Article 3. Right to Free Elections

The High Contracting Parties undertake to hold free elections at reasonable intervals by secret ballot, under conditions which will ensure the free expression of the opinion of the people in the choice of the legislature.

PART III
THE SIXTH PROTOCOL

Article 1. Abolition of the Death Penalty
The death penalty shall be abolished. No one shall be condemned to such penalty or executed.

Article 2. Death Penalty in Time of War
A State may make provision in its law for the death penalty in respect of acts committed in time of war or of imminent threat of war; such penalty shall be applied only in the instances laid down in the law and in accordance with its provisions. The State shall communicate to the Secretary General of the Council of Europe the relevant provisions of that law.

SCHEDULE 2
REMEDIAL ORDERS

1 Orders
(1) A remedial order may—

(a)   contain such incidental, supplemental, consequential or transitional provision as the person making it considers appropriate;

(b)   be made so as to have effect from a date earlier than that on which it is made;

(c)   make provision for the delegation of specific functions;

(d)   make different provision for different cases.

(2)   The power conferred by sub-paragraph (1)(a) includes—

(a)   power to amend primary legislation (including primary legislation other than that which contains the incompatible provision); and

(b)   power to amend or revoke subordinate legislation (including subordinate legislation other than that which contains the incompatible provision).

(3)   A remedial order may be made so as to have the same extent as the legislation which it affects.

(4)   No person is to be guilty of an offence solely as a result of the retrospective effect of a remedial order.

2 Procedure
No remedial order may be made unless—

(a)   a draft of the order has been approved by a resolution of each House of Parliament made after the end of the period of 60 days beginning with the day on which the draft was laid; or

(b)   it is declared in the order that it appears to the person making it that, because of the urgency of the matter, it is necessary to make the order without a draft being so approved.

3 Orders laid in draft
(1)   No draft may be laid under paragraph 2(a) unless—

(a)   the person proposing to make the order has laid before Parliament a document which contains a draft of the proposed order and the required information; and

(b)   the period of 60 days, beginning with the day on which the document required by this sub-paragraph was laid, has ended.

(2)   If representations have been made during that period, the draft laid under paragraph 2(a) must be accompanied by a statement containing—

(a)   a summary of the representations; and

(b)   if, as a result of the representations, the proposed order has been changed, details of the changes.

4   Urgent cases

(1)   If a remedial order ('the original order') is made without being approved in draft, the person making it must lay it before Parliament, accompanied by the required information, after it is made.

(2)   If representations have been made during the period of 60 days beginning with the day on which the original order was made, the person making it must (after the end of that period) lay before Parliament a statement containing—

(a)   a summary of the representations; and

(b)   if, as a result of the representations, he considers it appropriate to make changes to the original order, details of the changes.

(3)   If sub-paragraph (2)(b) applies, the person making the statement must—

(a)   make a further remedial order replacing the original order; and

(b)   lay the replacement order before Parliament.

(4)   If, at the end of the period of 120 days beginning with the day on which the original order was made, a resolution has not been passed by each House approving the original or replacement order, the order ceases to have effect (but without that affecting anything previously done under either order or the power to make a fresh remedial order).

5   Definitions

In this Schedule—

'representations' means representations about a remedial order (or proposed remedial order) made to the person making (or proposing to make) it and includes any relevant Parliamentary report or resolution; and

'required information' means—

(a)   an explanation of the incompatibility which the order (or proposed order) seeks to remove, including particulars of the relevant declaration, finding or order; and

(b)   a statement of the reasons for proceeding under section 10 and for making an order in those terms.

6   Calculating periods

In calculating any period for the purposes of this Schedule, no account is to be taken of any time during which—

(a)   Parliament is dissolved or prorogued; or

(b)   both Houses are adjourned for more than four days.

[7   (1)   This paragraph applies in relation to—

(a)   any remedial order made, and any draft of such an order proposed to be made,—

(i)   by the Scottish Ministers; or

(ii)   within devolved competence (within the meaning of the Scotland Act 1998) by Her Majesty in Council; and

(b)   any document or statement to be laid in connection with such an order (or proposed order).

(2)   This Schedule has effect in relation to any such order (or proposed order), document or statement subject to the following modifications.

(3)   Any reference to Parliament, each House of Parliament or both Houses of Parliament shall be construed as a reference to the Scottish Parliament.

(4)   Paragraph 6 does not apply and instead, in calculating any period for the purposes of this Schedule, no account is to be taken of any time during which the Scottish Parliament is dissolved or is in recess for more than four days.]

SCOTLAND ACT 1998
(1998, c 46)

126   Interpretation
(1)   In this Act—
'body' includes unincorporated association,
'constituencies' and 'regions', in relation to the Parliament, mean the constituencies and regions provided for by Schedule l,
'constituency member' means a member of the Parliament for a constituency,
'the Convention rights' has the same meaning as in the Human Rights Act 1998,
'document' means anything in which information is recorded in any form (and references to producing a document are to be read accordingly),
'enactment' includes an Act of the Scottish Parliament, Northern Ireland legislation (within the meaning of the Northern Ireland Act 1998) and an enactment comprised in subordinate legislation, and includes an enactment comprised in, or in subordinate legislation under, an Act of Parliament, whenever passed or made,
'financial year' means a year ending with 31st March,
'functions' includes powers and duties, and 'confer', in relation to functions, includes impose,
'government department' means any department of the Government of the United Kingdom,
'the Human Rights Convention' means—
    (a)   the Convention for the Protection of Human Rights and Fundamental Freedoms, agreed by the Council of Europe at Rome on 4th November 1950, and
    (b)   the Protocols to the Convention,
as they have effect for the time being in relation to the United Kingdom,
'Minister of the Crown' includes the Treasury,
'modify' includes amend or repeal,
'occupational pension scheme', 'personal pension scheme' and 'public service pension scheme' have the meanings given by section 1 of the Pension Schemes Act 1993, . . .
'the Parliament' means the Scottish Parliament,
'parliamentary', in relation to constituencies, elections and electors, is to be taken to refer to the Parliament of the United Kingdom,
'prerogative instrument' means an Order in Council, warrant, charter or other instrument made under the prerogative,
'the principal appointed day' means the day appointed by an order under section 130 which is designated by the order as the principal appointed day,
'proceedings', in relation to the Parliament, includes proceedings of any committee or sub-committee,
'property' includes rights and interests of any description,
'regional member' means a member of the Parliament for a region,
'Scotland' includes so much of the internal waters and territorial sea of the United Kingdom as are adjacent to Scotland,
'Scottish public authority' means any public body (except the Parliamentary corporation), public office or holder of such an office whose functions (in each case) are exercisable only in or as regards Scotland,
'the Scottish zone' means the sea within British fishery limits (that is, the limits set by or under section 1 of the Fishery Limits Act 1976) which is adjacent to Scotland,
'standing orders' means standing orders of the Parliament,
'subordinate legislation' has the same meaning as in the Interpretation Act 1978 and also includes an instrument made under an Act of the Scottish Parliament,

'tribunal' means any tribunal in which legal proceedings may be brought.

(2) Her Majesty may by Order in Council determine, or make provision for determining, for the purposes of this Act any boundary between waters which are to be treated as internal waters or territorial sea of the United Kingdom, or sea within British fishery limits, adjacent to Scotland and those which are not.

(3) For the purposes of this Act—

(a) the question whether any function of a body, government department, office or office-holder relates to reserved matters is to be determined by reference to the purpose for which the function is exercisable, having regard (among other things) to the likely effects in all the circumstances of any exercise of the function, but

(b) bodies to which paragraph 3 of Part III of Schedule 5 applies are to be treated as if all their functions were functions which relate to reserved matters.

(4) References in this Act to Scots private law are to the following areas of the civil law of Scotland—

(a) the general principles of private law (including private international law),

(b) the law of persons (including natural persons, legal persons and unincorporated bodies),

(c) the law of obligations (including obligations arising from contract, unilateral promise, delict, unjustified enrichment and negotiorum gestio),

(d) the law of property (including heritable and moveable property, trusts and succession), and

(e) the law of actions (including jurisdiction, remedies, evidence, procedure, diligence, recognition and enforcement of court orders, limitation of actions and arbitration),

and include references to judicial review of administrative action.

(5) References in this Act to Scots criminal law include criminal offences, jurisdiction, evidence, procedure and penalties and the treatment of offenders.

(6) References in this Act and in any other enactment to the Scottish Administration are to the office-holders in the Scottish Administration and the members of the staff of the Scottish Administration.

(7) For the purposes of this Act—

(a) references to office-holders in the Scottish Administration are to—

(i) members of the Scottish Executive and junior Scottish Ministers, and

(ii) the holders of offices in the Scottish Administration which are not ministerial offices, and

(b) references to members of the staff of the Scottish Administration are to the staff of the persons referred to in paragraph (a).

(8) For the purposes of this Act, the offices in the Scottish Administration which are not ministerial offices are—

(a) the Registrar General of Births, Deaths and Marriages for Scotland, the Keeper of the Registers of Scotland and the Keeper of the Records of Scotland, and

(b) any other office of a description specified in an Order in Council made by Her Majesty under this subsection.

(9) In this Act—

(a) all those rights, powers, liabilities, obligations and restrictions from time to time created or arising by or under the Community Treaties, and

(b) all those remedies and procedures from time to time provided for by or under the Community Treaties,

are referred to as 'Community law'.

(10) In this Act, 'international obligations' means any international obligations of the United Kingdom other than obligations to observe and implement Community law or the Convention rights.

(11) In this Act, 'by virtue of' includes 'by' and 'under'.

ADULTS WITH INCAPACITY (SCOTLAND) ACT 2000
(2000, asp 4)

PART 5
MEDICAL TREATMENT AND RESEARCH

47　Authority of persons responsible for medical treatment

(1)　This section applies where the medical practitioner primarily responsible for the medical treatment of an adult—

　　(a)　is of the opinion that the adult is incapable in relation to a decision about the medical treatment in question; and

　　(b)　has certified in accordance with subsection (5) that he is of this opinion.

(2)　Without prejudice to any authority conferred by any other enactment or rule of law, and subject to sections 49 and 50 and to the following provisions of this section, the medical practitioner primarily responsible for the medical treatment of the adult shall have, during the period specified in the certificate, authority to do what is reasonable in the circumstances, in relation to the medical treatment, to safeguard or promote the physical or mental health of the adult.

(3)　The authority conferred by subsection (2) shall be exercisable also by any other person who is authorised by the medical practitioner primarily responsible for the medical treatment of the adult to carry out medical treatment and who is acting—

　　(a)　on his behalf under his instructions; or

　　(b)　with his approval or agreement.

(4)　In this Part 'medical treatment' includes any procedure or treatment designed to safeguard or promote physical or mental health.

(5)　A certificate for the purposes of subsection (1) shall be in the prescribed form and shall specify the period during which the authority conferred by subsection (2) shall subsist, being a period which—

　　(a)　the medical practitioner primarily responsible for the medical treatment of the adult considers appropriate to the condition or circumstances of the adult; but

　　(b)　does not exceed one year from the date of the examination on which the certificate is based.

(6)　If after issuing a certificate, the medical practitioner primarily responsible for the medical treatment of the adult is of the opinion that the condition or circumstances of the adult have changed he may—

　　(a)　revoke the certificate;

　　(b)　issue a new certificate specifying such period not exceeding one year from the date of revocation of the old certificate as he considers appropriate to the new condition or circumstances of the adult.

(7)　The authority conferred by subsection (2) shall not authorise—

　　(a)　the use of force or detention, unless it is immediately necessary and only for so long as is necessary in the circumstances;

　　(b)　action which would be inconsistent with any decision by a competent court;

　　(c)　placing an adult in a hospital for the treatment of mental disorder against his will.

(8)　The authority conferred by subsection (2) shall not authorise medical treatment prescribed in regulations made under section 48.

(9)　Subject to subsection (10), where any question as to the authority of any person to provide medical treatment in pursuance of subsection (2)—

　　(a)　is the subject of proceedings in any court (other than for the purposes of any application to the court made under regulations made under section 48); and

　　(b)　has not been determined,

medical treatment authorised by subsection (2) shall not be given unless it is

authorised by any other enactment or rule of law for the preservation of the life of
the adult or the prevention of serious deterioration in his medical condition.

(10)   Nothing in subsection (9) shall authorise the provision of any medical
treatment where an interdict has been granted and continues to have effect prohibiting the provision of such medical treatment.

ELECTRONIC COMMUNICATIONS ACT 2000
(2000, c 7)

PART I
CRYPTOGRAPHY SERVICE PROVIDERS

1 Register of approved providers

(1)   It shall be the duty of the Secretary of State to establish and maintain a
register of approved providers of cryptography support services.

(2)   The Secretary of State shall secure that the register contains particulars of
every person who is for the time being approved under any arrangements in force
under section 2.

(3)   The particulars that must be recorded in every entry in the register relating
to an approved person are—

(a)   the name and address of that person;

(b)   the services in respect of which that person is approved; and

(c)   the conditions of the approval.

(4)   It shall be the duty of the Secretary of State to ensure that such arrangements are in force as he considers appropriate for—

(a)   allowing members of the public to inspect the contents of the register;
and

(b)   securing that such publicity is given to any withdrawal or modification
of an approval as will bring it to the attention of persons likely to be interested
in it.

2 Arrangements for the grant of approvals

(1)   It shall be the duty of the Secretary of State to secure that there are arrangements in force for granting approvals to persons who—

(a)   are providing cryptography support services in the United Kingdom or
are proposing to do so; and

(b)   seek approval in respect of any such services that they are providing, or
are proposing to provide, whether in the United Kingdom or elsewhere.

(2)   The arrangements must—

(a)   allow for an approval to be granted either in respect of all the services in
respect of which it is sought or in respect of only some of them;

(b)   ensure that an approval is granted to a person in respect of any services
only if the condition for the grant of an approval to that person is fulfilled in
accordance with subsection (3);

(c)   provide for an approval granted to any person to have effect subject to
such conditions (whether or not connected with the provision of the services
in respect of which the approval is granted) as may be contained in the
approval;

(d)   enable a person to whom the Secretary of State is proposing to grant an
approval to refuse it if the proposal is in different terms from the approval
which was sought;

(e)   make provision for the handling of complaints and disputes which—

(i)   are required by the conditions of an approved person's approval to be
dealt with in accordance with a procedure maintained by him in pursuance of
those conditions; but

(ii) are not disposed of by the application of that procedure;

(f) provide for the modification and withdrawal of approvals.

(3) The condition that must be fulfilled before an approval is granted to any person is that the Secretary of State is satisfied that that person—

(a) will comply, in providing the services in respect of which he is approved, with such technical and other requirements as may be prescribed;

(b) is a person in relation to whom such other requirements as may be prescribed are, and will continue to be, satisfied;

(c) is, and will continue to be, able and willing to comply with any requirements that the Secretary of State is proposing to impose by means of conditions of the approval; and

(d) is otherwise a fit and proper person to be approved in respect of those services.

(4) Regulations made by virtue of paragraph (a) or (b) of subsection (3) may frame a requirement for the purposes of that subsection by reference to the opinion of a person specified in the regulations, or of a person chosen in a manner determined in accordance with the regulations.

(5) The requirements which (subject to subsection (6)) may be imposed by conditions contained in an approval in accordance with the arrangements include—

(a) requirements to provide information to such persons, in such form, at such times and in response to such requests as may be specified in or determined under the terms of the condition;

(b) requirements that impose obligations that will continue or recur notwithstanding the withdrawal (in whole or in part) of the approval;

(c) requirements framed by reference to the opinion or directions of a person specified in or chosen in accordance with provision contained in the conditions.

(6) Nothing in the arrangements shall authorise the imposition, by conditions contained in an approval, of any requirements for—

(a) the provision of information, or

(b) the maintenance of a procedure for handling complaints or disputes, in relation to any matter other than one appearing to the Secretary of State to be relevant to the matters mentioned in subsection (3)(a) to (d).

(7) Any requirement to provide information that is imposed in accordance with the arrangements on any person by the conditions of his approval shall be enforceable at the suit or instance of the Secretary of State.

(8) Where any arrangements under this section so provide, a person who—

(a) seeks an approval under the arrangements,

(b) applies for a modification of such an approval,

(c) is for the time being approved under the arrangements, or

(d) has his approval under the arrangements modified wholly or partly in consequence of an application made by him, shall pay to the Secretary of State, at such time or times as may be prescribed, such fee or fees as may be prescribed in relation to that time or those times.

(9) Sums received by the Secretary of State by virtue of subsection (8) shall be paid into the Consolidated Fund.

(10) For the purposes of subsection (1) cryptography support services are provided in the United Kingdom if—

(a) they are provided from premises in the United Kingdom;

(b) they are provided to a person who is in the United Kingdom when he makes use of the services; or

(c) they are provided to a person who makes use of the services for the purposes of a business carried on in the United Kingdom or from premises in the United Kingdom.

3 Delegation of approval functions

(1) The Secretary of State may appoint any person to carry out, in his place, such of his functions under the preceding provisions of this Part (other than any power of his to make regulations) as may be specified in the appointment.

(2) An appointment under this section—

(a) shall have effect only to such extent, and subject to such conditions, as may be set out in the appointment; and

(b) may be revoked or varied at any time by a notice given by the Secretary of State to the appointed person.

(3) A person appointed under this section shall, in the carrying out of the functions specified in his appointment, comply with all such general directions as may be given to him from time to time by the Secretary of State.

(4) Subject to any order under subsection (5) and to any directions given by the Secretary of State, where a body established by or under any enactment or the holder of any office created by or under any enactment is appointed to carry out any functions of the Secretary of State under this Part—

(a) the enactments relating to the functions of that body or office shall have effect as if the functions of that body or office included the functions specified in the appointment; and

(b) the body or office-holder shall be taken to have power to do anything which is calculated to facilitate, or is incidental or conducive to, the carrying out of the functions so specified.

(5) The Secretary of State may, by order made by statutory instrument, provide for enactments relating to any such body or office as is mentioned in subsection (4) to have effect, so far as appears to him appropriate for purposes connected with the carrying out of functions that have been or may be conferred on the body or office-holder under this section, with such modifications as may be provided for in the order.

(6) An order shall not be made under subsection (5) unless a draft of it has first been laid before Parliament and approved by a resolution of each House.

(7) It shall be the duty of the Secretary of State to secure—

(a) that any appointment made under this section is published in such manner as he considers best calculated to bring it to the attention of persons likely to be interested in it;

(b) that any variation or revocation of such an appointment is also so published; and

(c) that the time fixed for any notice varying or revoking such an appointment to take effect allows a reasonable period after the giving of the notice for the making of any necessary incidental or transitional arrangements.

(8) Nothing in this section, or in anything done under this section, shall prejudice—

(a) any power of the Secretary of State, apart from this Act, to exercise functions through a Minister or official in his department;

(b) any power of any person by virtue of subsection (4), or by virtue of an order under subsection (5), to act on behalf of a body or office-holder in connection with the carrying out of any function;

(c) any provision by virtue of section 2(4) or (5)(c) that imposes a requirement by reference to the opinion of any person or determines the manner of choosing a person whose opinion is to be referred to.

4 Restrictions on disclosure of information

(1) Subject to the following provisions of this section, no information which—

(a) has been obtained under or by virtue of the provisions of this Part, and

(b) relates to the private affairs of any individual or to any particular business, shall, during the lifetime of that individual or so long as that business continues to be carried on, be disclosed without the consent of that individual or the person for the time being carrying on that business.

(2) Subsection (1) does not apply to any disclosure of information which is made—

(a) for the purpose of facilitating the carrying out of any functions under this Part, or any prescribed functions, of the Secretary of State or a person appointed under section 3;

(b) for the purpose of facilitating the carrying out of any functions of a local weights and measures authority in Great Britain;

(c) for the purpose of facilitating the carrying out of prescribed public functions of any person;

(d) in connection with the investigation of any criminal offence or for the purposes of any criminal proceedings;

(e) for the purposes of any civil proceedings which—

(i) relate to the provision of cryptography support services; and

(ii) are proceedings to which a person approved in accordance with arrangements under section 2 is a party; or

(f) in pursuance of a Community obligation.

(3) In subsection (2)(a) the reference to functions under this Part does not include a reference to any power of the Secretary of State to make regulations.

(4) In subsection (2)(c) 'public functions' includes any function conferred by or in accordance with any provision contained in or made under any enactment or Community legislation.

(5) If information is disclosed to the public in circumstances in which the disclosure does not contravene this section, this section shall not prevent its further disclosure by any person.

(6) Any person who discloses any information in contravention of this section shall be guilty of an offence and liable—

(a) on summary conviction, to a fine not exceeding the statutory maximum;

(b) on conviction on indictment, to imprisonment for a term not exceeding two years or a fine, or to both.

5 Regulations under Part I

(1) In this Part 'prescribed' means prescribed by regulations made by the Secretary of State, or determined in such manner as may be provided for in any such regulations.

(2) The powers of the Secretary of State to make regulations under this Part shall be exercisable by statutory instrument, which (except in the case of the initial regulations) shall be subject to annulment in pursuance of a resolution of either House of Parliament.

(3) The initial regulations shall not be made unless a draft of them has been laid before Parliament and approved by a resolution of each House.

(4) In this section 'the initial regulations' means the regulations made on the first occasion on which the Secretary of State exercises his powers to make regulations under this Part.

(5) Before making any regulations by virtue of section 2(3)(a) or (b) the Secretary of State shall consult—

(a) such persons appearing to him to be likely to be affected by those regulations, and

(b) such persons appearing to him to be representative of persons likely to be so affected,

as he thinks fit.

(6) Regulations made by the Secretary of State under any provision of this Part—

(a) may make different provision for different cases; and

(b)   may contain such incidental, supplemental, consequential and transitional provision as the Secretary of State thinks fit.

6   Provision of cryptography support services

(1)   In this Part 'cryptography support service' means any service which is provided to the senders or recipients of electronic communications, or to those storing electronic data, and is designed to facilitate the use of cryptographic techniques for the purpose of—

(a)   securing that such communications or data can be accessed, or can be put into an intelligible form, only by certain persons; or

(b)   securing that the authenticity or integrity of such communications or data is capable of being ascertained.

(2)   References in this Part to the provision of a cryptography support service do not include references to the supply of, or of any right to use, computer software or computer hardware except where the supply is integral to the provision of cryptography support services not consisting in such a supply.

PART II
FACILITATION OF ELECTRONIC COMMERCE, DATA STORAGE, ETC

7   Electronic signatures and related certificates

(1)   In any legal proceedings—

(a)   an electronic signature incorporated into or logically associated with a particular electronic communication or particular electronic data, and

(b)   the certification by any person of such a signature,

shall each be admissible in evidence in relation to any question as to the authenticity of the communication or data or as to the integrity of the communication or data.

(2)   For the purposes of this section an electronic signature is so much of anything in electronic form as—

(a)   is incorporated into or otherwise logically associated with any electronic communication or electronic data; and

(b)   purports to be so incorporated or associated for the purpose of being used in establishing the authenticity of the communication or data, the integrity of the communication or data, or both.

(3)   For the purposes of this section an electronic signature incorporated into or associated with a particular electronic communication or particular electronic data is certified by any person if that person (whether before or after the making of the communication) has made a statement confirming that—

(a)   the signature,

(b)   a means of producing, communicating or verifying the signature, or

(c)   a procedure applied to the signature,

is (either alone or in combination with other factors) a valid means of establishing the authenticity of the communication or data, the integrity of the communication or data, or both.

8   Power to modify legislation

(1)   Subject to subsection (3), the appropriate Minister may by order made by statutory instrument modify the provisions of—

(a)   any enactment or subordinate legislation, or

(b)   any scheme, licence, authorisation or approval issued, granted or given by or under any enactment or subordinate legislation,

in such manner as he may think fit for the purpose of authorising or facilitating the use of electronic communications or electronic storage (instead of other forms of communication or storage) for any purpose mentioned in subsection (2).

(2)   Those purposes are—

(a)   the doing of anything which under any such provisions is required to be or may be done or evidenced in writing or otherwise using a document, notice or instrument;

(b)   the doing of anything which under any such provisions is required to be or may be done by post or other specified means of delivery;

(c)   the doing of anything which under any such provisions is required to be or may be authorised by a person's signature or seal, or is required to be delivered as a deed or witnessed;

(d)   the making of any statement or declaration which under any such provisions is required to be made under oath or to be contained in a statutory declaration;

(e)   the keeping, maintenance or preservation, for the purposes or in pursuance of any such provisions, of any account, record, notice, instrument or other document;

(f)   the provision, production or publication under any such provisions of any information or other matter;

(g)   the making of any payment that is required to be or may be made under any such provisions.

(3)   The appropriate Minister shall not make an order under this section authorising the use of electronic communications or electronic storage for any purpose, unless he considers that the authorisation is such that the extent (if any) to which records of things done for that purpose will be available will be no less satisfactory in cases where use is made of electronic communications or electronic storage than in other cases.

(4)   Without prejudice to the generality of subsection (1), the power to make an order under this section shall include power to make an order containing any of the following provisions—

(a)   provision as to the electronic form to be taken by any electronic communications or electronic storage the use of which is authorised by an order under this section;

(b)   provision imposing conditions subject to which the use of electronic communications or electronic storage is so authorised;

(c)   provision, in relation to cases in which any such conditions are not satisfied, for treating anything for the purposes of which the use of such communications or storage is so authorised as not having been done;

(d)   provision, in connection with anything so authorised, for a person to be able to refuse to accept receipt of something in electronic form except in such circumstances as may be specified in or determined under the order;

(e)   provision, in connection with any use of electronic communications so authorised, for intermediaries to be used, or to be capable of being used, for the transmission of any data or for establishing the authenticity or integrity of any data;

(f)   provision, in connection with any use of electronic storage so authorised, for persons satisfying such conditions as may be specified in or determined under the regulations to carry out functions in relation to the storage;

(g)   provision, in relation to cases in which the use of electronic communications or electronic storage is so authorised, for the determination of any of the matters mentioned in subsection (5), or as to the manner in which they may be proved in legal proceedings;

(h)   provision, in relation to cases in which fees or charges are or may be imposed in connection with anything for the purposes of which the use of electronic communications or electronic storage is so authorised, for different fees or charges to apply where use is made of such communications or storage;

(i)   provision, in relation to any criminal or other liabilities that may arise (in respect of the making of false or misleading statements or otherwise) in connection with anything for the purposes of which the use of electronic communications or electronic storage is so authorised, for corresponding liabilities to arise in corresponding circumstances where use is made of such communications or storage;

(j)   provision requiring persons to prepare and keep records in connection with any use of electronic communications or electronic storage which is so authorised;

(k)   provision requiring the production of the contents of any records kept in accordance with an order under this section;

(l)   provision for a requirement imposed by virtue of paragraph (j) or (k) to be enforceable at the suit or instance of such person as may be specified in or determined in accordance with the order;

(m)   any such provision, in relation to electronic communications or electronic storage the use of which is authorised otherwise than by an order under this section, as corresponds to any provision falling within any of the preceding paragraphs that may be made where it is such an order that authorises the use of the communications or storage.

(5)   The matters referred to in subsection (4)(g) are—

(a)   whether a thing has been done using an electronic communication or electronic storage;

(b)   the time at which, or date on which, a thing done using any such communication or storage was done;

(c)   the place where a thing done using such communication or storage was done;

(d)   the person by whom such a thing was done; and

(e)   the contents, authenticity or integrity of any electronic data.

(6)   An order under this section—

(a)   shall not (subject to paragraph (b)) require the use of electronic communications or electronic storage for any purpose; but

(b)   may make provision that a period of notice specified in the order must expire before effect is given to a variation or withdrawal of an election or other decision which—

(i)   has been made for the purposes of such an order; and

(ii)   is an election or decision to make use of electronic communications or electronic storage.

(7)   The matters in relation to which provision may be made by an order under this section do not include any matter under the care and management of the Commissioners of Inland Revenue or any matter under the care and management of the Commissioners of Customs and Excise.

(8)   In this section references to doing anything under the provisions of any enactment include references to doing it under the provisions of any subordinate legislation the power to make which is conferred by that enactment.

9   Section 8 orders

(1)   In this Part 'the appropriate Minister' means (subject to subsections (2) and (7) and section 10(1))—

(a)   in relation to any matter with which a department of the Secretary of State is concerned, the Secretary of State;

(b)   in relation to any matter with which the Treasury is concerned, the Treasury; and

(c)   in relation to any matter with which any Government department other than a department of the Secretary of State or the Treasury is concerned, the Minister in charge of the other department.

(2)   Where in the case of any matter—

(a)   that matter falls within more than one paragraph of subsection (1),

(b)   there is more than one such department as is mentioned in paragraph (c) of that subsection that is concerned with that matter, or

(c)   both paragraphs (a) and (b) of this subsection apply, references, in relation to that matter, to the appropriate Minister are references to any one or more of the appropriate Ministers acting (in the case of more than one) jointly.

(3) Subject to subsection (4) and section 10(6), a statutory instrument containing an order under section 8 shall be subject to annulment in pursuance of a resolution of either House of Parliament.

(4) Subsection (3) does not apply in the case of an order a draft of which has been laid before Parliament and approved by a resolution of each House.

(5) An order under section 8 may—

(a) provide for any conditions or requirements imposed by such an order to be framed by reference to the directions of such persons as may be specified in or determined in accordance with the order;

(b) provide that any such condition or requirement is to be satisfied only where a person so specified or determined is satisfied as to specified matters.

(6) The provision made by such an order may include—

(a) different provision for different cases;

(b) such exceptions and exclusions as the person making the order may think fit; and

(c) any such incidental, supplemental, consequential and transitional provision as he may think fit;

and the provision that may be made by virtue of paragraph (c) includes provision modifying any enactment or subordinate legislation or any scheme, licence, authorisation or approval issued, granted or given by or under any enactment or subordinate legislation.

(7) In the case of any matter which is not one of the reserved matters within the meaning of the Scotland Act 1998 or in respect of which functions are, by virtue of section 63 of that Act, exercisable by the Scottish Ministers instead of by or concurrently with a Minister of the Crown, this section and section 8 shall apply to Scotland subject to the following modifications—

(a) subsections (1) and (2) of this section are omitted;

(b) any reference to the appropriate Minister is to be read as a reference to the Secretary of State;

(c) any power of the Secretary of State, by virtue of paragraph (b), to make an order under section 8 may also be exercised by the Scottish Ministers with the consent of the Secretary of State; and

(d) where the Scottish Ministers make an order under section 8—

(i) any reference to the Secretary of State (other than a reference in this subsection) shall be construed as a reference to the Scottish Ministers; and

(ii) any reference to Parliament or to a House of Parliament shall be construed as a reference to the Scottish Parliament.

[10   *Modifications in relation to Welsh matters*]

PART III
MISCELLANEOUS AND SUPPLEMENTAL

Telecommunications licences

[*Amends Telecommunications Act 1984.*]

Supplemental

13   Ministerial expenditure etc

There shall be paid out of money provided by Parliament—

(a) any expenditure incurred by the Secretary of State for or in connection with the carrying out of his functions under this Act; and

(b)   any increase attributable to this Act in the sums which are payable out of money so provided under any other Act.

14   Prohibition on key escrow requirements

(1)   Subject to subsection (2), nothing in this Act shall confer any power on any Minister of the Crown, on the Scottish Ministers, on the National Assembly for Wales or on any person appointed under section 3—

(a)   by conditions of an approval under Part I, or

(b)   by any regulations or order under this Act,

to impose a requirement on any person to deposit a key for electronic data with another person.

(2)   Subsection (1) shall not prohibit the imposition by an order under section 8 of—

(a)   a requirement to deposit a key for electronic data with the intended recipient of electronic communications comprising the data; or

(b)   a requirement for arrangements to be made, in cases where a key for data is not deposited with another person, which otherwise secure that the loss of a key, or its becoming unusable, does not have the effect that the information contained in a record kept in pursuance of any provision made by or under any enactment or subordinate legislation becomes inaccessible or incapable of being put into an intelligible form.

(3)   In this section 'key', in relation to electronic data, means any code, password, algorithm, key or other data the use of which (with or without other keys)—

(a)   allows access to the electronic data, or

(b)   facilitates the putting of the electronic data into an intelligible form;

and references in this section to depositing a key for electronic data with a person include references to doing anything that has the effect of making the key available to that person.

15   General interpretation

(1)   In this Act, except in so far as the context otherwise requires—

'document' includes a map, plan, design, drawing, picture or other image;

'communication' includes a communication comprising sounds or images or both and a communication effecting a payment;

'electronic communication' means a communication transmitted (whether from one person to another, from one device to another or from a person to a device or vice versa)—

(a)   by means of a telecommunication system (within the meaning of the Telecommunications Act 1984); or

(b)   by other means but while in an electronic form;

'enactment' includes—

(a)   an enactment passed after the passing of this Act,

(b)   an enactment comprised in an Act of the Scottish Parliament, and

(c)   an enactment contained in Northern Ireland legislation,

but does not include an enactment contained in Part I or II of this Act;

'modification' includes any alteration, addition or omission, and cognate expressions shall be construed accordingly;

'record' includes an electronic record; and

'subordinate legislation' means—

(a)   any subordinate legislation (within the meaning of the Interpretation Act 1978);

(b)   any instrument made under an Act of the Scottish Parliament; or

(c)   any statutory rules (within the meaning of the Statutory Rules (Northern Ireland) Order 1979).

(2)   In this Act—

(a)   references to the authenticity of any communication or data are references to any one or more of the following—

(i) whether the communication or data comes from a particular person or other source;

(ii) whether it is accurately timed and dated;

(iii) whether it is intended to have legal effect; and

(b) references to the integrity of any communication or data are references to whether there has been any tampering with or other modification of the communication or data.

(3) References in this Act to something's being put into an intelligible form include references to its being restored to the condition in which it was before any encryption or similar process was applied to it.

16 Short title, commencement, extent

(1) This Act may be cited as the Electronic Communications Act 2000.

(2) Part I of this Act and sections 7, 11 and 12 shall come into force on such day as the Secretary of State may by order made by statutory instrument appoint; and different days may be appointed under this subsection for different purposes.

(3) An order shall not be made for bringing any of Part I of this Act into force for any purpose unless a draft of the order has been laid before Parliament and approved by a resolution of each House.

(4) If no order for bringing Part I of this Act into force has been made under subsection (2) by the end of the period of five years beginning with the day on which this Act is passed, that Part shall, by virtue of this subsection, be repealed at the end of that period.

(5) This Act extends to Northern Ireland.

<h2 style="text-align:center">CIVIL PARTNERSHIP ACT 2004
(2004, c 33)</h2>

128 Promise or agreement to enter into civil partnership

No promise or agreement to enter into civil partnership creates any rights or obligations under the law of Scotland; and no action for breach of such a promise or agreement may be brought in any court in Scotland, whatever the law applicable to the promise or agreement.

<h2 style="text-align:center">GAMBLING ACT 2005
(2005, c 19)</h2>

PART 1
INTERPRETATION OF KEY CONCEPTS

Principal concepts

3 Gambling

In this Act 'gambling' means—

(a) gaming (within the meaning of section 6),

(b) betting (within the meaning of section 9), and

(c) participating in a lottery (within the meaning of section 14 and subject to section 15).

Gaming

6 Gaming & game of chance

(1) In this Act 'gaming' means playing a game of chance for a prize.

(2) In this Act 'game of chance'—

(a) includes—

(i) a game that involves both an element of chance and an element of skill,

(ii)   a game that involves an element of chance that can be eliminated by superlative skill, and

(iii)   a game that is presented as involving an element of chance, but

(b)   does not include a sport.

(3)   For the purposes of this Act a person plays a game of chance if he participates in a game of chance—

(a)   whether or not there are other participants in the game, and

(b)   whether or not a computer generates images or data taken to represent the actions of other participants in the game.

(4)   For the purposes of this Act a person plays a game of chance for a prize—

(a)   if he plays a game of chance and thereby acquires a chance of winning a prize, and

(b)   whether or not he risks losing anything at the game.

(5)   In this Act 'prize' in relation to gaming (except in the context of a gaming machine)—

(a)   means money or money's worth, and

(b)   includes both a prize provided by a person organising gaming and winnings of money staked.

(6)   The Secretary of State may by regulations provide that a specified activity, or an activity carried on in specified circumstances, is or is not to be treated for the purposes of this Act as—

(a)   a game;

(b)   a game of chance;

(c)   a sport.

Betting

9   Betting: general

(1)   In this Act 'betting' means making or accepting a bet on—

(a)   the outcome of a race, competition or other event or process,

(b)   the likelihood of anything occurring or not occurring, or

(c)   whether anything is or is not true.

(2)   A transaction that relates to the outcome of a race, competition or other event or process may be a bet within the meaning of subsection (1) despite the facts that—

(a)   the race, competition, event or process has already occurred or been completed, and

(b)   one party to the transaction knows the outcome.

(3)   A transaction that relates to the likelihood of anything occurring or not occurring may be a bet within the meaning of subsection (1) despite the facts that—

(a)   the thing has already occurred or failed to occur, and

(b)   one party to the transaction knows that the thing has already occurred or failed to occur.

Lottery

14   Lottery

(1)   For the purposes of this Act an arrangement is a lottery, irrespective of how it is described, if it satisfies one of the descriptions of lottery in subsections (2) and (3).

(2)   An arrangement is a simple lottery if—

(a)   persons are required to pay in order to participate in the arrangement,

(b)   in the course of the arrangement one or more prizes are allocated to one or more members of a class, and

(c)   the prizes are allocated by a process which relies wholly on chance.

(3)   An arrangement is a complex lottery if—

(a)   persons are required to pay in order to participate in the arrangement,

(b)   in the course of the arrangement one or more prizes are allocated to one or more members of a class,

(c)   the prizes are allocated by a series of processes, and

(d)   the first of those processes relies wholly on chance.

(4)   In this Act 'prize' in relation to lotteries includes any money, articles or services—

(a)   whether or not described as a prize, and

(b)   whether or not consisting wholly or partly of money paid, or articles or services provided, by the members of the class among whom the prize is allocated.

(5)   A process which requires persons to exercise skill or judgment or to display knowledge shall be treated for the purposes of this section as relying wholly on chance if—

(a)   the requirement cannot reasonably be expected to prevent a significant proportion of persons who participate in the arrangement of which the process forms part from receiving a prize, and

(b)   the requirement cannot reasonably be expected to prevent a significant proportion of persons who wish to participate in that arrangement from doing so.

(6)   Schedule 2 makes further provision about when an arrangement is to be or not to be treated for the purposes of this section as requiring persons to pay.

(7)   The Secretary of State may by regulations provide that an arrangement of a specified kind is to be or not to be treated as a lottery for the purposes of this Act; and—

(a)   the power in this subsection is not constrained by subsections (1) to (6) or Schedule 2, and

(b)   regulations under this subsection may amend other provisions of this section or Schedule 2.

15   National Lottery

(1)   Participating in a lottery which forms part of the National Lottery is not gambling for the purposes of this Act (despite section 3(c) but subject to subsections (2) and (3) below).

(2)   Participating in a lottery which forms part of the National Lottery is gambling for the purposes of—

(a)   section 42, and

(b)   section 335.

(3)   Where participating in a lottery which forms part of the National Lottery would also constitute gaming within the meaning of section 6, it shall be treated as gaming for the purposes of this Act if and only if a person participating in the lottery is required to participate in, or to be successful in, more than three processes before becoming entitled to a prize.

(4)   Participating in a lottery which forms part of the National Lottery shall not be treated as betting for the purposes of this Act where it would—

(a)   satisfy the definition of pool betting in section 12, or

(b)   satisfy the definition of betting in section 9 by virtue of section 11.

(5)   Schedule 3 shall have effect.

PART 17

LEGALITY AND ENFORCEMENT OF GAMBLING CONTRACTS

. . .

335   Enforceability of gambling contracts

(1)   The fact that a contract relates to gambling shall not prevent its enforcement.

(2)   Subsection (1) is without prejudice to any rule of law preventing the enforcement of a contract on the grounds of unlawfulness (other than a rule relating specifically to gambling).

PART 18
MISCELLANEOUS AND GENERAL

. . .

361   Extent

(1)   The following provisions of this Act extend to England and Wales, Scotland and Northern Ireland—

(a)   section 43,

(b)   section 331, and

(c)   section 340 (and the related entry in Schedule 17).

(2)   The other provisions of this Act shall extend only to—

(a)   England and Wales, and

(b)   Scotland.

(3)   This section is subject to section 356.

PART II
STATUTORY INSTRUMENTS

PROVISION AND USE OF WORK EQUIPMENT REGULATIONS 1998
(SI 1998/2306)

2 Interpretation

(1)   In these Regulations, unless the context otherwise requires—

'the 1974 Act' means the Health and Safety at Work etc Act 1974;

'employer' except in regulation 3(2) and (3) includes a person to whom the requirements imposed by the Regulations apply by virtue of regulation 3(3)(a) and (b);

'essential requirements' means requirements described in regulation 10(1);

'the Executive' means the Health and Safety Executive;

'inspection' in relation to an inspection under paragraph (1) or (2) of regulation 6—

(a)   means such visual or more rigorous inspection by a competent person as is appropriate for the purpose described in the paragraph;

(b)   where it is appropriate to carry out testing for the purpose, includes testing the nature and extent of which are appropriate for the purpose;

'power press' means a press or press brake for the working of metal by means of tools, or for die proving, which is power driven and which embodies a flywheel and clutch;

'thorough examination' in relation to a thorough examination under paragraph (1), (2), (3) or (4) of regulation 32—

(a)   means a thorough examination by a competent person;

(b)   includes testing the nature and extent of which are appropriate for the purpose described in the paragraph;

'use' in relation to work equipment means any activity involving work equipment and includes starting, stopping, programming, setting, transporting, repairing, modifying, maintaining, servicing and cleaning;

'work equipment' means any machinery, appliance, apparatus, tool or installation for use at work (whether exclusively or not);

and related expressions shall be construed accordingly.

4 Suitability of work equipment

(1)   Every employer shall ensure that work equipment is so constructed or adapted as to be suitable for the purpose for which it is used or provided.

(2)   In selecting work equipment, every employer shall have regard to the working conditions and to the risks to the health and safety of persons which exist in the premises or undertaking in which that work equipment is to be used and any additional risk posed by the use of that work equipment.

(3)   Every employer shall ensure that work equipment is used only for operations for which, and under conditions for which, it is suitable.

(4)   In this regulation 'suitable' [—

(a)   subject to paragraph (b), means suitable in any respect which it is reasonably foreseeable will affect the health and safety of any person; . . .]

5 Maintenance

(1)   Every employer shall ensure that work equipment is maintained in an efficient state, in efficient working order and in good repair.

(2)   Every employer shall ensure that where any machinery has a maintenance log, the log is kept up to date.

6 Inspection

(1)   Every employer shall ensure that, where the safety of work equipment depends on the installation conditions, it is inspected—

  (a)   after installation and before being put into service for the first time; or

  (b)   after assembly at a new site or in a new location,

to ensure that it has been installed correctly and is safe to operate.

(2)   Every employer shall ensure that work equipment exposed to conditions causing deterioration which is liable to result in dangerous situations is inspected—

  (a)   at suitable intervals; and

  (b)   each time that exceptional circumstances which are liable to jeopardise the safety of the work equipment have occurred,

to ensure that health and safety conditions are maintained and that any deterioration can be detected and remedied in good time.

(3)   Every employer shall ensure that the result of an inspection made under this regulation is recorded and kept until the next inspection under this regulation is recorded.

(4)   Every employer shall ensure that no work equipment—

  (a)   leaves his undertaking; or

  (b)   if obtained from the undertaking of another person, is used in his undertaking, unless it is accompanied by physical evidence that the last inspection required to be carried out under this regulation has been carried out.

7 Specific risks

(1)   Where the use of work equipment is likely to involve a specific risk to health or safety, every employer shall ensure that—

  (a)   the use of that work equipment is restricted to those persons given the task of using it; and

  (b)   repairs, modifications, maintenance or servicing of that work equipment is restricted to those persons who have been specifically designated to perform operations of that description (whether or not also authorised to perform other operations).

(2)   The employer shall ensure that the persons designated for the purposes of sub-paragraph (b) of paragraph (1) have received adequate training related to any operations in respect of which they have been so designated.

8 Information and instructions

(1)   Every employer shall ensure that all persons who use work equipment have available to them adequate health and safety information and, where appropriate, written instructions pertaining to the use of the work equipment.

(2)   Every employer shall ensure that any of his employees who supervises or manages the use of work equipment has available to him adequate health and safety information and, where appropriate, written instructions pertaining to the use of the work equipment.

(3)   Without prejudice to the generality of paragraph (1) or (2), the information and instructions required by either of those paragraphs shall include information and, where appropriate, written instructions on—

  (a)   the conditions in which and the methods by which the work equipment may be used;

  (b)   foreseeable abnormal situations and the action to be taken if such a situation were to occur; and

(c)   any conclusions to be drawn from experience in using the work equipment.

(4)   Information and instructions required by this regulation shall be readily comprehensive to those concerned.

9   Training

(1)   Every employer shall ensure that all persons who use work equipment have received adequate training for purposes of health and safety, including training in the methods which may be adopted when using the work equipment, any risks which such use may entail and precautions to be taken.

(2)   Every employer shall ensure that any of his employees who supervises or manages the use of work equipment has received adequate training for purposes of health and safety, including training in the methods which may be adopted when using the work equipment, any risks which such use may entail and precautions to be taken.

10   Conformity with Community requirements

(1)   Every employer shall ensure that an item of work equipment has been designed and constructed in compliance with any essential requirements, that is to say requirements relating to its design or construction in any of the instruments listed in Schedule 1 (being instruments which give effect to Community directives concerning the safety of products).

(2)   Where an essential requirement applied to the design or construction of an item of work equipment, the requirements of regulations 11 to 19 and 22 to 29 shall apply in respect of that item only to the extent that the essential requirement did not apply to it.

(3)   This regulation applies to items of work equipment provided for use in the premises or undertaking of the employer for the first time after 31 December 1992.

11   Dangerous parts of machinery

(1)   Every employer shall ensure that measures are taken in accordance with paragraph (2) which are effective—

(a)   to prevent access to any dangerous part of machinery or to any rotating stock-bar; or

(b)   to stop the movement of any dangerous part of machinery or rotating stock-bar before any part of a person enters a danger zone.

(2)   The measures required by paragraph (1) shall consist of—

(a)   the provision of fixed guards enclosing every dangerous part or rotating stock-bar where and to the extent that it is practicable to do so, but where or to the extent that it is not, then

(b)   the provision of other guards or protection devices where and to the extent that it is practicable to do so, but where or to the extent that it is not, then

(c)   the provision of jigs, holders, push-sticks or similar protection appliances used in conjunction with the machinery where and to the extent that it is practicable to do so, but where or to the extent that it is not, then

(d)   the provision of information, instruction, training and supervision.

(3)   All guards and protection devices provided under sub-paragraphs (a) or (b) of paragraph (2) shall—

(a)   be suitable for the purpose for which they are provided;

(b)   be of good construction, sound material and adequate strength;

(c)   be maintained in an efficient state, in efficient working order and in good repair;

(d)   not give rise to any increased risk to health or safety;

(e)   not be easily bypassed or disabled;

(f)   be situated at sufficient distance from the danger zone;

(g)   not unduly restrict the view of the operating cycle of the machinery, where such a view is necessary;

(h)   be so constructed or adapted that they allow operations necessary to fit or replace parts and for maintenance work, restricting access so that it is allowed only to the area where the work is to be carried out and, if possible, without having to dismantle the guard or protection device.

(4)   All protection appliances provided under sub-paragraph (c) of paragraph (2) shall comply with sub-paragraphs (a) to (d) and (g) of paragraph (3).

(5)   In this regulation—

'danger zone' means any zone in or around machinery in which a person is exposed to a risk to health or safety from contact with a dangerous part of machinery or a rotating stock-bar;

'stock-bar' means any part of a stock-bar which projects beyond the head-stock of a lathe.

12   Protection against specified hazards

(1)   Every employer shall take measures to ensure that the exposure of a person using work equipment to any risk to his health or safety from any hazard specified in paragraph (3) is either prevented, or, where that is not reasonably practicable, adequately controlled.

(2)   The measures required by paragraph (1) shall—

(a)   be measures other than the provision of personal protective equipment or of information, instruction, training and supervision, so far as is reasonably practicable; and

(b)   include, where appropriate, measures to minimise the effects of the hazard as well as to reduce the likelihood of the hazard occurring.

(3)   The hazards referred to in paragraph (1) are—

(a)   any article or substance falling or being ejected from work equipment;

(b)   rupture or disintegration of parts of work equipment;

(c)   work equipment catching fire or overheating;

(d)   the unintended or premature discharge of any article or of any gas, dust, liquid, vapour or other substance which, in each case, is produced, used or stored in the work equipment;

(e)   the unintended or premature explosion of the work equipment or any article or substance produced, used or stored in it.

(4)   For the purposes of this regulation 'adequately' means adequately having regard only to the nature of the hazard and the nature and degree of exposure to the risk.

(5)   This regulation shall not apply where any of the following Regulations apply in respect of any risk to a person's health or safety for which such Regulations require measures to be taken to prevent or control such risk, namely—

(a)   the Ionising Radiations Regulations 1985;

(b)   the Control of Asbestos at Work Regulations 1987;

(c)   the Control of Substances Hazardous to Health Regulations 1994;

(d)   the Noise at Work Regulations 1989;

(e)   the Construction (Head Protection) Regulations 1989;

(f)   the Control of Lead at Work Regulations 1998.

13   High or very low temperature

Every employer shall ensure that work equipment, parts of work equipment and any article or substance produced, used or stored in work equipment which, in each case, is at a high or very low temperature shall have protection where appropriate so as to prevent injury to any person by burn, scald or sear.

14   Controls for starting or making a significant change in operating conditions

(1)   Every employer shall ensure that, where appropriate, work equipment is provided with one or more controls for the purposes of—

(a)   starting the work equipment (including re-starting after a stoppage for any reason); or

(b)   controlling any change in the speed, pressure or other operating conditions of the work equipment where such conditions after the change result in risk to health and safety which is greater than or of a different nature from such risks before the change.

(2)   Subject to paragraph (3), every employer shall ensure that, where a control is required by paragraph (1), it shall not be possible to perform any operation mentioned in sub-paragraph (a) or (b) of that paragraph except by a deliberate action on such control.

(3)   Paragraph (1) shall not apply to re-starting or changing operating conditions as a result of the normal operating cycle of an automatic device.

15   Stop controls

(1)   Every employer shall ensure that, where appropriate, work equipment is provided with one or more readily accessible controls the operation of which will bring the work equipment to a safe condition in a safe manner.

(2)   Any control required by paragraph (1) shall bring the work equipment to a complete stop where necessary for reasons of health and safety.

(3)   Any control required by paragraph (1) shall, if necessary for reasons of health and safety, switch off all sources of energy after stopping the functioning of the work equipment.

(4)   Any control required by paragraph (1) shall operate in priority to any control which starts or changes the operating conditions of the work equipment.

16   Emergency stop controls

(1)   Every employer shall ensure that, where appropriate, work equipment is provided with one or more readily accessible emergency stop controls unless it is not necessary by reason of the nature of the hazards and the time taken for the work equipment to come to a complete stop as a result of the action of any control provided by virtue of regulation 15(1).

(2)   Any control required by paragraph (1) shall operate in priority to any control required by regulation 15(1).

17   Controls

(1)   Every employer shall ensure that all controls for work equipment are clearly visible and identifiable, including by appropriate marking where necessary.

(2)   Except where necessary, the employer shall ensure that no control for work equipment is in a position where any person operating the control is exposed to a risk to his health or safety.

(3)   Every employer shall ensure where appropriate—

(a)   that, so far as is reasonably practicable, the operator of any control is able to ensure from the position of that control that no person is in a place where he would be exposed to any risk to his health or safety as a result of the operation of that control, but where or to the extent that it is not reasonably practicable;

(b)   that, so far as is reasonably practicable, systems of work are effective to ensure that, when work equipment is about to start, no person is in a place where he would be exposed to a risk to his health or safety as a result of the work equipment starting, but where neither of these is reasonably practicable;

(c)   that an audible, visible or other suitable warning is given by virtue of regulation 24 whenever work equipment is about to start,

(4)   Every employer shall take appropriate measures to ensure that any person who is in a place where he would be exposed to a risk to his health or safety as a result of the starting or stopping of work equipment has sufficient time and suitable means to avoid that risk.

18   Control systems

(1)   Every employer shall—

(a)   ensure, so far as is reasonably practicable, that all control systems of work equipment are safe; and

(b)   are chosen making due allowance for the failures, faults and constraints to be expected in the planned circumstances of use.

(2)   Without prejudice to the generality of paragraph (1), a control system shall not be safe unless—

(a)   its operation does not create any increased risk to health or safety;

(b)   it ensures, so far as is reasonably practicable, that any fault in or damage to any part of the control system or the loss of supply of any source of energy used by the work equipment cannot result in additional or increased risk to health or safety;

(c)   it does not impede the operation of any control required by regulation 15 or 16.

19   Isolation from sources of energy

(1)   Every employer shall ensure that where appropriate work equipment is provided with suitable means to isolate it from all its sources of energy.

(2)   Without prejudice to the generality of paragraph (1), the means mentioned in that paragraph shall not be suitable unless they are clearly identifiable and readily accessible.

(3)   Every employer shall take appropriate measures to ensure that re-connection of any energy source to work equipment does not expose any person using the work equipment to any risk to his health or safety.

20   Stability

Every employer shall ensure that work equipment or any part of work equipment is stabilised by clamping or otherwise where necessary for purposes of health or safety.

21   Lighting

Every employer shall ensure that suitable and sufficient lighting, which takes account of the operations to be carried out, is provided at any place where a person uses work equipment.

22   Maintenance operations

Every employer shall take appropriate measures to ensure that work equipment is so constructed or adapted that, so far as is reasonably practicable, maintenance operations which involve a risk to health or safety can be carried out while the work equipment is shut down, or in other cases—

(a)   maintenance operations can be carried out without exposing the person carrying them out to a risk to his health or safety; or

(b)   appropriate measures can be taken for the protection of any person carrying out maintenance operations which involve a risk to his health or safety.

23   Markings

Every employer shall ensure that work equipment is marked in a clearly visible manner with any marking appropriate for reasons of health and safety.

24   Warnings

(1)   Every employer shall ensure that work equipment incorporates any warnings or warning devices which are appropriate for reasons of health and safety.

(2)   Without prejudice to the generality of paragraph (1), warnings given by warning devices on work equipment shall not be appropriate unless they are unambiguous, easily perceived and easily understood.

EMPLOYERS' LIABILITY (COMPULSORY INSURANCE) REGULATIONS 1998
(SI 1998/2573)

1 Citation, commencement and interpretation

...

(2) In these Regulations—
'the 1969 Act' means the Employers' Liability (Compulsory Insurance) Act 1969;
...

2 Prohibition of certain conditions in policies of insurance

(1) For the purposes of the 1969 Act, there is prohibited in any contract of insurance any condition which provides (in whatever terms) that no liability (either generally or in respect of a particular claim) shall arise under the policy, or that any such liability so arising shall cease, if—

(a) some specified thing is done or omitted to be done after the happening of the event giving rise to a claim under the policy,

(b) the policy holder does not take reasonable care to protect his employees against the risk of bodily injury or disease in the course of their employment;

(c) the policy holder fails to comply with the requirements of any enactment for the protection of employees against the risk of bodily injury or disease in the course of their employment; or

(d) the policy holder does not keep specified records or fails to provide the insurer with or make available to him information from such records.

(2) For the purposes of the 1969 Act there is also prohibited in a policy of insurance any condition which requires—

(a) a relevant employee to pay; or

(b) an insured employer to pay the relevant employee,

the first amount of any claim or any aggregation of claims.

(3) Paragraphs (1) and (2) above do not prohibit for the purposes of the 1969 Act a condition in a policy of insurance which requires the employer to pay or contribute any sum to the insurer in respect of the satisfaction of any claim made under the contract of insurance by a relevant employee or any costs and expenses incurred in relation to any such claim.

3 Limit of amount of compulsory insurance

(1) Subject to paragraph (2) below, the amount for which an employer is required by the 1969 Act to insure and maintain insurance in respect of relevant employees under one or more policies of insurance shall be, or shall in aggregate be not less than £5 million in respect of—

(a) a claim relating to any one or more of those employees arising out of any one occurrence; and

(b) any costs and expenses incurred in relation to any such claim.

UNFAIR TERMS IN CONSUMER CONTRACTS REGULATIONS 1999
(SI 1999/2083)

3 Interpretation

(1) In these Regulations—

'the Community' means the European Community;

'consumer' means any natural person who, in contracts covered by these Regulations, is acting for purposes which are outside his trade, business or profession;

'court' in relation to England and Wales and Northern Ireland means a county court or the High Court, and in relation to Scotland, the Sheriff or the Court of Session;

'Director' means the Director General of Fair Trading;*

'EEA Agreement' means the Agreement on the European Economic Area signed at Oporto on 2nd May 1992 as adjusted by the protocol signed at Brussels on 17th March 1993;

'Member State' means a State which is a contracting party to the EEA Agreement;

'notified' means notified in writing;

'qualifying body' means a person specified in Schedule 1;

'seller or supplier' means any natural or legal person who, in contracts covered by these Regulations, is acting for purposes relating to his trade, business or profession, whether publicly owned or privately owned;

'unfair terms' means the contractual terms referred to in regulation 5.

[(1A)   The references—

(a)   in regulation 4(1) to a seller or a supplier, and

(b)   in regulation 8(1) to a seller or supplier,

include references to a distance supplier and to an intermediary.

(1B)   In paragraph (1A) and regulation 5(6)—

'distance supplier' means—

(a)   a supplier under a distance contract within the meaning of the Financial Services (Distance Marketing) Regulations 2004, or

(b)   a supplier of unsolicited financial services within regulation 15 of those Regulations; and

'intermediary' has the same meaning as in those Regulations.]

(2)   In the application of these Regulations to Scotland for references to an 'injunction' or an 'interim injunction' there shall be substituted references to an 'interdict' or 'interim interdict' respectively.

4   Terms to which these Regulations apply

(1)   These Regulations apply in relation to unfair terms in contracts concluded between a seller or a supplier and a consumer.

(2)   These Regulations do not apply to contractual terms which reflect—

(a)   mandatory statutory or regulatory provisions (including such provisions under the law of any Member State or in Community legislation having effect in the United Kingdom without further enactment);

(b)   the provisions or principles of international conventions to which the Member States or the Community are party.

5   Unfair terms

(1)   A contractual term which has not been individually negotiated shall be regarded as unfair if, contrary to the requirement of good faith, it causes a significant imbalance in the parties' rights and obligations arising under the contract, to the detriment of the consumer.

(2)   A term shall always be regarded as not having been individually negotiated where it has been drafted in advance and the consumer has therefore not been able to influence the substance of the term.

(3)   Notwithstanding that a specific term or certain aspects of it in a contract has been individually negotiated, these Regulations shall apply to the rest of a contract if an overall assessment of it indicates that it is a pre-formulated standard contract.

(4)   It shall be for any seller or supplier who claims that a term was individually negotiated to show that it was.

(5)   Schedule 2 to these Regulations contains an indicative and non-exhaustive list of the terms which may be regarded as unfair.

* All references to 'the Director' have effect as if they were references to 'the OFT': Enterprise Act 2002, s 2.

[(6)   Any contractual term providing that the consumer bears the burden of proof in respect of showing that the supplier complied with any or all of the obligations upon him resulting from the Directive and any rule or enactment implementing it shall always be regarded as unfair.

(7)   In paragraph (6)—
'the Directive' means Directive 2002/65/EC of the European Parliament and of the Council of 23 September 2002 concerning the distance marketing of consumer financial services and amending Council Directive 90/619/EEC and Directive 97/7/EC and 98/27/EC; and

'rule' means a rule made by the Financial Services Authority under the Financial Services and Markets Act 2000 or by a designated professional body within the meaning of section 326(2) of that Act.]

6   Assessment of unfair terms

(1)   Without prejudice to regulation 12, the unfairness of a contractual term shall be assessed, taking into account the nature of the goods or services for which the contract was concluded and by referring, at the time of conclusion of the contract, to all the circumstances attending the conclusion of the contract and to all the other terms of the contract or of another contract on which it is dependent.

(2)   In so far as it is in plain intelligible language, the assessment of fairness of a term shall not relate—
(a)   to the definition of the main subject matter of the contract, or
(b)   to the adequacy of the price or remuneration, as against the goods or services supplied in exchange.

7   Written contracts

(1)   A seller or supplier shall ensure that any written term of a contract is expressed in plain, intelligible language.

(2)   If there is doubt about the meaning of a written term, the interpretation which is most favourable to the consumer shall prevail but this rule shall not apply in proceedings brought under regulation 12.

8   Effect of unfair term

(1)   An unfair term in a contract concluded with a consumer by a seller or supplier shall not be binding on the consumer.

(2)   The contract shall continue to bind the parties if it is capable of continuing in existence without the unfair term.

9   Choice of law clauses

These Regulations shall apply notwithstanding any contract term which applies or purports to apply the law of a non-Member State, if the contract has a close connection with the territory of the Member States.

10   Complaints—consideration by Director

(1)   It shall be the duty of the Director to consider any complaint made to him that any contract term drawn up for general use is unfair, unless—
(a)   the complaint appears to the Director to be frivolous or vexatious; or
(b)   a qualifying body has notified the Director that it agrees to consider the complaint.

(2)   The Director shall give reasons for his decision to apply or not to apply, as the case may be, for an injunction under regulation 12 in relation to any complaint which these Regulations require him to consider.

(3)   In deciding whether or not to apply for an injunction in respect of a term which the Director considers to be unfair, he may, if he considers it appropriate to do so, have regard to any undertakings given to him by or on behalf of any person as to the continued use of such a term in contracts concluded with consumers.

11   Complaints—consideration by qualifying bodies

(1)   If a qualifying body specified in Part One of Schedule I notifies the Director

that it agrees to consider a complaint that any contract term drawn up for general use is unfair, it shall be under a duty to consider that complaint.

(2)   Regulation 10(2) and (3) shall apply to a qualifying body which is under a duty to consider a complaint as they apply to the Director.

12   Injunctions to prevent continued use of unfair terms

(1)   The Director or, subject to paragraph (2), any qualifying body may apply for an injunction (including an interim injunction) against any person appearing to the Director or that body to be using, or recommending use of, an unfair term drawn up for general use in contracts concluded with consumers.

(2)   A qualifying body may apply for an injunction only where—

(a)   it has notified the Director of its intention to apply at least fourteen days before the date on which the application is made, beginning with the date on which the notification was given; or

(b)   the Director consents to the application being made within a shorter period.

(3)   The court on an application under this regulation may grant an injunction on such terms as it thinks fit.

(4)   An injunction may relate not only to use of a particular contract term drawn up for general use but to any similar term, or a term having like effect, used or recommended for use by any person.

13   Powers of the Director and qualifying bodies to obtain documents and information

(1)   The Director may exercise the power conferred by this regulation for the purpose of—

(a)   facilitating his consideration of a complaint that a contract term drawn up for general use is unfair; or

(b)   ascertaining whether a person has complied with an undertaking or court order as to the continued use, or recommendation for use, of a term in contracts concluded with consumers.

(2)   A qualifying body specified in Part One of Schedule 1 may exercise the power conferred by this regulation for the purpose of—

(a)   facilitating its consideration of a complaint that a contract term drawn up for general use is unfair; or

(b)   ascertaining whether a person has complied with—

(i)   an undertaking given to it or to the court following an application by that body, or

(ii)   a court order made on an application by that body,

as to the continued use, or recommendation for use, of a term in contracts concluded with consumers.

(3)   The Director may require any person to supply to him, and a qualifying body specified in Part One of Schedule 1 may require any person to supply to it—

(a)   a copy of any document which that person has used or recommended for use, at the time the notice referred to in paragraph (4) below is given, as a pre-formulated standard contract in dealings with consumers;

(b)   information about the use, or recommendation for use, by that person of that document or any other such document in dealings with consumers.

(4)   The power conferred by this regulation is to be exercised by a notice in writing which may—

(a)   specify the way in which and the time within which it is to be complied with; and

(b)   be varied or revoked by a subsequent notice.

(5)   Nothing in this regulation compels a person to supply any document or information which he would be entitled to refuse to produce or give in civil proceedings before the court.

(6)   If a person makes default in complying with a notice under this regulation, the court may, on the application of the Director or of the qualifying body, make such order as the court thinks fit for requiring the default to be made good, and any such order may provide that all the costs or expenses of and incidental to the application shall be borne by the person in default or by any officers of a company or other association who are responsible for its default.

14   Notification of undertakings and orders to Director
A qualifying body shall notify the Director—
(a)   of any undertaking given to it by or on behalf of any person as to the continued use of a term which that body considers to be unfair in contracts concluded with consumers,
(b)   of the outcome of any application made by it under regulation 12, and of the terms of any undertaking given to, or order made by, the court;
(c)   of the outcome of any application made by it to enforce a previous order of the court.

15   Publication, information and advice
(1)   The Director shall arrange for the publication in such form and manner as he considers appropriate, of—
(a)   details of any undertaking or order notified to him under regulation 14;
(b)   details of any undertaking given to him by or on behalf of any persons to the continued use of a term which the Director considers to be unfair in contracts concluded with consumers;
(c)   details of any application made by him under regulation 12, and of the terms of any undertaking given to, or order made by, the court;
(d)   details of any application made by the Director to enforce a previous order of the court.
(2)   The Director shall inform any person on request whether a particular term to which these Regulations apply has been—
(a)   the subject of an undertaking given to the Director or notified to him by a qualifying body; or
(b)   the subject of an order of the court made upon application by him or notified to him by a qualifying body;
and shall give that person details of the undertaking or a copy of the order, as the case may be, together with a copy of any amendments which the person giving the undertaking has agreed to make to the term in question.
(3)   The Director may arrange for the dissemination in such form and manner as he considers appropriate of such information and advice concerning the operation of these Regulations as may appear to him to be expedient to give to the public and to all persons likely to be affected by these Regulations.

[16   The functions of the Financial Services Authority
The functions of the Financial Services Authority under these Regulations shall be treated as functions of the Financial Services Authority under the [Financial Services and Markets Act 2000.]

Regulation 3   SCHEDULE 1. QUALIFYING BODIES

PART ONE

[1.   The Information Commissioner.
2.   The Gas and Electricity Markets Authority.
3.   The Director General of Electricity Supply for Northern Ireland.
4.   The Director General of Gas for Northern Ireland.
5.   The Director General of Telecommunications.
6.   The Director General of Water Services.

7. The Rail Regulator.
8. Every weights and measures authority in Great Britain.
9. The Department of Enterprise, Trade and Investment in Northern Ireland.
10. The Financial Services Authority.

PART TWO

11. Consumers' Association.]

Regulation 5(5)   SCHEDULE 2

INDICATIVE AND NON-EXHAUSTIVE LIST OF TERMS WHICH MAY BE
REGARDED AS UNFAIR

1. Terms which have the object or effect of—
    (a) excluding or limiting the legal liability of a seller or supplier in the event of the death of a consumer or personal injury to the latter resulting from an act or omission of that seller or supplier;
    (b) inappropriately excluding or limiting the legal rights of the consumer vis-à-vis the seller or supplier or another party in the event of total or partial non-performance or inadequate performance by the seller or supplier of any of the contractual obligations, including the option of offsetting a debt owed to the seller or supplier against any claim which the consumer may have against him;
    (c) making an agreement binding on the consumer whereas provision of services by the seller or supplier is subject to a condition whose realisation depends on his own will alone;
    (d) permitting the seller or supplier to retain sums paid by the consumer where the latter decides not to conclude or perform the contract, without providing for the consumer to receive compensation of an equivalent amount from the seller or supplier where the latter is the party cancelling the contract;
    (e) requiring any consumer who fails to fulfil his obligation to pay a disproportionately high sum in compensation;
    (f) authorising the seller or supplier to dissolve the contract on a discretionary basis where the same facility is not granted to the consumer, or permitting the seller or supplier to retain the sums paid for services not yet supplied by him where it is the seller or supplier himself who dissolves the contract;
    (g) enabling the seller or supplier to terminate a contract of indeterminate duration without reasonable notice except where there are serious grounds for doing so;
    (h) automatically extending a contract of fixed duration where the consumer does not indicate otherwise, when the deadline fixed for the consumer to express his desire not to extend the contract is unreasonably early;
    (i) irrevocably binding the consumer to terms with which he had no real opportunity of becoming acquainted before the conclusion of the contract;
    (j) enabling the seller or supplier to alter the terms of the contract unilaterally without a valid reason which is specified in the contract;
    (k) enabling the seller or supplier to alter unilaterally without a valid reason any characteristics of the product or service to be provided;
    (l) providing for the price of goods to be determined at the time of delivery or allowing a seller of goods or supplier of services to increase their price without in both cases giving the consumer the corresponding right to cancel the contract if the final price is too high in relation to the price agreed when the contract was concluded;
    (m) giving the seller or supplier the right to determine whether the goods or services supplied are in conformity with the contract, or giving him the exclusive right to interpret any term of the contract;

(n) limiting the seller's or supplier's obligation to respect commitments undertaken by his agents or making his commitments subject to compliance with a particular formality;

(o) obliging the consumer to fulfil all his obligations where the seller or supplier does not perform his;

(p) giving the seller or supplier the possibility of transferring his rights and obligations under the contract, where this may serve to reduce the guarantees for the consumer, without the latter's agreement,

(q) excluding or hindering the consumer's right to take legal action or exercise any other legal remedy, particularly by requiring the consumer to take disputes exclusively to arbitration not covered by legal provisions, unduly restricting the evidence available to him or imposing on him a burden of proof which, according to the applicable law, should lie with another party to the contract.

2. Scope of paragraphs 1(g), (j) and (1)—

(a) Paragraph 1(g) is without hindrance to terms by which a supplier of financial services reserves the right to terminate unilaterally a contract of indeterminate duration without notice where there is a valid reason provided that the supplier is required to inform the other contracting party or parties thereof immediately.

(b) Paragraph 1(j) is without hindrance to terms under which a supplier of financial services reserves the right to alter the rate of interest payable by the consumer or due to the latter, or the amount of other charges for financial services without notice where there is a valid reason, provided that the supplier is required to inform the other contracting party or parties thereof at the earliest opportunity and that the latter are free to dissolve the contract immediately.

Paragraph 1(j) is also without hindrance to terms under which a seller or supplier reserves the right to alter unilaterally the conditions of a contract of indeterminate duration, provided that he is required to inform the consumer with reasonable notice and that the consumer is free to dissolve the contract.

(c) Paragraphs 1(g), (j) and (l) do not apply to:

—transactions in transferable securities, financial instruments and other products or services where the price is linked to fluctuations in a stock exchange quotation or index or a financial market rate that the seller or supplier does not control;

—contracts for the purchase or sale of foreign currency, traveller's cheques or international money orders denominated in foreign currency;

(d) Paragraph 1(1) is without hindrance to price indexation clauses, where lawful, provided that the method by which prices vary is explicitly described.

CONSUMER PROTECTION (DISTANCE SELLING) REGULATIONS 2000
(SI 2000/2334)
(as amended by the Consumer Protection (Distance Selling) (Amendment) Regulations 2005 (SI 2005/689))

3 Interpretation
(1) In these Regulations—

['the 2000 Act' means the Financial Services and Markets Act 2000;

'appointed representative' has the same meaning as in section 39(2) of the 2000 Act;

'authorised person' has the same meaning as in section 31(2) of the 2000 Act;]

'breach' means contravention by a supplier of a prohibition in, or failure to comply with a requirement of, these Regulations;

'business' includes a trade or profession;

'consumer' means any natural person who, in contracts to which these Regulations apply, is acting for purposes which are outside his business;

'court' in relation to England and Wales and Northern Ireland means a county court or the High Court, and in relation to Scotland means the Sheriff Court or the Court of Session;

'credit' includes a cash loan and any other form of financial accommodation, and for this purpose 'cash' includes money in any form;

'Director' means the Director General of Fair Trading;*

'distance contract' means any contract concerning goods or services concluded between a supplier and a consumer under an organised distance sales or service provision scheme run by the supplier who, for the purpose of the contract, makes exclusive use of one or more means of distance communication up to and including the moment at which the contract is concluded;

'EEA Agreement' means the Agreement on the European Economic Area signed at Oporto on 2 May 1992 as adjusted by the Protocol signed at Brussels on 17 March 1993;

'enactment' includes an enactment comprised in, or in an instrument made under, an Act of the Scottish Parliament;

'enforcement authority' means the Director, every weights and measures authority in Great Britain, and the Department of Enterprise, Trade and Investment in Northern Ireland;

'excepted contract' means a contract such as is mentioned in regulation 5(1);

['financial service' means any service of a banking, credit, insurance, personal pension, investment or payment nature;]

'means of distance communication' means any means which, without the simultaneous physical presence of the supplier and the consumer, may be used for the conclusion of a contract between those parties; and an indicative list of such means is contained in Schedule 1;

'Member State' means a State which is a contracting party to the EEA Agreement;

'operator of a means of communication' means any public or private person whose business involves making one or more means of distance communication available to suppliers;

'period for performance' has the meaning given by regulation 19(2);

'personal credit agreement' has the meaning given by regulation 14(8);

['regulated activity' means an activity which is a regulated activity within the meaning of section 22 of the 2000 Act, read with any relevant order under that section and Schedule 2 to that Act;]

'related credit agreement' has the meaning given by regulation 15(5);

'supplier' means any person who, in contracts to which these Regulations apply, is acting in his commercial or professional capacity; and

'working days' means all days other than Saturdays, Sundays and public holidays.

(2)   In the application of these Regulations to Scotland, for references to an 'injunction' or an 'interim injunction' there shall be substituted references to an 'interdict' or an 'interim interdict' respectively.

4   Contracts to which these Regulations apply
These Regulations apply, subject to regulation 6, to distance contracts other than excepted contracts.

5   Excepted contracts
(1)   The following are excepted contracts, namely any contract—

(a)   for the sale or other disposition of an interest in land except for a rental agreement;

---

* All references to 'the Director' have effect as if they were references to 'the OFT': Enterprise Act 2002, s 2.

(b)   for the construction of a building where the contract also provides for a sale or other disposition of an interest in land on which the building is constructed, except for a rental agreement;

(c)   relating to financial services; [. . .]

(d)   concluded by means of an automated vending machine or automated commercial premises;

(e)   concluded with a telecommunications operator through the use of a public pay-phone;

(f)   concluded at an auction.

(2)   References in paragraph (1) to a rental agreement—

(a)   if the land is situated in England and Wales, are references to any agreement which does not have to be made in writing (whether or not in fact made in writing) because of section 2(5)(a) of the Law of Property (Miscellaneous Provisions) Act 1989;

(b)   if the land is situated in Scotland, are references to any agreement for the creation, transfer, variation or extinction of an interest in land, which does not have to be made in writing (whether or not in fact made in writing) as provided for in section 1(2) and (7) of the Requirements of Writing (Scotland) Act 1995; and

(c)   if the land is situated in Northern Ireland, are references to any agreement which is not one to which section II of the Statute of Frauds, (Ireland) 1695 applies.

(3)   Paragraph (2) shall not be taken to mean that a rental agreement in respect of land situated outside the United Kingdom is not capable of being a distance contract to which these Regulations apply.

[(4)   Regulations 7 to 14, 17 to 20, and 22 to 29 shall not apply to any contract which is made by an authorised person, the making or performance of which constitutes or is part of a regulated activity carried on by him.

(5)   Regulations 7 to 9, 17 to 20, and 22 to 29 shall not apply to any contract which is made by an appointed representative, the making or performance of which constitutes or is part of a regulated activity carried on by him.]

6   Contracts to which only part of these Regulations apply

(1)   Regulations 7 to 20 shall not apply to a contract which is a 'timeshare agreement' within the meaning of the Timeshare Act 1992 and to which that Act applies.

(2)   Regulations 7 to 19(1) shall not apply to—

(a)   contracts for the supply of food, beverages or other goods intended for everyday consumption supplied to the consumer's residence or to his workplace by regular roundsmen; or

(b)   contracts for the provision of accommodation, transport, catering or leisure services, where the supplier undertakes, when the contract is concluded, to provide these services on a specific date or within a specific period.

(3)   Regulations 19(2) to (8) and 20 do not apply to a contract for a 'package' within the meaning of the Package Travel, Package Holidays and Package Tours Regulations 1992 which is sold or offered for sale in the territory of the Member States.

[(4)   Regulations 7 to 14, 17 to 20 and 25 do not apply to any contract which is made, and regulation 24 does not apply to any unsolicited services which are supplied, by an unauthorised person where the making or performance of that contract or the supply of those services, as the case may be, constitutes or is part of a regulated activity carried on by him.

(5)   Regulations 7 to 9, 17 to 20 and 25 do not apply to any contract which is made, and regulation 24 does not apply to any unsolicited services which are supplied, by an appointed representative where the making or performance of that contract or the supply of those services, as the case may be, constitutes or is part of a regulated activity carried on by him.]

7   Information required prior to the conclusion of the contract

(1)   Subject to paragraph (4), in good time prior to the conclusion of the contract the supplier shall—

(a)   provide to the consumer the following information—

(i)   the identity of the supplier and, where the contract requires payment in advance, the supplier's address;

(ii)   a description of the main characteristics of the goods or services;

(iii)   the price of the goods or services including all taxes;

(iv)   delivery costs where appropriate;

(v)   the arrangements for payment, delivery or performance;

(vi)   the existence of a right of cancellation except in the cases referred to in regulation 13;

(vii)   the cost of using the means of distance communication where it is calculated other than at the basic rate;

(viii)   the period for which the offer or the price remains valid; and

(ix)   where appropriate, the minimum duration of the contract, in the case of contracts for the supply of goods or services to be performed permanently or recurrently;

(b)   inform the consumer if he proposes, in the event of the goods or services ordered by the consumer being unavailable, to provide substitute goods or services (as the case may be) of equivalent quality and price; and

(c)   inform the consumer that the cost of returning any such substitute goods to the supplier in the event of cancellation by the consumer would be met by the supplier.

(2)   The supplier shall ensure that the information required by paragraph (1) is provided in a clear and comprehensible manner appropriate to the means of distance communication used, with due regard in particular to the principles of good faith in commercial transactions and the principles governing the protection of those who are unable to give their consent such as minors.

(3)   Subject to paragraph (4), the supplier shall ensure that his commercial purpose is made clear when providing the information required by paragraph (1).

(4)   In the case of a telephone communication, the identity of the supplier and the commercial purpose of the call shall be made clear at the beginning of the conversation with the consumer.

8   Written and additional information

(1)   Subject to regulation 9, the supplier shall provide to the consumer in writing, or in another durable medium which is available and accessible to the consumer, the information referred to in paragraph (2), either—

(a)   prior to the conclusion of the contract, or

(b)   thereafter, in good time and in any event—

(i)   during the performance of the contract, in the case of services;

(ii)   at the latest at the time of delivery where goods not for delivery to third parties are concerned;

[(iii)   in the case of a contract for the supply of services, information as to how the right to cancel may be affected by the consumer agreeing to performance of the services beginning before the end of the seven working day period referred to in regulation 12.]

(2)   The information required to be provided by paragraph (1) is—

(a)   the information set out in paragraphs (i) to (vi) of regulation 7(1)(a);

(b)   information about the conditions and procedures for exercising the right to cancel under regulation 10, including—

(i)   where a term of the contract requires (or the supplier intends that it will require) that the consumer shall return the goods to the supplier in the event of cancellation, notification of that requirement; and

(ii)   information as to whether the consumer or the supplier would be responsible under these Regulations for the cost of returning any goods to the supplier, or the cost of his recovering them, if the consumer cancels the contract under regulation 10;

(c)   the geographical address of the place of business of the supplier to which the consumer may address any complaints;

(d)   information about any after-sales services and guarantees; and

(e)   the conditions for exercising any contractual right to cancel the contract, where the contract is of an unspecified duration or a duration exceeding one year.

[. . .]

9   Services performed through the use of a means of distance communication

(1)   Regulation 8 shall not apply to a contract for the supply of services which are performed through the use of a means of distance communication, where those services are supplied on only one occasion and are invoiced by the operator of the means of distance communication.

(2)   But the supplier shall take all necessary steps to ensure that a consumer who is a party to a contract to which paragraph (1) applies is able to obtain the supplier's geographical address and the place of business to which the consumer may address any complaints.

10   Right to cancel

(1)   Subject to regulation 13, if within the cancellation period set out in regulations 11 and 12, the consumer gives a notice of cancellation to the supplier, or any other person previously notified by the supplier to the consumer as a person to whom notice of cancellation may be given, the notice of cancellation shall operate to cancel the contract.

(2)   Except as otherwise provided by these Regulations, the effect of a notice of cancellation is that the contract shall be treated as if it had not been made.

(3)   For the purposes of these Regulations, a notice of cancellation is a notice in writing or in another durable medium available and accessible to the supplier (or to the other person to whom it is given) which, however expressed, indicates the intention of the consumer to cancel the contract.

(4)   A notice of cancellation given under this regulation by a consumer to a supplier or other person is to be treated as having been properly given if the consumer—

(a)   leaves it at the address last known to the consumer and addressed to the supplier or other person by name (in which case it is to be taken to have been given on the day on which it was left);

(b)   sends it by post to the address last known to the consumer and addressed to the supplier or other person by name (in which case, it is to be taken to have been given on the day on which it was posted);

(c)   sends it by facsimile to the business facsimile number last known to the consumer (in which case it is to be taken to have been given on the day on which it is sent); or

(d)   sends it by electronic mail, to the business electronic mail address last known to the consumer (in which case it is to be taken to have been given on the day on which it is sent).

(5)   Where a consumer gives a notice in accordance with paragraph (4)(a) or (b) to a supplier who is a body corporate or a partnership, the notice is to be treated as having been properly given if—

(a)   in the case of a body corporate, it is left at the address of, or sent to, the secretary or clerk of that body; or

(b)   in the case of a partnership, it is left with or sent to a partner or a person having control or management of the partnership business.

11   Cancellation period in the case of contracts for the supply of goods

(1)   For the purposes of regulation 10, the cancellation period in the case of contracts for the supply of goods begins with the day on which the contract is concluded and ends as provided in paragraphs (2) to (5).

(2)   Where the supplier complies with regulation 8, the cancellation period ends on the expiry of the period of seven working days beginning with the day after the day on which the consumer receives the goods.

(3)   Where a supplier who has not complied with regulation 8 provides to the consumer the information referred to in regulation 8(2), and does so in writing or in another durable medium available and accessible to the consumer, within the period of three months beginning with the day after the day on which the consumer receives the goods, the cancellation period ends on the expiry of the period of seven working days beginning with the day after the day on which the consumer receives the information.

(4)   Where neither paragraph (2) nor (3) applies, the cancellation period ends on the expiry of the period of three months and seven working days beginning with the day after the day on which the consumer receives the goods.

(5)   In the case of contracts for goods for delivery to third parties, paragraphs (2) to (4) shall apply as if the consumer had received the goods on the day on which they were received by the third party.

12   Cancellation period in the case of contracts for the supply of services

(1)   For the purposes of regulation 10, the cancellation period in the case of contracts for the supply of services begins with the day on which the contract is concluded and ends as provided in paragraphs (2) to (4).

(2)   Where the supplier complies with regulation 8 on or before the day on which the contract is concluded, the cancellation period ends on the expiry of the period of seven working days beginning with the day after the day on which the contract is concluded.

(3)   [Subject to paragraph (3A)] where a supplier who has not complied with regulation 8 on or before the day on which the contract is concluded provides to the consumer the information referred to in regulation 8(2) [. . .], and does so in writing or in another durable medium available and accessible to the consumer, within the period of three months beginning with the day after the day on which the contract is concluded, the cancellation period ends on the expiry of the period of seven working days beginning with the day after the day on which the consumer receives the information.

[(3A)   Where the performance of the contract has begun with the consumer's agreement before the expiry of the period of seven working days beginning with the day after the day on which the contract was concluded and the supplier has not complied with regulation 8 on or before the day on which performance began, but provides to the consumer the information referred to in regulation 8(2) in good time during the performance of the contract, the cancellation period ends—

(a)   on the expiry of the period of seven working days beginning with the day after the day on which the consumer receives the information; or

(b)   if the performance of the contract is completed before the expiry of the period referred to in sub-paragraph (a), on the day when the performance of the contract is completed.]

(4)   Where [none of paragraphs (2) to (3A) applies], the cancellation period ends on the expiry of the period of three months and seven working days beginning with the day after the day on which the contract is concluded.

13   Exceptions to the right to cancel

(1)   Unless the parties have agreed otherwise, the consumer will not have the right to cancel the contract by giving notice of cancellation pursuant to regulation 10 in respect of contracts—

[(a) for the supply of services if the performance of the contract has begun with the consumer's agreement—

(i) before the end of the cancellation period applicable under regulation 12(2); and

(ii) after the supplier has provided the information referred to in regulation 8(2).]

(b) for the supply of goods or services the price of which is dependent on fluctuations in the financial market which cannot be controlled by the supplier;

(c) for the supply of goods made to the consumer's specifications or clearly personalised or which by reason of their nature cannot be returned or are liable to deteriorate or expire rapidly;

(d) for the supply of audio or video recordings or computer software if they are unsealed by the consumer;

(e) for the supply of newspapers, periodicals or magazines; or

(f) for gaming, betting or lottery services.

14 Recovery of sums paid by or on behalf of the consumer on cancellation, and return of security

(1) On the cancellation of a contract under regulation 10; the supplier shall reimburse any sum paid by or on behalf of the consumer under or in relation to the contract to the person by whom it was made free of any charge, less any charge made in accordance with paragraph (5).

(2) The reference in paragraph (1) to any sum paid on behalf of the consumer includes any sum paid by a creditor who is not the same person as the supplier under a personal credit agreement with the consumer.

(3) The supplier shall make the reimbursement referred to in paragraph (1) as soon as possible and in any case within a period not exceeding 30 days beginning with the day on which the notice of cancellation was given.

(4) Where any security has been provided in relation to the contract, the security (so far as it is so provided) shall, on cancellation under regulation 10, be treated as never having had effect and any property lodged with the supplier solely for the purposes of the security as so provided shall be returned by him forthwith.

(5) Subject to paragraphs (6) and (7), the supplier may make a charge, not exceeding the direct costs of recovering any goods supplied under the contract, where a term of the contract provides that the consumer must return any goods supplied if he cancels the contract under regulation 10 but the consumer does not comply with this provision or returns the goods at the expense of the supplier.

(6) Paragraph (5) shall not apply where—

(a) the consumer cancels in circumstances where he has the right to reject the goods under a term of the contract, including a term implied by virtue of any enactment, or

(b) the term requiring the consumer to return any goods supplied if he cancels the contract is an 'unfair term' within the meaning of the Unfair Terms in Consumer Contracts Regulations 1999.

(7) Paragraph (5) shall not apply to the cost of recovering any goods which were supplied as substitutes for the goods ordered by the consumer.

(8) For the purposes of these Regulations, a personal credit agreement is an agreement between the consumer and any other person ('the creditor') by which the creditor provides the consumer with credit of any amount.

15 Automatic cancellation of a related credit agreement

(1) Where a notice of cancellation is given under regulation 10 which has the effect of cancelling the contract, the giving of the notice shall also have the effect of cancelling any related credit agreement.

(2) Where a related credit agreement is cancelled by virtue of paragraph (1), the supplier shall, if he is not the same person as the creditor under that agree-

ment, forthwith on receipt of the notice of cancellation inform the creditor that the notice has been given.

(3)   Where a related credit agreement is cancelled by virtue of paragraph (1)—

(a)   any sum paid by or on behalf of the consumer under, or in relation to, the credit agreement which the supplier is not obliged to reimburse under regulation 14(1) shall be reimbursed, except for any sum which, if it had not already been paid, would have to be paid under sub-paragraph (b);

(b)   the agreement shall continue in force so far as it relates to repayment of the credit and payment of interest, subject to regulation 16; and

(c)   subject to sub-paragraph (b), the agreement shall cease to be enforceable.

(4)   Where any security has been provided under a related credit agreement, the security, so far as it is so provided, shall be treated as never having had effect and any property lodged with the creditor solely for the purposes of the security as so provided shall be returned by him forthwith.

(5)   For the purposes of this regulation and regulation 16, a 'related credit agreement' means an agreement under which fixed sum credit which fully or partly covers the price under a contract cancelled under regulation 10 is granted—

(a)   by the supplier, or

(b)   by another person, under an arrangement between that person and the supplier.

(6)   For the purposes of this regulation and regulation 16—

(a)   'creditor' is a person who grants credit under a related credit agreement;

(b)   'fixed sum credit' has the same meaning as in section 10 of the Consumer Credit Act 1974;

(c)   'repayment' in relation to credit means repayment of money received by the consumer, and cognate expressions shall be construed accordingly; and

(d)   'interest' means interest on money so received.

16   Repayment of credit and interest after cancellation of a related credit agreement

(1)   This regulation applies following the cancellation of a related credit agreement by virtue of regulation 15(1).

(2)   If the consumer repays the whole or a portion of the credit—

(a)   before the expiry of one month following the cancellation of the credit agreement, or

(b)   in the case of a credit repayable by instalments, before the date on which the first instalment is due,

no interest shall be payable on the amount repaid.

(3)   If the whole of a credit repayable by instalments is not repaid on or before the date referred to in paragraph (2)(b), the consumer shall not be liable to repay any of the credit except on receipt of a request in writing, signed by the creditor, stating the amounts of the remaining instalments (recalculated by the creditor as nearly as may be in accordance with the agreement and without extending the repayment period), but excluding any sum other than principal and interest.

(4)   Where any security has been provided under a related credit agreement the duty imposed on the consumer to repay credit and to pay interest shall not be enforceable before the creditor has discharged any duty imposed on him by regulation 15(4) to return any property lodged with him as security on cancellation.

17   Restoration of goods by consumer after cancellation

(1)   This regulation applies where a contract is cancelled under regulation 10 after the consumer has acquired possession of any goods under the contract other than any goods mentioned in regulation 13(1)(b) to (e).

(2)   The consumer shall be treated as having been under a duty throughout the period prior to cancellation—

(a)   to retain possession of the goods, and

(b)   to take reasonable care of them.

(3)　On cancellation, the consumer shall be under a duty to restore the goods to the supplier in accordance with this regulation, and in the meanwhile to retain possession of the goods and take reasonable care of them.

(4)　The consumer shall not be under any duty to deliver the goods except at his own premises and in pursuance of a request in writing, or in another durable medium available and accessible to the consumer, from the supplier and given to the consumer either before, or at the time when, the goods are collected from those premises.

(5)　If the consumer—

(a)　delivers the goods (whether at his own premises or elsewhere) to any person to whom, under regulation 10(1), a notice of cancellation could have been given; or

(b)　sends the goods at his own expense to such a person,

he shall be discharged from any duty to retain possession of the goods or restore them to the supplier.

(6)　Where the consumer delivers the goods in accordance with paragraph (5)(a), his obligation to take care of the goods shall cease; and if he sends the goods in accordance with paragraph (5)(b), he shall be under a duty to take reasonable care to see that they are received by the supplier and not damaged in transit, but in other respects his duty to take care of the goods shall cease when he sends them.

(7)　Where, at any time during the period of 21 days beginning with the day notice of cancellation was given, the consumer receives such a request as is mentioned in paragraph (4), and unreasonably refuses or unreasonably fails to comply with it, his duty to retain possession and take reasonable care of the goods shall continue until he delivers or sends the goods as mentioned in paragraph (5), but if within that period he does not receive such a request his duty to take reasonable care of the goods shall cease at the end of that period.

(8)　Where—

(a)　a term of the contract provides that if the consumer cancels the contract, he must return the goods to the supplier, and

(b)　the consumer is not otherwise entitled to reject the goods under the terms of the contract or by virtue of any enactment,

paragraph (7) shall apply as if for the period of 21 days there were substituted the period of 6 months.

(9)　Where any security has been provided in relation to the cancelled contract, the duty to restore goods imposed on the consumer by this regulation shall not be enforceable before the supplier has discharged any duty imposed on him by regulation 14(4) to return any property lodged with him as security on cancellation.

(10)　Breach of a duty imposed by this regulation on a consumer is actionable as a breach of statutory duty.

18　Goods given in part-exchange

(1)　This regulation applies on the cancellation of a contract under regulation 10 where the supplier agreed to take goods in part-exchange (the 'part-exchange goods') and those goods have been delivered to him.

(2)　Unless, before the end of the period of 10 days beginning with the date of cancellation, the part-exchange goods are returned to the consumer in a condition substantially as good as when they were delivered to the supplier, the consumer shall be entitled to recover from the supplier a sum equal to the part-exchange allowance.

(3)　In this regulation the part-exchange allowance means the sum agreed as such in the cancelled contract, or if no such sum was agreed, such sum as it would have been reasonable to allow in respect of the part-exchange goods if no notice of cancellation had been served.

(4)　Where the consumer recovers from the supplier a sum equal to the part-exchange allowance, the title of the consumer to the part-exchange goods shall vest in the supplier (if it has not already done so) on recovery of that sum.

19 Performance

(1) Unless the parties agree otherwise, the supplier shall perform the contract within a maximum of 30 days beginning with the day after the day the consumer sent his order to the supplier.

(2) Subject to paragraphs (7) and (8), where the supplier is unable to perform the contract because the goods or services ordered are not available, within the period for performance referred to in paragraph (1) or such other period as the parties agree ('the period for performance'), he shall—

(a) inform the consumer; and

(b) reimburse any sum paid by or on behalf of the consumer under or in relation to the contract to the person by whom it was made.

(3) The reference in paragraph (2)(b) to any sum paid on behalf of the consumer includes any sum paid by a creditor who is not the same person as the supplier under a personal credit agreement with the consumer.

(4) The supplier shall make the reimbursement referred to in paragraph (2)(b) as soon as possible and in any event within a period of 30 days beginning with the day after the day on which the period for performance expired.

(5) A contract which has not been performed within the period for performance shall be treated as if it had not been made, save for any rights or remedies which the consumer has under it as a result of the non-performance.

(6) Where any security has been provided in relation to the contract, the security (so far as it is so provided) shall, where the supplier is unable to perform the contract within the period for performance, be treated as never having had any effect and any property lodged with the supplier solely for the purposes of the security as so provided shall be returned by him forthwith.

(7) Where the supplier is unable to supply the goods or services ordered by the consumer, the supplier may perform the contract for the purposes of these Regulations by providing substitute goods or services (as the case may be) of equivalent quality and price provided that—

(a) this possibility was provided for in the contract;

(b) prior to the conclusion of the contract the supplier gave the consumer the information required by regulation 7(1)(b) and (c) in the manner required by regulation 7(2).

(8) In the case of outdoor leisure events which by their nature cannot be rescheduled, paragraph 2(b) shall not apply where the consumer and the supplier so agree.

20 Effect of non-performance on related credit agreement

Where a supplier is unable to perform the contract within the period for performance—

(a) regulations 15 and 16 shall apply to any related credit agreement as if the consumer had given a valid notice of cancellation under regulation 10 on the expiry of the period for performance; and

(b) the reference in regulation 15(3)(a) to regulation 14(1) shall be read, for the purposes of this regulation, as a reference to regulation 19(2).

21 Payment by card

(1) Subject to paragraph (4), the consumer shall be entitled to cancel a payment where fraudulent use has been made of his payment card in connection with a contract to which this regulation applies by another person not acting, or to be treated as acting, as his agent.

(2) Subject to paragraph (4), the consumer shall be entitled to be recredited, or to have all sums returned by the card issuer, in the event of fraudulent use of his

payment card in connection with a contract to which this regulation applies by another person not acting, or to be treated as acting, as the consumer's agent.

(3) Where paragraphs (1) and (2) apply, in any proceedings if the consumer alleges that any use made of the payment card was not authorised by him it is for the card issuer to prove that the use was so authorised.

(4) Paragraphs (1) and (2) shall not apply to an agreement to which section 83(1) of the Consumer Credit Act 1974 applies.

(5) [amends Consumer Credit Act 1974].

(6) For the purposes of this regulation—

'card issuer' means the owner of the card; and

'payment card' includes credit cards, charge cards, debit cards and store cards.

22 *[Amends the Unsolicited Goods and Services Act 1971.]*

23 *[Amends the Unsolicited Goods and Services (Northern Ireland) Order 1976.]*

24 Inertia selling

(1) Paragraphs (2) and (3) apply if—

(a) unsolicited goods are sent to a person ('the recipient') with a view to his acquiring them;

(b) the recipient has no reasonable cause to believe that they were sent with a view to their being acquired for the purposes of a business; and

(c) the recipient has neither agreed to acquire nor agreed to return them.

(2) The recipient may, as between himself and the sender, use, deal with or dispose of the goods as if they were an unconditional gift to him.

(3) The rights of the sender to the goods are extinguished.

(4) A person who, not having reasonable cause to believe there is a right to payment, in the course of any business makes a demand for payment, or asserts a present or prospective right to payment, for what he knows are—

(a) unsolicited goods sent to another person with a view to his acquiring them for purposes other than those of his business, or

(b) unsolicited services supplied to another person for purposes other than those of his business,

is guilty of an offence and liable, on summary conviction, to a fine not exceeding level 4 on the standard scale.

(5) A person who, not having reasonable cause to believe there is a right to payment, in the course of any business and with a view to obtaining payment for what he knows are unsolicited goods sent or services supplied as mentioned in paragraph (4)—

(a) threatens to bring any legal proceedings, or

(b) places or causes to be placed the name of any person on a list of de-faulters or debtors or threatens to do so, or

(c) invokes or causes to be invoked any other collection procedure or threatens to do so,

is guilty of an offence and liable, on summary conviction, to a fine not exceeding level 5 on the standard scale.

(6) In this regulation—

'acquire' includes hire;

'send' includes deliver;

'sender', in relation to any goods, includes—

(a) any person on whose behalf or with whose consent the goods are sent;

(b) any other person claiming through or under the sender or any person mentioned in paragraph (a); and

(c) any person who delivers the goods; and

'unsolicited' means, in relation to goods sent or services supplied to any person, that they are sent or supplied without any prior request made by or on behalf of the recipient.

(7)   For the purposes of this regulation, an invoice or similar document which—

     (a)   states the amount of a payment, and

     (b)   fails to comply with the [conditions set out in Part 2 of the Schedule to the Regulatory Reform (Unsolicited Goods and Services Act 1971) (Directory Entries and Demands for Payment) Order 2005] or, as the case may be, [the requirements of regulations made under] Article 6 of the Unsolicited Goods and Services (Northern Ireland) Order 1976 applicable to it,

is to be regarded as asserting a right to the payment.

(8)   Section 3A of the Unsolicited Goods and Services Act 1971 applies for the purposes of this regulation in its application to England, Wales and Scotland as it applies for the purposes of that Act.

(9)   Article 6 of the Unsolicited Goods and Services (Northern Ireland) Order 1976 applies for the purposes of this regulation in its application to Northern Ireland as it applies for the purposes of that Order.

(10)   This regulation applies only to goods sent and services supplied after the date on which it comes into force.

25   No contracting-out

(1)   A term contained in any contract to which these Regulations apply is void if, and to the extent that, it is inconsistent with a provision for the protection of the consumer contained in these Regulations.

(2)   Where a provision of these Regulations specifies a duty or liability of the consumer in certain circumstances, a term contained in a contract to which these Regulations apply, other than a term to which paragraph (3) applies, is inconsistent with that provision if it purports to impose, directly or indirectly, an additional duty or liability on him in those circumstances.

(3)   This paragraph applies to a term which requires the consumer to return any goods supplied to him under the contract if he cancels it under regulation 10.

(4)   A term to which paragraph (3) applies shall, in the event of cancellation by the consumer under regulation 10, have effect only for the purposes of regulations 14(5) and 17(8).

(5)   These Regulations shall apply notwithstanding any contract term which applies or purports to apply the law of a non-Member State if the contract has a close connection with the territory of a Member State.

26   Consideration of complaints

(1)   It shall be the duty of an enforcement authority to consider any complaint made to it about a breach unless—

     (a)   the complaint appears to the authority to be frivolous or vexatious; or

     (b)   another enforcement authority has notified the Director that it agrees to consider the complaint.

(2)   If an enforcement authority notifies the Director that it agrees to consider a complaint made to another enforcement authority, the first mentioned authority shall be under a duty to consider the complaint.

(3)   An enforcement authority which is under a duty to consider a complaint shall give reasons for its decision to apply or not to apply, as the case may be, for an injunction under regulation 27.

(4)   In deciding whether or not to apply for an injunction in respect of a breach an enforcement authority may, if it considers it appropriate to do so, have regard to any undertaking given to it or another enforcement authority by or on behalf of any person as to compliance with these Regulations.

27   Injunctions to secure compliance with these Regulations

(1)   The Director or, subject to paragraph (2), any other enforcement authority

may apply for an injunction (including an interim injunction) against any person who appears to the Director or that authority to be responsible for a breach.

(2)   An enforcement authority other than the Director may apply for an injunction only where—

(a)   it has notified the Director of its intention to apply at least fourteen days before the date on which the application is to be made, beginning with the date on which the notification was given; or

(b)   the Director consents to the application being made within a shorter period.

(3)   The court on an application under this regulation may grant an injunction on such terms as it thinks fit to secure compliance with these Regulations.

28   Notification of undertakings and orders to the Director

An enforcement authority other than the Director shall notify the Director—

(a)   of any undertaking given to it by or on behalf of any person who appears to it to be responsible for a breach;

(b)   of the outcome of any application made by it under regulation 27 and of the terms of any undertaking given to or order made by the court;

(c)   of the outcome of any application made by it to enforce a previous order of the court.

29   Publication, information and advice

(1)   The Director shall arrange for the publication in such form and manner as he considers appropriate of—

(a)   details of any undertaking or order notified to him under regulation 28;

(b)   details of any undertaking given to him by or on behalf of any person as to compliance with these Regulations;

(c)   details of any application made by him under regulation 27, and of the terms of any undertaking given to, or order made by, the court;

(d)   details of any application made by the Director to enforce a previous order of the court.

(2)   The Director may arrange for the dissemination in such form and manner as he considers appropriate of such information and advice concerning the operation of these Regulations as it may appear to him to be expedient to give to the public and to all persons likely to be affected by these Regulations.

Regulation 3   SCHEDULE 1

INDICATIVE LIST OF MEANS OF DISTANCE COMMUNICATION

1.   Unaddressed printed matter.
2.   Addressed printed matter.
3.   Letter.
4.   Press advertising with order form.
5.   Catalogue.
6.   Telephone with human intervention.
7.   Telephone without human intervention (automatic calling machine, audio-text).
8.   Radio.
9.   Videophone (telephone with screen).
10.   Videotext (microcomputer and television screen) with keyboard or touch screen.
11.   Electronic mail.
12.   Facsimile machine (fax).
13.   Television (teleshopping).

LATE PAYMENT OF COMMERCIAL DEBTS (SCOTLAND) REGULATIONS 2002
(SSI 2002/335)

1 Citation, commencement and extent
(1)   These Regulations may be cited as the Late Payment of Commercial Debts (Scotland) Regulations 2002 and shall come into force on 7th August 2002.
(2)   These Regulations extend to Scotland only.

2 [*amends Late Payment of Commercial Debts (Interest) Act 1998*]

3 Proceedings restraining use of grossly unfair terms
(1)   In this regulation—
      (a)   'small and medium-sized enterprises' means those enterprises defined in Annex 1 to Commission Regulation (EC) No 70/2001 of 12th January 2001 on the application of Articles 87 and 88 of the EC Treaty to State aid to small and medium-sized enterprises;
      (b)   'representative body' means an organisation established to represent the collective interests of small and medium-sized enterprises in general or in a particular sector or area.
(2)   This regulation applies where a person acting in the course of a business has written standard terms on which he or she enters (or intends to enter) as purchaser into contracts to which the Late Payment of Commercial Debts (Interest) Act 1998 applies which include a term purporting to oust or vary the right to statutory interest in relation to qualifying debts created by those contracts.
(3)   If it appears to the Court of Session that in all or any circumstances the purported use of such a term in a relevant contract would be void under the Late Payment of Commercial Debts (Interest) Act 1998, the court on the application of a representative body may grant an interdict against that person prohibiting that person in those circumstances from using the offending term, on such terms as the court may think fit.
(4)   Only a representative body may apply to the Court of Session under this regulation.

4 Saving for existing contracts
These Regulations do not affect contracts made before 7th August 2002.

LATE PAYMENT OF COMMERCIAL DEBTS (RATE OF INTEREST) (SCOTLAND) ORDER 2002
(SSI 2002/336)

1 Citation, commencement and extent
(1)   This Order may be cited as the Late Payment of Commercial Debts (Rate of Interest) (Scotland) Order 2002 and shall come into force on 7th August 2002.
(2)   This Order extends to Scotland only.

2 Revocation
The Late Payment of Commercial Debts (Rate of Interest) (No 2) Order 1998 is revoked.

3 Interpretation
In this Order, 'the official dealing rate' means the rate announced from time to time by the Monetary Policy Committee of the Bank of England ('the Bank') and for the time being in force as the official dealing rate, being the rate at which the Bank is willing to enter into transactions for providing short term liquidity in the money markets.

4 Rate of statutory interest
The rate of interest for the purposes of the Late Payment of Commercial Debts

(Interest) Act 1998 shall be 8 per cent per annum over the official dealing rate in force on the 30th June (in respect of interest which starts to run between 1st July and 31st December) or the 31st December (in respect of interest which starts to run between 1st January and 30th June) immediately before the day on which statutory interest starts to run.

ELECTRONIC COMMERCE (EC DIRECTIVE) REGULATIONS 2002
(SI 2002/2013)

9 Information to be provided where contracts are concluded by electronic means

(1) Unless parties who are not consumers have agreed otherwise, where a contract is to be concluded by electronic means a service provider shall, prior to an order being placed by the recipient of a service, provide to that recipient in a clear, comprehensible and unambiguous manner the information set out in (a) to (d) below—

(a) the different technical steps to follow to conclude the contract;

(b) whether or not the concluded contract will be filed by the service provider and whether it will be accessible;

(c) the technical means for identifying and correcting input errors prior to the placing of the order; and

(d) the languages offered for the conclusion of the contract.

(2) Unless parties who are not consumers have agreed otherwise, a service provider shall indicate which relevant codes of conduct he subscribes to and give information on how those codes can be consulted electronically.

(3) Where the service provider provides terms and conditions applicable to the contract to the recipient, the service provider shall make them available to him in a way that allows him to store and reproduce them.

(4) The requirements of paragraphs (1) and (2) above shall not apply to contracts concluded exclusively by exchange of electronic mail or by equivalent individual communications.

10 Other information requirements

Regulations 6, 7, 8 and 9(1) have effect in addition to any other information requirements in legislation giving effect to Community law.

11 Placing of the order

(1) Unless parties who are not consumers have agreed otherwise, where the recipient of the service places his order through technological means, a service provider shall—

(a) acknowledge receipt of the order to the recipient of the service without undue delay and by electronic means; and

(b) make available to the recipient of the service appropriate, effective and accessible technical means allowing him to identify and correct input errors prior to the placing of the order.

(2) For the purposes of paragraph (1)(a) above—

(a) the order and the acknowledgement of receipt will be deemed to be received when the parties to whom they are addressed are able to access them; and

(b) the acknowledgement of receipt may take the form of the provision of the service paid for where that service is an information society service.

(3) The requirements of paragraph (1) above shall not apply to contracts concluded exclusively by exchange of electronic mail or by equivalent individual communications.

GENERAL PRODUCT SAFETY REGULATIONS 2005
(SI 2005/1803)

PART 1. GENERAL

1 Citation, commencement and revocation

(1)   These Regulations may be cited as the General Product Safety Regulations 2005 and shall come into force on 1st October 2005 with the exception of the reference to a civil partner in regulation 43(2) which shall come into force on 5th December 2005.

(2)   The General Product Safety Regulations 1994 are hereby revoked.

2 Interpretation

In these Regulations—

'the 1987 Act' means the Consumer Protection Act 1987;

'Community law' includes a law in any part of the United Kingdom which implements a Community obligation;

'contravention' includes a failure to comply and cognate expressions shall be construed accordingly;

'dangerous product' means a product other than a safe product;

'distributor' means a professional in the supply chain whose activity does not affect the safety properties of a product;

'enforcement authority' means the Secretary of State, any other Minister of the Crown in charge of a government department, any such department and any authority or council mentioned in regulation 10;

'general safety requirement' means the requirement that only safe products should be placed on the market;

'the GPS Directive' means Directive 2001/95/EC of the European Parliament and of the Council of 3 December 2001 on general product safety;

'magistrates' court' in relation to Northern Ireland, means a court of summary jurisdiction;

'Member State' means a Member State, Norway, Iceland or Liechtenstein;

'notice' means a notice in writing;

'officer', in relation to an enforcement authority, means a person authorised in writing to assist the authority in carrying out its functions under or for the purposes of the enforcement of these Regulations and safety notices, except in relation to an enforcement authority which is a government department where it means an officer of that department;

'producer' means—

(a)   the manufacturer of a product, when he is established in a Member State and any other person presenting himself as the manufacturer by affixing to the product his name, trade mark or other distinctive mark, or the person who reconditions the product;

(b)   when the manufacturer is not established in a Member State—

(i)   if he has a representative established in a Member State, the representative,

(ii)   in any other case, the importer of the product from a state that is not a Member State into a Member State;

(c)   other professionals in the supply chain, insofar as their activities may affect the safety properties of a product;

'product' means a product which is intended for consumers or likely, under reasonably foreseeable conditions, to be used by consumers even if not intended for them and which is supplied or made available, whether for consideration or not, in the course of a commercial activity and whether it is new, used or reconditioned and includes a product that is supplied or made available to consumers for their own use in the context of providing a service. 'Product' does not include equipment used by service providers themselves to supply a service to consumers, in particular equipment on which consumers ride or travel which is operated by a service provider;

'recall' means any measure aimed at achieving the return of a dangerous product that has already been supplied or made available to consumers;

'recall notice' means a notice under regulation 15;

'record' includes any book or document and any record in any form;

'requirement to mark' means a notice under regulation 12;

'requirement to warn' means a notice under regulation 13;

'safe product' means a product which, under normal or reasonably foreseeable conditions of use including duration and, where applicable, putting into service, installation and maintenance requirements, does not present any risk or only the minimum risks compatible with the product's use, considered to be acceptable and consistent with a high level of protection for the safety and health of persons. In determining the foregoing, the following shall be taken into account in particular—

(a)   the characteristics of the product, including its composition, packaging, instructions for assembly and, where applicable, instructions for installation and maintenance,

(b)   the effect of the product on other products, where it is reasonably foreseeable that it will be used with other products,

(c)   the presentation of the product, the labelling, any warnings and instructions for its use and disposal and any other indication or information regarding the product, and

(d)   the categories of consumers at risk when using the product, in particular children and the elderly.

The feasibility of obtaining higher levels of safety or the availability of other products presenting a lesser degree of risk shall not constitute grounds for considering a product to be a dangerous product;

'safety notice' means a suspension notice, a requirement to mark, a requirement to warn, a withdrawal notice or a recall notice;

'serious risk' means a serious risk, including one the effects of which are not immediate, requiring rapid intervention;

'supply' in relation to a product includes making it available, in the context of providing a service, for use by consumers;

'suspension notice' means a notice under regulation 11;

'withdrawal' means any measure aimed at preventing the distribution, display or offer of a dangerous product to a consumer;

'withdrawal notice' means a notice under regulation 14.

3 Application

(1)   Each provision of these Regulations applies to a product in so far as there are no specific provisions with the same objective in rules of Community law governing the safety of the product other than the GPS Directive.

(2)   Where a product is subject to specific safety requirements imposed by rules of Community law other than the GPS Directive, these Regulations shall apply only to the aspects and risks or category of risks not covered by those requirements. This means that:

(a)   the definition of 'safe product' and 'dangerous product' in regulation 2 and regulations 5 and 6 shall not apply to such a product in so far as concerns the risks or category of risks covered by the specific rules, and

(b)   the remainder of these Regulations shall apply except where there are specific provisions governing the aspects covered by those regulations with the same objective.

4   These Regulations do not apply to a second-hand product supplied as a product to be repaired or reconditioned prior to being used, provided the supplier clearly informs the person to whom he supplies the product to that effect.

PART 2. OBLIGATIONS OF PRODUCERS AND DISTRIBUTORS

5 General safety requirement

(1) No producer shall place a product on the market unless the product is a safe product.

(2) No producer shall offer or agree to place a product on the market or expose or possess a product for placing on the market unless the product is a safe product.

(3) No producer shall offer or agree to supply a product or expose or possess a product for supply unless the product is a safe product.

(4) No producer shall supply a product unless the product is a safe product.

6 Presumption of conformity

(1) Where, in the absence of specific provisions in rules of Community law governing the safety of a product, the product conforms to the specific rules of the law of part of the United Kingdom laying down the health and safety requirements which the product must satisfy in order to be marketed in the United Kingdom, the product shall be deemed safe so far as concerns the aspects covered by such rules.

(2) Where a product conforms to a voluntary national standard of the United Kingdom giving effect to a European standard the reference of which has been published in the Official Journal of the European Union in accordance with Article 4 of the GPS Directive, the product shall be presumed to be a safe product so far as concerns the risks and categories of risk covered by that national standard. The Secretary of State shall publish the reference number of such national standards in such manner as he considers appropriate.

(3) In circumstances other than those referred to in paragraphs (1) and (2), the conformity of a product to the general safety requirement shall be assessed taking into account—

(a) any voluntary national standard of the United Kingdom giving effect to a European standard, other than one referred to in paragraph (2),

(b) other national standards drawn up in the United Kingdom,

(c) recommendations of the European Commission setting guidelines on product safety assessment,

(d) product safety codes of good practice in the sector concerned,

(e) the state of the art and technology, and

(f) reasonable consumer expectations concerning safety.

(4) Conformity of a product with the criteria designed to ensure the general safety requirement is complied with, in particular the provisions mentioned in paragraphs (1) to (3), shall not bar an enforcement authority from exercising its powers under these Regulations in relation to that product where there is evidence that, despite such conformity, it is dangerous.

7 Other obligations of producers

(1) Within the limits of his activities, a producer shall provide consumers with the relevant information to enable them—

(a) to assess the risks inherent in a product throughout the normal or reasonably foreseeable period of its use, where such risks are not immediately obvious without adequate warnings, and

(b) to take precautions against those risks.

(2) The presence of warnings does not exempt any person from compliance with the other requirements of these Regulations.

(3) Within the limits of his activities, a producer shall adopt measures commensurate with the characteristics of the products which he supplies to enable him to—

(a) be informed of the risks which the products might pose, and

(b) take appropriate action including, where necessary to avoid such risks, withdrawal, adequately and effectively warning consumers as to the risks or, as a last resort, recall.

(4)   The measures referred to in paragraph (3) include—

(a)   except where it is not reasonable to do so, an indication by means of the product or its packaging of—

(i)   the name and address of the producer, and

(ii)   the product reference or where applicable the batch of products to which it belongs; and

(b)   where and to the extent that it is reasonable to do so—

(i)   sample testing of marketed products,

(ii)   investigating and if necessary keeping a register of complaints concerning the safety of the product, and

(iii)   keeping distributors informed of the results of such monitoring where a product presents a risk or may present a risk.

8   Obligations of distributors

(1)   A distributor shall act with due care in order to help ensure compliance with the applicable safety requirements and in particular he—

(a)   shall not expose or possess for supply or offer or agree to supply, or supply, a product to any person which he knows or should have presumed, on the basis of the information in his possession and as a professional, is a dangerous product; and

(b)   shall, within the limits of his activities, participate in monitoring the safety of a product placed on the market, in particular by—

(i)   passing on information on the risks posed by the product,

(ii)   keeping the documentation necessary for tracing the origin of the product,

(iii)   producing the documentation necessary for tracing the origin of the product, and (iv) cooperating in action taken by a producer or an enforcement authority to avoid the risks.

(2)   Within the limits of his activities, a distributor shall take measures enabling him to co-operate efficiently in the action referred to in paragraph (1)(b)(iii).

9   Obligations of producers and distributors

(1)   Subject to paragraph (2), where a producer or a distributor knows that a product he has placed on the market or supplied poses risks to the consumer that are incompatible with the general safety requirement, he shall forthwith notify an enforcement authority in writing of that information and—

(a)   the action taken to prevent risk to the consumer; and

(b)   where the product is being or has been marketed or otherwise supplied to consumers outside the United Kingdom, of the identity of each Member State in which, to the best of his knowledge, it is being or has been so marketed or supplied.

(2)   Paragraph (1) shall not apply—

(a)   in the case of a second-hand product supplied as an antique or as a product to be repaired or reconditioned prior to being used, provided the supplier clearly informed the person to whom he supplied the product to that effect,

(b)   in conditions concerning isolated circumstances or products.

(3)   In the event of a serious risk the notification under paragraph (1) shall include the following—

(a)   information enabling a precise identification of the product or batch of products in question,

(b)   a full description of the risks that the product presents,

(c)   all available information relevant for tracing the product, and

(d)   a description of the action undertaken to prevent risks to the consumer.

(4)   Within the limits of his activities, a person who is a producer or a distributor shall co-operate with an enforcement authority (at the enforcement auth-

ority's request) in action taken to avoid the risks posed by a product which he supplies or has supplied. Every enforcement authority shall maintain procedures for such co-operation, including procedures for dialogue with the producers and distributors concerned on issues related to product safety.

PART 3. ENFORCEMENT

10 Enforcement

(1)   It shall be the duty of every authority to which paragraph (4) applies to enforce within its area these Regulations and safety notices.

(2)   An authority in England or Wales to which paragraph (4) applies shall have the power to investigate and prosecute for an alleged contravention of any provision imposed by or under these Regulations which was committed outside its area in any part of England and Wales.

(3)   A district council in Northern Ireland shall have the power to investigate and prosecute for an alleged contravention of any provision imposed by or under these Regulations which was committed outside its area in any part of Northern Ireland.

(4)   The authorities to which this paragraph applies are:

(a)   in England, a county council, district council, London Borough Council, the Common Council of the City of London in its capacity as a local authority and the Council of the Isles of Scilly,

(b)   in Wales, a county council or a county borough council,

(c)   in Scotland, a council constituted under section 2 of the Local Government etc (Scotland) Act 1994,

(d)   in Northern Ireland any district council.

(5)   An enforcement authority shall in enforcing these Regulations act in a manner proportionate to the seriousness of the risk and shall take due account of the precautionary principle. In this context, it shall encourage and promote voluntary action by producers and distributors. Notwithstanding the foregoing, an enforcement authority may take any action under these Regulations urgently and without first encouraging and promoting voluntary action if a product poses a serious risk.

11 Suspension notices

(1)   Where an enforcement authority has reasonable grounds for suspecting that a requirement of these Regulations has been contravened in relation to a product, the authority may, for the period needed to organise appropriate safety evaluations, checks and controls, serve a notice ('a suspension notice') prohibiting the person on whom it is served from doing any of the following things without the consent of the authority, that is to say—

(a)   placing the product on the market, offering to place it on the market, agreeing to place it on the market or exposing it for placing on the market, or

(b)   supplying the product, offering to supply it, agreeing to supply it or exposing it for supply.

(2)   A suspension notice served by an enforcement authority in relation to a product may require the person on whom it is served to keep the authority informed of the whereabouts of any such product in which he has an interest.

(3)   A consent given by the enforcement authority for the purposes of paragraph (1) may impose such conditions on the doing of anything for which the consent is required as the authority considers appropriate.

12 Requirements to mark

(1)   Where an enforcement authority has reasonable grounds for believing that a product is a dangerous product in that it could pose risks in certain conditions, the authority may serve a notice ('a requirement to mark') requiring the person on

whom the notice is served at his own expense to undertake either or both of the following, as specified in the notice—

(a)   to ensure that the product is marked in accordance with requirements specified in the notice with warnings as to the risks it may present,

(b)   to make the marketing of the product subject to prior conditions as specified in the notice so as to ensure the product is a safe product.

(2)   The requirements referred to in paragraph (1)(a) shall be such as to ensure that the product is marked with a warning which is suitable, clearly worded and easily comprehensible.

13   Requirements to warn

Where an enforcement authority has reasonable grounds for believing that a product is a dangerous product in that it could pose risks for certain persons, the authority may serve a notice ('a requirement to warn') requiring the person on whom the notice is served at his own expense to undertake one or more of the following, as specified in the notice—

(a)   where and to the extent it is practicable to do so, to ensure that any person who could be subject to such risks and who has been supplied with the product be given warning of the risks in good time and in a form specified in the notice,

(b)   to publish a warning of the risks in such form and manner as is likely to bring those risks to the attention of any such person,

(c)   to ensure that the product carries a warning of the risks in a form specified in the notice.

14   Withdrawal notices

(1)   Where an enforcement authority has reasonable grounds for believing that a product is a dangerous product, the authority may serve a notice ('a withdrawal notice') prohibiting the person on whom it is served from doing any of the following things without the consent of the authority, that is to say—

(a)   placing the product on the market, offering to place it on the market, agreeing to place it on the market or exposing it for placing on the market, or

(b)   supplying the product, offering to supply it, agreeing to supply it or exposing it for supply.

(2)   A withdrawal notice may require the person on whom it is served to take action to alert consumers to the risks that the product presents.

(3)   In relation to a product that is already on the market, a withdrawal notice may only be served by an enforcement authority where the action being undertaken by the producer or the distributor concerned in fulfilment of his obligations under these Regulations is unsatisfactory or insufficient to prevent the risks concerned to the health and safety of persons.

(4)   Paragraph (3) shall not apply in the case of a product posing a serious risk requiring, in the view of the enforcement authority, urgent action.

(5)   A withdrawal notice served by an enforcement authority in relation to a product may require the person on whom it is served to keep the authority informed of the whereabouts of any such product in which he has an interest.

(6)   A consent given by the enforcement authority for the purposes of paragraph (1) may impose such conditions on the doing of anything for which the consent is required as the authority considers appropriate.

15   Recall notices

(1)   Subject to paragraph (4), where an enforcement authority has reasonable grounds for believing that a product is a dangerous product and that it has already been supplied or made available to consumers, the authority may serve a notice ('a recall notice') requiring the person on whom it is served to use his

reasonable endeavours to organise the return of the product from consumers to that person or to such other person as is specified in the notice.

(2)   A recall notice may require—

(a)   the recall to be effected in accordance with a code of practice applicable to the product concerned, or

(b)   the recipient of the recall notice to—

(i)   contact consumers who have purchased the product in order to inform them of the recall, where and to the extent it is practicable to do so,

(ii)   publish a notice in such form and such manner as is likely to bring to the attention of purchasers of the product the risk the product poses and the fact of the recall, or

(iii)   make arrangements for the collection or return of the product from consumers who have purchased it or for its disposal,

and may impose such additional requirements on the recipient of the notice as are reasonable and practicable with a view to achieving the return of the product from consumers to the person specified in the notice or its disposal.

(3)   In determining what requirements to include in a recall notice, the enforcement authority shall take into consideration the need to encourage distributors, users and consumers to contribute to its implementation.

(4)   A recall notice may only be issued by an enforcement authority where—

(a)   other action which it may require under these Regulations would not suffice to prevent the risks concerned to the health and safety of persons,

(b)   the action being undertaken by the producer or the distributor concerned in fulfilment of his obligations under these Regulations is unsatisfactory or insufficient to prevent the risks concerned to the health and safety of persons, and

(c)   the authority has given not less than seven days' notice to the person on whom the recall notice is to be served of its intention to serve such a notice and where that person has before the expiry of that period by notice required the authority to seek the advice of such person as the Institute determines on the questions of—

(i)   whether the product is a dangerous product,

(ii)   whether the issue of a recall notice is proportionate to the seriousness of the risk,

and the authority has taken account of such advice.

(5)   Paragraphs (4)(b) and (c) shall not apply in the case of a product posing a serious risk requiring, in the view of the enforcement authority, urgent action.

(6)   Where a person requires an enforcement authority to seek advice as referred to in paragraph (4)(c), that person shall be responsible for the fees, costs and expenses of the Institute and of the person appointed by the Institute to advise the authority.

(7)   In paragraphs 4(c) and (6) 'the Institute' means the charitable organisation with registered number 803725 and known as the Chartered Institute of Arbitrators.

(8)   A recall notice served by an enforcement authority in relation to a product may require the person on whom it is served to keep the authority informed of the whereabouts of any such product to which the recall notice relates, so far as he is able to do so.

(9)   Where the conditions in paragraph (1) for serving a recall notice are satisfied and either the enforcement authority has been unable to identify any person on whom to serve a recall notice, or the person on whom such a notice has been served has failed to comply with it, then the authority may itself take such action as could have been required by a recall notice.

(10)   Where—

(a)   an authority has complied with the requirements of paragraph (4); and

(b)   the authority has exercised its powers under paragraph (9) to take action

following the failure of the person on whom the recall notice has been served to
comply with that notice,

then the authority may recover from the person on whom the notice was served
summarily as a civil debt, any costs or expenses reasonably incurred by it in
undertaking the action referred to in sub-paragraph (b).

(11)   A civil debt recoverable under the preceding paragraph may be recovered—

(a)   in England and Wales by way of complaint (as mentioned in section 58
of the Magistrates' Courts Act 1980,

(b)   in Northern Ireland in proceedings under Article 62 of the Magistrates'
Courts (Northern Ireland) Order 1981.

16   Supplementary provisions relating to safety notices

(1)   Whenever feasible, prior to serving a safety notice the authority shall give
an opportunity to the person on whom the notice is to be served to submit his
views to the authority. Where, due to the urgency of the situation, this is not
feasible the person shall be given an opportunity to submit his views to the
authority after service of the notice.

(2)   A safety notice served by an enforcement authority in respect of a product
shall—

(a)   describe the product in a manner sufficient to identify it;

(b)   state the reasons on which the notice is based;

(c)   indicate the rights available to the recipient of the notice under these
Regulations and (where applicable) the time limits applying to their exercise;
and

(d)   in the case of a suspension notice, state the period of time for which it
applies.

(3)   A safety notice shall have effect throughout the United Kingdom.

(4)   Where an enforcement authority serves a suspension notice in respect of a
product, the authority shall be liable to pay compensation to a person having an
interest in the product in respect of any loss or damage suffered by reason of the
notice if—

(a)   there has been no contravention of any requirement of these Regulations
in relation to the product; and

(b)   the exercise by the authority of the power to serve the suspension notice
was not attributable to any neglect or default by that person.

(5)   Where an enforcement authority serves a withdrawal notice in respect of a
product, the authority shall be liable to pay compensation to a person having an
interest in the product in respect of any loss or damage suffered by reason of the
notice if—

(a)   the product was not a dangerous product; and

(b)   the exercise by the authority of the power to serve the withdrawal notice
was not attributable to any neglect or default by that person.

(6)   Where an enforcement authority serves a recall notice in respect of a product, the authority shall be liable to pay compensation to the person on whom the
notice was served in respect of any loss or damage suffered by reason of the notice
if—

(a)   the product was not a dangerous product; and

(b)   the exercise by the authority of the power to serve the recall notice was
not attributable to any neglect or default by that person.

(7)   An enforcement authority may vary or revoke a safety notice which
it has served provided that the notice is not made more restrictive for the
person on whom it is served or more onerous for that person to comply
with.

(8)   Wherever feasible prior to varying a safety notice the authority shall give
an opportunity to the person on whom the original notice was served to submit
his views to the authority.

17   Appeals against safety notices

(1)   A person on whom a safety notice has been served and a person having an interest in a product in respect of which a safety notice (other than a recall notice) has been served may, before the end of the period of 21 days beginning with the day on which the notice was served, apply for an order to vary or set aside the terms of the notice.

(2)   On an application under paragraph (1) the court or the sheriff, as the case may be, shall make an order setting aside the notice only if satisfied that—

(a)   in the case of a suspension notice, there has been no contravention in relation to the product of any requirement of these Regulations,

(b)   in the case of a requirement to mark or a requirement to warn, the product is not a dangerous product,

(c)   in the case of a withdrawal notice—

(i)   the product is not a dangerous product, or

(ii)   where applicable, regulation 14(3) has not been complied with by the enforcement authority concerned,

(d)   in the case of a recall notice—

(i)   the product is not a dangerous product, or

(ii)   regulation 15(4) has not been complied with,

(e)   in any case, the serving of the safety notice concerned was not proportionate to the seriousness of the risk.

(3)   On an application concerning the period of time specified in a suspension notice as the period for which it applies, the court or the sheriff, as the case may be, may reduce the period to such period as it considers sufficient for organising appropriate safety evaluations, checks and controls.

(4)   On an application to vary the terms of a notice, the court or the sheriff, as the case may be, may vary the requirements specified in the notice as it considers appropriate.

(5)   A person on whom a recall notice has been served and who proposes to make an application under paragraph (1) in relation to the notice may, before the end of the period of seven days beginning with the day on which the notice was served, apply to the court or the sheriff for an order suspending the effect of the notice and the court or the sheriff may, in any case where it considers it appropriate to do so, make an order suspending the effect of the notice.

(6)   If the court or the sheriff makes an order suspending the effect of a recall notice under paragraph (5) in the absence of the enforcement authority, the enforcement authority may apply for the revocation of such order.

(7)   An order under paragraph (5) shall take effect from the time it is made until—

(a)   it is revoked under paragraph (6),

(b)   where no application is made under paragraph (1) in respect of the recall notice within the time specified in that paragraph, the expiration of that time,

(c)   where such an application is made but is withdrawn or dismissed for want of prosecution, the date of dismissal or withdrawal of the application, or

(d)   where such an application is made and is not withdrawn or dismissed for want of prosecution, the determination of the application.

(8)   Subject to paragraph (6), in Scotland the sheriff's decision under paragraph (5) shall be final.

(9)   An application under this regulation may be made—

(a)   by way of complaint to any magistrates' court in which proceedings have been brought in England and Wales or Northern Ireland—

(i)   in respect of a contravention in relation to the product of a requirement imposed by or under these Regulations; or

(ii)   for the forfeiture of the product under regulation 18;

(b)   where no such proceedings have been brought, by way of complaint to any magistrates' court; or

(c)   in Scotland, by summary application to the sheriff.

(10)   A person aggrieved by an order made pursuant to an application under paragraph (1) by a magistrates' court in England, Wales or Northern Ireland, or by a decision of such a court not to make such an order, may appeal against that order or decision—

(a)   in England and Wales, to the Crown Court;

(b)   in Northern Ireland, to the county court.

[18   *Does not apply to Scotland*]

19   Forfeiture: Scotland

(1)   In Scotland a sheriff may make an order for forfeiture of a product on the grounds that the product is a dangerous product—

(a)   on an application by a procurator-fiscal made in the manner specified in section 134 of the Criminal Procedure (Scotland) Act 1995, or

(b)   where a person is convicted of any offence in respect of a contravention in relation to the product of a requirement imposed by or under these Regulations, in addition to any other penalty which the sheriff may impose.

(2)   The procurator-fiscal making an application under paragraph (1)(a) shall serve on any person appearing to him to be the owner of, or otherwise to have an interest in, the product to which the application relates a copy of the application, together with a notice giving him the opportunity to appear at the hearing of the application to show cause why the product should not be forfeited.

(3)   Service under paragraph (2) shall be carried out, and such service may be proved, in the manner specified for citation of an accused in summary proceedings under the Criminal Procedure (Scotland) Act 1995.

(4)   A person upon whom notice is served under paragraph (2) and any other person claiming to be the owner of, or otherwise to have an interest in, the product to which the application relates shall be entitled to appear at the hearing of the application to show cause why the product should not be forfeited.

(5)   The sheriff shall not make an order following an application under paragraph (1)(a)—

(a)   if any person on whom notice is served under paragraph (2) does not appear, unless service of the notice on that person is proved; or

(b)   if no notice under paragraph (2) has been served, unless the sheriff is satisfied that in the circumstances it was reasonable not to serve notice on any person.

(6)   The sheriff may make an order under this regulation only if he is satisfied that the product is a dangerous product.

(7)   Where an order for the forfeiture of a product is made following an application by the procurator-fiscal under paragraph (1)(a), any person who appeared, or was entitled to appear to show cause why the product should not be forfeited may, within twenty-one days of the making of the order, appeal to the High Court by Bill of Suspension on the ground of an alleged miscarriage of justice; and section 182(5)(a) to (e) of the Criminal Procedure (Scotland) Act 1995 shall apply to an appeal under this paragraph as it applies to a stated case under Part X of that Act.

(8)   An order following an application under paragraph (1)(a) shall not take effect—

(a)   until the end of the period of twenty-one days beginning with the day after the day on which the order is made; or

(b)   if an appeal is made under paragraph (7) within that period, until the appeal is determined or abandoned.

(9)   An order under paragraph (1)(b) shall not take effect—

(a)   until the end of the period within which an appeal against the order could be brought under the Criminal Procedure (Scotland) Act 1995; or

(b)   if an appeal is made within that period, until the appeal is determined or abandoned.

(10) Subject to paragraph (11), a product forfeited under this regulation shall be destroyed in accordance with such directions as the sheriff may give.

(11) If he thinks fit, the sheriff may direct that the product be released to such person as he may specify, on condition that that person does not supply the product to any other person otherwise than as mentioned in paragraph (11) of regulation 18.

20 Offences

(1) A person who contravenes regulations 5 or 8(1)(a) shall be guilty of an offence and liable on conviction on indictment to imprisonment for a term not exceeding 12 months or to a fine not exceeding £20,000 or to both, or on summary conviction to imprisonment for a term not exceeding three months or to a fine not exceeding the statutory maximum or to both.

(2) A person who contravenes regulation 7(1), 7(3) (by failing to take any of the measures specified in regulation 7(4)), 8(1)(b)(i), (ii) or (iii) or 9(1) shall be guilty of an offence and liable on summary conviction to imprisonment for a term not exceeding three months or to a fine not exceeding level 5 on the standard scale or to both.

(3) A producer or distributor who does not give notice to an enforcement authority under regulation 9(1) in respect of a product he has placed on the market or supplied commits an offence where it is proved that he ought to have known that the product poses risks to consumers that are incompatible with the general safety requirement and he shall be liable on summary conviction to imprisonment for a term not exceeding three months or to a fine not exceeding level 5 on the standard scale or to both.

(4) A person who contravenes a safety notice shall be guilty of an offence and liable on conviction on indictment to imprisonment for a term not exceeding 12 months or to a fine not exceeding £20,000 or to both, or on summary conviction to imprisonment for a term not exceeding three months or to a fine not exceeding the statutory maximum or to both.

21 Test purchases

(1) An enforcement authority shall have power to organise appropriate checks on the safety properties of a product, on an adequate scale, up to the final stage of use or consumption and for that purpose may make a purchase of a product or authorise an officer of the authority to make a purchase of a product.

(2) Where a product purchased under paragraph (1) is submitted to a test and the test leads to—

(a) the bringing of proceedings for an offence in respect of a contravention in relation to the product of any requirement imposed by or under these Regulations or for the forfeiture of the product under regulation 18 or 19, or

(b) the serving of a safety notice in respect of the product, and

(c) the authority is requested to do so and it is practicable for the authority to comply with the request,

then the authority shall allow the person from whom the product was purchased, a person who is a party to the proceedings, on whom the notice was served or who has an interest in the product to which the notice relates, to have the product tested.

22 Powers of entry and search etc

(1) An officer of an enforcement authority may at any reasonable hour and on production, if required, of his credentials exercise any of the powers conferred by the following provisions of this regulation.

(2) The officer may, for the purposes of ascertaining whether there has been a contravention of a requirement imposed by or under these Regulations, enter any premises other than premises occupied only as a person's residence and inspect any record or product.

(3)   The officer may, for the purpose of ascertaining whether there has been a contravention of a requirement imposed by or under these Regulations, examine any procedure (including any arrangements for carrying out a test) connected with the production of a product.

(4)   If the officer has reasonable grounds for suspecting that the product has not been placed on the market or supplied in the United Kingdom since it was manufactured or imported he may for the purpose of ascertaining whether there has been a contravention in relation to the product of a requirement imposed by or under these Regulations—

(a)   require a person carrying on a commercial activity, or employed in connection with a commercial activity, to supply all necessary information relating to the activity, including by the production of records,

(b)   require any record which is stored in an electronic form and is accessible from the premises to be produced in a form —

(i)   in which it can be taken away, and

(ii)   in which it is visible and legible.

(c)   for the purpose of ascertaining (by testing or otherwise) whether there has been any such contravention, seize and detain samples of the product,

(d)   take copies of, or of an entry in, any records produced by virtue of sub-paragraph (a).

(5)   If the officer has reasonable grounds for suspecting that there has been a contravention in relation to a product of a requirement imposed by or under these Regulations, he may—

(a)   for the purpose of ascertaining whether there has been any such contravention, require a person carrying on a commercial activity, or employed in connection with a commercial activity, to supply all necessary information relating to the activity, including by the production of records,

(b)   for the purpose of ascertaining whether there has been any such contravention, require any record which is stored in an electronic form and is accessible from the premises to be produced in a form—

(i)   in which it can be taken away, and

(ii)   in which it is visible and legible,

(c)   for the purpose of ascertaining (by testing or otherwise) whether there has been any such contravention, seize and detain samples of the product,

(d)   take copies of, or of an entry in, any records produced by virtue of sub-paragraph (a).

(6)   The officer may seize and detain any products or records which he has reasonable grounds for believing may be required as evidence in proceedings for an offence in respect of a contravention of any requirement imposed by or under these Regulations.

(7)   If and to the extent that it is reasonably necessary to do so to prevent a contravention of any requirement imposed by or under these Regulations, the officer may, for the purpose of exercising his power under paragraphs (4) to (6) to seize products or records—

(a)   require any person having authority to do so to open any container or to open any vending machine; and

(b)   himself open or break open any such container or machine where a requirement made under sub-paragraph (a) in relation to the container or machine has not been complied with.

23   Provisions supplemental to regulation 22 and search warrants etc

(1)   An officer seizing any products or records shall, before he leaves the premises, provide to the person from whom they were seized a written notice—

(a)   specifying the products (including the quantity thereof) and records seized,

(b)   stating the reasons for their seizure, and

(c)   explaining the right of appeal under regulation 25.

(2)   References in paragraph (1) and regulation 25 to the person from whom something has been seized, in relation to a case in which the power of seizure was exercisable by reason of the product having been found on any premises, are references to the occupier of the premises at the time of the seizure.

(3)   If a justice of the peace—

(a)   is satisfied by written information on oath that there are reasonable grounds for believing either—

(i)   that any products or records which an officer has power to inspect under regulation 22 are on any premises and that their inspection is likely to disclose evidence that there has been a contravention of any requirement imposed by or under these Regulations, or

(ii)   that such a contravention has taken place, is taking place or is about to take place on any premises, and

(b)   is also satisfied by such information either—

(i)   that admission to the premises has been or is likely to be refused and that notice of the intention to apply for a warrant under this paragraph has been given to the occupier, or

(ii)   that an application for admission, or the giving of such a notice, would defeat the object of the entry or that the premises are unoccupied or that the occupier is temporarily absent and it might defeat the object of the entry to await his return,

the justice may by warrant under his hand, which shall continue in force for a period of one month, authorise any officer of an enforcement authority to enter the premises, if need be by force.

(4)   An officer entering premises by virtue of regulation 22 or a warrant under paragraph (3) may take with him such other persons and equipment as may appear to him necessary.

(5)   On leaving any premises which a person is authorised to enter by a warrant under paragraph (3), that person shall, if the premises are unoccupied or the occupier is temporarily absent—

(a)   leave the premises as effectively secured against trespassers as he found them,

(b)   attach a notice such as is mentioned in paragraph (1) in a prominent place at the premises.

(6)   Where a product seized by an officer of an enforcement authority under regulation 22 or 23 is submitted to a test, the authority shall inform the person mentioned in paragraph (1) of the result of the test and, if—

(a)   proceedings are brought for an offence in respect of a contravention in relation to the product of any requirement imposed by or under these Regulations or for the forfeiture of the product under regulation 18 or 19; or

(b)   a safety notice is served in respect of the product; and

(c)   the authority is requested to do so and it is practicable for him to comply with the request,

then the authority shall allow a person who is a party to the proceedings or on whom the notice was served or who has an interest in the product to which the notice relates to have the product tested.

(7)   If a person who is not an officer of an enforcement authority purports to act as such under regulation 22 or under this regulation he shall be guilty of an offence and liable on summary conviction to a fine not exceeding level 5 on the standard scale.

(8)   In the application of this section to Scotland, the reference in paragraph (3) to a justice of the peace shall include a reference to a sheriff and the reference to written information on oath shall be construed as a reference to evidence on oath.

(9)   In the application of this section to Northern Ireland, the reference in para-

graph (3) to a justice of the peace shall include a reference to a lay magistrate and the references to an information on oath shall be construed as a reference to a complaint on oath.

24   Obstruction of officers

(1)   A person who—

(a)   intentionally obstructs an officer of an enforcement authority who is acting in pursuance of any provision of regulation 22 or 23; or

(b)   intentionally fails to comply with a requirement made of him by an officer of an enforcement authority under any provision of those regulations; or

(c)   without reasonable cause fails to give an officer of an enforcement authority who is so acting any other assistance or information which the officer may reasonably require of him for the purposes of the exercise of the officer's functions under any provision of those regulations,

shall be guilty of an offence and liable on summary conviction to a fine not exceeding level 5 on the standard scale.

(2)   A person shall be guilty of an offence if, in giving any information which is required by him by virtue of paragraph (1)(c)—

(a)   he makes a statement which he knows is false in a material particular; or

(b)   he recklessly makes a statement which is false in a material particular.

(3)   A person guilty of an offence under paragraph (2) shall be liable—

(a)   on conviction on indictment, to a fine;

(b)   on summary conviction, to a fine not exceeding the statutory maximum.

25   Appeals against detention of products and records

(1)   A person referred to in regulation 23(1) may apply for an order requiring any product or record which is for the time being detained under regulation 22 or 23 by an enforcement authority or by an officer of such an authority to be released to him or to another person.

(2)   An application under the preceding paragraph may be made—

(a)   to any magistrates' court in which proceedings have been brought in England and Wales or Northern Ireland—

(i)   for an offence in respect of a contravention in relation to the product of a requirement imposed by or under these Regulations, or

(ii)   for the forfeiture of the product under regulation 18,

(b)   where no such proceedings have been brought, by way of complaint to a magistrates' court;

(c)   in Scotland, by summary application to the sheriff.

(3)   On an application under paragraph (1) to a magistrates' court or to the sheriff, the court or the sheriff may make an order requiring a product or record to be released only if the court or sheriff is satisfied—

(a)   that proceedings—

(i)   for an offence in respect of any contravention in relation to the product or, in the case of a record, the product to which the record relates, of any requirement imposed by or under these Regulations; or

(ii)   for the forfeiture of the product or, in the case of a record, the product to which the record relates, under regulation 18 or 19,

have not been brought or, having been brought, have been concluded without the product being forfeited; and

(b)   where no such proceedings have been brought, that more than six months have elapsed since the product or records was seized.

(4)   In determining whether to make an order under this regulation requiring the release of a product or record the court or sheriff shall take all the circumstances into account including the results of any tests on the product which have been carried out by or on behalf of the enforcement authority and any statement made by the enforcement authority to the court or sheriff as to its intention to

bring proceedings for an offence in respect of a contravention in relation to the product of any requirement imposed by or under these Regulations.

(5)   Where—

(a)   more than 12 months have elapsed since a product or records were seized and the enforcement authority has not commenced proceedings for an offence in respect of a contravention in relation to the product (or, in the case of records, the product to which the records relate) of any requirement imposed by or under these Regulations or for the forfeiture of the product under regulation 18 or 19, or

(b)   an enforcement authority has brought proceedings for an offence as mentioned in sub-paragraph (a) and the proceedings were dismissed and all rights of appeal have been exercised or the time for appealing has expired,

the authority shall be under a duty to return the product or records detained under regulation 22 or 23 to the person from whom they were seized.

(6)   Where the authority is satisfied that some other person has a better right to a product or record than the person from whom it was seized, the authority shall, instead of the duty in paragraph (5), be under a duty to return it to that other person or, as the case may be, to the person appearing to the authority to have the best right to the product or record in question.

(7)   Where different persons claim to be entitled to the return of a product or record that is required to be returned under paragraph (5), then it may be retained for as long as is reasonably necessary for the determination in accordance with paragraph (6) of the person to whom it must be returned.

(8)   A person aggrieved by an order made under this regulation by a magistrates' court in England and Wales or Northern Ireland, or by a decision of such a court not to make such an order, may appeal against that order or decision—

(a)   in England and Wales, to the Crown Court;

(b)   in Northern Ireland, to the county court;

and an order so made may contain such provision as appears to the court to be appropriate for delaying the coming into force of the order pending the making and determination of any appeal (including any application under section 111 of the Magistrates' Courts Act 1980 or article 146 of the Magistrates' Courts (Northern Ireland) Order 1981 (statement of case)).

26   Compensation for seizure and detention

Where an officer of an enforcement authority exercises any power under regulation 22 or 23 to seize and detain a product, the enforcement authority shall be liable to pay compensation to any person having an interest in the product in respect of any loss or damage caused by reason of the exercise of the power if—

(a)   there has been no contravention in relation to the product of any requirement imposed by or under these Regulations, and

(b)   the exercise of the power is not attributable to any neglect or default by that person.

27   Recovery of expenses of enforcement

(1)   This regulation shall apply where a court—

(a)   convicts a person of an offence in respect of a contravention in relation to a product of any requirement imposed by or under these Regulations, or

(b)   makes an order under regulation 18 or 19 for the forfeiture of a product.

(2)   The court may (in addition to any other order it may make as to costs or expenses) order the person convicted or, as the case may be, any person having an interest in the product to reimburse an enforcement authority for any expenditure which has been or may be incurred by that authority—

(a)   in connection with any seizure or detention of the product by or on behalf of the authority, or

(b)   in connection with any compliance by the authority with directions given by the court for the purposes of any order for the forfeiture of the product.

28   Power of Secretary of State to obtain information

(1)   If the Secretary of State considers that, for the purposes of deciding whether to serve a safety notice, or to vary or revoke a safety notice which he has already served, he requires information or a sample of a product he may serve on a person a notice requiring him—

(a)   to furnish to the Secretary of State, within a period specified in the notice, such information as is specified;

(b)   to produce such records as are specified in the notice at a time and place so specified (and to produce any such records which are stored in any electronic form in a form in which they are visible and legible) and to permit a person appointed by the Secretary of State for that purpose to take copies of the records at that time and place;

(c)   to produce such samples of a product as are specified in the notice at a time and place so specified.

(2)   A person shall be guilty of an offence if he—

(a)   fails, without reasonable cause, to comply with a notice served on him under paragraph (1); or

(b)   in purporting to comply with a requirement which by virtue of paragraph (1)(a) or (b) is contained in such a notice—

(i)   furnishes information or records which he knows are false in a material particular, or

(ii)   recklessly furnishes information or records which are false in a material particular.

(3)   A person guilty of an offence under paragraph (2) shall—

(a)   in the case of an offence under sub-paragraph (a) of that paragraph, be liable on summary conviction to a fine not exceeding level 5 on the standard scale; and

(b)   in the case of an offence under sub-paragraph (b) of that paragraph, be liable—

(i)   on conviction on indictment, to a fine;

(ii)   on summary conviction, to a fine not exceeding the statutory maximum.

29   Defence of due diligence

(1)   Subject to the following provisions of this regulation, in proceedings against a person for an offence under these Regulations it shall be a defence for that person to show that he took all reasonable steps and exercised all due diligence to avoid committing the offence.

(2)   Where in any proceedings against any person for such an offence the defence provided by paragraph (1) involves an allegation that the commission of the offence was due—

(a)   to the act or default of another, or

(b)   to reliance on information given by another,

that person shall not, without the leave of the court, be entitled to rely on the defence unless, not less than seven clear days before, in England, Wales and Northern Ireland, the hearing of the proceedings or, in Scotland, the trial diet, he has served a notice under paragraph (3) on the person bringing the proceedings.

(3)   A notice under this paragraph shall give such information identifying or assisting in the identification of the person who—

(a)   committed the act or default, or

(b)   gave the information,

as is in the possession of the person serving the notice at the time he serves it.

(4)   A person may not rely on the defence provided by paragraph (1) by reason

of his reliance on information supplied by another, unless he shows that it was reasonable in all the circumstances to have relied on the information, having regard in particular—

(a)   to the steps which he took, and those which might reasonably have been taken, for the purpose of verifying the information; and

(b)   to whether he had any reason to disbelieve the information.

30   Defence in relation to antiques

(1)   This regulation shall apply in proceedings against any person for an offence under regulation 20(1) in respect of the supply, offer or agreement to supply or exposure or possession for supply of second hand products supplied as antiques.

(2)   It shall be a defence for that person to show that the terms on which he supplied the product or agreed or offered to supply the product or, in the case of a product which he exposed or possessed for supply, the terms on which he intended to supply the product, contemplated the acquisition of an interest in the product by the person supplied or to be supplied.

(3)   Paragraph (2) applies only if the producer or distributor clearly informed the person to whom he supplied the product, or offered or agreed to supply the product or, in the case of a product which he exposed or possessed for supply, he intended to so inform that person, that the product is an antique.

31   Liability of person other than principal offender

(1)   Where the commission by a person of an offence under these Regulations is due to an act or default committed by some other person in the course of a commercial activity of his, the other person shall be guilty of the offence and may be proceeded against and punished by virtue of this paragraph whether or not proceedings are taken against the first-mentioned person.

(2)   Where a body corporate is guilty of an offence under these Regulations (including where it is so guilty by virtue of paragraph (1)) in respect of any act or default which is shown to have been committed with the consent or connivance of, or to be attributable to any neglect on the part of, any director, manager, secretary or other similar officer of the body corporate or any person who was purporting to act in any such capacity he, as well as the body corporate, shall be guilty of that offence and shall be liable to be proceeded against and punished accordingly.

(3)   Where the affairs of a body corporate are managed by its members, paragraph (2) shall apply in relation to the acts and defaults of a member in connection with his functions of management as if he were a director of the body corporate.

(4)   Where a Scottish partnership is guilty of an offence under these Regulations (including where it is so guilty by virtue of paragraph (1)) in respect of any act or default which is shown to have been committed with the consent or connivance of, or to be attributable to any neglect on the part of, a partner in the partnership, he, as well as the partnership, shall be guilty of that offence and shall be liable to be proceeded against and punished accordingly.

PART 4. MISCELLANEOUS

32   Reports

(1)   It shall be the duty of the Secretary of State to lay before each House of Parliament a report on the exercise during the period to which the report relates of the functions which are exercisable by enforcement authorities under these Regulations.

(2)   The first such report shall relate to the period beginning on the day on which these Regulations come into force and ending on 31 March 2008 and subsequent reports shall relate to a period of not more than five years beginning on the day after the day on which the period to which the previous report relates ends.

(3)   The Secretary of State may from time to time prepare and lay before each

House of Parliament such other reports on the exercise of those functions as he considers appropriate.

(4)   The Secretary of State may direct an enforcement authority to report at such intervals as he may specify in the direction on the discharge by that authority of the functions exercisable by it under these Regulations.

(5)   A report under paragraph (4) shall be in such form and shall contain such particulars as are specified in the direction of the Secretary of State.

33   Duty to notify Secretary of State and Commission

(1)   An enforcement authority which has received a notification under regulation 9(1) shall immediately pass the same on to the Secretary of State, who shall immediately pass it on to the competent authorities appointed for the purpose in the Member States where the product in question is or has been marketed or otherwise supplied to consumers.

(2)   Where an enforcement authority takes a measure which restricts the placing on the market of a product, or requires its withdrawal or recall, it shall immediately notify the Secretary of State, specifying its reasons for taking the action. It shall also immediately notify the Secretary of State of any modification or lifting of such a measure.

(3)   On receiving a notification under paragraph (2), or if he takes a measure which restricts the placing on the market of a product, or requires its withdrawal or recall, the Secretary of State shall (to the extent that such notification is not required under article 12 of the GPS Directive or any other Community legislation) immediately notify the European Commission of the measure taken, specifying the reasons for taking it. The Secretary of State shall also immediately notify the European Commission of any modification or lifting of such a measure. If the Secretary of State considers that the effects of the risk do not or cannot go beyond the territory of the United Kingdom, he shall notify the European Commission of the measure concerned insofar as it involves information likely to be of interest to Member States from the product safety standpoint, and in particular if it is in response to a new risk which has not yet been reported in other notifications.

(4)   Where an enforcement authority adopts or decides to adopt, recommend or agree with producers and distributors, whether on a compulsory or voluntary basis, a measure or action to prevent, restrict or impose specific conditions on the possible marketing or use of a product (other than a pharmaceutical product) by reason of a serious risk, it shall immediately notify the Secretary of State. It shall also immediately notify the Secretary of State of any modification or withdrawal of any such measure or action.

(5)   On receiving a notification under paragraph (4), or if he adopts or decides to adopt, recommend or agree with producers and distributors, whether on a compulsory or voluntary basis, a measure or action to prevent, restrict or impose specific conditions on the possible marketing or use of a product (other than a pharmaceutical product) by reason of a serious risk, the Secretary of State shall immediately notify the European Commission of it through the Community Rapid Information System, known as RAPEX. The Secretary of State shall also inform the European Commission without delay of any modification or withdrawal of any such measure or action.

(6)   If the Secretary of State considers that the effects of the risk do not or cannot go beyond the territory of the United Kingdom, he shall notify the European Commission of the measures or action concerned insofar as they involve information likely to be of interest to Member States of the European Union from the product safety standpoint, and in particular if they are in response to a new risk which has not been reported in other notifications.

(7)   Before deciding to adopt such a measure or take such an action as is referred to in paragraph (5), the Secretary of State may pass on to the European

Commission any information in his possession regarding the existence of a serious risk. Where he does so, he must inform the European Commission, within 45 days of the day of passing the information to it, whether he confirms or modifies that information.

(8)   Upon receipt of a notification from the European Commission under article 12(2) of the GPS Directive, the Secretary of State shall notify the Commission of the following—

(a)   whether the product the subject of the notification has been marketed in the United Kingdom;

(b)   what measure concerning the product the enforcement authorities in the United Kingdom may be adopting, stating the reasons, including any differing assessment of risk or any other special circumstance justifying the decision as to the measure, in particular lack of action or follow-up; and

(c)   any relevant supplementary information he has obtained on the risk involved, including the results of any test or analysis carried out.

(9)   The Secretary of State shall notify the European Commission without delay of any modification or withdrawal of any measures notified to it under paragraph (8)(b).

(10)   In this regulation—

(a)   references to a product excludes a second hand product supplied as an antique or as a product to be repaired or reconditioned prior to being used, provided the supplier clearly informs the person to whom he supplies the product to that effect;

(b)   'pharmaceutical product' means a product falling within Council Directive 2001/83/EC of the European Parliament and of the Council on the Community code relating to medicinal products for human use.

34   Provisions supplemental to regulation 33

(1)   A notification under regulation 33(2) to (6), (8) or (9) to the Secretary of State or the Commission shall be in writing and shall provide all available details and at least the following information—

(a)   information enabling the product to be identified,

(b)   a description of the risk involved, including a summary of the results of any test or analysis and of their conclusions which are relevant to assessing the level of risk,

(c)   the nature and the duration of the measures or action taken or decided on, if applicable,

(d)   information on supply chains and distribution of the product, in particular on destination countries.

(2)   Where a measure notified to the Commission under regulation 33 seeks to limit the marketing or use of a chemical substance or preparation, the Secretary of State shall provide to the Commission as soon as possible either a summary or the references of the relevant data relating to the substance or preparation considered and to known and available substitutes, where such information is available. The Secretary of State shall also notify the Commission of the anticipated effects of the measure on consumer health and safety together with the assessment of the risk carried out in accordance with the general principles for the risk evaluation of chemical substances as referred to in article 10(4) of Council Regulation (EEC) No 793/93 of 23 March 1993 on the evaluation and control of the risks of existing substances, in the case of an existing substance, or in article 3(2) of Council Directive 67/548/EEC on the approximation of laws, regulations and administrative provisions relating to the classification, packaging and labelling of dangerous substances in the case of a new substance.

(3)   Where the Commission carries out an investigation under paragraph 5 of Annex II to the GPS Directive, the Secretary of State shall supply the Commission with such information as it requests, to the best of his ability.

35   Implementation of Commission decisions
(1)   This regulation applies where the Commission adopts a decision pursuant to article 13 of the GPS Directive.
(2)   The Secretary of State shall—
    (a)   take such action under these Regulations, or
    (b)   direct another enforcement authority to take such action under these Regulations, as is necessary to comply with the decision.
(3)   Where an enforcement authority serves a safety notice pursuant to paragraph (2), the following provisions of these Regulations shall not apply in relation to that notice, namely regulations 14(3), 15(4) to (6) and 16(1), 16(2)(c) and (d), 16(5) to (7) and 17.
(4)   Unless the Commission's decision provides otherwise, export from the Community of a dangerous product which is the subject of such a decision is prohibited with effect from the date the decision comes into force.
(5)   The enforcement of the prohibition in paragraph (4) shall be treated as an assigned matter within the meaning of section 1(1) of the Customs and Excise Management Act 1979.
(6)   The measures necessary to implement the decision shall be taken within 20 days, unless the decision specifies a different period.
(7)   The Secretary of State or, where the Secretary of State has directed another enforcement authority to take action under paragraph (2)(b), that enforcement authority shall, within one month, give the parties concerned an opportunity to submit their views and shall inform the Commission accordingly.

36   Market surveillance
In order to ensure a high level of consumer health and safety protection, enforcement authorities shall within the limits of their responsibility and to the extent of their ability undertake market surveillance of products employing appropriate means and procedures and co-operating with other enforcement authorities and competent authorities of other Member States which may include:
    (a)   establishment, periodical updating and implementation of sectoral surveillance programmes by categories of products or risks and the monitoring of surveillance activities, findings and results,
    (b)   follow-up and updating of scientific and technical knowledge concerning the safety of products,
    (c)   the periodical review and assessment of the functioning of the control activities and their effectiveness and, if necessary, revision of the surveillance approach and organisation put in place.

37   Complaints procedures
An enforcement authority shall maintain and publish a procedure by which complaints may be submitted by any person on product safety and on surveillance and control activities, which complaints shall be followed up as appropriate.

38   Co-operation between enforcement authorities
(1)   It shall be the duty of an enforcement authority to co-operate with other enforcement authorities in carrying out the functions conferred on them by these Regulations. In particular—
    (a)   enforcement authorities shall share their expertise and best practices with each other;
    (b)   enforcement authorities shall undertake collaborative working where they have a shared interest.
(2)   The Secretary of State shall inform the European Commission as to the arrangements for the enforcement of these Regulations, including which bodies are enforcement authorities.

39   Information
(1)   An enforcement authority shall in general make available to the public such

information as is available to it on the following matters relating to the risks to consumer health and safety posed by a product—

(a)   the nature of the risk,

(b)   the product identification,

and the measures taken in respect of the risk, without prejudice to the need not to disclose information for effective monitoring and investigation activities.

(2)   Paragraph (1) shall not apply to any information obtained by an enforcement authority for the purposes of these Regulations which, by its nature, is covered by professional secrecy, unless the circumstances require such information to be made public in order to protect the health and safety of consumers.

(3)   *[Amends Enterprise Act 2002 (Part 9 Restrictions on Disclosure of Information) (Amendment and Specification) Order 2003.]*

40   Service of documents

(1)   A document required or authorised by virtue of these Regulations to be served on a person may be so served—

(a)   on an individual by delivering it to him or by leaving it at his proper address or by sending it by post to him at that address;

(b)   on a body corporate other than a limited liability partnership, by serving it in accordance with sub-paragraph (a) on the secretary of the body;

(c)   on a limited liability partnership, by serving it in accordance with sub-paragraph (a) on a member of the partnership; or

(d)   on a partnership, by serving it in accordance with sub-paragraph (a) on a partner or a person having the control or management of the partnership business;

(e)   on any other person by leaving it at his proper address or by sending it by post to him at that address.

(2)   For the purposes of paragraph (1), and for the purposes of section 7 of the Interpretation Act 1978 (which relates to the service of documents by post) in its application to that paragraph, the proper address of a person on whom a document is to be served by virtue of these Regulations shall be his last known address except that—

(a)   in the case of a body corporate (other than a limited liability partnership) or its secretary, it shall be the address of the registered or principal office of the body;

(b)   in the case of a limited liability partnership or a member of the partnership, it shall be the address of the registered or principal office of the partnership;

(c)   in the case of a partnership or a partner or a person having the control or management of a partnership business, it shall be the address of the principal office of the partnership,

and for the purposes of this paragraph the principal officer of a company constituted under the law of a country or territory outside the United Kingdom or of a partnership carrying on business outside the United Kingdom is its principal office within the United Kingdom.

(3)   A document required or authorised by virtue of these Regulations to be served on a person may also be served by transmitting the request by any means of electronic communication to an electronic address (which includes a fax number and an e-mail address) being an address which the person has held out as an address at which he or it can be contacted for the purposes of receiving such documents.

(4)   A document transmitted by any means of electronic communication in accordance with the preceding paragraph is, unless the contrary is proved, deemed to be received on the business day after the notice was transmitted over a public electronic communications network.

41 Extension of time for bringing summary proceedings

(1) Notwithstanding section 127 of the Magistrates' Courts Act 1980 or article 19 of the Magistrates' Courts (Northern Ireland) Order 1981, in England, Wales and Northern Ireland a magistrates' court may try an information (in the case of England and Wales) or a complaint (in the case of Northern Ireland) in respect of an offence under these Regulations if (in the case of England and Wales) the information is laid or (in the case of Northern Ireland) the complaint is made within three years from the date of the offence or within one year from the discovery of the offence by the prosecutor whichever is the earlier.

(2) Notwithstanding section 136 of the Criminal Procedure (Scotland) Act 1995, in Scotland summary proceedings for an offence under these Regulations may be commenced within three years from the date of the offence or within one year from the discovery of the offence by the prosecutor whichever is the earlier.

(3) For the purposes of paragraph (2), section 136(3) of the Criminal Procedure (Scotland) Act 1995 shall apply as it applies for the purposes of that section.

42 Civil proceedings

These Regulations shall not be construed as conferring any right of action in civil proceedings in respect of any loss or damage suffered in consequence of a contravention of these Regulations.

43 Privileged information

(1) Nothing in these Regulations shall be taken as requiring a person to produce any records if he would be entitled to refuse to produce those records in any proceedings in any court on the grounds that they are the subject of legal professional privilege or, in Scotland, that they contain a confidential communication made by or to an advocate or solicitor in that capacity, or as authorising a person to take possession of any records which are in the possession of a person who would be so entitled.

(2) Nothing in these Regulations shall be construed as requiring a person to answer any question or give any information if to do so would incriminate that person or that person's spouse or civil partner.

44 Evidence in proceedings for offence relating to regulation 9(1)

(1) This regulation applies where a person has given a notification to an enforcement authority pursuant to regulation 9(1).

(2) No evidence relating to that statement may be adduced and no question relating to it may be asked by the prosecution in any criminal proceedings (other than proceedings in which that person is charged with an offence under regulation 20 for a contravention of regulation 9(1)), unless evidence relating to it is adduced, or a question relating to it is asked, in the proceedings by or on behalf of that person.

45 Transitional provisions

Where, in relation to a product, a suspension notice (within the meaning of the 1987 Act) has (by virtue of regulation 11(b) of the General Product Safety Regulations 1994) been served under section 14 of the 1987 Act and is in force immediately prior to the coming into force of these Regulations, it shall continue in force notwithstanding the revocation of the General Product Safety Regulations 1994 by these Regulations, and those Regulations shall continue to apply accordingly.

46–47 *[Amendment provisions]*

PART III
EC MATERIALS

COUNCIL DIRECTIVE OF 25 JULY 1985
on the approximation of the laws, regulations and administrative provisions
of the Member States concerning liability for defective products
(85/374/EEC)

(amended by Directive 99/34/EC)

THE COUNCIL OF THE EUROPEAN COMMUNITIES,

Having regard to the Treaty establishing the European Economic Community, and in particular Article 100 thereof,

Having regard to the proposal from the Commission,

Having regard to the opinion of the European Parliament,

Having regard to the opinion of the Economic and Social Committee,

Whereas approximation of the laws of the Member States concerning the liability of the producer for damage caused by the defectiveness of his products is necessary because the existing divergences may distort competition and affect the movement of goods within the common market and entail a differing degree of protection of the consumer against damage caused by a defective product to his health or property;

Whereas liability without fault on the part of the producer is the sole means of adequately solving the problem, peculiar to our age of increasing technicality, of a fair apportionment of the risks inherent in modern technological production;

Whereas liability without fault should apply only to movables which have been industrially produced;

Whereas, as a result, it is appropriate to exclude liability for agricultural products and game, except where they have undergone a processing of an industrial nature which could cause a defect in these products; whereas the liability provided for in this Directive should also apply to movables which are used in the construction of immovables or are installed in immovables;

Whereas protection of the consumer requires that all producers involved in the production process should be made liable, in so far as their finished product, component part or any raw material supplied by them was defective; whereas, for the same reason, liability should extend to importers of products into the Community and to persons who present themselves as producers by affixing their name, trade mark or other distinguishing feature or who supply a product the producer of which cannot be identified;

Whereas, in situations where several persons are liable for the same damage, the protection of the consumer requires that the injured person should be able to claim full compensation for the damage from any one of them;

Whereas, to protect the physical well-being and property of the consumer, the defectiveness of the product should be determined by reference not to its fitness for use but to the lack of the safety which the public at large is entitled to expect; whereas the safety is assessed by excluding any misuse of the product not reasonable under the circumstances;

Whereas a fair apportionment of risk between the injured person and the producer implies that the producer should be able to free himself from liability if he furnishes proof as to the existence of certain exonerating circumstances;

Whereas the protection of the consumer requires that the liability of the producer remains unaffected by acts or omissions of other persons having contributed to cause the damage; whereas, however, the contributory negligence of the injured person may be taken into account to reduce or disallow such liability;

Whereas the protection of the consumer requires compensation for death and personal injury as well as compensation for damage to property; whereas the latter should nevertheless be limited to goods for private use or consumption and be subject to a deduction of a lower threshold of a fixed amount in order to avoid litigation in an excessive number of cases; whereas this Directive should not prejudice compensation for pain and suffering and other non-material damages payable, where appropriate, under the law applicable to the case;

Whereas a uniform period of limitation for the bringing of action for compensation is in the interests both of the injured person and of the producer;

Whereas products age in the course of time, higher safety standards are developed and the state of science and technology progresses; whereas, therefore, it would not be reasonable to make the producer liable for an unlimited period for the defectiveness of his product; whereas, therefore, liability should expire after a reasonable length of time, without prejudice to claims pending at law;

Whereas, to achieve effective protection of consumers, no contractual derogation should be permitted as regards the liability of the producer in relation to the injured person;

Whereas under the legal systems of the Member States an injured party may have a claim for damages based on grounds of contractual liability or on grounds of non-contractual liability other than that provided for in this Directive; in so far as these provisions also serve to attain the objective of effective protection of consumers, they should remain unaffected by this Directive; whereas, in so far as effective protection of consumers in the sector of pharmaceutical products is already also attained in a Member State under a special liability system, claims based on this system should similarly remain possible;

Whereas, to the extent that liability for nuclear injury or damage is already covered in all Member States by adequate special rules, it has been possible to exclude damage of this type from the scope of this Directive;

Whereas, since the exclusion of primary agricultural products and game from the scope of this Directive may be felt, in certain Member States, in view of what is expected for the protection of consumers, to restrict unduly such protection, it should be possible for a Member State to extend liability to such products;

Whereas, for similar reasons, the possibility offered to a producer to free himself from liability if he proves that the state of scientific and technical knowledge at the time when he put the product into circulation was not such as to enable the existence of a defect to be discovered may be felt in certain Member States to restrict unduly the protection of the consumer; whereas it should therefore be possible for a Member State to maintain in its legislation or to provide by new legislation that this exonerating circumstance is not admitted; whereas, in the case of new legislation, making use of this derogation should, however, be subject to a Community stand-still procedure, in order to raise, if possible, the level of protection in a uniform manner throughout the Community;

Whereas, taking into account the legal traditions in most of the Member States, it is inappropriate to set any financial ceiling on the producer's liability without fault; whereas, in so far as there are, however, differing traditions, it seems possible to admit that a Member State may derogate from the principle of unlimited liability by providing a limit for the total liability of the producer for damage resulting from a death or personal injury and caused by identical items with the same defect, provided that this limit is established at a level sufficiently high to guarantee adequate protection of the consumer and the correct functioning of the common market;

Whereas the harmonization resulting from this cannot be total at the present stage, but opens the way towards greater harmonization; whereas it is therefore necessary that the Council receive at regular intervals, reports from the Commission on the application of this Directive, accompanied, as the case may be, by appropriate proposals;

Whereas it is particularly important in this respect that a re-examination be carried out of those parts of the Directive relating to the derogations open to the Member States, at the expiry of a period of sufficient length to gather practical experience on the effects of these derogations on the protection of consumers and on the functioning of the common market,

HAS ADOPTED THIS DIRECTIVE:

Article 1
The producer shall be liable for damage caused by a defect in his product.

[Article 2
For the purpose of this Directive 'product' means all movables even if incorporated into another movable or into an immovable. 'Product' includes electricity.]

Article 3
1. 'Producer' means the manufacturer of a finished product, the producer of any raw material or the manufacturer of a component part and any person who, by putting his name, trade mark or other distinguishing feature on the product presents himself as its producer.

2. Without prejudice to the liability of the producer, any person who imports into the Community a product for sale, hire, leasing or any form of distribution in the course of his business shall be deemed to be a producer within the meaning of this Directive and shall be responsible as a producer.

3. Where the producer of the product cannot be identified, each supplier of the product shall be treated as its producer unless he informs the injured person, within a reasonable time, of the identity of the producer or of the person who supplied him with the product. The same shall apply, in the case of an imported product, if this product does not indicate the identity of the importer referred to in paragraph 2, even if the name of the producer is indicated.

Article 4
The injured person shall be required to prove the damage, the defect and the causal relationship between defect and damage.

Article 5
Where, as a result of the provisions of this Directive, two or more persons are liable for the same damage, they shall be liable jointly and severally, without prejudice to the provisions of national law concerning the rights of contribution or recourse.

Article 6
1. A product is defective when it does not provide the safety which a person is entitled to expect, taking all circumstances into account, including:
    (a)   the presentation of the product;
    (b)   the use to which it could reasonably be expected that the product would be put;
    (c)   the time when the product was put into circulation.

2. A product shall not be considered defective for the sole reason that a better product is subsequently put into circulation.

Article 7
The producer shall not be liable as a result of this Directive if he proves:

(a) that he did not put the product into circulation; or

(b) that, having regard to the circumstances, it is probable that the defect which caused the damage did not exist at the time when the product was put into circulation by him or that this defect came into being afterwards; or

(c) that the product was neither manufactured by him for sale or any form of distribution for economic purpose nor manufactured or distributed by him in the course of his business; or

(d) that the defect is due to compliance of the product with mandatory regulations issued by the public authorities; or

(e) that the state of scientific and technical knowledge at the time when he put the product into circulation was not such as to enable the existence of the defect to be discovered; or

(f) in the case of a manufacturer of a component, that the defect is attributable to the design of the product in which the component has been fitted or to the instructions given by the manufacturer of the product.

Article 8

1. Without prejudice to the provisions of national law concerning the right of contribution or recourse, the liability of the producer shall not be reduced when the damage is caused both by a defect in product and by the act or omission of a third party.

2. The liability of the producer may be reduced or disallowed when, having regard to all the circumstances, the damage is caused both by a defect in the product and by the fault of the injured person or any person for whom the injured person is responsible.

Article 9

For the purpose of Article 1, 'damage' means:

(a) damage caused by death or by personal injuries;

(b) damage to, or destruction of, any item of property other than the defective product itself, with a lower threshold of 500 ECU, provided that the item of property:

(i) is of a type ordinarily intended for private use or consumption, and

(ii) was used by the injured person mainly for his own private use or consumption.

This Article shall be without prejudice to national provisions relating to non-material damage.

Article 10

1. Member States shall provide in their legislation that a limitation period of three years shall apply to proceedings for the recovery of damages as provided for in this Directive. The limitation period shall begin to run from the day on which the plaintiff became aware, or should reasonably have become aware, of the damage, the defect and the identity of the producer.

2. The laws of Member States regulating suspension or interruption of the limitation period shall not be affected by this Directive.

Article 11

Member States shall provide in their legislation that the rights conferred upon the injured person pursuant to this Directive shall be extinguished upon the expiry of a period of 10 years from the date on which the producer put into circulation the actual product which caused the damage, unless the injured person has in the meantime instituted proceedings against the producer.

Article 12

The liability of the producer arising from this Directive may not, in relation to the injured person, be limited or excluded by a provision limiting his liability or exempting him from liability.

Article 13
This Directive shall not affect any rights which an injured person may have according to the rules of the law of contractual or non-contractual liability or a special liability system existing at the moment when this Directive is notified.

Article 14
This Directive shall not apply to injury or damage arising from nuclear accidents and covered by international conventions ratified by the Member States.

Article 15
    1.   Each Member State may:
       (a) [. . .]
       (b) by way of derogation from Article 7(e), maintain or, subject to the procedure set out in paragraph 2 of this Article, provide in this legislation that the producer shall be liable even if he proves that the state of scientific and technical knowledge at the time when he put the product into circulation was not such as to enable the existence of a defect to be discovered.
    2.   A Member State wishing to introduce the measure specified in paragraph 1(b) shall communicate the text of the proposed measure to the Commission. The Commission shall inform the other Member States thereof.

The Member State concerned shall hold the proposed measure in abeyance for nine months after the Commission is informed and provided that in the meantime the Commission has not submitted to the Council a proposal amending this Directive on the relevant matter. However, if within three months of receiving the said information, the Commission does not advise the Member State concerned that it intends submitting such a proposal to the Council, the Member State may take the proposed measure immediately.

If the Commission does submit to the Council such a proposal amending this Directive within the aforementioned nine months, the Member State concerned shall hold the proposed measure in abeyance for a further period of 18 months from the date on which the proposal is submitted.
    3.   Ten years after the date of notification of this Directive, the Commission shall submit to the Council a report on the effect that rulings by the courts as to the application of Article 7(e) and of paragraph 1(b) of this Article have on consumer protection and the functioning of the common market. In the light of this report the Council, acting on a proposal from the Commission and pursuant to the terms of Article 100 of the Treaty, shall decide whether to repeal Article 7(e).

Article 16
    1.   Any Member State may provide that a producer's total liability for damage resulting from a death or personal injury and caused by identical items with the same defect shall be limited to an amount which may not be less than 70 million ECU.
    2.   Ten years after the date of notification of this Directive, the Commission shall submit to the Council a report on the effect on consumer protection and the functioning of the common market of the implementation of the financial limit on liability by those Member States which have used the option provided for in paragraph 1. In the light of this report the Council, acting on a proposal from the Commission and pursuant to the terms of Article 100 of the Treaty, shall decide whether to repeal paragraph 1.

Article 17
This Directive shall not apply to products put into circulation before the date on which the provisions referred to in Article 19 enter into force.

Article 18
    1.   For the purposes of this Directive, the ECU shall be that defined by Regulation (EEC) No 3180/78, as amended by Regulation (EEC) No 2626/84. The

equivalent in national currency shall initially be calculated at the rate obtaining on the date of adoption of this Directive.

2. Every five years the Council, acting on a proposal from the Commission, shall examine and, if need be, revise the amounts in this Directive, in the light of economic and monetary trends in the Community.

Article 19

1. Member States shall bring into force, not later than three years from the date of notification of this Directive, the laws, regulations and administrative provisions necessary to comply with this Directive. They shall forthwith inform the Commission thereof.

2. The procedure set out in Article 15(2) shall apply from the date of notification of this Directive.

Article 20

Member States shall communicate to the Commission the texts of the main provisions of national law which they subsequently adopt in the field governed by this Directive.

Article 21

Every five years the Commission shall present a report to the Council on the application of this Directive and, if necessary, shall submit appropriate proposals to it.

Article 22

This Directive is addressed to the Member States.

Done at Brussels, 25 July 1985.

DIRECTIVE 1999/93/EC OF THE EUROPEAN PARLIAMENT AND OF THE COUNCIL OF 13 DECEMBER 1999 ON A COMMUNITY FRAMEWORK FOR ELECTRONIC SIGNATURES

THE EUROPEAN PARLIAMENT AND THE COUNCIL OF THE EUROPEAN UNION,

Having regard to the Treaty establishing the European Community, and in particular Articles 47(2), 55 and 95 thereof,

Having regard to the proposal from the Commission,

Having regard to the opinion of the Economic and Social Committee,

Having regard to the opinion of the Committee of the Regions),

Acting in accordance with the procedure laid down in Article 251 of the Treaty,

Whereas:

(1) On 16 April 1997 the Commission presented to the European Parliament, the Council, the Economic and Social Committee and the Committee of the Regions a Communication on a European Initiative in Electronic Commerce;

(2) On 8 October 1997 the Commission presented to the European Parliament, the Council, the Economic and Social Committee and the Committee of the Regions a Communication on ensuring security and trust in electronic communication – towards a European framework for digital signatures and encryption;

(3) On 1 December 1997 the Council invited the Commission to submit as soon as possible a proposal for a Directive of the European Parliament and of the Council on digital signatures;

(4) Electronic communication and commerce necessitate 'electronic signatures' and related services allowing data authentication; divergent rules with respect to legal recognition of electronic signatures and the accreditation of certification-service providers in the Member States may create a significant barrier to the use

of electronic communications and electronic commerce; on the other hand, a clear Community framework regarding the conditions applying to electronic signatures will strengthen confidence in, and general acceptance of, the new technologies; legislation in the Member States should not hinder the free movement of goods and services in the internal market;

(5) The interoperability of electronic-signature products should be promoted; in accordance with Article 14 of the Treaty, the internal market comprises an area without internal frontiers in which the free movement of goods is ensured; essential requirements specific to electronic-signature products must be met in order to ensure free movement within the internal market and to build trust in electronic signatures, without prejudice to Council Regulation (EC) No 3381/94 of 19 December 1994 setting up a Community regime for the control of exports of dual-use goods and Council Decision 94/942/CFSP of 19 December 1994 on the joint action adopted by the Council concerning the control of exports of dual-use goods;

(6) This Directive does not harmonise the provision of services with respect to the confidentiality of information where they are covered by national provisions concerned with public policy or public security;

(7) The internal market ensures the free movement of persons, as a result of which citizens and residents of the European Union increasingly need to deal with authorities in Member States other than the one in which they reside; the availability of electronic communication could be of great service in this respect;

(8) Rapid technological development and the global character of the Internet necessitate an approach which is open to various technologies and services capable of authenticating data electronically;

(9) Electronic signatures will be used in a large variety of circumstances and applications, resulting in a wide range of new services and products related to or using electronic signatures; the definition of such products and services should not be limited to the issuance and management of certificates, but should also encompass any other service and product using, or ancillary to, electronic signatures, such as registration services, time-stamping services, directory services, computing services or consultancy services related to electronic signatures;

(10) The internal market enables certification-service-providers to develop their cross-border activities with a view to increasing their competitiveness, and thus to offer consumers and businesses new opportunities to exchange information and trade electronically in a secure way, regardless of frontiers; in order to stimulate the Community-wide provision of certification services over open networks, certification-service-providers should be free to provide their services without prior authorisation; prior authorisation means not only any permission whereby the certification-service-provider concerned has to obtain a decision by national authorities before being allowed to provide its certification services, but also any other measures having the same effect;

(11) Voluntary accreditation schemes aiming at an enhanced level of service-provision may offer certification-service-providers the appropriate framework for developing further their services towards the levels of trust, security and quality demanded by the evolving market; such schemes should encourage the development of best practice among certification-service-providers; certification-service-providers should be left free to adhere to and benefit from such accreditation schemes;

(12) Certification services can be offered either by a public entity or a legal or natural person, when it is established in accordance with the national law; whereas Member States should not prohibit certification-service-providers from operating outside voluntary accreditation schemes; it should be ensured that such accreditation schemes do not reduce competition for certification services;

(13) Member States may decide how they ensure the supervision of compliance with the provisions laid down in this Directive; this Directive does not preclude the establishment of private-sector-based supervision systems; this Directive does

not oblige certification-service-providers to apply to be supervised under any applicable accreditation scheme;

(14) It is important to strike a balance between consumer and business needs;

(15) Annex III covers requirements for secure signature-creation devices to ensure the functionality of advanced electronic signatures; it does not cover the entire system environment in which such devices operate; the functioning of the internal market requires the Commission and the Member States to act swiftly to enable the bodies charged with the conformity assessment of secure signature devices with Annex III to be designated; in order to meet market needs conformity assessment must be timely and efficient;

(16) This Directive contributes to the use and legal recognition of electronic signatures within the Community; a regulatory framework is not needed for electronic signatures exclusively used within systems, which are based on voluntary agreements under private law between a specified number of participants; the freedom of parties to agree among themselves the terms and conditions under which they accept electronically signed data should be respected to the extent allowed by national law; the legal effectiveness of electronic signatures used in such systems and their admissibility as evidence in legal proceedings should be recognised;

(17) This Directive does not seek to harmonise national rules concerning contract law, particularly the formation and performance of contracts, or other formalities of a non-contractual nature concerning signatures; for this reason the provisions concerning the legal effect of electronic signatures should be without prejudice to requirements regarding form laid down in national law with regard to the conclusion of contracts or the rules determining where a contract is concluded;

(18) The storage and copying of signature-creation data could cause a threat to the legal validity of electronic signatures;

(19) Electronic signatures will be used in the public sector within national and Community administrations and in communications between such administrations and with citizens and economic operators, for example in the public procurement, taxation, social security, health and justice systems;

(20) Harmonised criteria relating to the legal effects of electronic signatures will preserve a coherent legal framework across the Community; national law lays down different requirements for the legal validity of hand-written signatures; whereas certificates can be used to confirm the identity of a person signing electronically; advanced electronic signatures based on qualified certificates aim at a higher level of security; advanced electronic signatures which are based on a qualified certificate and which are created by a secure-signature-creation device can be regarded as legally equivalent to hand-written signatures only if the requirements for hand-written signatures are fulfilled;

(21) In order to contribute to the general acceptance of electronic authentication methods it has to be ensured that electronic signatures can be used as evidence in legal proceedings in all Member States; the legal recognition of electronic signatures should be based upon objective criteria and not be linked to authorisation of the certification-service-provider involved; national law governs the legal spheres in which electronic documents and electronic signatures may be used; this Directive is without prejudice to the power of a national court to make a ruling regarding conformity with the requirements of this Directive and does not affect national rules regarding the unfettered judicial consideration of evidence;

(22) Certification-service-providers providing certification-services to the public are subject to national rules regarding liability;

(23) The development of international electronic commerce requires cross-border arrangements involving third countries; in order to ensure interoperability at a global level, agreements on multilateral rules with third countries on mutual recognition of certification services could be beneficial;

(24) In order to increase user confidence in electronic communication and elec-

tronic commerce, certification-service-providers must observe data protection legislation and individual privacy;

(25) Provisions on the use of pseudonyms in certificates should not prevent Member States from requiring identification of persons pursuant to Community or national law;

(26) The measures necessary for the implementation of this Directive are to be adopted in accordance with Council Decision 1999/468/EC of 28 June 1999 laying down the procedures for the exercise of implementing powers conferred on the Commission;

(27) Two years after its implementation the Commission will carry out a review of this Directive so as, inter alia, to ensure that the advance of technology or changes in the legal environment have not created barriers to achieving the aims stated in this Directive; it should examine the implications of associated technical areas and submit a report to the European Parliament and the Council on this subject;

(28) In accordance with the principles of subsidiarity and proportionality as set out in Article 5 of the Treaty, the objective of creating a harmonised legal framework for the provision of electronic signatures and related services cannot be sufficiently achieved by the Member States and can therefore be better achieved by the Community; this Directive does not go beyond what is necessary to achieve that objective,

HAVE ADOPTED THIS DIRECTIVE:

Article 1. Scope
The purpose of this Directive is to facilitate the use of electronic signatures and to contribute to their legal recognition. It establishes a legal framework for electronic signatures and certain certification-services in order to ensure the proper functioning of the internal market.

It does not cover aspects related to the conclusion and validity of contracts or other legal obligations where there are requirements as regards form prescribed by national or Community law nor does it affect rules and limits, contained in national or Community law, governing the use of documents.

Article 2. Definitions
For the purpose of this Directive:

1. 'electronic signature' means data in electronic form which are attached to or logically associated with other electronic data and which serve as a method of authentication;

2. 'advanced electronic signature' means an electronic signature which meets the following requirements:
   (a) it is uniquely linked to the signatory;
   (b) it is capable of identifying the signatory;
   (c) it is created using means that the signatory can maintain under his sole control; and
   (d) it is linked to the data to which it relates in such a manner that any subsequent change of the data is detectable;

3. 'signatory' means a person who holds a signature-creation device and acts either on his own behalf or on behalf of the natural or legal person or entity he represents;

4. 'signature-creation data' means unique data, such as codes or private cryptographic keys, which are used by the signatory to create an electronic signature;

5. 'signature-creation device' means configured software or hardware used to implement the signature-creation data;

6. 'secure-signature-creation device' means a signature-creation device which meets the requirements laid down in Annex III;

7. 'signature-verification-data' means data, such as codes or public crypto-graphic keys, which are used for the purpose of verifying an electronic signature;

8. 'signature-verification device' means configured software or hardware used to implement the signature-verification-data;

9. 'certificate' means an electronic attestation which links signature-verification data to a person and confirms the identity of that person;

10. 'qualified certificate' means a certificate which meets the requirements laid down in Annex I and is provided by a certification-service-provider who fulfils the requirements laid down in Annex II;

11. 'certification-service-provider' means an entity or a legal or natural person who issues certificates or provides other services related to electronic signatures;

12. 'electronic-signature product' means hardware or software, or relevant components thereof, which are intended to be used by a certification-service-provider for the provision of electronic-signature services or are intended to be used for the creation or verification of electronic signatures;

13. 'voluntary accreditation' means any permission, setting out rights and obli-gations specific to the provision of certification services, to be granted upon request by the certification-service-provider concerned, by the public or private body charged with the elaboration of, and supervision of compliance with, such rights and obligations, where the certification-service-provider is not entitled to exercise the rights stemming from the permission until it has received the decision by the body.

Article 3. Market access

1. Member States shall not make the provision of certification services subject to prior authorisation.

2. Without prejudice to the provisions of paragraph 1, Member States may introduce or maintain voluntary accreditation schemes aiming at enhanced levels of certification-service provision. All conditions related to such schemes must be objective, transparent, proportionate and non-discriminatory. Member States may not limit the number of accredited certification-service-providers for reasons which fall within the scope of this Directive.

3. Each Member State shall ensure the establishment of an appropriate system that allows for supervision of certification-service-providers which are established on its territory and issue qualified certificates to the public.

4. The conformity of secure signature-creation-devices with the requirements laid down in Annex III shall be determined by appropriate public or private bodies designated by Member States. The Commission shall, pursuant to the pro-cedure laid down in Article 9, establish criteria for Member States to determine whether a body should be designated.

A determination of conformity with the requirements laid down in Annex III made by the bodies referred to in the first subparagraph shall be recognised by all Member States.

5. The Commission may, in accordance with the procedure laid down in Article 9, establish and publish reference numbers of generally recognised stan-dards for electronic-signature products in the Official Journal of the European Communities. Member States shall presume that there is compliance with the requirements laid down in Annex II, point (f), and Annex III when an electronic signature product meets those standards.

6. Member States and the Commission shall work together to promote the development and use of signature-verification devices in the light of the recom-mendations for secure signature-verification laid down in Annex IV and in the interests of the consumer.

7. Member States may make the use of electronic signatures in the public sector subject to possible additional requirements. Such requirements shall be objective, transparent, proportionate and non-discriminatory and shall relate only to the

specific characteristics of the application concerned. Such requirements may not constitute an obstacle to cross-border services for citizens.

Article 4. Internal market principles

1. Each Member State shall apply the national provisions which it adopts pursuant to this Directive to certification-service-providers established on its territory and to the services which they provide. Member States may not restrict the provision of certification-services originating in another Member State in the fields covered by this Directive.

2. Member States shall ensure that electronic-signature products which comply with this Directive are permitted to circulate freely in the internal market.

Article 5. Legal effects of electronic signatures

1. Member States shall ensure that advanced electronic signatures which are based on a qualified certificate and which are created by a secure-signature-creation device:

   (a) satisfy the legal requirements of a signature in relation to data in electronic form in the same manner as a handwritten signature satisfies those requirements in relation to paper-based data; and

   (b) are admissible as evidence in legal proceedings.

2. Member States shall ensure that an electronic signature is not denied legal effectiveness and admissibility as evidence in legal proceedings solely on the grounds that it is:

– in electronic form, or

– not based upon a qualified certificate, or

– not based upon a qualified certificate issued by an accredited certification-service-provider, or

– not created by a secure signature-creation device.

Article 6. Liability

1. As a minimum, Member States shall ensure that by issuing a certificate as a qualified certificate to the public or by guaranteeing such a certificate to the public a certification-service-provider is liable for damage caused to any entity or legal or natural person who reasonably relies on that certificate:

   (a) as regards the accuracy at the time of issuance of all information contained in the qualified certificate and as regards the fact that the certificate contains all the details prescribed for a qualified certificate;

   (b) for assurance that at the time of the issuance of the certificate, the signatory identified in the qualified certificate held the signature-creation data corresponding to the signature-verification data given or identified in the certificate;

   (c) for assurance that the signature-creation data and the signature-verification data can be used in a complementary manner in cases where the certification-service-provider generates them both; unless the certification-service-provider proves that he has not acted negligently.

2. As a minimum Member States shall ensure that a certification-service-provider who has issued a certificate as a qualified certificate to the public is liable for damage caused to any entity or legal or natural person who reasonably relies on the certificate for failure to register revocation of the certificate unless the certification-service-provider proves that he has not acted negligently.

3. Member States shall ensure that a certification-service-provider may indicate in a qualified certificate limitations on the use of that certificate, provided that the limitations are recognisable to third parties. The certification-service-provider shall not be liable for damage arising from use of a qualified certificate which exceeds the limitations placed on it.

4. Member States shall ensure that a certification-service-provider may indicate in the qualified certificate a limit on the value of transactions for which the certificate can be used, provided that the limit is recognisable to third parties.

The certification-service-provider shall not be liable for damage resulting from this maximum limit being exceeded.

5.   The provisions of paragraphs 1 to 4 shall be without prejudice to Council Directive 93/13/EEC of 5 April 1993 on unfair terms in consumer contracts.

Article 7. International aspects

1.   Member States shall ensure that certificates which are issued as qualified certificates to the public by a certification-service-provider established in a third country are recognised as legally equivalent to certificates issued by a certification-service-provider established within the Community if:

(a)   the certification-service-provider fulfils the requirements laid down in this Directive and has been accredited under a voluntary accreditation scheme established in a Member State; or

(b)   a certification-service-provider established within the Community which fulfils the requirements laid down in this Directive guarantees the certificate; or

(c)   the certificate or the certification-service-provider is recognised under a bilateral or multilateral agreement between the Community and third countries or international organisations.

2.   In order to facilitate cross-border certification services with third countries and legal recognition of advanced electronic signatures originating in third countries, the Commission shall make proposals, where appropriate, to achieve the effective implementation of standards and international agreements applicable to certification services. In particular, and where necessary, it shall submit proposals to the Council for appropriate mandates for the negotiation of bilateral and multilateral agreements with third countries and international organisations. The Council shall decide by qualified majority.

3.   Whenever the Commission is informed of any difficulties encountered by Community undertakings with respect to market access in third countries, it may, if necessary, submit proposals to the Council for an appropriate mandate for the negotiation of comparable rights for Community undertakings in these third countries. The Council shall decide by qualified majority.

Measures taken pursuant to this paragraph shall be without prejudice to the obligations of the Community and of the Member States under relevant international agreements.

Article 8. Data protection

1.   Member States shall ensure that certification-service-providers and national bodies responsible for accreditation or supervision comply with the requirements laid down in Directive 95/46/EC of the European Parliament and of the Council of 24 October 1995 on the protection of individuals with regard to the processing of personal data and on the free movement of such data.

2.   Member States shall ensure that a certification-service-provider which issues certificates to the public may collect personal data only directly from the data subject, or after the explicit consent of the data subject, and only insofar as it is necessary for the purposes of issuing and maintaining the certificate. The data may not be collected or processed for any other purposes without the explicit consent of the data subject.

3.   Without prejudice to the legal effect given to pseudonyms under national law, Member States shall not prevent certification service providers from indicating in the certificate a pseudonym instead of the signatory's name.

Article 9. Committee

1.   The Commission shall be assisted by an 'Electronic-Signature Committee', hereinafter referred to as 'the committee'.

2.   Where reference is made to this paragraph, Articles 4 and 7 of Decision 1999/468/EC shall apply, having regard to the provisions of Article 8 thereof.

The period laid down in Article 4(3) of Decision 1999/468/EC shall be set at three months.

3. The Committee shall adopt its own rules of procedure.

Article 10. Tasks of the committee

The committee shall clarify the requirements laid down in the Annexes of this Directive, the criteria referred to in Article 3(4) and the generally recognised standards for electronic signature products established and published pursuant to Article 3(5), in accordance with the procedure laid down in Article 9(2).

Article 11. Notification

1. Member States shall notify to the Commission and the other Member States the following:

(a) information on national voluntary accreditation schemes, including any additional requirements pursuant to Article 3(7);

(b) the names and addresses of the national bodies responsible for accreditation and supervision as well as of the bodies referred to in Article 3(4);

(c) the names and addresses of all accredited national certification service providers.

2. Any information supplied under paragraph 1 and changes in respect of that information shall be notified by the Member States as soon as possible.

Article 12. Review

1. The Commission shall review the operation of this Directive and report thereon to the European Parliament and to the Council by 19 July 2003 at the latest.

2. The review shall inter alia assess whether the scope of this Directive should be modified, taking account of technological, market and legal developments. The report shall in particular include an assessment, on the basis of experience gained, of aspects of harmonisation. The report shall be accompanied, where appropriate, by legislative proposals.

Article 13. Implementation

1. Member States shall bring into force the laws, regulations and administrative provisions necessary to comply with this Directive before 19 July 2001. They shall forthwith inform the Commission thereof.

When Member States adopt these measures, they shall contain a reference to this Directive or shall be accompanied by such a reference on the occasion of their official publication. The methods of making such reference shall be laid down by the Member States.

2. Member States shall communicate to the Commission the text of the main provisions of domestic law which they adopt in the field governed by this Directive.

Article 14. Entry into force

This Directive shall enter into force on the day of its publication in the Official Journal of the European Communities

Article 15. Addressees

This Directive is addressed to the Member States.

Done at Brussels, 13 December 1999.

ANNEX I
REQUIREMENTS FOR QUALIFIED CERTIFICATES

Qualified certificates must contain:

(a) an indication that the certificate is issued as a qualified certificate;

(b) the identification of the certification-service-provider and the State in which it is established;

(c)   the name of the signatory or a pseudonym, which shall be identified as such;

(d)   provision for a specific attribute of the signatory to be included if relevant, depending on the purpose for which the certificate is intended;

(e)   signature-verification data which correspond to signature-creation data under the control of the signatory;

(f)   an indication of the beginning and end of the period of validity of the certificate;

(g)   the identity code of the certificate;

(h)   the advanced electronic signature of the certification-service-provider issuing it;

(i)   limitations on the scope of use of the certificate, if applicable; and

(j)   limits on the value of transactions for which the certificate can be used, if applicable.

ANNEX II
REQUIREMENTS FOR CERTIFICATION-SERVICE-PROVIDERS ISSUING QUALIFIED CERTIFICATES

Certification-service-providers must:

(a)   demonstrate the reliability necessary for providing certification services;

(b)   ensure the operation of a prompt and secure directory and a secure and immediate revocation service;

(c)   ensure that the date and time when a certificate is issued or revoked can be determined precisely;

(d)   verify, by appropriate means in accordance with national law, the identity and, if applicable, any specific attributes of the person to which a qualified certificate is issued;

(e)   employ personnel who possess the expert knowledge, experience, and qualifications necessary for the services provided, in particular competence at managerial level, expertise in electronic signature technology and familiarity with proper security procedures; they must also apply administrative and management procedures which are adequate and correspond to recognised standards;

(f)   use trustworthy systems and products which are protected against modification and ensure the technical and cryptographic security of the process supported by them;

(g)   take measures against forgery of certificates, and, in cases where the certification-service-provider generates signature-creation data, guarantee confidentiality during the process of generating such data;

(h)   maintain sufficient financial resources to operate in conformity with the requirements laid down in the Directive, in particular to bear the risk of liability for damages, for example, by obtaining appropriate insurance;

(i)   record all relevant information concerning a qualified certificate for an appropriate period of time, in particular for the purpose of providing evidence of certification for the purposes of legal proceedings. Such recording may be done electronically;

(j)   not store or copy signature-creation data of the person to whom the certification-service-provider provided key management services;

(k)   before entering into a contractual relationship with a person seeking a certificate to support his electronic signature inform that person by a durable means of communication of the precise terms and conditions regarding the use of the certificate, including any limitations on its use, the existence of a voluntary accreditation scheme and procedures for complaints and dispute settlement. Such information, which may be transmitted electronically, must be in writing and in readily understandable language. Relevant parts of this information must also be made available on request to third parties relying on the certificate;

    (l)   use trustworthy systems to store certificates in a verifiable form so that:

       – only authorised persons can make entries and changes,

       – information can be checked for authenticity,

       – certificates are publicly available for retrieval in only those cases for which the certificate-holder's consent has been obtained, and

       – any technical changes compromising these security requirements are apparent to the operator.

ANNEX III
REQUIREMENTS FOR SECURE SIGNATURE-CREATION DEVICES

1.   Secure signature-creation devices must, by appropriate technical and procedural means, ensure at the least that:

    (a)   the signature-creation-data used for signature generation can practically occur only once, and that their secrecy is reasonably assured;

    (b)   the signature-creation-data used for signature generation cannot, with reasonable assurance, be derived and the signature is protected against forgery using currently available technology;

    (c)   the signature-creation-data used for signature generation can be reliably protected by the legitimate signatory against the use of others.

2.   Secure signature-creation devices must not alter the data to be signed or prevent such data from being presented to the signatory prior to the signature process.

ANNEX IV
RECOMMENDATIONS FOR SECURE SIGNATURE VERIFICATION

During the signature-verification process it should be ensured with reasonable certainty that:

    (a)   the data used for verifying the signature correspond to the data displayed to the verifier;

    (b)   the signature is reliably verified and the result of that verification is correctly displayed;

    (c)   the verifier can, as necessary, reliably establish the contents of the signed data;

    (d)   the authenticity and validity of the certificate required at the time of signature verification are reliably verified;

    (e)   the result of verification and the signatory's identity are correctly displayed;

    (f)   the use of a pseudonym is clearly indicated; and

    (g)   any security-relevant changes can be detected.

DIRECTIVE 2000/35/EC OF THE EUROPEAN PARLIAMENT AND OF THE COUNCIL OF 29 JUNE 2000
on combating late payment in commercial transactions

THE EUROPEAN PARLIAMENT AND THE COUNCIL OF THE EUROPEAN UNION,

Having regard to the Treaty establishing the European Community, and in particular Article 95 thereof,

    Having regard to the proposal from the Commission,

    Having regard to the opinion of the Economic and Social Committee,

    Acting in accordance with the procedure laid down in Article 251 of the Treaty, in the light of the joint text approved by the Conciliation Committee on 4 May 2000,

Whereas:

(1)   In its resolution on the integrated programme in favour of SMEs and the craft sector, the European Parliament urged the Commission to submit proposals to deal with the problem of late payment.

(2)   On 12 May 1995 the Commission adopted a recommendation on payment periods in commercial transactions.

(3)   In its resolution on the Commission recommendation on payment periods in commercial transactions, the European Parliament called on the Commission to consider transforming its recommendation into a proposal for a Council directive to be submitted as soon as possible.

(4)   On 29 May 1997 the Economic and Social Committee adopted an opinion on the Commission's Green Paper on Public Procurement in the European Union: Exploring the way forward.

(5)   On 4 June 1997 the Commission published an action plan for the single market, which underlined that late payment represents an increasingly serious obstacle for the success of the single market.

(6)   On 17 July 1997 the Commission published a report on late payments in commercial transactions, summarising the results of an evaluation of the effects of the Commission's recommendation of 12 May 1995.

(7)   Heavy administrative and financial burdens are placed on businesses, particularly small and medium-sized ones, as a result of excessive payment periods and late payment. Moreover, these problems are a major cause of insolvencies threatening the survival of businesses and result in numerous job losses.

(8)   In some Member States contractual payment periods differ significantly from the Community average.

(9)   The differences between payment rules and practices in the Member States constitute an obstacle to the proper functioning of the internal market.

(10)   This has the effect of considerably limiting commercial transactions between Member States. This is in contradiction with Article 14 of the Treaty as entrepreneurs should be able to trade throughout the internal market under conditions which ensure that transborder operations do not entail greater risks than domestic sales. Distortions of competition would ensue if substantially different rules applied to domestic and transborder operations.

(11)   The most recent statistics indicate that there has been, at best, no improvement in late payments in many Member States since the adoption of the recommendation of 12 May 1995.

(12)   The objective of combating late payments in the internal market cannot be sufficiently achieved by the Member States acting individually and can, therefore, be better achieved by the Community. This Directive does not go beyond what is necessary to achieve that objective. This Directive complies therefore, in its entirety, with the requirements of the principles of subsidiarity and proportionality as laid down in Article 5 of the Treaty.

(13)   This Directive should be limited to payments made as remuneration for commercial transactions and does not regulate transactions with consumers, interest in connection with other payments, eg payments under the laws on cheques and bills of exchange, payments made as compensation for damages including payments from insurance companies.

(14)   The fact that the liberal professions are covered by this Directive does not mean that Member States have to treat them as undertakings or merchants for purposes not covered by this Directive.

(15)   This Directive only defines the term 'enforceable title' but does not regulate the various procedures of forced execution of such a title and the conditions under which forced execution of such a title can be stopped or suspended.

(16)   Late payment constitutes a breach of contract which has been made

financially attractive to debtors in most Member States by low interest rates on late payments and/or slow procedures for redress. A decisive shift, including compensation of creditors for the costs incurred, is necessary to reverse this trend and to ensure that the consequences of late payments are such as to discourage late payment.

(17) The reasonable compensation for the recovery costs has to be considered without prejudice to national provisions according to which a national judge can award to the creditor any additional damage caused by the debtor's late payment, taking also into account that such incurred costs may be already compensated for by the interest for late payment.

(18) This Directive takes into account the issue of long contractual payment periods and, in particular, the existence of certain categories of contracts where a longer payment period in combination with a restriction of freedom of contract or a higher interest rate can be justified.

(19) This Directive should prohibit abuse of freedom of contract to the disadvantage of the creditor. Where an agreement mainly serves the purpose of procuring the debtor additional liquidity at the expense of the creditor, or where the main contractor imposes on his suppliers and subcontractors terms of payment which are not justified on the grounds of the terms granted to himself, these may be considered to be factors constituting such an abuse. This Directive does not affect national provisions relating to the way contracts are concluded or regulating the validity of contractual terms which are unfair to the debtor.

(20) The consequences of late payment can be dissuasive only if they are accompanied by procedures for redress which are rapid and effective for the creditor. In conformity with the principle of non-discrimination contained in Article 12 of the Treaty, those procedures should be available to all creditors who are established in the Community.

(21) It is desirable to ensure that creditors are in a position to exercise a retention of title on a non-discriminatory basis throughout the Community, if the retention of title clause is valid under the applicable national provisions designated by private international law.

(22) This Directive should regulate all commercial transactions irrespective of whether they are carried out between private or public undertakings or between undertakings and public authorities, having regard to the fact that the latter handle a considerable volume of payments to business. It should therefore also regulate all commercial transactions between main contractors and their suppliers and subcontractors.

(23) Article 5 of this Directive requires that the recovery procedure for unchallenged claims be completed within a short period of time in conformity with national legislation, but does not require Member States to adopt a specific procedure or to amend their existing legal procedures in a specific way.

HAVE ADOPTED THIS DIRECTIVE:

Article 1. Scope
This Directive shall apply to all payments made as remuneration for commercial transactions.

Article 2. Definitions
For the purposes of this Directive:

1. 'commercial transactions' means transactions between undertakings or between undertakings and public authorities which lead to the delivery of goods or the provision of services for remuneration,

'public authority' means any contracting authority or entity, as defined by the Public Procurement Directives (92/50/EEC, 93/36/EEC, 93/37/EEC and 93/38/EEC), 'undertaking' means any organisation acting in the course of its independent economic or professional activity, even where it is carried on by a single person;

2.   'late payment' means exceeding the contractual or statutory period of payment;

3.   'retention of title' means the contractual agreement according to which the seller retains title to the goods in question until the price has been paid in full;

4.   'interest rate applied by the European Central Bank to its main refinancing operations' means the interest rate applied to such operations in the case of fixed-rate tenders. In the event that a main refinancing operation was conducted according to a variable-rate tender procedure, this interest rate refers to the marginal interest rate which resulted from that tender. This applies both in the case of single-rate and variable-rate auctions;

5.   'enforceable title' means any decision, judgment or order for payment issued by a court or other competent authority, whether for immediate payment or payment by instalments, which permits the creditor to have his claim against the debtor collected by means of forced execution; it shall include a decision, judgment or order for payment that is provisionally enforceable and remains so even if the debtor appeals against it.

Article 3. Interest in case of late payment

1.   Member States shall ensure that:

(a)   interest in accordance with point (d) shall become payable from the day following the date or the end of the period for payment fixed in the contract;

(b)   if the date or period for payment is not fixed in the contract, interest shall become payable automatically without the necessity of a reminder:

(i)   30 days following the date of receipt by the debtor of the invoice or an equivalent request for payment; or

(ii)   if the date of the receipt of the invoice or the equivalent request for payment is uncertain, 30 days after the date of receipt of the goods or services; or

(iii)   if the debtor receives the invoice or the equivalent request for payment earlier than the goods or the services, 30 days after the receipt of the goods or services; or

(iv)   if a procedure of acceptance or verification, by which the conformity of the goods or services with the contract is to be ascertained, is provided for by statute or in the contract and if the debtor receives the invoice or the equivalent request for payment earlier or on the date on which such acceptance or verification takes place, 30 days after this latter date;

(c)   the creditor shall be entitled to interest for late payment to the extent that:

(i)   he has fulfilled his contractual and legal obligations; and

(ii)   he has not received the amount due on time, unless the debtor is not responsible for the delay;

(d)   the level of interest for late payment ('the statutory rate'), which the debtor is obliged to pay, shall be the sum of the interest rate applied by the European Central Bank to its most recent main refinancing operation carried out before the first calendar day of the half-year in question ('the reference rate'), plus at least seven percentage points ('the margin'), unless otherwise specified in the contract. For a Member State which is not participating in the third stage of economic and monetary union, the reference rate referred to above shall be the equivalent rate set by its national central bank. In both cases, the reference rate in force on the first calendar day of the half-year in question shall apply for the following six months;

(e)   unless the debtor is not responsible for the delay, the creditor shall be entitled to claim reasonable compensation from the debtor for all relevant recovery costs incurred through the latter's late payment. Such recovery costs shall respect the principles of transparency and proportionality as regards the debt in question. Member States may, while respecting the principles referred to above, fix maximum amounts as regards the recovery costs for different levels of debt.

2. For certain categories of contracts to be defined by national law, Member States may fix the period after which interest becomes payable to a maximum of 60 days provided that they either restrain the parties to the contract from exceeding this period or fix a mandatory interest rate that substantially exceeds the statutory rate.

3. Member States shall provide that an agreement on the date for payment or on the consequences of late payment which is not in line with the provisions of paragraphs 1(b) to (d) and 2 either shall not be enforceable or shall give rise to a claim for damages if, when all circumstances of the case, including good commercial practice and the nature of the product, are considered, it is grossly unfair to the creditor. In determining whether an agreement is grossly unfair to the creditor, it will be taken, inter alia, into account whether the debtor has any objective reason to deviate from the provisions of paragraphs 1(b) to (d) and 2. If such an agreement is determined to be grossly unfair, the statutory terms will apply, unless the national courts determine different conditions which are fair.

4. Member States shall ensure that, in the interests of creditors and of competitors, adequate and effective means exist to prevent the continued use of terms which are grossly unfair within the meaning of paragraph 3.

5. The means referred to in paragraph 4 shall include provisions whereby organisations officially recognised as, or having a legitimate interest in, representing small and medium-sized enterprises may take action according to the national law concerned before the courts or before competent administrative bodies on the grounds that contractual terms drawn up for general use are grossly unfair within the meaning of paragraph 3, so that they can apply appropriate and effective means to prevent the continued use of such terms.

Article 4. Retention of title

1. Member States shall provide in conformity with the applicable national provisions designated by private international law that the seller retains title to goods until they are fully paid for if a retention of title clause has been expressly agreed between the buyer and the seller before the delivery of the goods.

2. Member States may adopt or retain provisions dealing with down payments already made by the debtor.

Article 5. Recovery procedures for unchallenged claims

1. Member States shall ensure that an enforceable title can be obtained, irrespective of the amount of the debt, normally within 90 calendar days of the lodging of the creditor's action or application at the court or other competent authority, provided that the debt or aspects of the procedure are not disputed. This duty shall be carried out by Member States in conformity with their respective national legislation, regulations and administrative provisions.

2. The respective national legislation, regulations and administrative provisions shall apply the same conditions for all creditors who are established in the European Community.

3. The 90 calendar day period referred to in paragraph 1 shall not include the following:

  (a) periods for service of documents;

  (b) any delays caused by the creditor, such as periods devoted to correcting applications.

4. This Article shall be without prejudice to the provisions of the Brussels Convention on jurisdiction and enforcement of judgments in civil and commercial matters.

Article 6. Transposition

1. Member States shall bring into force the laws, regulations and administrative provisions necessary to comply with this Directive before 8 August 2002. They shall forthwith inform the Commission thereof.

When Member States adopt these measures, they shall contain a reference to this Directive or shall be accompanied by such reference on the occasion of their official publication. The methods of making such reference shall be laid down by Member States.

2. Member States may maintain or bring into force provisions which are more favourable to the creditor than the provisions necessary to comply with this Directive.

3. In transposing this Directive, Member States may exclude:

  (a) debts that are subject to insolvency proceedings instituted against the debtor;

  (b) contracts that have been concluded prior to 8 August 2002; and

  (c) claims for interest of less than EUR 5.

4. Member States shall communicate to the Commission the text of the main provisions of national law which they adopt in the field covered by this Directive.

5. The Commission shall undertake two years after 8 August 2002 a review of, inter alia, the statutory rate, contractual payment periods and late payments, to assess the impact on commercial transactions and the operation of the legislation in practice. The results of this review and of other reviews will be made known to the European Parliament and the Council, accompanied where appropriate by proposals for improvement of this Directive.

Article 7. Entry into force

This Directive shall enter into force on the day of its publication in the Official Journal of the European Communities.

Article 8. Addressees

This Directive is addressed to the Member States.

Done at Luxembourg, 29 June 2000.

DIRECTIVE 2000/31/EC OF THE EUROPEAN PARLIAMENT AND OF THE COUNCIL OF 8 JUNE 2000
ON CERTAIN LEGAL ASPECTS OF INFORMATION SOCIETY SERVICES, IN PARTICULAR ELECTRONIC COMMERCE, IN THE INTERNAL MARKET (DIRECTIVE ON ELECTRONIC COMMERCE)

THE EUROPEAN PARLIAMENT AND THE COUNCIL OF THE EUROPEAN UNION,

Having regard to the Treaty establishing the European Community, and in particular Articles 47(2), 55 and 95 thereof,

  Having regard to the proposal from the Commission,

  Having regard to the opinion of the Economic and Social Committee,

  Acting in accordance with the procedure laid down in Article 251 of the Treaty,

  Whereas:

  (1) The European Union is seeking to forge ever closer links between the States and peoples of Europe, to ensure economic and social progress; in accordance with Article 14(2) of the Treaty, the internal market comprises an area without internal frontiers in which the free movements of goods, services and the freedom of establishment are ensured; the development of information society services within the area without internal frontiers is vital to eliminating the barriers which divide the European peoples.

  (2) The development of electronic commerce within the information society

offers significant employment opportunities in the Community, particularly in small and medium-sized enterprises, and will stimulate economic growth and investment in innovation by European companies, and can also enhance the competitiveness of European industry, provided that everyone has access to the Internet.

(3)   Community law and the characteristics of the Community legal order are a vital asset to enable European citizens and operators to take full advantage, without consideration of borders, of the opportunities afforded by electronic commerce; this Directive therefore has the purpose of ensuring a high level of Community legal integration in order to establish a real area without internal borders for information society services.

(4)   It is important to ensure that electronic commerce could fully benefit from the internal market and therefore that, as with Council Directive 89/552/EEC of 3 October 1989 on the coordination of certain provisions laid down by law, regulation or administrative action in Member States concerning the pursuit of television broadcasting activities, a high level of Community integration is achieved.

(5)   The development of information society services within the Community is hampered by a number of legal obstacles to the proper functioning of the internal market which make less attractive the exercise of the freedom of establishment and the freedom to provide services; these obstacles arise from divergences in legislation and from the legal uncertainty as to which national rules apply to such services; in the absence of coordination and adjustment of legislation in the relevant areas, obstacles might be justified in the light of the case-law of the Court of Justice of the European Communities; legal uncertainty exists with regard to the extent to which Member States may control services originating from another Member State.

(6)   In the light of Community objectives, of Articles 43 and 49 of the Treaty and of secondary Community law, these obstacles should be eliminated by coordinating certain national laws and by clarifying certain legal concepts at Community level to the extent necessary for the proper functioning of the internal market; by dealing only with certain specific matters which give rise to problems for the internal market, this Directive is fully consistent with the need to respect the principle of subsidiarity as set out in Article 5 of the Treaty.

(7)   In order to ensure legal certainty and consumer confidence, this Directive must lay down a clear and general framework to cover certain legal aspects of electronic commerce in the internal market.

(8)   The objective of this Directive is to create a legal framework to ensure the free movement of information society services between Member States and not to harmonise the field of criminal law as such.

(9)   The free movement of information society services can in many cases be a specific reflection in Community law of a more general principle, namely freedom of expression as enshrined in Article 10(1) of the Convention for the Protection of Human Rights and Fundamental Freedoms, which has been ratified by all the Member States; for this reason, directives covering the supply of information society services must ensure that this activity may be engaged in freely in the light of that Article, subject only to the restrictions laid down in paragraph 2 of that Article and in Article 46(1) of the Treaty; this Directive is not intended to affect national fundamental rules and principles relating to freedom of expression.

(10)   In accordance with the principle of proportionality, the measures provided for in this Directive are strictly limited to the minimum needed to achieve the objective of the proper functioning of the internal market; where action at Community level is necessary, and in order to guarantee an area which is truly without internal frontiers as far as electronic commerce is concerned, the Directive must ensure a high level of protection of objectives of general interest, in particular the protection of minors and human dignity, consumer protection and the protection of public health; according to Article 152 of the Treaty, the protection of public health is an essential component of other Community policies.

(11) This Directive is without prejudice to the level of protection for, in particular, public health and consumer interests, as established by Community acts; amongst others, Council Directive 93/13/EEC of 5 April 1993 on unfair terms in consumer contracts and Directive 97/7/EC of the European Parliament and of the Council of 20 May 1997 on the protection of consumers in respect of distance contracts form a vital element for protecting consumers in contractual matters; those Directives also apply in their entirety to information society services; that same Community acquis, which is fully applicable to information society services, also embraces in particular Council Directive 84/450/EEC of 10 September 1984 concerning misleading and comparative advertising, Council Directive 87/102/EEC of 22 December 1986 for the approximation of the laws, regulations and administrative provisions of the Member States concerning consumer credit, Council Directive 93/22/EEC of 10 May 1993 on investment services in the securities field, Council Directive 90/314/EEC of 13 June 1990 on package travel, package holidays and package tours, Directive 98/6/EC of the European Parliament and of the Council of 16 February 1998 on consumer production in the indication of prices of products offered to consumers, Council Directive 92/59/EEC of 29 June 1992 on general product safety, Directive 94/47/EC of the European Parliament and of the Council of 26 October 1994 on the protection of purchasers in respect of certain aspects on contracts relating to the purchase of the right to use immovable properties on a timeshare basis, Directive 98/27/EC of the European Parliament and of the Council of 19 May 1998 on injunctions for the protection of consumers' interests, Council Directive 85/374/EEC of 25 July 1985 on the approximation of the laws, regulations and administrative provisions concerning liability for defective products, Directive 1999/44/EC of the European Parliament and of the Council of 25 May 1999 on certain aspects of the sale of consumer goods and associated guarantees, the future Directive of the European Parliament and of the Council concerning the distance marketing of consumer financial services and Council Directive 92/28/EEC of 31 March 1992 on the advertising of medicinal products; this Directive should be without prejudice to Directive 98/43/EC of the European Parliament and of the Council of 6 July 1998 on the approximation of the laws, regulations and administrative provisions of the Member States relating to the advertising and sponsorship of tobacco products adopted within the framework of the internal market, or to directives on the protection of public health; this Directive complements information requirements established by the above-mentioned Directives and in particular Directive 97/7/EC.

(12) It is necessary to exclude certain activities from the scope of this Directive, on the grounds that the freedom to provide services in these fields cannot, at this stage, be guaranteed under the Treaty or existing secondary legislation; excluding these activities does not preclude any instruments which might prove necessary for the proper functioning of the internal market; taxation, particularly value added tax imposed on a large number of the services covered by this Directive, must be excluded from the scope of this Directive.

(13) This Directive does not aim to establish rules on fiscal obligations nor does it pre-empt the drawing up of Community instruments concerning fiscal aspects of electronic commerce.

(14) The protection of individuals with regard to the processing of personal data is solely governed by Directive 95/46/EC of the European Parliament and of the Council of 24 October 1995 on the protection of individuals with regard to the processing of personal data and on the free movement of such data and Directive 97/66/EC of the European Parliament and of the Council of 15 December 1997 concerning the processing of personal data and the protection of privacy in the telecommunications sector which are fully applicable to information society services; these Directives already establish a Community legal framework in the field of personal data and therefore it is not necessary to cover this issue in this Directive in order to ensure the smooth functioning of the internal market, in particular

the free movement of personal data between Member States; the implementation and application of this Directive should be made in full compliance with the principles relating to the protection of personal data, in particular as regards unsolicited commercial communication and the liability of intermediaries; this Directive cannot prevent the anonymous use of open networks such as the Internet.

(15)   The confidentiality of communications is guaranteed by Article 5 Directive 97/66/EC; in accordance with that Directive, Member States must prohibit any kind of interception or surveillance of such communications by others than the senders and receivers, except when legally authorised.

(16)   The exclusion of gambling activities from the scope of application of this Directive covers only games of chance, lotteries and betting transactions, which involve wagering a stake with monetary value; this does not cover promotional competitions or games where the purpose is to encourage the sale of goods or services and where payments, if they arise, serve only to acquire the promoted goods or services.

(17)   The definition of information society services already exists in Community law in Directive 98/34/EC of the European Parliament and of the Council of 22 June 1998 laying down a procedure for the provision of information in the field of technical standards and regulations and of rules on information society services and in Directive 98/84/EC of the European Parliament and of the Council of 20 November 1998 on the legal protection of services based on, or consisting of, conditional access; this definition covers any service normally provided for remuneration, at a distance, by means of electronic equipment for the processing (including digital compression) and storage of data, and at the individual request of a recipient of a service; those services referred to in the indicative list in Annex V to Directive 98/34/EC which do not imply data processing and storage are not covered by this definition.

(18)   Information society services span a wide range of economic activities which take place on-line; these activities can, in particular, consist of selling goods on-line; activities such as the delivery of goods as such or the provision of services off-line are not covered; information society services are not solely restricted to services giving rise to on-line contracting but also, in so far as they represent an economic activity, extend to services which are not remunerated by those who receive them, such as those offering on-line information or commercial communications, or those providing tools allowing for search, access and retrieval of data; information society services also include services consisting of the transmission of information via a communication network, in providing access to a communication network or in hosting information provided by a recipient of the service; television broadcasting within the meaning of Directive EEC/89/552 and radio broadcasting are not information society services because they are not provided at individual request; by contrast, services which are transmitted point to point, such as video-on-demand or the provision of commercial communications by electronic mail are information society services; the use of electronic mail or equivalent individual communications for instance by natural persons acting outside their trade, business or profession including their use for the conclusion of contracts between such persons is not an information society service; the contractual relationship between an employee and his employer is not an information society service; activities which by their very nature cannot be carried out at a distance and by electronic means, such as the statutory auditing of company accounts or medical advice requiring the physical examination of a patient are not information society services.

(19)   The place at which a service provider is established should be determined in conformity with the case-law of the Court of Justice according to which the concept of establishment involves the actual pursuit of an economic activity through a fixed establishment for an indefinite period; this requirement is also fulfilled where a company is constituted for a given period; the place of establishment of a com-

pany providing services via an Internet website is not the place at which the technology supporting its website is located or the place at which its website is accessible but the place where it pursues its economic activity; in cases where a provider has several places of establishment it is important to determine from which place of establishment the service concerned is provided; in cases where it is difficult to determine from which of several places of establishment a given service is provided, this is the place where the provider has the centre of his activities relating to this particular service.

(20) The definition of 'recipient of a service' covers all types of usage of information society services, both by persons who provide information on open networks such as the Internet and by persons who seek information on the Internet for private or professional reasons.

(21) The scope of the coordinated field is without prejudice to future Community harmonisation relating to information society services and to future legislation adopted at national level in accordance with Community law; the coordinated field covers only requirements relating to on-line activities such as on-line information, on-line advertising, on-line shopping, on-line contracting and does not concern Member States' legal requirements relating to goods such as safety standards, labelling obligations, or liability for goods, or Member States' requirements relating to the delivery or the transport of goods, including the distribution of medicinal products; the coordinated field does not cover the exercise of rights of pre-emption by public authorities concerning certain goods such as works of art.

(22) Information society services should be supervised at the source of the activity, in order to ensure an effective protection of public interest objectives; to that end, it is necessary to ensure that the competent authority provides such protection not only for the citizens of its own country but for all Community citizens; in order to improve mutual trust between Member States, it is essential to state clearly this responsibility on the part of the Member State where the services originate; moreover, in order to effectively guarantee freedom to provide services and legal certainty for suppliers and recipients of services, such information society services should in principle be subject to the law of the Member State in which the service provider is established.

(23) This Directive neither aims to establish additional rules on private international law relating to conflicts of law nor does it deal with the jurisdiction of Courts; provisions of the applicable law designated by rules of private international law must not restrict the freedom to provide information society services as established in this Directive.

(24) In the context of this Directive, notwithstanding the rule on the control at source of information society services, it is legitimate under the conditions established in this Directive for Member States to take measures to restrict the free movement of information society services.

(25) National courts, including civil courts, dealing with private law disputes can take measures to derogate from the freedom to provide information society services in conformity with conditions established in this Directive.

(26) Member States, in conformity with conditions established in this Directive, may apply their national rules on criminal law and criminal proceedings with a view to taking all investigative and other measures necessary for the detection and prosecution of criminal offences, without there being a need to notify such measures to the Commission.

(27) This Directive, together with the future Directive of the European Parliament and of the Council concerning the distance marketing of consumer financial services, contributes to the creating of a legal framework for the on-line provision of financial services; this Directive does not pre-empt future initiatives in the area of financial services in particular with regard to the harmonisation of rules of conduct in this field; the possibility for Member States, established in this Directive, under certain circumstances of restricting the freedom to provide information

society services in order to protect consumers also covers measures in the area of financial services in particular measures aiming at protecting investors.

(28)   The Member States' obligation not to subject access to the activity of an information society service provider to prior authorisation does not concern postal services covered by Directive 97/67/EC of the European Parliament and of the Council of 15 December 1997 on common rules for the development of the internal market of Community postal services and the improvement of quality of service consisting of the physical delivery of a printed electronic mail message and does not affect voluntary accreditation systems, in particular for providers of electronic signature certification service.

(29)   Commercial communications are essential for the financing of information society services and for developing a wide variety of new, charge-free services; in the interests of consumer protection and fair trading, commercial communications, including discounts, promotional offers and promotional competitions or games, must meet a number of transparency requirements; these requirements are without prejudice to Directive 97/7/EC; this Directive should not affect existing Directives on commercial communications, in particular Directive 98/43/EC.

(30)   The sending of unsolicited commercial communications by electronic mail may be undesirable for consumers and information society service providers and may disrupt the smooth functioning of interactive networks; the question of consent by recipient of certain forms of unsolicited commercial communications is not addressed by this Directive, but has already been addressed, in particular, by Directive 97/7/EC and by Directive 97/66/EC; in Member States which authorise unsolicited commercial communications by electronic mail, the setting up of appropriate industry filtering initiatives should be encouraged and facilitated; in addition it is necessary that in any event unsolicited commercial communications are clearly identifiable as such in order to improve transparency and to facilitate the functioning of such industry initiatives; unsolicited commercial communications by electronic mail should not result in additional communication costs for the recipient.

(31)   Member States which allow the sending of unsolicited commercial communications by electronic mail without prior consent of the recipient by service providers established in their territory have to ensure that the service providers consult regularly and respect the opt-out registers in which natural persons not wishing to receive such commercial communications can register themselves.

(32)   In order to remove barriers to the development of cross-border services within the Community which members of the regulated professions might offer on the Internet, it is necessary that compliance be guaranteed at Community level with professional rules aiming, in particular, to protect consumers or public health; codes of conduct at Community level would be the best means of determining the rules on professional ethics applicable to commercial communication; the drawing-up or, where appropriate, the adaptation of such rules should be encouraged without prejudice to the autonomy of professional bodies and associations.

(33)   This Directive complements Community law and national law relating to regulated professions maintaining a coherent set of applicable rules in this field.

(34)   Each Member State is to amend its legislation containing requirements, and in particular requirements as to form, which are likely to curb the use of contracts by electronic means; the examination of the legislation requiring such adjustment should be systematic and should cover all the necessary stages and acts of the contractual process, including the filing of the contract; the result of this amendment should be to make contracts concluded electronically workable; the legal effect of electronic signatures is dealt with by Directive 1999/93/EC of the European Parliament and of the Council of 13 December 1999 on a Community framework for electronic signatures; the acknowledgement of receipt by a service provider may take the form of the on-line provision of the service paid for.

(35)   This Directive does not affect Member States' possibility of maintaining or establishing general or specific legal requirements for contracts which can be fulfilled by electronic means, in particular requirements concerning secure electronic signatures.

(36)   Member States may maintain restrictions for the use of electronic contracts with regard to contracts requiring by law the involvement of courts, public authorities, or professions exercising public authority; this possibility also covers contracts which require the involvement of courts, public authorities, or professions exercising public authority in order to have an effect with regard to third parties as well as contracts requiring by law certification or attestation by a notary.

(37)   Member States' obligation to remove obstacles to the use of electronic contracts concerns only obstacles resulting from legal requirements and not practical obstacles resulting from the impossibility of using electronic means in certain cases.

(38)   Member States' obligation to remove obstacles to the use of electronic contracts is to be implemented in conformity with legal requirements for contracts enshrined in Community law.

(39)   The exceptions to the provisions concerning the contracts concluded exclusively by electronic mail or by equivalent individual communications provided for by this Directive, in relation to information to be provided and the placing of orders, should not enable, as a result, the by-passing of those provisions by providers of information society services.

(40)   Both existing and emerging disparities in Member States' legislation and case-law concerning liability of service providers acting as intermediaries prevent the smooth functioning of the internal market, in particular by impairing the development of cross-border services and producing distortions of competition; service providers have a duty to act, under certain circumstances, with a view to preventing or stopping illegal activities; this Directive should constitute the appropriate basis for the development of rapid and reliable procedures for removing and disabling access to illegal information; such mechanisms could be developed on the basis of voluntary agreements between all parties concerned and should be encouraged by Member States; it is in the interest of all parties involved in the provision of information society services to adopt and implement such procedures; the provisions of this Directive relating to liability should not preclude the development and effective operation, by the different interested parties, of technical systems of protection and identification and of technical surveillance instruments made possible by digital technology within the limits laid down by Directives 95/46/EC and 97/66/EC.

(41)   This Directive strikes a balance between the different interests at stake and establishes principles upon which industry agreements and standards can be based.

(42)   The exemptions from liability established in this Directive cover only cases where the activity of the information society service provider is limited to the technical process of operating and giving access to a communication network over which information made available by third parties is transmitted or temporarily stored, for the sole purpose of making the transmission more efficient; this activity is of a mere technical, automatic and passive nature, which implies that the information society service provider has neither knowledge of nor control over the information which is transmitted or stored.

(43)   A service provider can benefit from the exemptions for 'mere conduit' and for 'caching' when he is in no way involved with the information transmitted; this requires among other things that he does not modify the information that he transmits; this requirement does not cover manipulations of a technical nature which take place in the course of the transmission as they do not alter the integrity of the information contained in the transmission.

(44)   A service provider who deliberately collaborates with one of the recipients

of his service in order to undertake illegal acts goes beyond the activities of 'mere conduit' or 'caching' and as a result cannot benefit from the liability exemptions established for these activities.

(45) The limitations of the liability of intermediary service providers established in this Directive do not affect the possibility of injunctions of different kinds; such injunctions can in particular consist of orders by courts or administrative authorities requiring the termination or prevention of any infringement, including the removal of illegal information or the disabling of access to it.

(46) In order to benefit from a limitation of liability, the provider of an information society service, consisting of the storage of information, upon obtaining actual knowledge or awareness of illegal activities has to act expeditiously to remove or to disable access to the information concerned; the removal or disabling of access has to be undertaken in the observance of the principle of freedom of expression and of procedures established for this purpose at national level; this Directive does not affect Member States' possibility of establishing specific requirements which must be fulfilled expeditiously prior to the removal or disabling of information.

(47) Member States are prevented from imposing a monitoring obligation on service providers only with respect to obligations of a general nature; this does not concern monitoring obligations in a specific case and, in particular, does not affect orders by national authorities in accordance with national legislation.

(48) This Directive does not affect the possibility for Member States of requiring service providers, who host information provided by recipients of their service, to apply duties of care, which can reasonably be expected from them and which are specified by national law, in order to detect and prevent certain types of illegal activities.

(49) Member States and the Commission are to encourage the drawing-up of codes of conduct; this is not to impair the voluntary nature of such codes and the possibility for interested parties of deciding freely whether to adhere to such codes.

(50) It is important that the proposed directive on the harmonisation of certain aspects of copyright and related rights in the information society and this Directive come into force within a similar time scale with a view to establishing a clear framework of rules relevant to the issue of liability of intermediaries for copyright and relating rights infringements at Community level.

(51) Each Member State should be required, where necessary, to amend any legislation which is liable to hamper the use of schemes for the out-of-court settlement of disputes through electronic channels; the result of this amendment must be to make the functioning of such schemes genuinely and effectively possible in law and in practice, even across borders.

(52) The effective exercise of the freedoms of the internal market makes it necessary to guarantee victims effective access to means of settling disputes; damage which may arise in connection with information society services is characterised both by its rapidity and by its geographical extent; in view of this specific character and the need to ensure that national authorities do not endanger the mutual confidence which they should have in one another, this Directive requests Member States to ensure that appropriate court actions are available; Member States should examine the need to provide access to judicial procedures by appropriate electronic means.

(53) Directive 98/27/EC, which is applicable to information society services, provides a mechanism relating to actions for an injunction aimed at the protection of the collective interests of consumers; this mechanism will contribute to the free movement of information society services by ensuring a high level of consumer protection.

(54) The sanctions provided for under this Directive are without prejudice to any other sanction or remedy provided under national law; Member States are not

obliged to provide criminal sanctions for infringement of national provisions adopted pursuant to this Directive.

(55)   This Directive does not affect the law applicable to contractual obligations relating to consumer contracts; accordingly, this Directive cannot have the result of depriving the consumer of the protection afforded to him by the mandatory rules relating to contractual obligations of the law of the Member State in which he has his habitual residence.

(56)   As regards the derogation contained in this Directive regarding contractual obligations concerning contracts concluded by consumers, those obligations should be interpreted as including information on the essential elements of the content of the contract, including consumer rights, which have a determining influence on the decision to contract.

(57)   The Court of Justice has consistently held that a Member State retains the right to take measures against a service provider that is established in another Member State but directs all or most of his activity to the territory of the first Member State if the choice of establishment was made with a view to evading the legislation that would have applied to the provider had he been established on the territory of the first Member State.

(58)   This Directive should not apply to services supplied by service providers established in a third country; in view of the global dimension of electronic commerce, it is, however, appropriate to ensure that the Community rules are consistent with international rules; this Directive is without prejudice to the results of discussions within international organisations (amongst others WTO, OECD, Uncitral) on legal issues.

(59)   Despite the global nature of electronic communications, coordination of national regulatory measures at European Union level is necessary in order to avoid fragmentation of the internal market, and for the establishment of an appropriate European regulatory framework; such coordination should also contribute to the establishment of a common and strong negotiating position in international forums.

(60)   In order to allow the unhampered development of electronic commerce, the legal framework must be clear and simple, predictable and consistent with the rules applicable at international level so that it does not adversely affect the competitiveness of European industry or impede innovation in that sector.

(61)   If the market is actually to operate by electronic means in the context of globalisation, the European Union and the major non-European areas need to consult each other with a view to making laws and procedures compatible.

(62)   Cooperation with third countries should be strengthened in the area of electronic commerce, in particular with applicant countries, the developing countries and the European Union's other trading partners.

(63)   The adoption of this Directive will not prevent the Member States from taking into account the various social, societal and cultural implications which are inherent in the advent of the information society; in particular it should not hinder measures which Member States might adopt in conformity with Community law to achieve social, cultural and democratic goals taking into account their linguistic diversity, national and regional specificities as well as their cultural heritage, and to ensure and maintain public access to the widest possible range of information society services; in any case, the development of the information society is to ensure that Community citizens can have access to the cultural European heritage provided in the digital environment.

(64)   Electronic communication offers the Member States an excellent means of providing public services in the cultural, educational and linguistic fields.

(65)   The Council, in its resolution of 19 January 1999 on the consumer dimension of the information society, stressed that the protection of consumers deserved special attention in this field; the Commission will examine the degree to which existing consumer protection rules provide insufficient protection in the context of

the information society and will identify, where necessary, the deficiencies of this legislation and those issues which could require additional measures; if need be, the Commission should make specific additional proposals to resolve such deficiencies that will thereby have been identified,

HAVE ADOPTED THIS DIRECTIVE:

CHAPTER I
GENERAL PROVISIONS

Article 1. Objective and scope

1.   This Directive seeks to contribute to the proper functioning of the internal market by ensuring the free movement of information society services between the Member States.

2.   This Directive approximates, to the extent necessary for the achievement of the objective set out in paragraph 1, certain national provisions on information society services relating to the internal market, the establishment of service providers, commercial communications, electronic contracts, the liability of intermediaries, codes of conduct, out-of-court dispute settlements, court actions and cooperation between Member States.

3.   This Directive complements Community law applicable to information society services without prejudice to the level of protection for, in particular, public health and consumer interests, as established by Community acts and national legislation implementing them in so far as this does not restrict the freedom to provide information society services.

4.   This Directive does not establish additional rules on private international law nor does it deal with the jurisdiction of Courts.

5.   This Directive shall not apply to:

(a)   the field of taxation;

(b)   questions relating to information society services covered by Directives 95/46/EC and 97/66/EC;

(c)   questions relating to agreements or practices governed by cartel law;

(d)   the following activities of information society services:

– the activities of notaries or equivalent professions to the extent that they involve a direct and specific connection with the exercise of public authority,

– the representation of a client and defence of his interests before the courts,

– gambling activities which involve wagering a stake with monetary value in games of chance, including lotteries and betting transactions.

6.   This Directive does not affect measures taken at Community or national level, in the respect of Community law, in order to promote cultural and linguistic diversity and to ensure the defence of pluralism.

Article 2. Definitions

For the purpose of this Directive, the following terms shall bear the following meanings:

(a)   'information society services': services within the meaning of Article 1(2) of Directive 98/34/EC as amended by Directive 98/48/EC;

(b)   'service provider': any natural or legal person providing an information society service;

(c)   'established service provider': a service provider who effectively pursues an economic activity using a fixed establishment for an indefinite period. The presence and use of the technical means and technologies required to provide the service do not, in themselves, constitute an establishment of the provider;

(d)   'recipient of the service': any natural or legal person who, for professional ends or otherwise, uses an information society service, in particular for the purposes of seeking information or making it accessible;

(e) 'consumer': any natural person who is acting for purposes which are outside his or her trade, business or profession;

(f) 'commercial communication': any form of communication designed to promote, directly or indirectly, the goods, services or image of a company, organisation or person pursuing a commercial, industrial or craft activity or exercising a regulated profession. The following do not in themselves constitute commercial communications:

– information allowing direct access to the activity of the company, organisation or person, in particular a domain name or an electronic-mail address,

– communications relating to the goods, services or image of the company, organisation or person compiled in an independent manner, particularly when this is without financial consideration;

(g) 'regulated profession': any profession within the meaning of either Article 1(d) of Council Directive 89/48/EEC of 21 December 1988 on a general system for the recognition of higher-education diplomas awarded on completion of professional education and training of at least three-years' duration or of Article 1(f) of Council Directive 92/51/EEC of 18 June 1992 on a second general system for the recognition of professional education and training to supplement Directive 89/48/EEC;

(h) 'coordinated field': requirements laid down in Member States' legal systems applicable to information society service providers or information society services, regardless of whether they are of a general nature or specifically designed for them.

(i) The coordinated field concerns requirements with which the service provider has to comply in respect of:

– the taking up of the activity of an information society service, such as requirements concerning qualifications, authorisation or notification,

– the pursuit of the activity of an information society service, such as requirements concerning the behaviour of the service provider, requirements regarding the quality or content of the service including those applicable to advertising and contracts, or requirements concerning the liability of the service provider;

(ii) The coordinated field does not cover requirements such as:

– requirements applicable to goods as such,

– requirements applicable to the delivery of goods,

– requirements applicable to services not provided by electronic means.

Article 3. Internal market

1. Each Member State shall ensure that the information society services provided by a service provider established on its territory comply with the national provisions applicable in the Member State in question which fall within the coordinated field.

2. Member States may not, for reasons falling within the coordinated field, restrict the freedom to provide information society services from another Member State.

3. Paragraphs 1 and 2 shall not apply to the fields referred to in the Annex.

4. Member States may take measures to derogate from paragraph 2 in respect of a given information society service if the following conditions are fulfilled:

(a) the measures shall be:

(i) necessary for one of the following reasons:

– public policy, in particular the prevention, investigation, detection and prosecution of criminal offences, including the protection of minors and the fight against any incitement to hatred on grounds of race, sex, religion or nationality, and violations of human dignity concerning individual persons,

– the protection of public health,

– public security, including the safeguarding of national security and defence,

– the protection of consumers, including investors;

(ii) taken against a given information society service which prejudices the objectives referred to in point (i) or which presents a serious and grave risk of prejudice to those objectives;

(iii) proportionate to those objectives;

(b) before taking the measures in question and without prejudice to court proceedings, including preliminary proceedings and acts carried out in the framework of a criminal investigation, the Member State has:

– asked the Member State referred to in paragraph 1 to take measures and the latter did not take such measures, or they were inadequate,

– notified the Commission and the Member State referred to in paragraph 1 of its intention to take such measures.

5. Member States may, in the case of urgency, derogate from the conditions stipulated in paragraph 4(b). Where this is the case, the measures shall be notified in the shortest possible time to the Commission and to the Member State referred to in paragraph 1, indicating the reasons for which the Member State considers that there is urgency.

6. Without prejudice to the Member State's possibility of proceeding with the measures in question, the Commission shall examine the compatibility of the notified measures with Community law in the shortest possible time; where it comes to the conclusion that the measure is incompatible with Community law, the Commission shall ask the Member State in question to refrain from taking any proposed measures or urgently to put an end to the measures in question.

CHAPTER II
PRINCIPLES

Section 1: Establishment and information requirements

Article 4. Principle excluding prior authorisation

1. Member States shall ensure that the taking up and pursuit of the activity of an information society service provider may not be made subject to prior authorisation or any other requirement having equivalent effect.

2. Paragraph 1 shall be without prejudice to authorisation schemes which are not specifically and exclusively targeted at information society services, or which are covered by Directive 97/13/EC of the European Parliament and of the Council of 10 April 1997 on a common framework for general authorisations and individual licences in the field of telecommunications services.

Article 5. General information to be provided

1. In addition to other information requirements established by Community law, Member States shall ensure that the service provider shall render easily, directly and permanently accessible to the recipients of the service and competent authorities, at least the following information:

(a) the name of the service provider;

(b) the geographic address at which the service provider is established;

(c) the details of the service provider, including his electronic mail address, which allow him to be contacted rapidly and communicated with in a direct and effective manner;

(d) where the service provider is registered in a trade or similar public register, the trade register in which the service provider is entered and his registration number, or equivalent means of identification in that register;

(e) where the activity is subject to an authorisation scheme, the particulars of the relevant supervisory authority;

(f) as concerns the regulated professions:

 – any professional body or similar institution with which the service provider is registered,

 – the professional title and the Member State where it has been granted,

 – a reference to the applicable professional rules in the Member State of establishment and the means to access them;

(g)   where the service provider undertakes an activity that is subject to VAT, the identification number referred to in Article 22(1) of the sixth Council Directive 77/388/EEC of 17 May 1977 on the harmonisation of the laws of the Member States relating to turnover taxes—Common system of value added tax: uniform basis of assessment.

2.   In addition to other information requirements established by Community law, Member States shall at least ensure that, where information society services refer to prices, these are to be indicated clearly and unambiguously and, in particular, must indicate whether they are inclusive of tax and delivery costs.

Section 2: Commercial communications

Article 6. Information to be provided

In addition to other information requirements established by Community law, Member States shall ensure that commercial communications which are part of, or constitute, an information society service comply at least with the following conditions:

(a)   the commercial communication shall be clearly identifiable as such;

(b)   the natural or legal person on whose behalf the commercial communication is made shall be clearly identifiable;

(c)   promotional offers, such as discounts, premiums and gifts, where permitted in the Member State where the service provider is established, shall be clearly identifiable as such, and the conditions which are to be met to qualify for them shall be easily accessible and be presented clearly and unambiguously;

(d)   promotional competitions or games, where permitted in the Member State where the service provider is established, shall be clearly identifiable as such, and the conditions for participation shall be easily accessible and be presented clearly and unambiguously.

Article 7. Unsolicited commercial communication

1.   In addition to other requirements established by Community law, Member States which permit unsolicited commercial communication by electronic mail shall ensure that such commercial communication by a service provider established in their territory shall be identifiable clearly and unambiguously as such as soon as it is received by the recipient.

2.   Without prejudice to Directive 97/7/EC and Directive 97/66/EC, Member States shall take measures to ensure that service providers undertaking unsolicited commercial communications by electronic mail consult regularly and respect the opt-out registers in which natural persons not wishing to receive such commercial communications can register themselves.

Article 8. Regulated professions

1.   Member States shall ensure that the use of commercial communications which are part of, or constitute, an information society service provided by a member of a regulated profession is permitted subject to compliance with the professional rules regarding, in particular, the independence, dignity and honour of the profession, professional secrecy and fairness towards clients and other members of the profession.

2.   Without prejudice to the autonomy of professional bodies and associations, Member States and the Commission shall encourage professional associations and bodies to establish codes of conduct at Community level in order to determine the types of information that can be given for the purposes of commercial communication in conformity with the rules referred to in paragraph 1.

3.   When drawing up proposals for Community initiatives which may become necessary to ensure the proper functioning of the Internal Market with regard to the information referred to in paragraph 2, the Commission shall take due account of codes of conduct applicable at Community level and shall act in close cooperation with the relevant professional associations and bodies.

4.   This Directive shall apply in addition to Community Directives concerning access to, and the exercise of, activities of the regulated professions.

Section 3: Contracts concluded by electronic means

Article 9. Treatment of contracts

1.   Member States shall ensure that their legal system allows contracts to be concluded by electronic means. Member States shall in particular ensure that the legal requirements applicable to the contractual process neither create obstacles for the use of electronic contracts nor result in such contracts being deprived of legal effectiveness and validity on account of their having been made by electronic means.

2.   Member States may lay down that paragraph 1 shall not apply to all or certain contracts falling into one of the following categories:

(a)   contracts that create or transfer rights in real estate, except for rental rights;

(b)   contracts requiring by law the involvement of courts, public authorities or professions exercising public authority;

(c)   contracts of suretyship granted and on collateral securities furnished by persons acting for purposes outside their trade, business or profession;

(d)   contracts governed by family law or by the law of succession.

3.   Member States shall indicate to the Commission the categories referred to in paragraph 2 to which they do not apply paragraph 1. Member States shall submit to the Commission every five years a report on the application of paragraph 2 explaining the reasons why they consider it necessary to maintain the category referred to in paragraph 2(b) to which they do not apply paragraph 1.

Article 10. Information to be provided

1.   In addition to other information requirements established by Community law, Member States shall ensure, except when otherwise agreed by parties who are not consumers, that at least the following information is given by the service provider clearly, comprehensibly and unambiguously and prior to the order being placed by the recipient of the service:

(a)   the different technical steps to follow to conclude the contract;

(b)   whether or not the concluded contract will be filed by the service provider and whether it will be accessible;

(c)   the technical means for identifying and correcting input errors prior to the placing of the order;

(d)   the languages offered for the conclusion of the contract.

2.   Member States shall ensure that, except when otherwise agreed by parties who are not consumers, the service provider indicates any relevant codes of conduct to which he subscribes and information on how those codes can be consulted electronically.

3.   Contract terms and general conditions provided to the recipient must be made available in a way that allows him to store and reproduce them.

4.   Paragraphs 1 and 2 shall not apply to contracts concluded exclusively by exchange of electronic mail or by equivalent individual communications.

Article 11. Placing of the order

1.   Member States shall ensure, except when otherwise agreed by parties who

are not consumers, that in cases where the recipient of the service places his order through technological means, the following principles apply:

– the service provider has to acknowledge the receipt of the recipient's order without undue delay and by electronic means,

– the order and the acknowledgement of receipt are deemed to be received when the parties to whom they are addressed are able to access them.

2. Member States shall ensure that, except when otherwise agreed by parties who are not consumers, the service provider makes available to the recipient of the service appropriate, effective and accessible technical means allowing him to identify and correct input errors, prior to the placing of the order.

3. Paragraph 1, first indent, and paragraph 2 shall not apply to contracts concluded exclusively by exchange of electronic mail or by equivalent individual communications.

Section 4: Liability of intermediary service providers

Article 12. 'Mere conduit'

1. Where an information society service is provided that consists of the transmission in a communication network of information provided by a recipient of the service, or the provision of access to a communication network, Member States shall ensure that the service provider is not liable for the information transmitted, on condition that the provider:

(a)   does not initiate the transmission;

(b)   does not select the receiver of the transmission; and

(c)   does not select or modify the information contained in the transmission.

2. The acts of transmission and of provision of access referred to in paragraph 1 include the automatic, intermediate and transient storage of the information transmitted in so far as this takes place for the sole purpose of carrying out the transmission in the communication network, and provided that the information is not stored for any period longer than is reasonably necessary for the transmission.

3. This Article shall not affect the possibility for a court or administrative authority, in accordance with Member States' legal systems, of requiring the service provider to terminate or prevent an infringement.

Article 13. 'Caching'

1. Where an information society service is provided that consists of the transmission in a communication network of information provided by a recipient of the service, Member States shall ensure that the service provider is not liable for the automatic, intermediate and temporary storage of that information, performed for the sole purpose of making more efficient the information's onward transmission to other recipients of the service upon their request, on condition that:

(a)   the provider does not modify the information;

(b)   the provider complies with conditions on access to the information;

(c)   the provider complies with rules regarding the updating of the information, specified in a manner widely recognised and used by industry;

(d)   the provider does not interfere with the lawful use of technology, widely recognised and used by industry, to obtain data on the use of the information; and

(e)   the provider acts expeditiously to remove or to disable access to the information it has stored upon obtaining actual knowledge of the fact that the information at the initial source of the transmission has been removed from the network, or access to it has been disabled, or that a court or an administrative authority has ordered such removal or disablement.

2. This Article shall not affect the possibility for a court or administrative authority, in accordance with Member States' legal systems, of requiring the service provider to terminate or prevent an infringement.

Article 14. Hosting

1.   Where an information society service is provided that consists of the storage of information provided by a recipient of the service, Member States shall ensure that the service provider is not liable for the information stored at the request of a recipient of the service, on condition that:

(a)   the provider does not have actual knowledge of illegal activity or information and, as regards claims for damages, is not aware of facts or circumstances from which the illegal activity or information is apparent; or

(b)   the provider, upon obtaining such knowledge or awareness, acts expeditiously to remove or to disable access to the information.

2.   Paragraph 1 shall not apply when the recipient of the service is acting under the authority or the control of the provider.

3.   This Article shall not affect the possibility for a court or administrative authority, in accordance with Member States' legal systems, of requiring the service provider to terminate or prevent an infringement, nor does it affect the possibility for Member States of establishing procedures governing the removal or disabling of access to information.

Article 15. No general obligation to monitor

1.   Member States shall not impose a general obligation on providers, when providing the services covered by Articles 12, 13 and 14, to monitor the information which they transmit or store, nor a general obligation actively to seek facts or circumstances indicating illegal activity.

2.   Member States may establish obligations for information society service providers promptly to inform the competent public authorities of alleged illegal activities undertaken or information provided by recipients of their service or obligations to communicate to the competent authorities, at their request, information enabling the identification of recipients of their service with whom they have storage agreements.

CHAPTER III
IMPLEMENTATION

Article 16. Codes of conduct

1.   Member States and the Commission shall encourage:

(a)   the drawing up of codes of conduct at Community level, by trade, professional and consumer associations or organisations, designed to contribute to the proper implementation of Articles 5 to 15;

(b)   the voluntary transmission of draft codes of conduct at national or Community level to the Commission;

(c)   the accessibility of these codes of conduct in the Community languages by electronic means;

(d)   the communication to the Member States and the Commission, by trade, professional and consumer associations or organisations, of their assessment of the application of their codes of conduct and their impact upon practices, habits or customs relating to electronic commerce;

(e)   the drawing up of codes of conduct regarding the protection of minors and human dignity.

2.   Member States and the Commission shall encourage the involvement of associations or organisations representing consumers in the drafting and implementation of codes of conduct affecting their interests and drawn up in accordance with paragraph 1(a). Where appropriate, to take account of their specific needs, associations representing the visually impaired and disabled should be consulted.

Article 17. Out-of-court dispute settlement

1.   Member States shall ensure that, in the event of disagreement between an information society service provider and the recipient of the service, their legis-

lation does not hamper the use of out-of-court schemes, available under national law, for dispute settlement, including appropriate electronic means.

2.   Member States shall encourage bodies responsible for the out-of-court settlement of, in particular, consumer disputes to operate in a way which provides adequate procedural guarantees for the parties concerned.

3.   Member States shall encourage bodies responsible for out-of-court dispute settlement to inform the Commission of the significant decisions they take regarding information society services and to transmit any other information on the practices, usages or customs relating to electronic commerce.

Article 18. Court actions

1.   Member States shall ensure that court actions available under national law concerning information society services' activities allow for the rapid adoption of measures, including interim measures, designed to terminate any alleged infringement and to prevent any further impairment of the interests involved.

2.   The Annex to Directive 98/27/EC shall be supplemented as follows:

'11. Directive 2000/31/EC of the European Parliament and of the Council of 8 June 2000 on certain legal aspects on information society services, in particular electronic commerce, in the internal market (Directive on electronic commerce) (OJ L 178, 17.7.2000, p. 1).'

Article 19. Cooperation

1.   Member States shall have adequate means of supervision and investigation necessary to implement this Directive effectively and shall ensure that service providers supply them with the requisite information.

2.   Member States shall cooperate with other Member States; they shall, to that end, appoint one or several contact points, whose details they shall communicate to the other Member States and to the Commission.

3.   Member States shall, as quickly as possible, and in conformity with national law, provide the assistance and information requested by other Member States or by the Commission, including by appropriate electronic means.

4.   Member States shall establish contact points which shall be accessible at least by electronic means and from which recipients and service providers may:

(a)   obtain general information on contractual rights and obligations as well as on the complaint and redress mechanisms available in the event of disputes, including practical aspects involved in the use of such mechanisms;

(b)   obtain the details of authorities, associations or organisations from which they may obtain further information or practical assistance.

5.   Member States shall encourage the communication to the Commission of any significant administrative or judicial decisions taken in their territory regarding disputes relating to information society services and practices, usages and customs relating to electronic commerce. The Commission shall communicate these decisions to the other Member States.

Article 20. Sanctions

Member States shall determine the sanctions applicable to infringements of national provisions adopted pursuant to this Directive and shall take all measures necessary to ensure that they are enforced. The sanctions they provide for shall be effective, proportionate and dissuasive.

CHAPTER IV

FINAL PROVISIONS

Article 21. Re-examination

1.   Before 17 July 2003, and thereafter every two years, the Commission shall submit to the European Parliament, the Council and the Economic and Social Committee a report on the application of this Directive, accompanied, where necessary, by proposals for adapting it to legal, technical and economic develop-

ments in the field of information society services, in particular with respect to crime prevention, the protection of minors, consumer protection and to the proper functioning of the internal market.

2.   In examining the need for an adaptation of this Directive, the report shall in particular analyse the need for proposals concerning the liability of providers of hyperlinks and location tool services, 'notice and take down' procedures and the attribution of liability following the taking down of content. The report shall also analyse the need for additional conditions for the exemption from liability, provided for in Articles 12 and 13, in the light of technical developments, and the possibility of applying the internal market principles to unsolicited commercial communications by electronic mail.

Article 22. Transposition

1.   Member States shall bring into force the laws, regulations and administrative provisions necessary to comply with this Directive before 17 January 2002. They shall forthwith inform the Commission thereof.

2.   When Member States adopt the measures referred to in paragraph 1, these shall contain a reference to this Directive or shall be accompanied by such reference at the time of their official publication. The methods of making such reference shall be laid down by Member States.

Article 23. Entry into force

This Directive shall enter into force on the day of its publication in the Official Journal of the European Communities.

Article 24. Addressees

This Directive is addressed to the Member States.

Done at Luxemburg, 8 June 2000.

PART IV
CODES

DRAFT RULES ON UNJUSTIFIED ENRICHMENT
(SLC Discussion Paper No 99 (1996), Appendix)

1 General principle

A person who has been enriched at the expense of another person is bound, if the enrichment is unjustified, to redress the enrichment.

2 Enrichment

(1) A person is enriched if he acquires an economic benefit.

(2) A person acquires an economic benefit if his net worth is increased or is prevented from being decreased, and accordingly a person may be enriched, among other ways, by

    (a)   acquiring money or other property

    (b)   having value added to property

    (c)   being freed, in whole or in part, from an obligation, or

    (d)   being saved from a loss or expenditure

(3) A person is treated as acquiring an economic benefit under a void contract, or under a voidable contract which has been reduced, rescinded or otherwise set aside, or under a contract which has been terminated by frustration or rescission for breach or by some other means (apart from full performance) or under any other transaction or purported transaction which does not provide legal cause for the acquisition, if he would have acquired an economic benefit but for the fact that he gave consideration, and accordingly in such circumstances both parties to the transaction or purported transaction may be regarded as being enriched.

3 At the expense of another person

(1) The enrichment of one person is at the expense of another person if it is the direct result of

    (a)   a payment, grant, transfer, incurring of liability, or rendering of services by the other person

       (i)   to the enriched person

      (ii)   in fulfilment of an obligation of the enriched person

     (iii)   in adding value to the enriched person's property, or

     (iv)   in acquiring some other economic benefit for the enriched person, or

    (b)   in any case not covered by paragraph (a), an interference with the patrimonial rights of the other person otherwise than by the operation of natural forces.

(2) A person interferes with the patrimonial rights of another person if, among other things, he

    (a)   extinguishes those rights or acts in such a way that they are extinguished

    (b)   disposes or purports to dispose of property belonging to that other person

    (c)   uses property which that other person has the right to use to the exclusion of the interferer, or

    (d)   actively intercepts a benefit due to the other person

but a person does not interfere with the patrimonial rights of another person merely because he breaches a contract between himself and the other person.

(3)   A person who claims redress or any unjustified enrichment resulting from an interference with his patrimonial rights is treated for the purpose of any claims by or against third parties as thereby ratifying the interference.

(4)   A person who purchases property in good faith from someone who is not the owner of the property is not treated as being enriched at the expense of the owner or of any former owner by reason only of any economic benefit derived by him from the purchase of the property; and the same rule applies to any other acquirer, in good faith and for value, of the right, or of what purports to be the right, to deal with the property or rights of another, and to anyone deriving title from such a purchaser or acquirer.

(5)   Where a person (E) has been enriched indirectly as a result of performance by another person (C) under a contract between C and a third party (T), E's enrichment is not regarded as being at the expense of C, even if C is unable to recover under his contract with T.

(6)   This rule is subject to rule 8 (which deals with certain exceptional cases where redress is due for indirect enrichment).

4   Unjustified

An enrichment is unjustified unless it is justified under rules 5 or 6.

5   Enrichment justified by legal cause

(1)   An enrichment is justified if the enriched person is entitled to it by virtue of
    (a)   an enactment
    (b)   a rule of law
    (c)   a court decree
    (d)   a contract (whether or not the person claiming redress is a party) or unilateral voluntary obligation
    (e)   a will or trust
    (f)   a gift, or
    (g)   some other legal cause.

(2)   The reference to an enactment or rule of law in rule 5(1) is to an enactment or rule of law which confers rights directly and not to an enactment or rule of law in so far as it operates indirectly by regulating the effects of court decrees, contracts, wills, trusts, gifts or other legal causes.

(3)   A purported or apparent legal cause does not justify an enrichment if it is void or if, being voidable, it has been reduced, rescinded or otherwise set aside.

(4)   An acquisition of property is not a justified enrichment merely because legal title to the property has been acquired.

6   Enrichment justified by public policy

(1)   An enrichment is justified if it is the result of

(a)   work or expenditure which was undertaken or incurred by the other person for his own benefit, or for the benefit of a third party or the public at large, which has incidentally conferred a benefit on the enriched person, and which was undertaken or incurred when the person knew or could reasonably have been expected to know that there would be a benefit to the enriched person and accepted, or could reasonably be supposed to have accepted, the risk that the enriched person would not pay for the benefit

(b)   the voluntary and deliberate conferring by the other person of a benefit on the enriched person, in the knowledge that it is not due and in acceptance of the risk that the enriched person may choose not to pay or do anything in return

(c)   a voluntary performance by the other person of an obligation which has prescribed, even if he erroneously believed that the obligation was still due, provided that any due counter-performance has been given

(d)   a voluntary performance by the other person of an obligation which is invalid for some formal reason only, even if he erroneously believed that the obligation was valid, provided that any due counter-performance has been given or if there is some other consideration of public policy which requires it to be regarded as justified.

(2)   For the purpose of rule 6(1)(a) 'benefit', in relation to a person who has done work or provided services in tendering for a contract or in the anticipation of obtaining a contract, includes the benefit to the person of having, or improving, the chance of obtaining the contract.

7   Exceptions to rules 5 and 6

(1)   Rule 5(1)(b) does not apply in so far as the enrichment is the result of any rule of law on the acquisition of property by accession or specification, or any analogous rule whereby one person may acquire another's property when it becomes attached to or mixed with his own.

(2)   Rule 5(1)(d) does not apply in so far as the contract or obligation,

(a)   is unenforceable because of an enactment or rule of law (whether or not it is also illegal), unless allowing redress for the enrichment would contravene the policy underlying the enactment or rule of law,

(b)   has been terminated by rescission or frustration or some other means (apart from full performance) and the contract or obligation does not, expressly or impliedly, exclude redress in respect of the benefit in question.

(3)   For the purpose of rule 7(2)(b) a contract which provides for performance in several parts or stages is presumed, unless the contract indicates the contrary, to exclude redress in so far as performance by one party under, and substantially in accordance with, the contract has been met by performance by the other party under, and substantially in accordance with, the contract.

(4)   Rule 5(1)(f) does not apply where the gift

(a)   was made in error, whether of fact or law, or

(b)   was subject to a condition, which has been met, that it would be returned.

(5)   Rule 6(1)(a) and (b) do not apply where the other person has, in circumstances where it was reasonable to do so,

(a)   paid a monetary debt due by the enriched person

(b)   fulfilled an alimentary obligation due by the enriched person

(c)   incurred expenditure or performed services necessary for preserving the life, health or welfare of the enriched person, or

(d)   incurred expenditure or performed services urgently necessary for preserving the property of the enriched person or preventing it from being dangerous.

8   Redress for indirect enrichment

(1)(a)   Where a person (E) has acquired money or money's worth from a third party (T) by disposing or purporting to dispose of property belonging to another person (C), or by otherwise interfering with C's patrimonial rights, or by disposing of property acquired by him from C under a transaction voidable at C's instance, E's enrichment is treated, notwithstanding anything in the preceding rules, as being at the expense of C and as not being justified by any contract between himself and T.

(b)   Paragraph (a) does not apply if E was a purchaser in good faith of the property in question, or had otherwise acquired, in good faith and for value, the right, or what purported to be the right, to deal with the property or rights in question, or had derived title from such a purchaser or acquirer.

(2)   Where a person (T) has been enriched at the expense of another person (C) and T has transferred to another person (E) any benefit arising out of the enrichment then, notwithstanding anything in the preceding rules, E is taken to be enriched at the expense of C and neither the transfer by T to E, nor any voluntary obligation underlying the transfer, justifies the enrichment if

(a)   T's enrichment at the expense of C was unjustified or was justified only by a transaction voidable at C's instance

(b)   C is unable to recover from T, or cannot reasonably be expected to attempt to recover from T, and

(c)   the acquisition by E from T was not in good faith and for value.

(3)   Where a person (E) has been enriched by receiving a benefit from a trust estate or from the estate of a deceased person, the fact that E's enrichment is the result of a transfer from a trustee or executor does not prevent him from being liable to make redress to

(a)   a creditor of the estate to the extent that the creditor, because of the transfer to the beneficiary, has been unable to recover from the trustee or executor, or

(b)   a person (the true beneficiary) who is legally entitled to the benefit in question.

(4)   Where a debtor pays the wrong person, that person is enriched at the expense of the true creditor in so far as the payment extinguishes the liability of the debtor to the true creditor.

(5)   Nothing in these rules affects any procedural rule designed to avoid duplication of proceedings.

9   Redress due

(1)   The redress due by an enriched person under these rules is such transfer of property or payment of money, or both, as is required to redress the enriched person's unjustified enrichment at the expense of the claimant.

(2)   The redress due is assessed in accordance with the rules in the schedule in any case where those rules are applicable.

(3)   Where the enriched person has been enriched at the expense of the claimant in more than one way, the rules in the schedule apply cumulatively unless there would be double redress in respect of the same enrichment.

(4)   This rule is subject to the provisions of rule 10.

10   Court's powers to refuse or modify award

(1)   Where, in an action for unjustified enrichment, it appears to the court that each party is bound to make redress to the other, the court may

(a)   refuse to grant decree against the defender until satisfied that the pursuer has made, or will make, the redress due by him, or

(b)   where both obligations are to pay money, set off one entitlement against the other and grant decree for the difference.

(2)   Where, in an action for unjustified enrichment based on the passive receipt of a benefit by the enriched person, it appears to the court

(a)   that the enriched person had no reasonable opportunity to refuse the benefit

(b)   that the enriched person would have refused the benefit if he had had such an opportunity

(c)   that the enriched person cannot, or cannot reasonably be expected to, convert the value of the benefit into money or money's worth, and

(d)   that it would be inequitable to make a full award

the court may refuse or modify the award accordingly.

(3)   Where, in an action for unjustified enrichment based on the defender's acquisition of the pursuer's property by accession or specification or any analogous rule, it appears to the court that the pursuer has acted in good faith and that, having regard to the respective values of the properties involved, the conduct of the parties and all other relevant factors, the most appropriate and equitable solution would be for the defender to be ordered to sell to the pursuer such property at such a price as would enable the pursuer to regain his property without prejudice to the defender, the court may grant decree accordingly.

(4)   Notwithstanding anything in the preceding rules, a court deciding an

action for unjustified enrichment may refuse to make an award, or may make a reduced award, or may grant decree subject to conditions, if it considers

(a)   that the person enriched, where he did not know, and could not reasonably be expected to know, that redress was due, changed his position (whether by spending money, disposing of property, consuming property or its fruits, abandoning rights, failing to exercise rights in time, or otherwise) in reliance on his enrichment, and it would for that reason be inequitable to make a full award or grant decree unconditionally

(b)   that the claimant was so culpable or negligent in causing the unjustified enrichment that it would be inequitable or contrary to public policy to make a full award or grant decree unconditionally

(c)   that the claimant would be unjustly enriched if a full award were made or if decree were granted unconditionally, or

(d)   that, for any other reason, it would be inequitable or contrary to public policy to make a full award or grant decree unconditionally.

11 Bars to proceedings

(1)(a)   An action for unjustified enrichment cannot be brought under these rules if there is, or was,

(i)   a special statutory or contractual procedure for dealing with the situation giving rise to the enrichment or

(ii)   another legal remedy for the enrichment

and if the claimant could reasonably have been expected to use that procedure or remedy.

(b)   Paragraph (a) does not apply if the enactment or contract providing the other procedure or remedy indicates expressly or impliedly that it is intended to be in addition to any remedy available under the general law on unjustified enrichment.

(c)   The availability of damages for loss does not preclude an action for redress of unjustified enrichment but, without prejudice to his right to claim damages for any consequential or other loss, the claimant cannot claim both redress of the other party's unjustified enrichment and damages for his corresponding loss.

(2)(a)   A person who, before a court decision in proceedings to which he was not a party, has made a payment or transfer which was apparently due under the law as it was commonly supposed to be at that time cannot bring an action for unjustified enrichment in respect of that payment or transfer on the ground that the decision has shown that the law was not as it was commonly supposed to be and that the payment or transfer was accordingly not in fact due.

(b)   In the preceding paragraph, 'decision' in any case where a decision is affirmed or restored on appeal means the decision so affirmed or restored and not the decision affirming or restoring it.

(3)   The bars mentioned in this rule are in addition to any bar resulting from the operation of the general law on personal bar.

12 Areas of law not affected

(1)   These rules replace the existing Scottish common law on unjustified enrichment, including

(a)   the common law on restitution in so far as it is part of the law on unjustified enrichment

(b)   the common law on repetition and recompense, and

(c)   the *condictio indebiti*; the *condictio causa data causa non secuta*; the *condictio ob turpem vel iniustam causam*; the *condictio ob non causam*; the *condictio sine causa*; the *actio in quantum locupletior factus est*; and the *actio de in rem verso* in so far as they form part of the existing law.

(2)   Nothing in these rules affects

(a)   any enacted law

(b)   the law on rights of relief of cautioners and co-obligants

(c)   the law on subrogation of insurers or those who have paid an indemnity

(d)   the law derived from the case of *Walker v Milne* (whereby loss suffered or expenditure incurred in the expectation of a contract may in certain circumstances be recovered)

(e)   the law on the rights of a defrauded person as against the creditors of the person who defrauded him

(f)   the law on the recovery by a person of the possession or control of his own property or of any other property to the possession or control of which he is entitled

(g)   the law on the special obligations of those in a fiduciary position

(h)   the law on general average or salvage

(i)   the law on *negotiorum gestio*.

13   Interpretation

(1)   In these rules, and in the schedule where applicable,

(a)   'court decree' includes the decision of any tribunal, quasi-judicial body or arbiter having jurisdiction

(b)   'enactment' includes subordinate legislation

(c)   'gift' includes a gratuitous waiver, renunciation or discharge of a right

(d)   'he' means he, she or it; 'him' means him, her or it; and 'his' means his, hers or its

(e)   'patrimonial rights' include rights flowing from the ownership of property, rights to protect confidential information and other rights having an economic value but do not include purely personal rights, such as the rights to life, liberty, bodily integrity or reputation, and

(f)   'property' means property of any kind, corporeal or incorporeal, heritable or moveable.

(2)   Any reference in these rules to a contract which has been terminated by rescission or frustration includes a reference to a contract which has been substantially terminated by rescission or frustration and a reference to a severable part of a contract which has been terminated by rescission or frustration.

SCHEDULE. REDRESS DUE

PART I

E acquires benefit directly from C

1.   This part of the schedule applies where the enriched person (E) has been enriched by acquiring a benefit directly from the claimant (C).

2(1)   Where the unjustified enrichment resulted from the acquisition of money by E from C, the redress due by E to C is the amount acquired, with interest from the time of acquisition.

(2)   Where the unjustified enrichment resulted from the acquisition of other property by E from C, the redress due by E to C is

(a)   if the property is corporeal and can be returned in substantially the same condition as it was in at the time of the acquisition, the return of the property in that condition along with a sum of money to take account of any benefit derived by E from the ownership, use or possession of the property and interest on that sum where appropriate

(b)   if the property is corporeal and cannot be returned in substantially the same condition as it was in at the time of the acquisition, the amount which it would have been reasonable to expect E to pay C for the property at the time of its acquisition by E, with interest on that amount from the time of acquisition

(c)   if the property is incorporeal, the return of the property where possible and, whether or not return is possible, a sum of money to take account of any benefit derived by E from the ownership of the property and interest on that sum where appropriate.

3. Where the unjustified enrichment resulted from the addition of value by C to E's property, the redress due by E to C is the amount which it would have been reasonable to expect E to pay C for his work or expenditure in adding that value, or the amount of value added (at the time when the addition was made), if less, with interest where appropriate.

4. Where the unjustified enrichment resulted from the discharge or reduction of any liability of E by means of a payment by C, the redress due by E to C is the amount paid, with interest from the date of payment.

5. Where the unjustified enrichment resulted from E's being saved a loss or expenditure by receiving C's services, the redress due by E to C is the amount which it would have been reasonable to expect E to pay for those services, or the amount of loss or expenditure saved, if less, with interest where appropriate.

6(1) Where the unjustified enrichment resulted from E's being saved a loss or expenditure by using or possessing C's property, the redress due by E to C is the amount which it would have been reasonable to expect E to pay for that use or possession, or the amount of loss or expenditure saved, if less, with interest where appropriate.

(2) Where the unjustified enrichment resulted from E's being saved a loss or expenditure by consuming C's property, the redress due by E to C is the amount which it would have been reasonable to expect E to pay for the property at the time of consumption, or the amount of loss or expenditure saved, if less, with interest where appropriate.

(3) Where the unjustified enrichment resulted from E's being saved a loss or expenditure by interfering with C's patrimonial rights in any other way, the redress due by E to C is the amount which it would have been reasonable to expect E to pay C, at the time of the interference, for permission to interfere with those rights in that way in the circumstances, or the amount of loss or expenditure saved, if less, with interest where appropriate.

7. Where the unjustified enrichment resulted from the acquisition of any other benefit by E from C, the redress due by E to C is the amount which it would have been reasonable to expect E to pay C for the benefit at the time or acquisition, or the amount of E's actual enrichment, if less, with interest where appropriate.

PART II

E acquires benefit from T at indirect expense of C

8. This part of the schedule applies where the enriched person (E) has been enriched indirectly at the expense of the claimant (C).

9. Where E has enriched himself by using or disposing of C's property, or otherwise interfering with C's patrimonial rights, in order to obtain money or money's worth from a third party (T) the redress due by E to C is the amount which it would have been reasonable for E to pay C at the time of the use, disposal or interference for permission to use or dispose of C's property or to interfere with his rights in that way, or the amount of E's actual enrichment attributable to the use, disposal or interference, if less, with interest where appropriate.

10. Where E has been indirectly enriched at the expense of C as a result of the transfer of a benefit from a third party (T) in the circumstances covered by rule 8(2) (transfer of benefit arising from unjustified enrichment to person taking otherwise than in good faith and for value) T is treated as if he had been acting as E's agent and accordingly the redress due by E to C is the same, and is due on the same conditions, as it would have been if E had acquired the benefit directly from C.

11.   Where E has been indirectly enriched at the expense of C in the circumstances covered by rule 8(3) (transfers from trusts or executries) the redress due by E to C is

(1)   where C is a creditor claiming under rule 8(3)(a) the amount of the debt due to C out of the estate or the amount of E's enrichment out of the estate, whichever is the less, with interest where appropriate

(2)   where C is a true beneficiary claiming under rule 8(3)(b), and the benefit due to him out of the estate and received by E was a special legacy, the transfer of the subject matter of the legacy along with a sum to take account of any benefit derived by E from its use or possession or, if the subject matter of the legacy cannot be transferred in substantially the same condition as it was in when acquired by E, an amount representing its value when acquired by E, with interest from that date

(3)   where C is a true beneficiary claiming under rule 8(3)(b), and the benefit due to him out of the estate and received by E was not a special legacy, the amount of the benefit due to C out of the estate or the amount of E's unjustified enrichment out of the estate, whichever is the less, with interest where appropriate.

PART III

General

12.   Any reference in this schedule to the return of property includes a reference to a return by reconveyance or by any other means by which ownership can be restored to the other person.

13.   For the purposes of paragraph 2(2) corporeal property acquired by the enriched person by accession or specification, or any analogous rule whereby one person may acquire another's property when it becomes attached to or mixed with his own, is treated as property which cannot be returned in substantially the same condition as it was in at the time of acquisition.

14.   Where property is to be returned or transferred to the claimant by the enriched person under these rules, the expenses of the return or transfer are to be borne

(1)   by the claimant if the enrichment was in good faith, or

(2)   by the enriched person if the enrichment was in bad faith unless a court dealing with the claim orders otherwise.

15.   In assessing what it would have been reasonable for E to pay C for any interference with C's rights or for permission to interfere with those rights regard may be had to any factors which would have made C reluctant or unwilling to permit the interference.

PRINCIPLES OF EUROPEAN CONTRACT LAW*

CHAPTER 1. GENERAL PROVISIONS

Section 1. Scope of the Principles

Article 1:101   Application of the principles
(1)   These Principles are intended to be applied as general rules of contract law in the European Union.

---

(2)   These Principles will apply when the parties have agreed to incorporate them into their contract or that their contract is to be governed by them.

(3)   These Principles may be applied when the parties:

(a)   have agreed that their contract is to be governed by 'general principles of law', the 'lex mercatoria' or the like; or

(b)   have not chosen any system or rules of law to govern their contract.

(4)   These Principles may provide a solution to the issue raised where the system or rules of law applicable do not do so.

Article 1:102   Freedom of contract

(1)   Parties are free to enter into a contract and to determine its contents, subject to the requirements of good faith and fair dealing, and the mandatory rules established by these Principles.

(2)   The parties may exclude the application of any of the Principles or derogate from or vary their effects, except as otherwise provided by these Principles.

Article 1:103   Mandatory law

(1)   Where the law otherwise applicable so allows, the parties may choose to have their contract governed by the Principles, with the effect that national mandatory rules are not applicable.

(2)   Effect should nevertheless be given to those mandatory rules of national, supranational and international law which, according to the relevant rules of private international law, are applicable irrespective of the law governing the contract.

Article 1:104   Application to questions of consent

(1)   The existence and validity of the agreement of the parties to adopt or incorporate these Principles shall be determined by these Principles.

(2)   Nevertheless, a party may rely upon the law of the country in which it has its habitual residence to establish that it did not consent if it appears from the circumstances that it would not be reasonable to determine the effect of its conduct in accordance with these Principles.

Article 1:105   Usages and practices

(1)   The parties are bound by any usage to which they have agreed and by any practice they have established between themselves.

(2)   The parties are bound by a usage which would be considered generally applicable by persons in the same situation as the parties, except where the application of such usage would be unreasonable.

Article 1:106   Interpretation and supplementation

(1)   These Principles should be interpreted and developed in accordance with their purposes. In particular, regard should be had to the need to promote good faith and fair dealing, certainty in contractual relationships and uniformity of application.

(2)   Issues within the scope of these Principles but not expressly settled by them are so far as possible to be settled in accordance with the ideas underlying the Principles. Failing this, the legal system applicable by virtue of the rules of private international law is to be applied.

Article 1:107   Application of the principles by way of analogy

These Principles apply with appropriate modifications to agreements to modify or end a contract, to unilateral promises and other statements and conduct indicating intention.

Section 2. General duties

Article 1:201   Good faith and fair dealing

(1)   Each party must act in accordance with good faith and fair dealing.

(2)   The parties may not exclude or limit this duty.

Article 1:202   Duty to co-operate
Each party owes to the other a duty to co-operate in order to give full effect to the contract.

Section 3. Terminology and other provisions

Article 1:301   Meaning of terms
In these Principles, except where the context otherwise requires:
   (1)   'act' includes omission;
   (2)   'court' includes arbitral tribunal;
   (3)   an 'intentional' act includes an act done recklessly;
   (4)   'non-performance' denotes any failure to perform an obligation under the contract, whether or not excused, and includes delayed performance, defective performance and failure to co-operate in order to give full effect to the contract;
   (5)   a matter is 'material' if it is one which a reasonable person in the same situation as one party ought to have known would influence the other party in its decision whether to contract on the proposed terms or to contract at all;
   (6)   'written' statements include communications made by telegram, telex, telefax and electronic mail and other means of communication capable of providing a readable record of the statement on both sides.

Article 1:302   Reasonableness
Under these Principles reasonableness is to be judged by what persons acting in good faith and in the same situation as the parties would consider to be reasonable. In particular, in assessing what is reasonable the nature and purpose of the contract, the circumstances of the case, and the usages and practices of the trades or professions involved should be taken into account.

Article 1:303   Notice
   (1)   Any notice may be given by any means, whether in writing or otherwise, appropriate to the circumstances.
   (2)   Subject to paragraphs (4) and (5), any notice becomes effective when it reaches the addressee.
   (3)   A notice reaches the addressee when it is delivered to it or to its place of business or mailing address, or, if it does not have a place of business or mailing address, to its habitual residence.
   (4)   If one party gives notice to the other because of the other's non-performance or because such non-performance is reasonably anticipated by the first party, and the notice is properly dispatched or given, a delay or inaccuracy in the transmission of the notice or its failure to arrive does not prevent it from having effect. The notice shall have effect from the time at which it would have arrived in normal circumstances.
   (5)   A notice has no effect if a withdrawal of it reaches the addressee before or at the same time as the notice.
   (6)   In this Article, 'notice' includes the communication of a promise, statement, offer, acceptance, demand, request or other declaration.

Article 1:304   Computation of time
   (1)   A period of time set by a party in a written document for the addressee to reply or take other action begins to run from the date stated as the date of the document. If no date is shown, the period begins to run from the moment the document reaches the addressee.
   (2)   Official holidays and official non-working days occurring during the period are included in calculating the period. However, if the last day of the period is an official holiday or official non-working day at the address of the addressee, or at the place where a prescribed act is to be performed, the period is extended until the first following working day in that place.
   (3)   Periods of time expressed in days, weeks, months or years shall begin at

00.00 on the next day and shall end at 24.00 on the last day of the period; but any reply that has to reach the party who set the period must arrive, or other act which is to be done must be completed, by the normal close of business in the relevant place on the last day of the period.

Article 1:305   Imputed knowledge and intention
If any person who with a party's assent was involved in making a contract, or who was entrusted with performance by a party or who performed with its assent:

(a)   knew or foresaw a fact, or ought to have known or foreseen it; or

(b)   acted intentionally or with gross negligence, or not in accordance with good faith and fair dealing,

this knowledge, foresight or behaviour is imputed to the party itself.

CHAPTER 2. FORMATION

Section 1. General provisions

Article 2:101   Conditions for the conclusion of a contract
(1)   A contract is concluded if:

(a)   the parties intend to be legally bound, and

(b)   they reach a sufficient agreement

without any further requirement.

(2)   A contract need not be concluded or evidenced in writing nor is it subject to any other requirement as to form. The contract may be proved by any means, including witnesses.

Article 2:102   Intention
The intention of a party to be legally bound by contract is to be determined from the party's statements or conduct as they were reasonably understood by the other party.

Article 2:103   Sufficient agreement
(1)   There is sufficient agreement if the terms:

(a)   have been sufficiently defined by the parties so that the contract can be enforced, or

(b)   can be determined under these Principles.

(2)   However, if one of the parties refuses to conclude a contract unless the parties have agreed on some specific matter, there is no contract unless agreement on that matter has been reached.

Article 2:104   Terms not individually negotiated
(1)   Contract terms which have not been individually negotiated may be invoked against a party who did not know of them only if the party invoking them took reasonable steps to bring them to the other party's attention before or when the contract was concluded.

(2)   Terms are not brought appropriately to a party's attention by a mere reference to them in a contract document, even if that party signs the document.

Article 2:105   Merger clause
(1)   If a written contract contains an individually negotiated clause stating that the writing embodies all the terms of the contract (a merger clause), any prior statements, undertakings or agreements which are not embodied in the writing do not form part of the contract.

(2)   If the merger clause is not individually negotiated it will only establish a presumption that the parties intended that their prior statements, undertakings or agreements were not to form part of the contract. This rule may not be excluded or restricted.

(3)   The parties' prior statements may be used to interpret the contract. This rule may not be excluded or restricted except by an individually negotiated clause.

(4)   A party may by its statements or conduct be precluded from asserting a merger clause to the extent that the other party has reasonably relied on them.

Article 2:106   Written modification only
(1)   A clause in a written contract requiring any modification or ending by agreement to be made in writing establishes only a presumption that an agreement to modify or end the contract is not intended to be legally binding unless it is in writing.
(2)   A party may by its statements or conduct be precluded from asserting such a clause to the extent that the other party has reasonably relied on them.

Article 2:107   Promises binding without acceptance
A promise which is intended to be legally binding without acceptance is binding.

Section 2. Offer and Acceptance

Article 2:201   Offer
(1)   A proposal amounts to an offer if:
   (a)   it is intended to result in a contract if the other party accepts it, and
   (b)   it contains sufficiently definite terms to form a contract.
(2)   An offer may be made to one or more specific persons or to the public.
(3)   A proposal to supply goods or services at stated prices made by a professional supplier in a public advertisement or a catalogue, or by a display of goods, is presumed to be an offer to sell or supply at that price until the stock of goods, or the supplier's capacity to supply the service, is exhausted.

Article 2:202   Revocation of an offer
(1)   An offer may be revoked if the revocation reaches the offeree before it has dispatched its acceptance or, in cases of acceptance by conduct, before the contract has been concluded under Article 2.205(2) or (3).
(2)   An offer made to the public can be revoked by the same means as were used to make the offer.
(3)   However, a revocation of an offer is ineffective if:
   (a)   the offer indicates that it is irrevocable; or
   (b)   it states a fixed time for its acceptance; or
   (c)   it was reasonable for the offeree to rely on the offer as being irrevocable and the offeree has acted in reliance on the offer.

Article 2:203   Rejection
When a rejection of an offer reaches the offeror, the offer lapses.

Article 2:204   Acceptance
(1)   Any form of statement or conduct by the offeree is an acceptance if it indicates assent to the offer.
(2)   Silence or inactivity does not in itself amount to acceptance.

Article 2:205   Time of conclusion of the contract
(1)   If an acceptance has been dispatched by the offeree the contract is concluded when the acceptance reaches the offeror.
(2)   In case of acceptance by conduct, the contract is concluded when notice of the conduct reaches the offeror.
(3)   If by virtue of the offer, of practices which the parties have established between themselves, or of a usage, the offeree may accept the offer by performing an act without notice to the offeror, the contract is concluded when the performance of the act begins.

Article 2:206   Time limit for acceptance
(1)   In order to be effective, acceptance of an offer must reach the offeror within the time fixed by it.

(2)   If no time has been fixed by the offeror acceptance must reach it within a reasonable time.

(3)   In the case of an acceptance by an act of performance under article 2.205(3), that act must be performed within the time for acceptance fixed by the offeror or, if no such time is fixed, within a reasonable time.

Article 2:207   Late acceptance

(1)   A late acceptance is nonetheless effective as an acceptance if without delay the offeror informs the offeree that he treats it as such.

(2)   If a letter or other writing containing a late acceptance shows that it has been sent in such circumstances that if its transmission had been normal it would have reached the offeror in due time, the late acceptance is effective as an acceptance unless, without delay, the offeror informs the offeree that it considers its offer as having lapsed.

Article 2:208   Modified acceptance

(1)   A reply by the offeree which states or implies additional or different terms which would materially alter the terms of the offer is a rejection and a new offer.

(2)   A reply which gives a definite assent to an offer operates as an acceptance even if it states or implies additional or different terms, provided these do not materially alter the terms of the offer. The additional or different terms then become part of the contract.

(3)   However, such a reply will be treated as a rejection of the offer if:
   (a)   the offer expressly limits acceptance to the terms of the offer; or
   (b)   the offeror objects to the additional or different terms without delay; or
   (c)   the offeree makes its acceptance conditional upon the offeror's assent to the additional or different terms, and the assent does not reach the offeree within a reasonable time.

Article 2:209   Conflicting general conditions

(1)   If the parties have reached agreement except that the offer and acceptance refer to conflicting general conditions of contract, a contract is nonetheless formed. The general conditions form part of the contract to the extent that they are common in substance.

(2)   However, no contract is formed if one party:
   (a)   has indicated in advance, explicitly, and not by way of general conditions, that it does not intend to be bound by a contract on the basis of paragraph (1); or
   (b)   without delay, informs the other party that it does not intend to be bound by such contract.

(3)   General conditions of contract are terms which have been formulated in advance for an indefinite number of contracts of a certain nature, and which have not been individually negotiated between the parties.

Article 2:210   Professional's written confirmation

If professionals have concluded a contract but have not embodied it in a final document, and one without delay sends the other a writing which purports to be a confirmation of the contract but which contains additional or different terms, such terms will become part of the contract unless:
   (a)   the terms materially alter the terms of the contract, or
   (b)   the addressee objects to them without delay.

Article 2:211   Contracts not concluded through offer and acceptance

The rules in this section apply with appropriate adaptations even though the process of conclusion of a contract cannot be analysed into offer and acceptance.

Section 3. Liability for Negotiations

Article 2:301 Negotiations contrary to good faith

(1) A party is free to negotiate and is not liable for failure to reach an agreement.

(2) However, a party who has negotiated or broken off negotiations contrary to good faith and fair dealing is liable for the losses caused to the other party.

(3) It is contrary to good faith and fair dealing, in particular, for a party to enter into or continue negotiations with no real intention of reaching an agreement with the other party.

Article 2:302 Breach of confidentiality

If confidential information is given by one party in the course of negotiations, the other party is under a duty not to disclose that information or use it for its own purposes whether or not a contract is subsequently concluded. The remedy for breach of this duty may include compensation for loss suffered and restitution of the benefit received by the other party.

CHAPTER 3. AUTHORITY OF AGENTS

Section 1. General provisions

Article 3:101 Scope of the chapter

(1) This Chapter governs the authority of an agent or other intermediary to bind its principal in relation to a contract with a third party.

(2) This Chapter does not govern an agent's authority bestowed by law or the authority of an agent appointed by a public or judicial authority.

(3) This Chapter does not govern the internal relationship between the agent or intermediary and its principal.

Article 3:102 Categories of representation

(1) Where an agent acts in the name of a principal, the rules on direct representation apply (Section 2). It is irrelevant whether the principal's identity is revealed at the time the agent acts or is to be revealed later.

(2) Where an intermediary acts on instructions and on behalf of, but not in the name of, a principal, or where the third party neither knows nor has reason to know that the intermediary acts as an agent, the rules on indirect representation apply (Section 3).

Section 2. Direct Representation

Article 3:201 Express, implied and apparent authority

(1) The principal's grant of authority to an agent to act in its name may be express or may be implied from the circumstances.

(2) The agent has authority to perform all acts necessary in the circumstances to achieve the purposes for which the authority was granted.

(3) A person is to be treated as having granted authority to an apparent agent if the person's statements or conduct induce the third party reasonably and in good faith to believe that the apparent agent has been granted authority for the act performed by it.

Article 3:202 Agent acting in exercise of its authority

Where an agent is acting within its authority as defined by article 3.201, its acts bind the principal and the third party directly to each other. The agent itself is not bound to the third party.

Article 3:203 Unidentified principal

If an agent enters into a contract in the name of a principal whose identity is to be revealed later, but fails to reveal that identity within a reasonable time after a request by the third party, the agent itself is bound by the contract.

Article 3:204   Agent acting without or outside its authority

(1)   Where a person acting as an agent acts without authority or outside the scope of its authority, its acts are not binding upon the principal and the third party.

(2)   Failing ratification by the principal according to article 3.207, the agent is liable to pay the third party such damages as will place the third party in the same position as if the agent had acted with authority. This does not apply if the third party knew or could not have been unaware of the agent's lack of authority.

Article 3:205   Conflict of interest

(1)   If a contract concluded by an agent involves the agent in a conflict of interests of which the third party knew or could not have been unaware, the principal may avoid the contract according to the provisions of articles 4.112 to 4.116.

(2)   There is presumed to be a conflict of interest where:

(a)   the agent also acted as agent for the third party; or

(b)   the contract was with itself in its personal capacity.

(3)   However, the principal may not avoid the contract:

(a)   if it had consented to, or could not have been unaware of, the agent's so acting; or

(b)   if the agent had disclosed the conflict of interest to it and it had not objected within a reasonable time.

Article 3:206   Subagency

An agent has implied authority to appoint a subagent to carry out tasks which are not of a personal character and which it is not reasonable to expect the agent to carry out itself. The rules of this Section apply to the subagency; acts of the subagent which are within its and the agent's authority bind the principal and the third party directly to each other.

Article 3:207   Ratification by principal

(1)   Where a person acting as an agent acts without authority or outside its authority, the principal may ratify the agent's acts.

(2)   Upon ratification, the agent's acts are considered as having been authorised, without prejudice to the rights of other persons.

Article 3:208   Third party's right with respect to confirmation of authority

Where the statements or conduct of the principal gave the third party reason to believe that an act performed by the agent was authorised, but the third party is in doubt about the authorisation, it may send a written confirmation to the principal or request ratification from it. If the principal does not object or answer the request without delay, the agent's act is treated as having been authorised.

Article 3:209   Duration of authority

(1)   An agent's authority continues until the third party knows or ought to know that:

(a)   the agent's authority has been brought to an end by the principal, the agent, or both; or

(b)   the acts for which the authority had been granted have been completed, or the time for which it had been granted has expired; or

(c)   the agent has become insolvent or, where a natural person, has died or become incapacitated; or

(d)   the principal has become insolvent.

(2)   The third party is considered to know that the agent's authority has been brought to an end under paragraph (1)(a) above if this has been communicated or publicised in the same manner in which the authority was originally communicated or publicised.

(3)   However, the agent remains authorised for a reasonable time to perform those acts which are necessary to protect the interests of the principal or its successors.

Section 3. Indirect Representation

Article 3:301   Intermediaries not acting in the name of a principal
(1)   Where an intermediary acts:
    (a)   on instructions and on behalf, but not in the name, of a principal, or
    (b)   on instructions from a principal but the third party does not know and has no reason to know this,
the intermediary and the third party are bound to each other.
(2)   The principal and the third party are bound to each other only under the conditions set out in Articles 3.302 to 3.304.

Article 3:302   Intermediary's insolvency or fundamental non-performance to principal
If the intermediary becomes insolvent, or if it commits a fundamental non-performance towards the principal, or if prior to the time for performance it is clear that there will be a fundamental non-performance:
    (a)   on the principal's demand, the intermediary shall communicate the name and address of the third party to the principal; and
    (b)   the principal may exercise against the third party the rights acquired on the principal's behalf by the intermediary, subject to any defences which the third party may set up against the intermediary.

Article 3:303   Intermediary's insolvency or fundamental non-performance to third party
If the intermediary becomes insolvent, or if it commits a fundamental non-performance towards the third party, or if prior to the time for performance it is clear that there will be a fundamental non-performance:
    (a)   on the third party's demand, the intermediary shall communicate the name and address of the principal to the third party; and
    (b)   the third party may exercise against the principal the rights which the third party has against the intermediary, subject to any defences which the intermediary may set up against the third party and those which the principal may set up against the intermediary.

Article 3:304   Requirement of notice
The rights under Articles 3.302 and 3.303 may be exercised only if notice of intention to exercise them is given to the intermediary and to the third party or principal, respectively. Upon receipt of the notice, the third party or the principal is no longer entitled to render performance to the intermediary.

CHAPTER 4. VALIDITY

Article 4:101   Matters not covered
This Chapter does not deal with invalidity arising from illegality, immorality or lack of capacity.

Article 4:102   Initial impossibility
A contract is not invalid merely because at the time it was concluded performance of the obligation assumed was impossible, or because a party was not entitled to dispose of the assets to which the contract relates.

Article 4:103   Mistake as to facts or law
(1)   A party may avoid a contract for mistake of fact or law existing when the contract was concluded if:
    (a) (i)   the mistake was caused by information given by the other party; or

(ii) the other party knew or ought to have known of the mistake and it was contrary to good faith and fair dealing to leave the mistaken party in error; or

(iii) the other party made the same mistake, and

(b) the other party knew or ought to have known that the mistaken party, had it known the truth, would not have entered the contract or would have done so only on fundamentally different terms.

(2) However a party may not avoid the contract if:

(a) in the circumstances its mistake was inexcusable, or

(b) the risk of the mistake was assumed, or in the circumstances should be borne, by it.

Article 4:104   Inaccuracy in communication

An inaccuracy in the expression or transmission of a statement is to be treated as a mistake of the person who made or sent the statement and Article 4.103 applies.

Article 4:105   Adaptation of contract

(1) If a party is entitled to avoid the contract for mistake but the other party indicates that it is willing to perform, or actually does perform, the contract as it was understood by the party entitled to avoid it, the contract is to be treated as if it had been concluded as the that [sic] party understood it. The other party must indicate its willingness to perform, or render such performance, promptly after being informed of the manner in which the party entitled to avoid it understood the contract and before that party acts in reliance on any notice of avoidance.

(2) After such indication or performance the right to avoid is lost and any earlier notice of avoidance is ineffective.

(3) Where both parties have made the same mistake, the court may at the request of either party bring the contract into accordance with what might reasonably have been agreed had the mistake not occurred.

Article 4:106   Incorrect information

A party who has concluded a contract relying on incorrect information given it by the other party may recover damages in accordance with Article 4.117(2) and (3) even if the information does not give rise to a right to avoid the contract on the ground of mistake under Article 4.103, unless the party who gave the information had reason to believe that the information was correct.

Article 4:107   Fraud

(1) A party may avoid a contract when it has been led to conclude it by the other party's fraudulent representation, whether by words or conduct, or fraudulent non-disclosure of any information which in accordance with good faith and fair dealing it should have disclosed.

(2) A party's representation or non-disclosure is fraudulent if it was intended to deceive.

(3) In determining whether good faith and fair dealing required that a party disclose particular information, regard should be had to all the circumstances, including:

(a) whether the party had special expertise;

(b) the cost to it of acquiring the relevant information;

(c) whether the other party could reasonably acquire the information for itself; and

(d) the apparent importance of the information to the other party.

Article 4:108   Threats

A party may avoid a contract when it has been led to conclude it by the other party's imminent and serious threat of an act:

(a) which is wrongful in itself, or

(b)   which it is wrongful to use as a means to obtain the conclusion of the contract, unless in the circumstances the first party had a reasonable alternative.

Article 4:109   Excessive benefit or unfair advantage
(1)   A party may avoid a contract if, at the time of the conclusion of the contract:

(a)   it was dependent on or had a relationship of trust with the other party, was in economic distress or had urgent needs, was improvident, ignorant, inexperienced or lacking in bargaining skill, and

(b)   the other party knew or ought to have known of this and, given the circumstances and purpose of the contract, took advantage of the first party's situation in a way which was grossly unfair or took an excessive benefit.

(2)   Upon the request of the party entitled to avoidance, a court may if it is appropriate adapt the contract in order to bring it into accordance with what might have been agreed had the requirements of good faith and fair dealing been followed.

(3)   A court may similarly adapt the contract upon the request of a party receiving notice of avoidance for excessive benefit or unfair advantage, provided that this party informs the party who gave the notice promptly after receiving it and before that party has acted in reliance on it.

Article 4:110   Unfair terms not individually negotiated
(1)   A party may avoid a term which has not been individually negotiated if, contrary to the requirements of good faith and fair dealing, it causes a significant imbalance in the parties' rights and obligations arising under the contract to the detriment of that party, taking into account the nature of the performance to be rendered under the contract, all the other terms of the contract and the circumstances at the time the contract was concluded.

(2)   This Article does not apply to:

(a)   a term which defines the main subject matter of the contract, provided the term is in plain and intelligible language; or to

(b)   the adequacy in value of one party's obligations compared to the value of the obligations of the other party.

Article 4:111   Third persons
(1)   Where a third person for whose acts a party is responsible, or who with a party's assent is involved in the making of a contract:

(a)   causes a mistake by giving information, or knows of or ought to have known of a mistake,

(b)   gives incorrect information,

(c)   commits fraud,

(d)   makes a threat, or

(e)   takes excessive benefit or unfair advantage,

remedies under this Chapter will be available under the same conditions as if the behaviour or knowledge had been that of the party itself.

(2)   Where any other third person:

(a)   gives incorrect information,

(b)   commits fraud,

(c)   makes a threat, or

(d)   takes excessive benefit or unfair advantage,

remedies under this Chapter will be available if the party knew or ought to have known of the relevant facts, or at the time of avoidance it has not acted in reliance on the contract.

Article 4:112   Notice of avoidance
Avoidance must be by notice to the other party.

Article 4:113 Time limits

(1) Notice of avoidance must be given within a reasonable time, with due regard to the circumstances, after the avoiding party knew or ought to have known of the relevant facts or became capable of acting freely.

(2) However, a party may avoid an individual term under Article 4.110 if it gives notice of avoidance within a reasonable time after the other party has invoked the term.

Article 4:114 Confirmation

If the party who is entitled to avoid a contract confirms it, expressly or impliedly, after it knows of the ground for avoidance, or becomes capable of acting freely, avoidance of the contract is excluded.

Article 4:115 Effect of avoidance

On avoidance either party may claim restitution of whatever it has supplied under the contract, provided it makes concurrent restitution of whatever it has received. If restitution cannot be made in kind for any reason, a reasonable sum must be paid for what has been received.

Article 4:116 Partial avoidance

If a ground of avoidance affects only particular terms of a contract, the effect of an avoidance is limited to those terms unless, giving due consideration to all the circumstances of the case, it is unreasonable to uphold the remaining contract.

Article 4:117 Damages

(1) A party who avoids a contract under this Chapter may recover from the other party damages so as to put the avoiding party as nearly as possible into the same position as if it had not concluded the contract, provided that the other party knew or ought to have known of the mistake, fraud, threat or taking of excessive benefit or unfair advantage.

(2) If a party has the right to avoid a contract under this Chapter, but does not exercise its right, or has lost its right under the provisions of Articles 4.113 or 4.114, it may recover, subject to paragraph (1), damages limited to the loss caused to it by the mistake, fraud, threat or taking of excessive benefit or unfair advantage. The same measure of damages shall apply when the party was misled by incorrect information in the sense of Article 4.106.

(3) In other respects, the damages shall be in accordance with the relevant provisions of Chapter 9, Section 5, with appropriate adaptations.

Article 4:118 Exclusion or restriction of remedies

(1) Remedies for fraud, threats and excessive benefit or unfair advantage-taking, and the right to avoid an unfair term which has not been individually negotiated, cannot be excluded or restricted.

(2) Remedies for mistake and incorrect information may be excluded or restricted unless the exclusion or restriction is contrary to good faith and fair dealing.

Article 4:119 Remedies for non-performance

A party who is entitled to a remedy under this Chapter in circumstances which afford that party a remedy for non-performance may pursue either remedy.

CHAPTER 5. INTERPRETATION

Article 5:101 General rules of interpretation

(1) A contract is to be interpreted according to the common intention of the parties even if this differs from the literal meaning of the words.

(2) If it is established that one party intended the contract to have a particular meaning, and at the time of the conclusion of the contract the other party could

not have been unaware of the first party's intention, the contract is to be interpreted in the way intended by the first party.

(3)   If an intention cannot be established according to (1) or (2), the contract is to be interpreted according to the meaning that reasonable persons of the same kind as the parties would give to it in the same circumstances.

Article 5:102   Relevant circumstances
In interpreting the contract, regard shall be had, in particular, to:

(a)   the circumstances in which it was concluded, including the preliminary negotiations;

(b)   the conduct of the parties, even subsequent to the conclusion of the contract;

(c)   the nature and purpose of the contract;

(d)   the interpretation which has already been given to similar clauses by the parties and the practices they have established between themselves;

(e)   the meaning commonly given to terms and expressions in the branch of activity concerned and the interpretation similar clauses may already have received;

(f)   usages; and

(g)   good faith and fair dealing.

Article 5:103   Contra proferentem rule
Where there is doubt about the meaning of a contract term not individually negotiated, an interpretation of the term against the party who supplied it is to be preferred.

Article 5:104   Preference to negotiated terms
Terms which have been individually negotiated take preference over those which are not.

Article 5:105   Reference to contract as a whole
Terms are to be interpreted in the light of the whole contract in which they appear.

Article 5:106   Terms to be given effect
An interpretation which renders the terms of the contract lawful, or effective, is to be preferred to one which would not.

Article 5:107   Linguistic discrepancies
Where a contract is drawn up in two or more language versions none of which is stated to be authoritative, there is, in case of discrepancy between the versions, a preference for the interpretation according to the version in which the contract was originally drawn up.

CHAPTER 6. CONTENTS AND EFFECTS

Article 6:101   Statements giving rise to contractual obligations
(1)   A statement made by one party before or when the contract is concluded is to be treated as giving rise to a contractual obligation if that is how the other party reasonably understood it in the circumstances, taking into account:

(a)   the apparent importance of the statement to the other party;

(b)   whether the party was making the statement in the course of business; and

(c)   the relative expertise of the parties.

(2)   If one of the parties is a professional supplier who gives information about the quality or use of services or goods or other property when marketing or advertising them or otherwise before the contract for them is concluded, the statement is to be treated as giving rise to a contractual obligation unless it is shown that the other party knew or could not have been unaware that the statement was incorrect.

(3)   Such information and other undertakings given by a person advertising or marketing services, goods or other property for the professional supplier, or by a person in earlier links of the business chain, are to be treated as giving rise to a contractual obligation on the part of the professional supplier unless it did not know and had no reason to know of the information or undertaking.

Article 6:102   Implied terms

In addition to the express terms, a contract may contain implied terms which stem from
   (a)   the intention of the parties,
   (b)   the nature and purpose of the contract, and
   (c)   good faith and fair dealing.

Article 6:103   Simulation

When the parties have concluded an apparent contract which was not intended to reflect their true agreement, as between the parties the true agreement prevails.

Article 6:104   Determination of price

Where the contract does not fix the price or the method of determining it, the parties are to be treated as having agreed on a reasonable price.

Article 6:105   Unilateral determination by a party

Where the price or any other contractual term is to be determined by one party whose determination is grossly unreasonable, then notwithstanding any provision to the contrary, a reasonable price or other term shall be substituted.

Article 6:106   Determination by a third person

(1)   Where the price or any other contractual term is to be determined by a third person, and it cannot or will not do so, the parties are presumed to have empowered the court to appoint another person to determine it.

(2)   If a price or other term fixed by a third person is grossly unreasonable, a reasonable price or term shall be substituted.

Article 6:107   Reference to a non-existent factor

Where the price or any other contractual term is to be determined by reference to a factor which does not exist or has ceased to exist or to be accessible, the nearest equivalent factor shall be substituted.

Article 6:108   Quality of performance

If the contract does not specify the quality, a party must tender performance of at least average quality.

Article 6:109   Contract for an indefinite period

A contract for an indefinite period may be ended by either party by giving notice of reasonable length.

Article 6:110   Stipulation in favour of a third party

(1)   A third party may require performance of a contractual obligation when its right to do so has been expressly agreed upon between the promisor and the promisee, or when such agreement is to be inferred from the purpose of the contract or the circumstances of the case. The third party need not be identified at the time the agreement is concluded.

(2)   If the third party renounces the right to performance the right is treated as never having accrued to it.

(3)   The promisee may by notice to the promisor deprive the third party of the right to performance unless:
   (a)   the third party has received notice from the promisee that the right has been made irrevocable, or
   (b)   the promisor or the promisee has received notice from the third party that the latter accepts the right.

Article 6:111   Change of circumstances
(1)   A party is bound to fulfil its obligations even if performance has become more onerous, whether because the cost of performance has increased or because the value of the performance it receives has diminished.
(2)   If, however, performance of the contract becomes excessively onerous because of a change of circumstances, the parties are bound to enter into negotiations with a view to adapting the contract or terminating it, provided that:
    (a)   the change of circumstances occurred after the time of conclusion of the contract,
    (b)   the possibility of a change of circumstances was not one which could reasonably have been taken into account at the time of conclusion of the contract, and
    (c)   the risk of the change of circumstances is not one which, according to the contract, the party affected should be required to bear.
(3)   If the parties fail to reach agreement within a reasonable period, the court may:
    (a)   terminate the contract at a date and on terms to be determined by the court; or
    (b)   adapt the contract in order to distribute between the parties in a just and equitable manner the losses and gains resulting from the change of circumstances.
In either case, the court may award damages for the loss suffered through a party refusing to negotiate or breaking off negotiations contrary to good faith and fair dealing.

CHAPTER 7. PERFORMANCE

Article 7:101   Place of performance
(1)   If the place of performance of a contractual obligation is not fixed by or determinable from the contract it shall be:
    (a)   in the case of an obligation to pay money, the creditor's place of business at the time of the conclusion of the contract;
    (b)   in the case of an obligation other than to pay money, the obligor's place of business at the time of the conclusion of the contract.
(2)   If a party has more than one place of business, the place of business for the purpose of the preceding paragraph is that which has the closest relationship to the contract, having regard to the circumstances known to or contemplated by the parties at the time of conclusion of the contract.
(3)   If a party does not have a place of business its habitual residence is to be treated as its place of business.

Article 7:102   Time of performance
A party has to effect its performance:
(1)   if a time is fixed by or determinable from the contract, at that time;
(2)   if a period of time is fixed by or determinable from the contract, at any time within that period unless the circumstances of the case indicate that the other party is to choose the time;
(3)   in any other case, within a reasonable time after the conclusion of the contract.

Article 7:103   Early performance
(1)   A party may decline a tender of performance made before it is due except where acceptance of the tender would not unreasonably prejudice its interests.
(2)   A party's acceptance of early performance does not affect the time fixed for the performance of its own obligation.

Article 7:104   Order of performance
To the extent that the performances of the parties can be rendered simultaneously,

the parties are bound to render them simultaneously unless the circumstances indicate otherwise.

Article 7:105   Alternative performance

(1)   Where an obligation may be discharged by one of alternative performances, the choice belongs to the party who is to perform, unless the circumstances indicate otherwise.

(2)   If the party who is to make the choice fails to do so by the time required by the contract, then:

(a)   if the delay in choosing is fundamental, the right to choose passes to the other party;

(b)   if the delay is not fundamental, the other party may give a notice fixing an additional period of reasonable length in which the party to choose must do so. If the latter fails to do so, the right to choose passes to the other party.

Article 7:106   Performance by a third person

(1)   Except where the contract requires personal performance the obligee cannot refuse performance by a third person if:

(a)   the third person acts with the assent of the obligor; or

(b)   the third person has a legitimate interest in performance and the obligor has failed to perform or it is clear that it will not perform at the time performance is due.

(2)   Performance by the third person in accordance with paragraph (1) discharges the obligor.

Article 7:107   Form of payment

(1)   Payment of money due may be made in any form used in the ordinary course of business.

(2)   A creditor who, pursuant to the contract or voluntarily, accepts a cheque or other order to pay or a promise to pay is presumed to do so only on condition that it will be honoured. The creditor may not enforce the original obligation to pay unless the order or promise is not honoured.

Article 7:108   Currency of payment

(1)   The parties may agree that payment shall be made only in a specified currency.

(2)   In the absence of such agreement, a sum of money expressed in a currency other than that of the place where payment is due may be paid in the currency of that place according to the rate of exchange prevailing there at the time when payment is due.

(3)   If, in a case falling within the preceding paragraph, the debtor has not paid at the time when payment is due, the creditor may require payment in the currency of the place where payment is due according to the rate of exchange prevailing there either at the time when payment is due or at the time of actual payment.

Article 7:109   Appropriation of performance

(1)   Where a party has to perform several obligations of the same nature and the performance tendered does not suffice to discharge all of the obligations, then subject to paragraph 4 the party may at the time of its performance declare to which obligation the performance is to be appropriated.

(2)   If the performing party does not make such a declaration, the other party may within a reasonable time appropriate the performance to such obligation as it chooses. It shall inform the performing party of the choice. However, any such appropriation to an obligation which:

(a)   is not yet due, or

(b)   is illegal, or

(c)   is disputed,

is invalid.

(3)   In the absence of an appropriation by either party, and subject to paragraph 4, the performance is appropriated to that obligation which satisfies one of the following criteria in the sequence indicated:
(a)   the obligation which is due or is the first to fall due;
(b)   the obligation for which the obligee has the least security;
(c)   the obligation which is the most burdensome for the obligor,
(d)   the obligation which has arisen first.
If none of the preceding criteria applies, the performance is appropriated proportionately to all obligations.
(4)   In the case of a monetary obligation, a payment by the debtor is to be appropriated, first, to expenses, secondly, to interest, and thirdly, to principal, unless the creditor makes a different appropriation.

Article 7:110   Property not accepted

(1)   A party who is left in possession of tangible property other than money because of the other party's failure to accept or retake the property must take reasonable steps to protect and preserve the property.
(2)   The party left in possession may discharge its duty to deliver or return:
(a)   by depositing the property on reasonable terms with a third person to be held to the order of the other party, and notifying the other party of this; or
(b)   by selling the property on reasonable terms after notice to the other party, and paying the net proceeds to that party.
(3)   Where, however, the property is liable to rapid deterioration or its preservation is unreasonably expensive, the party must take reasonable steps to dispose of it. It may discharge its duty to deliver or return by paying the net proceeds to the other party.
(4)   The party left in possession is entitled to be reimbursed or to retain out of the proceeds of sale any expenses reasonably incurred.

Article 7:111   Money not accepted

Where a party fails to accept money properly tendered by the other party, that party may after notice to the first party discharge its obligation to pay by depositing the money to the order of the first party in accordance with the law of the place where payment is due.

Article 7:112   Costs of performance

Each party shall bear the costs of performance of its obligations.

CHAPTER 8. NON-PERFORMANCE AND REMEDIES IN GENERAL

Article 8:101   Remedies available

(1)   Whenever a party does not perform an obligation under the contract and the non-performance is not excused under Article 8.108, the aggrieved party may resort to any of the remedies set out in Chapter 9.
(2)   Where a party's non-performance is excused under Article 8.108, the aggrieved party may resort to any of the remedies set out in Chapter 9 except claiming performance and damages.
(3)   A party may not resort to any of the remedies set out in Chapter 9 to the extent that its own act caused the other party's non-performance.

Article 8:102   Cumulation of remedies

Remedies which are not incompatible may be cumulated. In particular, a party is not deprived of its right to damages by exercising its right to any other remedy.

Article 8:103   Fundamental non-performance

A non-performance of an obligation is fundamental to the contract if:
(a)   strict compliance with the obligation is of the essence of the contract; or
(b)   the non-performance substantially deprives the aggrieved party of what

it was entitled to expect under the contract, unless the other party did not foresee and could not reasonably have foreseen that result; or

(c)   the non-performance is intentional and gives the aggrieved party reason to believe that it cannot rely on the other party's future performance.

Article 8:104   Cure by non-performing party
A party whose tender of performance is not accepted by the other party because it does not conform to the contract may make a new and conforming tender where the time for performance has not yet arrived or the delay would not be such as to constitute a fundamental non-performance.

Article 8:105   Assurance of performance
(1)   A party who reasonably believes that there will be a fundamental non-performance by the other party may demand adequate assurance of due performance and meanwhile may withhold performance of its own obligations so long as such reasonable belief continues.

(2)   Where this assurance is not provided within a reasonable time, the party demanding it may terminate the contract if it still reasonably believes that there will be a fundamental non-performance by the other party and gives notice of termination without delay.

Article 8:106   Notice fixing additional period for performance
(1)   In any case of non-performance the aggrieved party may by notice to the other party allow an additional period of time for performance.

(2)   During the additional period the aggrieved party may withhold performance of its own reciprocal obligations and may claim damages, but it may not resort to any other remedy. If it receives notice from the other party that the latter will not perform within that period, or if upon expiry of that period due performance has not been made, the aggrieved party may resort to any of the remedies that may be available under Chapter 9.

(3)   If in a case of delay in performance which is not fundamental the aggrieved party has given a notice fixing an additional period of time of reasonable length, it may terminate the contract at the end of the period of notice. The aggrieved party may in its notice provide that if the other party does not perform within the period fixed by the notice the contract shall terminate automatically. If the period stated is too short, the aggrieved party may terminate, or, as the case may be, the contract shall terminate automatically, only after a reasonable period from the time of the notice.

Article 8:107   Performance entrusted to another
A party who entrusts performance of the contract to another person remains responsible for performance.

Article 8:108   Excuse due to an impediment
(1)   A party's non-performance is excused if it proves that it is due to an impediment beyond its control and that it could not reasonably have been expected to take the impediment into account at the time of the conclusion of the contract, or to have avoided or overcome the impediment or its consequences.

(2)   Where the impediment is only temporary the excuse provided by this article has effect for the period during which the impediment exists. However, if the delay amounts to a fundamental non-performance, the obligee may treat it as such.

(3)   The non-performing party must ensure that notice of the impediment and of its effect on its ability to perform is received by the other party within a reasonable time after the non-performing party knew or ought to have known of these circumstances. The other party is entitled to damages for any loss resulting from the non-receipt of such notice.

Article 8:109   Clause excluding or restricting remedies
Remedies for non-performance may be excluded or restricted unless it would be contrary to good faith and fair dealing to invoke the exclusion or restriction.

CHAPTER 9. PARTICULAR REMEDIES FOR NON-PERFORMANCE

Section 1. Right to Performance

Article 9:101   Monetary obligations
(1)   The creditor is entitled to recover money which is due.
(2)   Where the creditor has not yet performed its obligation and it is clear that the debtor will be unwilling to receive performance, the creditor may nonetheless proceed with its performance and may recover any sum due under the contract unless:
    (a)   it could have made a reasonable substitute transaction without significant effort or expense; or
    (b)   performance would be unreasonable in the circumstances.

Article 9:102   Non-monetary obligations
(1)   The aggrieved party is entitled to specific performance of an obligation other than one to pay money, including the remedying of a defective performance.
(2)   Specific performance cannot, however, be obtained where:
    (a)   performance would be unlawful or impossible; or
    (b)   performance would cause the obligor unreasonable effort or expense; or
    (c)   the performance consists in the provision of services or work of a personal character or depends upon a personal relationship, or
    (d)   the aggrieved party may reasonably obtain performance from another source.
(3)   The aggrieved party will lose the right to specific performance if it fails to seek it within a reasonable time after it has or ought to have become aware of the non-performance.

Article 9:103   Damages not precluded
The fact that a right to performance is excluded under this Section does not preclude a claim for damages.

Section 2. Withholding Performance

Article 9:201   Right to withhold performance
(1)   A party who is to perform simultaneously with or after the other party may withhold performance until the other has tendered performance or has performed. The first party may withhold the whole of its performance or a part of it as may be reasonable in the circumstances.
(2)   A party may similarly withhold performance for as long as it is clear that there will be a non-performance by the other party when the other party's performance becomes due.

Section 3. Termination of the Contract

Article 9:301   Right to terminate the contract
(1)   A party may terminate the contract if the other party's non-performance is fundamental.
(2)   In the case of delay the aggrieved party may also terminate the contract under Article 8.106(3).

Article 9:302   Contract to be performed in parts
If the contract is to be performed in separate parts and in relation to a part to which a counter-performance can be apportioned, there is a fundamental non-

performance, the aggrieved party may exercise its right to terminate under this Section in relation to the part concerned. It may terminate the contract as a whole only if the non-performance is fundamental to the contract as a whole.

Article 9:303   Notice of termination

(1)   A party's right to terminate the contract is to be exercised by notice to the other party.

(2)   The aggrieved party loses its right to terminate the contract unless it gives notice within a reasonable time after it has or ought to have become aware of the non-performance.

(3)(a)   When performance has not been tendered by the time it was due, the aggrieved party need not give notice of termination before a tender has been made. If a tender is later made it loses its right to terminate if it does not give such notice within a reasonable time after it has or ought to have become aware of the tender.

(b)   If, however, the aggrieved party knows or has reason to know that the other party still intends to tender within a reasonable time, and the aggrieved party unreasonably fails to notify the other party that it will not accept performance, it loses its right to terminate if the other party in fact tenders within a reasonable time.

(4)   If a party is excused under Article 8.108 through an impediment which is total and permanent, the contract is terminated automatically and without notice at the time the impediment arises.

Article 9:304   Anticipatory non-performance

Where prior to the time for performance by a party it is clear that there will be a fundamental non-performance by it the other party may terminate the contract.

Article 9:305   Effects of termination in general

(1)   Termination of the contract releases both parties from their obligation to effect and to receive future performance, but, subject to Articles 9.306 to 9.308, does not affect the rights and liabilities that have accrued up to the time of termination.

(2)   Termination does not affect any provision of the contract for the settlement of disputes or any other provision which is to operate even after termination.

Article 9:306   Property reduced in value

A party who terminates the contract may reject property previously received from the other party if its value to the first party has been fundamentally reduced as a result of the other party's non-performance.

Article 9:307   Recovery of money paid

On termination of the contract a party may recover money paid for a performance which it did not receive or which it properly rejected.

Article 9:308   Recovery of property

On termination of the contract a party who has supplied property which can be returned and for which it has not received payment or other counter-performance may recover the property.

Article 9:309   Recovery for performance that cannot be returned

On termination of the contract a party who has rendered a performance which cannot be returned and for which it has not received payment or other counter-performance may recover a reasonable amount for the value of the performance to the other party.

Section 4. Price Reduction

Article 9:401   Right to reduce price

(1)   A party who accepts a tender of performance not conforming to the con-

tract may reduce the price. This reduction shall be proportionate to the decrease in the value of the performance at the time this was tendered compared to the value which a conforming tender would have had at that time.

(2)   A party who is entitled to reduce the price under the preceding paragraph and who has already paid a sum exceeding the reduced price may recover the excess from the other party.

(3)   A party who reduces the price cannot also recover damages for reduction in the value of the performance but remains entitled to damages for any further loss it has suffered so far as these are recoverable under Section 5 of this Chapter.

Section 5. Damages and Interest

Article 9:501   Right to damages

(1)   The aggrieved party is entitled to damages for loss caused by the other party's non-performance which is not excused under Article 8.108.

(2)   The loss for which damages are recoverable includes:
   (a)   non-pecuniary loss; and
   (b)   future loss which is reasonably likely to occur.

Article 9:502   General measure of damages

The general measure of damages is such sum as will put the aggrieved party as nearly as possible into the position in which it would have been if the contract had been duly performed. Such damages cover the loss which the aggrieved party has suffered and the gain of which it has been deprived.

Article 9:503   Foreseeability

The non-performing party is liable only for loss which it foresaw or could reasonably have foreseen at the time of conclusion of the contract as a likely result of its non-performance, unless the non-performance was intentional or grossly negligent.

Article 9:504   Loss attributable to aggrieved party

The non-performing party is not liable for loss suffered by the aggrieved party to the extent that the aggrieved party contributed to the non-performance or its effects.

Article 9:505   Reduction of loss

(1)   The non-performing party is not liable for loss suffered by the aggrieved party to the extent that the aggrieved party could have reduced the loss by taking reasonable steps.

(2)   The aggrieved party is entitled to recover any expenses reasonably incurred in attempting to reduce the loss.

Article 9:506   Substitute transaction

Where the aggrieved party has terminated the contract and has made a substitute transaction within a reasonable time and in a reasonable manner, it may recover the difference between the contract price and the price of the substitute transaction as well as damages for any further loss so far as these are recoverable under this Section.

Article 9:507   Current price

Where the aggrieved party has terminated the contract and has not made a substitute transaction but there is a current price for the performance contracted for, it may recover the difference between the contract price and the price current at the time the contract is terminated as well as damages for any further loss so far as these are recoverable under this Section.

Article 9:508   Delay in payment of money

(1)   If payment of a sum of money is delayed, the aggrieved party is entitled to interest on that sum from the time when payment is due to the time of payment at

the average commercial bank short-term lending rate to prime borrowers prevailing for the contractual currency of payment at the place where payment is due.

(2)   The aggrieved party may in addition recover damages for any further loss so far as these are recoverable under this Section.

Article 9:509   Agreed Payment for non-performance

(1)   Where the contract provides that a party who fails to perform is to pay a specified sum to the aggrieved party for such non-performance, the aggrieved party shall be awarded that sum irrespective of its actual loss.

(2)   However, despite any agreement to the contrary the specified sum may be reduced to a reasonable amount where it is grossly excessive in relation to the loss resulting from the non-performance and the other circumstances.

Article 9:510   Currency by which damages are to be measured

Damages are to be measured by the currency which most appropriately reflects the aggrieved party's loss.

CHAPTER 10. PLURALITY OF PARTIES

Section 1. Plurality of debtors

Article 10:101   Solidary, separate and communal obligations

(1)   Obligations are solidary when all the debtors are bound to render one and the same performance and the creditor may require it from any one of them until full performance has been received.

(2)   Obligations are separate when each debtor is bound to render only part of the performance and the creditor may require from each debtor only that debtor's part.

(3)   An obligation is communal when all the debtors are bound to render the performance together and the creditor may require it only from all of them.

Article 10:102   When solidary obligations arise

(1)   If several debtors are bound to render one and the same performance to a creditor under the same contract, they are solidarily liable, unless the contract or the law provides otherwise.

(2)   Solidary obligations also arise where several persons are liable for the same damage.

(3)   The fact that the debtors are not liable on the same terms does not prevent their obligations from being solidary.

Article 10:103   Liability under separate obligations

Debtors bound by separate obligations are liable in equal shares unless the contract or the law provides otherwise.

Article 10:104   Communal obligations: special rule when money claimed for non-performance

Notwithstanding Article 10:101(3), when money is claimed for non-performance of a communal obligation, the debtors are solidarily liable for payment to the creditor.

Article 10:105   Apportionment between solidary debtors

(1)   As between themselves, solidary debtors are liable in equal shares unless the contract or the law provides otherwise.

(2)   If two or more debtors are liable for the same damage under Article 10:102(2), their share of liability as between themselves is determined according to the law governing the event which gave rise to the liability.

Article 10:106   Recourse between solidary debtors

(1)   A solidary debtor who has performed more than that debtor's share may

claim the excess from any of the other debtors to the extent of each debtor's un-performed share, together with a share of any costs reasonably incurred.

(2)   A solidary debtor to whom paragraph (1) applies may also, subject to any prior right and interest of the creditor, exercise the rights and actions of the creditor, including accessory securities, to recover the excess from any of the other debtors to the extent of each debtor's unperformed share.

(3)   If a solidary debtor who has performed more than that debtor's share is unable, despite all reasonable efforts, to recover contribution from another solidary debtor, the share of the others, including the one who has performed, is increased proportionally.

Article 10:107   Performance, set-off and merger in solidary obligations

(1)   Performance or set-off by a solidary debtor or set-off by the creditor against one solidary debtor discharges the other debtors in relation to the creditor to the extent of the performance or set-off.

(2)   Merger of debts between a solidary debtor and the creditor discharges the other debtors only for the share of the debtor concerned.

Article 10:108   Release or settlement in solidary obligations

(1)   When the creditor releases, or reaches a settlement with, one solidary debtor, the other debtors are discharged of liability for the share of that debtor.

(2)   The debtors are totally discharged by the release or settlement if it so provides.

(3)   As between solidary debtors, the debtor who is discharged from that debtor's share is discharged only to the extent of the share at the time of the discharge and not from any supplementary share for which that debtor may subsequently become liable under Article 10:106(3).

Article 10:109   Effect of judgment in solidary obligations

A decision by a court as to the liability to the creditor of one solidary debtor does not affect:

(a)   the liability to the creditor of the other solidary debtors; or

(b)   the rights of recourse between the solidary debtors under Article 10:106.

Article 10:110   Prescription in solidary obligations

Prescription of the creditor's right to performance ('claim') against one solidary debtor does not affect:

(a)   the liability to the creditor of the other solidary debtors; or

(b)   the rights of recourse between the solidary debtors under Article 10:106.

Article 10:111   Opposability of other defences in solidary obligations

(1)   A solidary debtor may invoke against the creditor any defence which another solidary debtor can invoke, other than a defence personal to that other debtor. Invoking the defence has no effect with regard to the other solidary debtors.

(2)   A debtor from whom contribution is claimed may invoke against the claimant any personal defence that that debtor could have invoked against the creditor.

Section 2. Plurality of creditors

Article 10:201   Solidary, separate and communal claims

(1)   Claims are solidary when any of the creditors may require full performance from the debtor and when the debtor may render performance to any of the creditors.

(2)   Claims are separate when the debtor owes each creditor only that creditor's share of the claim and each creditor may require performance only of that creditor's share.

(3)   A claim is communal when the debtor must perform to all the creditors and any creditor may require performance only for the benefit of all.

Article 10:202   Apportionment of separate claims
Separate creditors are entitled to equal shares unless the contract or the law provides otherwise.

Article 10:203   Difficulties of executing a communal claim
If one of the creditors in a communal claim refuses, or is unable to receive, the performance, the debtor may discharge the obligation to perform by depositing the property or money with a third party according to Articles 7:110 or 7:111 of the Principles.

Article 10:204   Apportionment of solidary claims
(1)   Solidary creditors are entitled to equal shares unless the contract or the law provides otherwise.

(2)   A creditor who has received more than that creditor's share must transfer the excess to the other creditors to the extent of their respective shares.

Article 10:205   Regime of solidary claims
(1)   A release granted to the debtor by one of the solidary creditors has no effect on the other solidary creditors

(2)   The rules of Articles 10:107, 10:109, 10:110 and 10:111(1) apply, with appropriate adaptations, to solidary claims.

CHAPTER 11. ASSIGNMENT OF CLAIMS

Section 1. General Principles

Article 11:101   Scope of chapter
(1)   This Chapter applies to the assignment by agreement of a right to performance ('claim') under an existing or future contract.

(2)   Except where otherwise stated or the context otherwise requires, this Chapter also applies to the assignment by agreement of other transferable claims.

(3)   This Chapter does not apply:

   (a)   to the transfer of a financial instrument or investment security where, under the law otherwise applicable, such transfer must be by entry in a register maintained by or for the issuer; or

   (b)   to the transfer of a bill of exchange or other negotiable instrument or of a negotiable security or a document of title to goods where, under the law otherwise applicable, such transfer must be by delivery (with any necessary indorsement).

(4)   In this Chapter 'assignment' includes an assignment by way of security.

(5)   This Chapter also applies, with appropriate adaptations, to the granting by agreement of a right in security over a claim otherwise than by assignment.

Article 11:102   Contractual claims generally assignable
(1)   Subject to Articles 11:301 and 11:302, a party to a contract may assign a claim under it.

(2)   A future claim arising under an existing or future contract may be assigned if at the time when it comes into existence, or at such other time as the parties agree, it can be identified as the claim to which the assignment relates.

Article 11:103   Partial assignment
A claim which is divisible may be assigned in part, but the assignor is liable to the debtor for any increased costs which the debtor thereby incurs.

Article 11:104   Form of assignment
An assignment need not be in writing and is not subject to any other requirement as to form. It may be proved by any means, including witnesses.

Section 2. Effects of Assignment As Between Assignor and Assignee

Article 11:201   Rights transferred to assignee
(1)   The assignment of a claim transfers to the assignee:
  (a)   all the assignor's rights to performance in respect of the claim assigned; and
  (b)   all accessory rights securing such performance.
(2)   Where the assignment of a claim under a contract is associated with the substitution of the assignee as debtor in respect of any obligation owed by the assignor under the same contract, this Article takes effect subject to Article 12:201.

Article 11:202   When assignment takes effect
(1)   An assignment of an existing claim takes effect at the time of the agreement to assign or such later time as the assignor and assignee agree.
(2)   An assignment of a future claim is dependent upon the assigned claim coming into existence but thereupon takes effect from the time of the agreement to assign or such later time as the assignor and assignee agree.

Article 11:203   Preservation of assignee's rights against assignor
An assignment is effective as between the assignor and assignee, and entitles the assignee to whatever the assignor receives from the debtor, even if it is ineffective against the debtor under Article 11:301 or 11:302.

Article 11:204   Undertakings by assignor
By assigning or purporting to assign a claim the assignor undertakes to the assignee that:
  (a)   at the time when the assignment is to take effect the following conditions will be satisfied except as otherwise disclosed to the assignee:
    (i)   the assignor has the right to assign the claim;
    (ii)   the claim exists and the assignee's rights are not affected by any defences or rights (including any right of set-off) which the debtor might have against the assignor; and
    (iii)   the claim is not subject to any prior assignment or right in security in favour of any other party or to any other incumbrance;
  (b)   the claim and any contract under which it arises will not be modified without the consent of the assignee unless the modification is provided for in the assignment agreement or is one which is made in good faith and is of a nature to which the assignee could not reasonably object; and
  (c)   the assignor will transfer to the assignee all transferable rights intended to secure performance which are not accessory rights.

Section 3. Effects of Assignment As Between Assignee and Debtor

Article 11:301   Contractual prohibition of assignment
(1)   An assignment which is prohibited by or is otherwise not in conformity with the contract under which the assigned claim arises is not effective against the debtor unless:
  (a)   the debtor has consented to it; or
  (b)   the assignee neither knew nor ought to have known of the non-conformity; or
  (c)   the assignment is made under a contract for the assignment of future rights to payment of money.
(2)   Nothing in the preceding paragraph affects the assignor's liability for the non-conformity.

Article 11:302   Other ineffective assignments
An assignment to which the debtor has not consented is ineffective against the debtor so far as it relates to a performance which the debtor, by reason of the

nature of the performance or the relationship of the debtor and the assignor, could not reasonably be required to render to anyone except the assignor.

Article 11:303   Effect on debtor's obligation

(1)   Subject to Articles 11:301, 11:302, 11:307 and 11:308, the debtor is bound to perform in favour of the assignee if and only if the debtor has received a notice in writing from the assignor or the assignee which reasonably identifies the claim which has been assigned and requires the debtor to give performance to the assignee.

(2)   However, if such notice is given by the assignee, the debtor may within a reasonable time request the assignee to provide reliable evidence of the assignment, pending which the debtor may withhold performance.

(3)   Where the debtor has acquired knowledge of the assignment otherwise than by a notice conforming to paragraph (1), the debtor may either withhold performance from or give performance to the assignee.

(4)   Where the debtor gives performance to the assignor, the debtor is discharged if and only if the performance is given without knowledge of the assignment.

Article 11:304   Protection of debtor

A debtor who performs in favour of a person identified as assignee in a notice of assignment under Article 11:303 is discharged unless the debtor could not have been unaware that such person was not the person entitled to performance.

Article 11:305   Competing demands

A debtor who has received notice of two or more competing demands for performance may discharge liability by conforming to the law of the due place of performance, or, if the performances are due in different places, the law applicable to the claim.

Article 11:306   Place of performance

(1)   Where the assigned claim relates to an obligation to pay money at a particular place, the assignee may require payment at any place within the same country or, if that country is a Member State of the European Union, at any place within the European Union, but the assignor is liable to the debtor for any increased costs which the debtor incurs by reason of any change in the place of performance.

(2)   Where the assigned claim relates to a non-monetary obligation to be performed at a particular place, the assignee may not require performance at any other place.

Article 11:307   Defences and rights of set-off

(1)   The debtor may set up against the assignee all substantive and procedural defences to the assigned claim which the debtor could have used against the assignor.

(2)   The debtor may also assert against the assignee all rights of set-off which would have been available against the assignor under Chapter 13 in respect of any claim against the assignor:

(a)   existing at the time when a notice of assignment, whether or not conforming to Article 11:303(1), reaches the debtor; or

(b)   closely connected with the assigned claim.

Article 11:308   Unauthorised modification not binding on assignee

A modification of the claim made by agreement between the assignor and the debtor, without the consent of the assignee, after a notice of assignment, whether or not conforming to Article 11:303(1), reaches the debtor does not affect the rights of the assignee against the debtor unless the modification is provided for in the assignment agreement or is one which is made in good faith and is of a nature to which the assignee could not reasonably object.

Section 4. Order of Priority between Assignee and Competing Claimants

Article 11:401   Priorities

(1)   Where there are successive assignments of the same claim, the assignee whose assignment is first notified to the debtor has priority over any earlier assignee if at the time of the later assignment the assignee under that assignment neither knew nor ought to have known of the earlier assignment.

(2)   Subject to paragraph (1), the priority of successive assignments, whether of existing or future claims, is determined by the order in which they are made.

(3)   The assignee's interest in the assigned claim has priority over the interest of a creditor of the assignor who attaches that claim, whether by judicial process or otherwise, after the time the assignment has taken effect under Article 11:202.

(4)   In the event of the assignor's bankruptcy, the assignee's interest in the assigned claim has priority over the interest of the assignor's insolvency administrator and creditors, subject to any rules of the law applicable to the bankruptcy relating to:

(a)   publicity required as a condition of such priority;

(b)   the ranking of claims; or

(c)   the avoidance or ineffectiveness of transactions in the bankruptcy proceedings.

CHAPTER 12. SUBSTITUTION OF NEW DEBTOR: TRANSFER OF CONTRACT

Section 1. Substitution of New Debtor

Article 12:101   Substitution: general rules

(1)   A third person may undertake with the agreement of the debtor and the creditor to be substituted as debtor, with the effect that the original debtor is discharged.

(2)   A creditor may agree in advance to a future substitution. In such a case the substitution takes effect only when the creditor is given notice by the new debtor of the agreement between the new and the original debtor.

Article 12:102   Effects of substitution on defences and securities

(1)   The new debtor cannot invoke against the creditor any rights or defences arising from the relationship between the new debtor and the original debtor.

(2)   The discharge of the original debtor also extends to any security of the original debtor given to the creditor for the performance of the obligation, unless the security is over an asset which is transferred to the new debtor as part of a transaction between the original and the new debtor.

(3)   Upon discharge of the original debtor, a security granted by any person other than the new debtor for the performance of the obligation is released, unless that other person agrees that it should continue to be available to the creditor.

(4)   The new debtor may invoke against the creditor all defences which the original debtor could have invoked against the creditor.

Section 2. Transfer of Contract

Article 12:201   Transfer of contract

(1)   A party to a contract may agree with a third person that that person is to be substituted as the contracting party. In such a case the substitution takes effect only where, as a result of the other party's assent, the first party is discharged.

(2)   To the extent that the substitution of the third person as a contracting party involves a transfer of rights to performance ('claims'), the provisions of Chapter 11 apply; to the extent that obligations are transferred, the provisions of Section 1 of this Chapter apply.

CHAPTER 13. SET-OFF

Article 13:101   Requirements for set-off
If two parties owe each other obligations of the same kind, either party may set off that party's right to performance ('claim') against the other party's claim, if and to the extent that, at the time of set-off, the first party:
    (a)   is entitled to effect performance; and
    (b)   may demand the other party's performance.

Article 13:102   Unascertained claims
    (1)   A debtor may not set off a claim which is unascertained as to its existence or value unless the set-off will not prejudice the interests of the other party.
    (2)   Where the claims of both parties arise from the same legal relationship it is presumed that the other party's interests will not be prejudiced.

Article 13:103   Foreign currency set-off
Where parties owe each other money in different currencies, each party may set off that party's claim against the other party's claim, unless the parties have agreed that the party declaring set-off is to pay exclusively in a specified currency.

Article 13:104   Notice of set-off
The right of set-off is exercised by notice to the other party.

Article 13:105   Plurality of claims and obligations
    (1)   Where the party giving notice of set-off has two or more claims against the other party, the notice is effective only if it identifies the claim to which it relates.
    (2)   Where the party giving notice of set-off has to perform two or more obligations towards the other party, the rules in Article 7:109 apply with appropriate adaptations.

Article 13:106   Effect of set-off
Set-off discharges the obligations, as far as they are coextensive, as from the time of notice.

Article 13:107   Exclusion of right of set-off
Set-off cannot be effected:
    (a)   where it is excluded by agreement;
    (b)   against a claim to the extent that that claim is not capable of attachment; and
    (c)   against a claim arising from a deliberate wrongful act.

CHAPTER 14. PRESCRIPTION

Section 1. General Provision

Article 14:101   Claims subject to prescription
A right to performance of an obligation ('claim') is subject to prescription by the expiry of a period of time in accordance with these Principles.

Section 2. Periods of Prescription and their Commencement

Article 14:201   General period
The general period of prescription is three years.

Article 14:202   Period for a claim established by legal proceedings
    (1)   The period of prescription for a claim established by judgment is ten years.
    (2)   The same applies to a claim established by an arbitral award or other instrument which is enforceable as if it were a judgment.

Article 14:203   Commencement
    (1)   The general period of prescription begins to run from the time when the

debtor has to effect performance or, in the case of a right to damages, from the time of the act which gives rise to the claim.

(2)   Where the debtor is under a continuing obligation to do or refrain from doing something, the general period of prescription begins to run with each breach of the obligation.

(3)   The period of prescription set out in Article 14:202 begins to run from the time when the judgment or arbitral award obtains the effect of res judicata, or the other instrument becomes enforceable, though not before the debtor has to effect performance.

Section 3. Extension of Period

Article 14:301   Suspension in case of ignorance
The running of the period of prescription is suspended as long as the creditor does not know of, and could not reasonably know of:
(a)   the identity of the debtor; or
(b)   the facts giving rise to the claim including, in the case of a right to damages, the type of damage.

Article 14:302   Suspension in case of judicial and other proceedings
(1)   The running of the period of prescription is suspended from the time when judicial proceedings on the claim are begun.

(2)   Suspension lasts until a decision has been made which has the effect of res judicata, or until the case has been otherwise disposed of.

(3)   These provisions apply, with appropriate adaptations, to arbitration proceedings and to all other proceedings initiated with the aim of obtaining an instrument which is enforceable as if it were a judgment.

Article 14:303   Suspension in case of impediment beyond creditor's control
(1)   The running of the period of prescription is suspended as long as the creditor is prevented from pursuing the claim by an impediment which is beyond the creditor's control and which the creditor could not reasonably have been expected to avoid or overcome.

(2)   Paragraph (1) applies only if the impediment arises, or subsists, within the last six months of the prescription period.

Article 14:304   Postponement of expiry in case of negotiations
If the parties negotiate about the claim, or about circumstances from which a claim might arise, the period of prescription does not expire before one year has passed since the last communication made in the negotiations.

Article 14:305   Postponement of expiry in case of incapacity
(1)   If a person subject to an incapacity is without a representative, the period of prescription of a claim held by or against that person does not expire before one year has passed after either the incapacity has ended or a representative has been appointed.

(2)   The period of prescription of claims between a person subject to an incapacity and that person's representative does not expire before one year has passed after either the incapacity has ended or a new representative has been appointed.

Article 14:306   Postponement of expiry: deceased's estate
Where the creditor or debtor has died, the period of prescription of a claim held by or against the deceased's estate does not expire before one year has passed after the claim can be enforced by or against an heir, or by or against a representative of the estate.

Article 14:307   Maximum length of period
The period of prescription cannot be extended, by suspension of its running or

postponement of its expiry under these Principles, to more than ten years or, in case of claims for personal injuries, to more than thirty years. This does not apply to suspension under Article 14:302.

Section 4. Renewal of Periods

Article 14:401   Renewal by acknowledgement

(1)   If the debtor acknowledges the claim, vis-à-vis the creditor, by part payment, payment of interest, giving of security, or in any other manner, a new period of prescription begins to run.

(2)   The new period is the general period of prescription, regardless of whether the claim was originally subject to the general period of prescription or the ten year period under Article 14:202. In the latter case, however, this Article does not operate so as to shorten the ten year period.

Article 14:402   Renewal by attempted execution

The ten year period of prescription laid down in Article 14:202 begins to run again with each reasonable attempt at execution undertaken by the creditor.

Section 5. Effects of Prescription

Article 14:501   General effect

(1)   After expiry of the period of prescription the debtor is entitled to refuse performance.

(2)   Whatever has been performed in order to discharge a claim may not be reclaimed merely because the period of prescription had expired.

Article 14:502   Effect on ancillary claims

The period of prescription for a right to payment of interest, and other claims of an ancillary nature, expires not later than the period for the principal claim.

Article 14:503   Effect on set-off

A claim in relation to which the period of prescription has expired may nonetheless be set off, unless the debtor has invoked prescription previously or does so within two months of notification of set-off.

Section 6. Modification by Agreement

Article 14:601   Agreements concerning prescription

(1)   The requirements for prescription may be modified by agreement between the parties, in particular by either shortening or lengthening the periods of prescription.

(2)   The period of prescription may not, however, be reduced to less than one year or extended to more than thirty years after the time of commencement set out in Article 14:203.

CHAPTER 15. ILLEGALITY

Article 15:101   Contracts contrary to fundamental principles

A contract is of no effect to the extent that it is contrary to principles recognised as fundamental in the laws of the Member States of the European Union.

Article 15:102   Contracts infringing mandatory rules

(1)   Where a contract infringes a mandatory rule of law applicable under Article 1:103 of these Principles, the effects of that infringement upon the contract are the effects, if any, expressly prescribed by that mandatory rule.

(2)   Where the mandatory rule does not expressly prescribe the effects of an infringement upon a contract, the contract may be declared to have full effect, to have some effect, to have no effect, or to be subject to modification.

(3)   A decision reached under paragraph (2) must be an appropriate and pro-

portional response to the infringement, having regard to all relevant circumstances, including:

(a)   the purpose of the rule which has been infringed;

(b)   the category of persons for whose protection the rule exists;

(c)   any sanction that may be imposed under the rule infringed;

(d)   the seriousness of the infringement;

(e)   whether the infringement was intentional; and

(f)   the closeness of the relationship between the infringement and the contract.

Article 15:103   Partial ineffectiveness

(1)   If only part of a contract is rendered ineffective under Articles 15:101 or 15:102, the remaining part continues in effect unless, giving due consideration to all the circumstances of the case, it is unreasonable to uphold it.

(2)   Articles 15:104 and 15:105 apply, with appropriate adaptations, to a case of partial ineffectiveness.

Article 15:104   Restitution

(1)   When a contract is rendered ineffective under Articles 15:101 or 15:102, either party may claim restitution of whatever that party has supplied under the contract, provided that, where appropriate, concurrent restitution is made of whatever has been received.

(2)   When considering whether to grant restitution under paragraph (1), and what concurrent restitution, if any, would be appropriate, regard must be had to the factors referred to in Article 15:102(3).

(3)   An award of restitution may be refused to a party who knew or ought to have known of the reason for the ineffectiveness.

(4)   If restitution cannot be made in kind for any reason, a reasonable sum must be paid for what has been received.

Article 15:105   Damages

(1)   A party to a contract which is rendered ineffective under Articles 15:101 or 15:102 may recover from the other party damages putting the first party as nearly as possible into the same position as if the contract had not been concluded, provided that the other party knew or ought to have known of the reason for the ineffectiveness.

(2)   When considering whether to award damages under paragraph (1), regard must be had to the factors referred to in Article 15:102(3).

(3)   An award of damages may be refused where the first party knew or ought to have known of the reason for the ineffectiveness.

CHAPTER 16. CONDITIONS

Article 16:101   Types of condition

A contractual obligation may be made conditional upon the occurrence of an uncertain future event, so that the obligation takes effect only if the event occurs (suspensive condition) or comes to an end if the event occurs (resolutive condition).

Article 16:102   Interference with conditions

(1)   If fulfilment of a condition is prevented by a party, contrary to duties of good faith and fair dealing or co-operation, and if fulfilment would have operated to that party's disadvantage, the condition is deemed to be fulfilled.

(2)   If fulfilment of a condition is brought about by a party, contrary to duties of good faith and fair dealing or co-operation, and if fulfilment operates to that party's advantage, the condition is deemed not to be fulfilled.

Article 16:103   Effect of conditions
(1)   Upon fulfilment of a suspensive condition, the relevant obligation takes effect unless the parties otherwise agree.
(2)   Upon fulfilment of a resolutive condition, the relevant obligation comes to an end unless the parties otherwise agree.

CHAPTER 17. CAPITALISATION OF INTEREST

Article 17:101   When interest to be added to capital
(1)   Interest payable according to Article 9:508(1) is added to the outstanding capital every 12 months.
(2)   Paragraph (1) of this Article does not apply if the parties have provided for interest upon delay in payment.

UNIDROIT PRINCIPLES FOR INTERNATIONAL COMMERCIAL CONTRACTS 2004*

PREAMBLE

(Purpose of the Principles)
These Principles set forth general rules for international commercial contracts.

They shall be applied when the parties have agreed that their contract be governed by them.†)
They may be applied when the parties have agreed that their contract be governed by general principles of law, the *lex mercatoria* or the like.
They may be applied when the parties have not chosen any law to govern their contract.
They may be used to interpret or supplement international uniform law instruments.
They may be used to interpret or supplement domestic law.
They may serve as a model for national and international legislators.

CHAPTER 1. GENERAL PROVISIONS

Article 1.1   Freedom of contract
The parties are free to enter into a contract and to determine its content.

Article 1.2   No form required
Nothing in these Principles requires a contract, statement or any other act to be made in or evidenced by a particular form. It may be proved by any means, including witnesses.

The reader is reminded that the complete version of the Unidroit Principles contains not only the black-letter rules reproduced hereunder, but also detailed comments on each article and, where appropriate, illustrations. The volume may be ordered from Unidroit at <http://www.unidroit.org>.

For an update of international case law and bibliography relating to the Principles see <http://www.unilex.info>.

† Parties wishing to provide that their agreement be governed by the Principles might use the following words, adding any desired exceptions or modifications: 'This contract shall be governed by the Unidroit Principles (2004) [except as to Articles . . .]'.

Parties wishing to provide in addition for the application of the law of a particular jurisdiction might use the following words: 'This contract shall be governed by the Unidroit Principles (2004) [except as to Articles . . .]', supplemented when necessary by the law of [jurisdiction X].

Article 1.3   Binding character of contract

A contract validly entered into is binding upon the parties. It can only be modified or terminated in accordance with its terms or by agreement or as otherwise provided in these Principles.

Article 1.4   Mandatory rules

Nothing in these Principles shall restrict the application of mandatory rules, whether of national, international or supranational origin, which are applicable in accordance with the relevant rules of private international law.

Article 1.5   Exclusion or modification by the parties

The parties may exclude the application of these Principles or derogate from or vary the effect of any of their provisions, except as otherwise provided in the Principles.

Article 1.6   Interpretation and supplementation of the Principles

(1)   In the interpretation of these Principles, regard is to be had to their international character and to their purposes including the need to promote uniformity in their application.

(2)   Issues within the scope of these Principles but not expressly settled by them are as far as possible to be settled in accordance with their underlying general principles.

Article 1.7   Good faith and fair dealing

(1)   Each party must act in accordance with good faith and fair dealing in international trade.

(2)   The parties may not exclude or limit this duty.

Article 1.8   Inconsistent behaviour

A party cannot act inconsistently with an understanding it has caused the other party to have and upon which that other party reasonably has acted in reliance to its detriment.

Article 1.9   Usages and practices

(1)   The parties are bound by any usage to which they have agreed and by any practices which they have established between themselves.

(2)   The parties are bound by a usage that is widely known to and regularly observed in international trade by parties in the particular trade concerned except where the application of such a usage would be unreasonable.

Article 1.10   Notice

(1)   Where notice is required it may be given by any means appropriate to the circumstances.

(2)   A notice is effective when it reaches the person to whom it is given.

(3)   For the purpose of paragraph (2) a notice 'reaches' a person when given to that person orally or delivered at that person's place of business or mailing address.

(4)   For the purpose of this article 'notice' includes a declaration, demand, request or any other communication of intention.

Article 1.11   Definitions

In these Principles

– 'court' includes an arbitral tribunal;

– where a party has more than one place of business the relevant 'place of business' is that which has the closest relationship to the contract and its performance, having regard to the circumstances known to or contemplated by the parties at any time before or at the conclusion of the contract;

– 'obligor' refers to the party who is to perform an obligation and 'obligee' refers to the party who is entitled to performance of that obligation.

– 'writing' means any mode of communication that preserves a record of the information contained therein and is capable of being reproduced in tangible form.

Article 1.12 Computation of time set by parties

(1) Official holidays or non-business days occurring during a period set by parties for an act to be performed are included in calculating the period.

(2) However, if the last day of the period is an official holiday or a non-business day at the place of business of the party to perform the act, the period is extended until the first business day which follows, unless the circumstances indicate otherwise.

(3) The relevant time zone is that of the place of business of the party setting the time, unless the circumstances indicate otherwise.

CHAPTER 2 — FORMATION AND AUTHORITY OF AGENTS

Section 1: Formation

Article 2.1.1 Manner of formation

A contract may be concluded either by the acceptance of an offer or by conduct of the parties that is sufficient to show agreement.

Article 2.1.2 Definition of offer

A proposal for concluding a contract constitutes an offer if it is sufficiently definite and indicates the intention of the offeror to be bound in case of acceptance.

Article 2.1.3 Withdrawal of offer

(1) An offer becomes effective when it reaches the offeree.

(2) An offer, even if it is irrevocable, may be withdrawn if the withdrawal reaches the offeree before or at the same time as the offer.

Article 2.1.4 Revocation of offer

(1) Until a contract is concluded an offer may be revoked if the revocation reaches the offeree before it has dispatched an acceptance.

(2) However, an offer cannot be revoked
  (a) if it indicates, whether by stating a fixed time for acceptance or otherwise, that it is irrevocable; or
  (b) if it was reasonable for the offeree to rely on the offer as being irrevocable and the offeree has acted in reliance on the offer.

Article 2.1.5 Rejection of offer

An offer is terminated when a rejection reaches the offeror.

Article 2.1.6 Mode of acceptance

(1) A statement made by or other conduct of the offeree indicating assent to an offer is an acceptance. Silence or inactivity does not in itself amount to acceptance.

(2) An acceptance of an offer becomes effective when the indication of assent reaches the offeror.

(3) However, if, by virtue of the offer or as a result of practices which the parties have established between themselves or of usage, the offeree may indicate assent by performing an act without notice to the offeror, the acceptance is effective when the act is performed.

Article 2.1.7 Time of acceptance

An offer must be accepted within the time the offeror has fixed or, if no time is fixed, within a reasonable time having regard to the circumstances, including the rapidity of the means of communication employed by the offeror. An oral offer must be accepted immediately unless the circumstances indicate otherwise.

Article 2.1.8 Acceptance within a fixed period of time

A period of acceptance fixed by the offeror begins to run from the time that the offer is dispatched. A time indicated in the offer is deemed to be the time of dispatch unless the circumstances indicate otherwise.

Article 2.1.9   Late acceptance. Delay in transmission

(1)   A late acceptance is nevertheless effective as an acceptance if without undue delay the offeror so informs the offeree or gives notice to that effect.

(2)   If a communication containing a late acceptance shows that it has been sent in such circumstances that if its transmission had been normal it would have reached the offeror in due time, the late acceptance is effective as an acceptance unless, without undue delay, the offeror informs the offeree that it considers the offer as having lapsed.

Article 2.1.10   Withdrawal of acceptance

An acceptance may be withdrawn if the withdrawal reaches the offeror before or at the same time as the acceptance would have become effective.

Article 2.1.11   Modified acceptance

(1)   A reply to an offer which purports to be an acceptance but contains additions, limitations or other modifications is a rejection of the offer and constitutes a counter-offer.

(2)   However, a reply to an offer which purports to be an acceptance but contains additional or different terms which do not materially alter the terms of the offer constitutes an acceptance, unless the offeror, without undue delay, objects to the discrepancy. If the offeror does not object, the terms of the contract are the terms of the offer with the modifications contained in the acceptance.

Article 2.1.12   Writings in confirmation

If a writing which is sent within a reasonable time after the conclusion of the contract and which purports to be a confirmation of the contract contains additional or different terms, such terms become part of the contract, unless they materially alter the contract or the recipient, without undue delay, objects to the discrepancy.

Article 2.1.13   Conclusion of contract dependent on agreement on specific matters or in particular form

Where in the course of negotiations one of the parties insists that the contract is not concluded until there is agreement on specific matters or in a particular form, no contract is concluded before agreement is reached on those matters or in that form.

Article 2.1.14   Contract with terms deliberately left open

(1)   If the parties intend to conclude a contract, the fact that they intentionally leave a term to be agreed upon in further negotiations or to be determined by a third person does not prevent a contract from coming into existence.

(2)   The existence of the contract is not affected by the fact that subsequently

   (a)   the parties reach no agreement on the term; or

   (b)   the third person does not determine the term,

provided that there is an alternative means of rendering the term definite that is reasonable in the circumstances, having regard to the intention of the parties.

Article 2.1.15   Negotiations in bad faith

(1)   A party is free to negotiate and is not liable for failure to reach an agreement.

(2)   However, a party who negotiates or breaks off negotiations in bad faith is liable for the losses caused to the other party.

(3)   It is bad faith, in particular, for a party to enter into or continue negotiations when intending not to reach an agreement with the other party.

Article 2.1.16   Duty of confidentiality

Where information is given as confidential by one party in the course of negotiations, the other party is under a duty not to disclose that information or to use it improperly for its own purposes, whether or not a contract is subsequently concluded. Where appropriate, the remedy for breach of that duty may include compensation based on the benefit received by the other party.

Article 2.1.17   Merger clauses
A contract in writing which contains a clause indicating that the writing completely embodies the terms on which the parties have agreed cannot be contradicted or supplemented by evidence of prior statements or agreements. However, such statements or agreements may be used to interpret the writing.

Article 2.1.18   Modification in a particular form
A contract in writing which contains a clause requiring any modification or termination by agreement to be in a particular form may not be otherwise modified or terminated. However, a party may be precluded by its conduct from asserting such a clause to the extent that the other party has reasonably acted in reliance on that conduct.

Article 2.1.19   Contracting under standard terms
(1)   Where one party or both parties use standard terms in concluding a contract, the general rules on formation apply, subject to Articles 2.1.20–2.1.22.
(2)   Standard terms are provisions which are prepared in advance for general and repeated use by one party and which are actually used without negotiation with the other party.

Article 2.1.20   Surprising terms
(1)   No term contained in standard terms which is of such a character that the other party could not reasonably have expected it, is effective unless it has been expressly accepted by that party.
(2)   In determining whether a term is of such a character regard shall be had to its content, language and presentation.

Article 2.1.21   Conflict between standard terms and non-standard terms
In case of conflict between a standard term and a term which is not a standard term the latter prevails.

Article 2.1.22   Battle of forms
Where both parties use standard terms and reach agreement except on those terms, a contract is concluded on the basis of the agreed terms and of any standard terms which are common in substance unless one party clearly indicates in advance, or later and without undue delay informs the other party, that it does not intend to be bound by such a contract.

Section 2: Authority of Agents

Article 2.2.1   Scope of the Section
(1)   This Section governs the authority of a person ('the agent'), to affect the legal relations of another person ('the principal'), by or with respect to a contract with a third party, whether the agent acts in its own name or in that of the principal.
(2)   It governs only the relations between the principal or the agent on the one hand, and the third party on the other.
(3)   It does not govern an agent's authority conferred by law or the authority of an agent appointed by a public or judicial authority.

Article 2.2.2   Establishment and scope of the authority of the agent
(1)   The principal's grant of authority to an agent may be express or implied.
(2)   The agent has authority to perform all acts necessary in the circumstances to achieve the purposes for which the authority was granted.

Article 2.2.3   Agency disclosed

(1)   Where an agent acts within the scope of its authority and the third party knew or ought to have known that the agent was acting as an agent, the acts of the agent shall directly affect the legal relations between the principal and the third party and no legal relation is created between the agent and the third party.

(2)   However, the acts of the agent shall affect only the relations between the agent and the third party, where the agent with the consent of the principal undertakes to become the party to the contract.

Article 2.2.4   Agency undisclosed

(1)   Where an agent acts within the scope of its authority and the third party neither knew nor ought to have known that the agent was acting as an agent, the acts of the agent shall affect only the relations between the agent and the third party.

(2)   However, where such an agent, when contracting with the third party on behalf of a business, represents itself to be the owner of that business, the third party, upon discovery of the real owner of the business, may exercise also against the latter the rights it has against the agent.

Article 2.2.5   Agent acting without or exceeding its authority

(1)   Where an agent acts without authority or exceeds its authority, its acts do not affect the legal relations between the principal and the third party.

(2)   However, where the principal causes the third party reasonably to believe that the agent has authority to act on behalf of the principal and that the agent is acting within the scope of that authority, the principal may not invoke against the third party the lack of authority of the agent.

Article 2.2.6   Liability of agent acting without or exceeding its authority

(1)   An agent that acts without authority or exceeds its authority is, failing ratification by the principal, liable for damages that will place the third party in the same position as if the agent had acted with authority and not exceeded its authority.

(2)   However, the agent is not liable if the third party knew or ought to have known that the agent had no authority or was exceeding its authority.

Article 2.2.7   Conflict of interests

(1)   If a contract concluded by an agent involves the agent in a conflict of interests with the principal of which the third party knew or ought to have known, the principal may avoid the contract. The right to avoid is subject to Articles 3.12 and 3.14 to 3.17.

(2)   However, the principal may not avoid the contract

(a)   if the principal had consented to, or knew or ought to have known of, the agent's involvement in the conflict of interests; or

(b)   if the agent had disclosed the conflict of interests to the principal and the latter had not objected within a reasonable time.

Article 2.2.8   Sub-agency

An agent has implied authority to appoint a sub-agent to perform acts which it is not reasonable to expect the agent to perform itself. The rules of this Section apply to the sub-agency.

Article 2.2.9   Ratification

(1)   An act by an agent that acts without authority or exceeds its authority may be ratified by the principal. On ratification the act produces the same effects as if it had initially been carried out with authority.

(2)   The third party may by notice to the principal specify a reasonable period of time for ratification. If the principal does not ratify within that period of time it can no longer do so.

(3)   If, at the time of the agent's act, the third party neither knew nor ought to

have known of the lack of authority, it may, at any time before ratification, by notice to the principal indicate its refusal to become bound by a ratification.

Article 2.2.10   Termination of authority

(1)   Termination of authority is not effective in relation to the third party unless the third party knew or ought to have known of it.

(2)   Notwithstanding the termination of its authority, an agent remains authorised to perform the acts that are necessary to prevent harm to the principal's interests.

CHAPTER 3 — VALIDITY

Article 3.1   Matters not covered

These Principles do not deal with invalidity arising from
   (a)   lack of capacity;
   (b)   immorality or illegality.

Article 3.2   Validity of mere agreement

A contract is concluded, modified or terminated by the mere agreement of the parties, without any further requirement.

Article 3.3   Initial impossibility

(1)   The mere fact that at the time of the conclusion of the contract the performance of the obligation assumed was impossible does not affect the validity of the contract.

(2)   The mere fact that at the time of the conclusion of the contract a party was not entitled to dispose of the assets to which the contract relates does not affect the validity of the contract.

Article 3.4   Definition of mistake

Mistake is an erroneous assumption relating to facts or to law existing when the contract was concluded.

Article 3.5   Relevant mistake

(1)   A party may only avoid the contract for mistake if, when the contract was concluded, the mistake was of such importance that a reasonable person in the same situation as the party in error would only have concluded the contract on materially different terms or would not have concluded it at all if the true state of affairs had been known, and
   (a)   the other party made the same mistake, or caused the mistake, or knew or ought to have known of the mistake and it was contrary to reasonable commercial standards of fair dealing to leave the mistaken party in error; or
   (b)   the other party had not at the time of avoidance reasonably acted in reliance on the contract.

(2)   However, a party may not avoid the contract if
   (a)   it was grossly negligent in committing the mistake; or
   (b)   the mistake relates to a matter in regard to which the risk of mistake was assumed or, having regard to the circumstances, should be borne by the mistaken party.

Article 3.6   Error in expression or transmission

An error occurring in the expression or transmission of a declaration is considered to be a mistake of the person from whom the declaration emanated.

Article 3.7   Remedies for non-performance

A party is not entitled to avoid the contract on the ground of mistake if the circumstances on which that party relies afford, or could have afforded, a remedy for non-performance.

Article 3.8   Fraud

A party may avoid the contract when it has been led to conclude the contract by the other party's fraudulent representation, including language or practices, or fraudulent non-disclosure of circumstances which, according to reasonable commercial standards of fair dealing, the latter party should have disclosed.

Article 3.9   Threat

A party may avoid the contract when it has been led to conclude the contract by the other party's unjustified threat which, having regard to the circumstances, is so imminent and serious as to leave the first party no reasonable alternative. In particular, a threat is unjustified if the act or omission with which a party has been threatened is wrongful in itself, or it is wrongful to use it as a means to obtain the conclusion of the contract.

Article 3.10   Gross disparity

(1)   A party may avoid the contract or an individual term of it if, at the time of the conclusion of the contract, the contract or term unjustifiably gave the other party an excessive advantage. Regard is to be had, among other factors, to

(a)   the fact that the other party has taken unfair advantage of the first party's dependence, economic distress or urgent needs, or of its improvidence, ignorance, inexperience or lack of bargaining skill, and

(b)   the nature and purpose of the contract.

(2)   Upon the request of the party entitled to avoidance, a court may adapt the contract or term in order to make it accord with reasonable commercial standards of fair dealing.

(3)   A court may also adapt the contract or term upon the request of the party receiving notice of avoidance, provided that that party informs the other party of its request promptly after receiving such notice and before the other party has reasonably acted in reliance on it. The provisions of Article 3.13(2) apply accordingly.

Article 3.11   Third persons

(1)   Where fraud, threat, gross disparity or a party's mistake is imputable to, or is known or ought to be known by, a third person for whose acts the other party is responsible, the contract may be avoided under the same conditions as if the behaviour or knowledge had been that of the party itself.

(2)   Where fraud, threat or gross disparity is imputable to a third person for whose acts the other party is not responsible, the contract may be avoided if that party knew or ought to have known of the fraud, threat or disparity, or has not at the time of avoidance reasonably acted in reliance on the contract.

Article 3.12   Confirmation

If the party entitled to avoid the contract expressly or impliedly confirms the contract after the period of time for giving notice of avoidance has begun to run, avoidance of the contract is excluded.

Article 3.13   Loss of right to avoid

(1)   If a party is entitled to avoid the contract for mistake but the other party declares itself willing to perform or performs the contract as it was understood by the party entitled to avoidance, the contract is considered to have been concluded as the latter party understood it. The other party must make such a declaration or render such performance promptly after having been informed of the manner in which the party entitled to avoidance had understood the contract and before that party has reasonably acted in reliance on a notice of avoidance.

(2)   After such a declaration or performance the right to avoidance is lost and any earlier notice of avoidance is ineffective.

Article 3.14   Notice of avoidance

The right of a party to avoid the contract is exercised by notice to the other party.

Article 3.15   Time limits
(1)   Notice of avoidance shall be given within a reasonable time, having regard to the circumstances, after the avoiding party knew or could not have been unaware of the relevant facts or became capable of acting freely.

(2)   Where an individual term of the contract may be avoided by a party under Article 3.10, the period of time for giving notice of avoidance begins to run when that term is asserted by the other party.

Article 3.16   Partial avoidance
Where a ground of avoidance affects only individual terms of the contract, the effect of avoidance is limited to those terms unless, having regard to the circumstances, it is unreasonable to uphold the remaining contract.

Article 3.17   Retroactive effect of avoidance
(1)   Avoidance takes effect retroactively.

(2)   On avoidance either party may claim restitution of whatever it has supplied under the contract or the part of it avoided, provided that it concurrently makes restitution of whatever it has received under the contract or the part of it avoided or, if it cannot make restitution in kind, it makes an allowance for what it has received.

Article 3.18   Damages
Irrespective of whether or not the contract has been avoided, the party who knew or ought to have known of the ground for avoidance is liable for damages so as to put the other party in the same position in which it would have been if it had not concluded the contract.

Article 3.19   Mandatory character of the provisions
The provisions of this Chapter are mandatory, except insofar as they relate to the binding force of mere agreement, initial impossibility or mistake.

Article 3.20   Unilateral declarations
The provisions of this Chapter apply with appropriate adaptations to any communication of intention addressed by one party to the other.

CHAPTER 4 — INTERPRETATION

Article 4.1   Intention of the parties
(1)   A contract shall be interpreted according to the common intention of the parties.

(2)   If such an intention cannot be established, the contract shall be interpreted according to the meaning that reasonable persons of the same kind as the parties would give to it in the same circumstances.

Article 4.2   Interpretation of statements and other conduct
(1)   The statements and other conduct of a party shall be interpreted according to that party's intention if the other party knew or could not have been unaware of that intention.

(2)   If the preceding paragraph is not applicable, such statements and other conduct shall be interpreted according to the meaning that a reasonable person of the same kind as the other party would give to it in the same circumstances.

Article 4.3   Relevant circumstances
In applying Articles 4.1 and 4.2, regard shall be had to all the circumstances, including
- (a)   preliminary negotiations between the parties;
- (b)   practices which the parties have established between themselves;
- (c)   the conduct of the parties subsequent to the conclusion of the contract;
- (d)   the nature and purpose of the contract;

(e)   the meaning commonly given to terms and expressions in the trade concerned;
(f)   usages.

Article 4.4   Reference to contract or statement as a whole
Terms and expressions shall be interpreted in the light of the whole contract or statement in which they appear.

Article 4.5   All terms to be given effect
Contract terms shall be interpreted so as to give effect to all the terms rather than to deprive some of them of effect.

Article 4.6   Contra proferentem rule
If contract terms supplied by one party are unclear, an interpretation against that party is preferred.

Article 4.7   Linguistic discrepancies
Where a contract is drawn up in two or more language versions which are equally authoritative there is, in case of discrepancy between the versions, a preference for the interpretation according to a version in which the contract was originally drawn up.

Article 4.8   Supplying an omitted term
(1)   Where the parties to a contract have not agreed with respect to a term which is important for a determination of their rights and duties, a term which is appropriate in the circumstances shall be supplied.
(2)   In determining what is an appropriate term regard shall be had, among other factors, to
(a)   the intention of the parties;
(b)   the nature and purpose of the contract;
(c)   good faith and fair dealing;
(d)   reasonableness.

CHAPTER 5 — CONTENT AND THIRD PARTY RIGHTS

Section 1: Content

Article 5.1.1   Express and implied obligations
The contractual obligations of the parties may be express or implied.

Article 5.1.2   Implied obligations
Implied obligations stem from
(a)   the nature and purpose of the contract;
(b)   practices established between the parties and usages;
(c)   good faith and fair dealing;
(d)   reasonableness.

Article 5.1.3   Co-operation between the parties
Each party shall co-operate with the other party when such co-operation may reasonably be expected for the performance of that party's obligations.

Article 5.1.4   Duty to achieve a specific result. Duty of best efforts
(1)   To the extent that an obligation of a party involves a duty to achieve a specific result, that party is bound to achieve that result.
(2)   To the extent that an obligation of a party involves a duty of best efforts in the performance of an activity, that party is bound to make such efforts as would be made by a reasonable person of the same kind in the same circumstances.

Article 5.1.5   Determination of kind of duty involved
In determining the extent to which an obligation of a party involves a duty of best

efforts in the performance of an activity or a duty to achieve a specific result, regard shall be had, among other factors, to

    (a)   the way in which the obligation is expressed in the contract;

    (b)   the contractual price and other terms of the contract;

    (c)   the degree of risk normally involved in achieving the expected result;

    (d)   the ability of the other party to influence the performance of the obligation.

Article 5.1.6   Determination of quality of performance

Where the quality of performance is neither fixed by, nor determinable from, the contract a party is bound to render a performance of a quality that is reasonable and not less than average in the circumstances.

Article 5.1.7   Price determination

(1)   Where a contract does not fix or make provision for determining the price, the parties are considered, in the absence of any indication to the contrary, to have made reference to the price generally charged at the time of the conclusion of the contract for such performance in comparable circumstances in the trade concerned or, if no such price is available, to a reasonable price.

(2)   Where the price is to be determined by one party and that determination is manifestly unreasonable, a reasonable price shall be substituted notwithstanding any contract term to the contrary.

(3)   Where the price is to be fixed by a third person, and that person cannot or will not do so, the price shall be a reasonable price.

(4)   Where the price is to be fixed by reference to factors which do not exist or have ceased to exist or to be accessible, the nearest equivalent factor shall be treated as a substitute.

Article 5.1.8   Contract for an indefinite period

A contract for an indefinite period may be ended by either party by giving notice a reasonable time in advance.

Article 5.1.9   Release by agreement

(1)   An obligee may release its right by agreement with the obligor.

(2)   An offer to release a right gratuitously shall be deemed accepted if the obligor does not reject the offer without delay after having become aware of it.

Section 2: Third Party Rights

Article 5.2.1   Contracts in favour of third parties

(1)   The parties (the 'promisor' and the 'promisee') may confer by express or implied agreement a right on a third party (the 'beneficiary').

(2)   The existence and content of the beneficiary's right against the promisor are determined by the agreement of the parties and are subject to any conditions or other limitations under the agreement.

Article 5.2.2   Third party identifiable

The beneficiary must be identifiable with adequate certainty by the contract but need not be in existence at the time the contract is made.

Article 5.2.3   Exclusion and limitation clauses

The conferment of rights in the beneficiary includes the right to invoke a clause in the contract which excludes or limits the liability of the beneficiary.

Article 5.2.4   Defences

The promisor may assert against the beneficiary all defences which the promisor could assert against the promisee.

Article 5.2.5   Revocation

The parties may modify or revoke the rights conferred by the contract on the beneficiary until the beneficiary has accepted them or reasonably acted in reliance on them.

Article 5.2.6 Renunciation
The beneficiary may renounce a right conferred on it.

CHAPTER 6 — PERFORMANCE

Section 1: Performance in General

Article 6.1.1 Time of performance
A party must perform its obligations:

  (a) if a time is fixed by or determinable from the contract, at that time;

  (b) if a period of time is fixed by or determinable from the contract, at any time within that period unless circumstances indicate that the other party is to choose a time;

  (c) in any other case, within a reasonable time after the conclusion of the contract.

Article 6.1.2 Performance at one time or in instalments
In cases under Article 6.1.1(b) or (c), a party must perform its obligations at one time if that performance can be rendered at one time and the circumstances do not indicate otherwise.

Article 6.1.3 Partial performance
(1) The obligee may reject an offer to perform in part at the time performance is due, whether or not such offer is coupled with an assurance as to the balance of the performance, unless the obligee has no legitimate interest in so doing.

(2) Additional expenses caused to the obligee by partial performance are to be borne by the obligor without prejudice to any other remedy.

Article 6.1.4 Order of performance
(1) To the extent that the performances of the parties can be rendered simultaneously, the parties are bound to render them simultaneously unless the circumstances indicate otherwise.

(2) To the extent that the performance of only one party requires a period of time, that party is bound to render its performance first, unless the circumstances indicate otherwise.

Article 6.1.5 Earlier performance
(1) The obligee may reject an earlier performance unless it has no legitimate interest in so doing.

(2) Acceptance by a party of an earlier performance does not affect the time for the performance of its own obligations if that time has been fixed irrespective of the performance of the other party's obligations.

(3) Additional expenses caused to the obligee by earlier performance are to be borne by the obligor, without prejudice to any other remedy.

Article 6.1.6 Place of performance
(1) If the place of performance is neither fixed by, nor determinable from, the contract, a party is to perform:

  (a) a monetary obligation, at the obligee's place of business;

  (b) any other obligation, at its own place of business.

(2) A party must bear any increase in the expenses incidental to performance which is caused by a change in its place of business subsequent to the conclusion of the contract.

Article 6.1.7 Payment by cheque or other instrument
(1) Payment may be made in any form used in the ordinary course of business at the place for payment.

(2) However, an obligee who accepts, either by virtue of paragraph (1) or voluntarily, a cheque, any other order to pay or a promise to pay, is presumed to do so only on condition that it will be honoured.

Article 6.1.8   Payment by funds transfer
(1) Unless the obligee has indicated a particular account, payment may be made by a transfer to any of the financial institutions in which the obligee has made it known that it has an account.
(2) In case of payment by a transfer the obligation of the obligor is discharged when the transfer to the obligee's financial institution becomes effective.

Article 6.1.9   Currency of payment
(1) If a monetary obligation is expressed in a currency other than that of the place for payment, it may be paid by the obligor in the currency of the place for payment unless
    (a)   that currency is not freely convertible; or
    (b)   the parties have agreed that payment should be made only in the currency in which the monetary obligation is expressed.
(2) If it is impossible for the obligor to make payment in the currency in which the monetary obligation is expressed, the obligee may require payment in the currency of the place for payment, even in the case referred to in paragraph (1)(b).
(3) Payment in the currency of the place for payment is to be made according to the applicable rate of exchange prevailing there when payment is due.
(4) However, if the obligor has not paid at the time when payment is due, the obligee may require payment according to the applicable rate of exchange prevailing either when payment is due or at the time of actual payment.

Article 6.1.10   Currency not expressed
Where a monetary obligation is not expressed in a particular currency, payment must be made in the currency of the place where payment is to be made.

Article 6.1.11   Costs of performance
Each party shall bear the costs of performance of its obligations.

Article 6.1.12   Imputation of payments
(1) An obligor owing several monetary obligations to the same obligee may specify at the time of payment the debt to which it intends the payment to be applied. However, the payment discharges first any expenses, then interest due and finally the principal.
(2) If the obligor makes no such specification, the obligee may, within a reasonable time after payment, declare to the obligor the obligation to which it imputes the payment, provided that the obligation is due and undisputed.
(3) In the absence of imputation under paragraphs (1) or (2), payment is imputed to that obligation which satisfies one of the following criteria in the order indicated:
    (a)   an obligation which is due or which is the first to fall due;
    (b)   the obligation for which the obligee has least security;
    (c)   the obligation which is the most burdensome for the obligor;
    (d)   the obligation which has arisen first.
If none of the preceding criteria applies, payment is imputed to all the obligations proportionally.

Article 6.1.13   Imputation of non-monetary obligations
Article 6.1.12 applies with appropriate adaptations to the imputation of performance of non-monetary obligations.

Article 6.1.14   Application for public permission
Where the law of a State requires a public permission affecting the validity of the

contract or its performance and neither that law nor the circumstances indicate otherwise

(a)   if only one party has its place of business in that State, that party shall take the measures necessary to obtain the permission;

(b)   in any other case the party whose performance requires permission shall take the necessary measures.

Article 6.1.15   Procedure in applying for permission

(1)   The party required to take the measures necessary to obtain the permission shall do so without undue delay and shall bear any expenses incurred.

(2)   That party shall whenever appropriate give the other party notice of the grant or refusal of such permission without undue delay.

Article 6.1.16   Permission neither granted nor refused

(1)   If, notwithstanding the fact that the party responsible has taken all measures required, permission is neither granted nor refused within an agreed period or, where no period has been agreed, within a reasonable time from the conclusion of the contract, either party is entitled to terminate the contract.

(2)   Where the permission affects some terms only, paragraph (1) does not apply if, having regard to the circumstances, it is reasonable to uphold the remaining contract even if the permission is refused.

Article 6.1.17   Permission refused

(1)   The refusal of a permission affecting the validity of the contract renders the contract void. If the refusal affects the validity of some terms only, only such terms are void if, having regard to the circumstances, it is reasonable to uphold the remaining contract.

(2)   Where the refusal of a permission renders the performance of the contract impossible in whole or in part, the rules on non-performance apply.

Section 2: Hardship

Article 6.2.1   Contract to be observed

Where the performance of a contract becomes more onerous for one of the parties, that party is nevertheless bound to perform its obligations subject to the following provisions on hardship.

Article 6.2.2   Definition of hardship

There is hardship where the occurrence of events fundamentally alters the equilibrium of the contract either because the cost of a party's performance has increased or because the value of the performance a party receives has diminished, and

(a)   the events occur or become known to the disadvantaged party after the conclusion of the contract;

(b)   the events could not reasonably have been taken into account by the disadvantaged party at the time of the conclusion of the contract;

(c)   the events are beyond the control of the disadvantaged party; and

(d)   the risk of the events was not assumed by the disadvantaged party.

Article 6.2.3   Effects of hardship

(1)   In case of hardship the disadvantaged party is entitled to request renegotiations. The request shall be made without undue delay and shall indicate the grounds on which it is based.

(2)   The request for renegotiation does not in itself entitle the disadvantaged party to withhold performance.

(3)   Upon failure to reach agreement within a reasonable time either party may resort to the court.

(4)   If the court finds hardship it may, if reasonable,

(a)   terminate the contract at a date and on terms to be fixed, or

(b)   adapt the contract with a view to restoring its equilibrium.

CHAPTER 7 — NON-PERFORMANCE

Section 1: Non-Performance in General

Article 7.1.1   Non-performance defined
Non-performance is failure by a party to perform any of its obligations under the contract, including defective performance or late performance.

Article 7.1.2   Interference by the other party
A party may not rely on the non-performance of the other party to the extent that such non-performance was caused by the first party's act or omission or by another event as to which the first party bears the risk.

Article 7.1.3   Withholding performance
(1)   Where the parties are to perform simultaneously, either party may withhold performance until the other party tenders its performance.
(2)   Where the parties are to perform consecutively, the party that is to perform later may withhold its performance until the first party has performed.

Article 7.1.4   Cure by non-performing party
(1)   The non-performing party may, at its own expense, cure any non-performance, provided that
   (a)   without undue delay, it gives notice indicating the proposed manner and timing of the cure;
   (b)   cure is appropriate in the circumstances;
   (c)   the aggrieved party has no legitimate interest in refusing cure; and
   (d)   cure is effected promptly.
(2)   The right to cure is not precluded by notice of termination.
(3)   Upon effective notice of cure, rights of the aggrieved party that are inconsistent with the non-performing party's performance are suspended until the time for cure has expired.
(4)   The aggrieved party may withhold performance pending cure.
(5)   Notwithstanding cure, the aggrieved party retains the right to claim damages for delay as well as for any harm caused or not prevented by the cure.

Article 7.1.5   Additional period for performance
(1)   In a case of non-performance the aggrieved party may by notice to the other party allow an additional period of time for performance.
(2)   During the additional period the aggrieved party may withhold performance of its own reciprocal obligations and may claim damages but may not resort to any other remedy. If it receives notice from the other party that the latter will not perform within that period, or if upon expiry of that period due performance has not been made, the aggrieved party may resort to any of the remedies that may be available under this Chapter.
(3)   Where in a case of delay in performance which is not fundamental the aggrieved party has given notice allowing an additional period of time of reasonable length, it may terminate the contract at the end of that period. If the additional period allowed is not of reasonable length it shall be extended to a reasonable length. The aggrieved party may in its notice provide that if the other party fails to perform within the period allowed by the notice the contract shall automatically terminate.
(4)   Paragraph (3) does not apply where the obligation which has not been performed is only a minor part of the contractual obligation of the non-performing party.

Article 7.1.6   Exemption clauses
A clause which limits or excludes one party's liability for non-performance or which permits one party to render performance substantially different from what

the other party reasonably expected may not be invoked if it would be grossly unfair to do so, having regard to the purpose of the contract.

Article 7.1.7   Force majeure

(1)   Non-performance by a party is excused if that party proves that the non-performance was due to an impediment beyond its control and that it could not reasonably be expected to have taken the impediment into account at the time of the conclusion of the contract or to have avoided or overcome it or its consequences.

(2)   When the impediment is only temporary, the excuse shall have effect for such period as is reasonable having regard to the effect of the impediment on the performance of the contract.

(3)   The party who fails to perform must give notice to the other party of the impediment and its effect on its ability to perform. If the notice is not received by the other party within a reasonable time after the party who fails to perform knew or ought to have known of the impediment, it is liable for damages resulting from such non-receipt.

(4)   Nothing in this article prevents a party from exercising a right to terminate the contract or to withhold performance or request interest on money due.

Section 2: Right to Performance

Article 7.2.1   Performance of monetary obligation

Where a party who is obliged to pay money does not do so, the other party may require payment.

Article 7.2.2   Performance of non-monetary obligation

Where a party who owes an obligation other than one to pay money does not perform, the other party may require performance, unless

(a)   performance is impossible in law or in fact;

(b)   performance or, where relevant, enforcement is unreasonably burdensome or expensive;

(c)   the party entitled to performance may reasonably obtain performance from another source;

(d)   performance is of an exclusively personal character; or

(e)   the party entitled to performance does not require performance within a reasonable time after it has, or ought to have, become aware of the non-performance.

Article 7.2.3   Repair and replacement of defective performance

The right to performance includes in appropriate cases the right to require repair, replacement, or other cure of defective performance. The provisions of Articles 7.2.1 and 7.2.2 apply accordingly.

Article 7.2.4   Judicial penalty

(1)   Where the court orders a party to perform, it may also direct that this party pay a penalty if it does not comply with the order.

(2)   The penalty shall be paid to the aggrieved party unless mandatory provisions of the law of the forum provide otherwise. Payment of the penalty to the aggrieved party does not exclude any claim for damages.

Article 7.2.5   Change of remedy

(1)   An aggrieved party who has required performance of a non-monetary obligation and who has not received performance within a period fixed or otherwise within a reasonable period of time may invoke any other remedy.

(2)   Where the decision of a court for performance of a non-monetary obligation cannot be enforced, the aggrieved party may invoke any other remedy.

Section 3: Termination

Article 7.3.1   Right to terminate the contract

(1) A party may terminate the contract where the failure of the other party to perform an obligation under the contract amounts to a fundamental non-performance.

(2) In determining whether a failure to perform an obligation amounts to a fundamental non-performance regard shall be had, in particular, to whether

(a) the non-performance substantially deprives the aggrieved party of what it was entitled to expect under the contract unless the other party did not foresee and could not reasonably have foreseen such result;

(b) strict compliance with the obligation which has not been performed is of essence under the contract;

(c) the non-performance is intentional or reckless;

(d) the non-performance gives the aggrieved party reason to believe that it cannot rely on the other party's future performance;

(e) the non-performing party will suffer disproportionate loss as a result of the preparation or performance if the contract is terminated.

(3) In the case of delay the aggrieved party may also terminate the contract if the other party fails to perform before the time allowed it under Article 7.1.5 has expired.

Article 7.3.2   Notice of termination

(1) The right of a party to terminate the contract is exercised by notice to the other party.

(2) If performance has been offered late or otherwise does not conform to the contract the aggrieved party will lose its right to terminate the contract unless it gives notice to the other party within a reasonable time after it has or ought to have become aware of the offer or of the non-conforming performance.

Article 7.3.3   Anticipatory non-performance

Where prior to the date for performance by one of the parties it is clear that there will be a fundamental non-performance by that party, the other party may terminate the contract.

Article 7.3.4   Adequate assurance of due performance

A party who reasonably believes that there will be a fundamental non-performance by the other party may demand adequate assurance of due performance and may meanwhile withhold its own performance. Where this assurance is not provided within a reasonable time the party demanding it may terminate the contract.

Article 7.3.5   Effects of termination in general

(1) Termination of the contract releases both parties from their obligation to effect and to receive future performance.

(2) Termination does not preclude a claim for damages for non-performance.

(3) Termination does not affect any provision in the contract for the settlement of disputes or any other term of the contract which is to operate even after termination.

Article 7.3.6   Restitution

(1) On termination of the contract either party may claim restitution of whatever it has supplied, provided that such party concurrently makes restitution of whatever it has received. If restitution in kind is not possible or appropriate allowance should be made in money whenever reasonable.

(2) However, if performance of the contract has extended over a period of time and the contract is divisible, such restitution can only be claimed for the period after termination has taken effect.

Section 4: Damages

Article 7.4.1 Right to damages
Any non-performance gives the aggrieved party a right to damages either ex-clusively or in conjunction with any other remedies except where the non-performance is excused under these Principles.

Article 7.4.2 Full compensation
(1) The aggrieved party is entitled to full compensation for harm sustained as a result of the non-performance. Such harm includes both any loss which it suffered and any gain of which it was deprived, taking into account any gain to the aggrieved party resulting from its avoidance of cost or harm.

(2) Such harm may be non-pecuniary and includes, for instance, physical suf-fering or emotional distress.

Article 7.4.3 Certainty of harm
(1) Compensation is due only for harm, including future harm, that is estab-lished with a reasonable degree of certainty.

(2) Compensation may be due for the loss of a chance in proportion to the probability of its occurrence.

(3) Where the amount of damages cannot be established with a sufficient degree of certainty, the assessment is at the discretion of the court.

Article 7.4.4 Foreseeability of harm
The non-performing party is liable only for harm which it foresaw or could reasonably have foreseen at the time of the conclusion of the contract as being likely to result from its non-performance.

Article 7.4.5 Proof in harm in case of replacement transaction
Where the aggrieved party has terminated the contract and has made a replace-ment transaction within a reasonable time and in a reasonable manner it may recover the difference between the contract price and the price of the replacement transaction as well as damages for any further harm.

Article 7.4.6 Proof of harm by current price
(1) Where the aggrieved party has terminated the contract and has not made a replacement transaction but there is a current price for the performance contracted for, it may recover the difference between the contract price and the price current at the time the contract is terminated as well as damages for any further harm.

(2) Current price is the price generally charged for goods delivered or services rendered in comparable circumstances at the place where the contract should have been performed or, if there is no current price at that place, the current price at such other place that appears reasonable to take as a reference.

Article 7.4.7 Harm due in part to aggrieved party
Where the harm is due in part to an act or omission of the aggrieved party or to another event as to which that party bears the risk, the amount of damages shall be reduced to the extent that these factors have contributed to the harm, having regard to the conduct of each of the parties.

Article 7.4.8 Mitigation of harm
(1) The non-performing party is not liable for harm suffered by the aggrieved party to the extent that the harm could have been reduced by the latter party's taking reasonable steps.

(2) The aggrieved party is entitled to recover any expenses reasonably incurred in attempting to reduce the harm.

Article 7.4.9 Interest for failure to pay money
(1) If a party does not pay a sum of money when it falls due the aggrieved

party is entitled to interest upon that sum from the time when payment is due to the time of payment whether or not the non-payment is excused.

(2) The rate of interest shall be the average bank short-term lending rate to prime borrowers prevailing for the currency of payment at the place for payment, or where no such rate exists at that place, then the same rate in the State of the currency of payment. In the absence of such a rate at either place the rate of interest shall be the appropriate rate fixed by the law of the State of the currency of payment.

(3) The aggrieved party is entitled to additional damages if the non-payment caused it a greater harm.

Article 7.4.10   Interest on damages
Unless otherwise agreed, interest on damages for non-performance of non-monetary obligations accrues as from the time of non-performance.

Article 7.4.11   Manner of monetary redress
(1) Damages are to be paid in a lump sum. However, they may be payable in instalments where the nature of the harm makes this appropriate.

(2) Damages to be paid in instalments may be indexed.

Article 7.4.12   Currency in which to assess damages
Damages are to be assessed either in the currency in which the monetary obligation was expressed or in the currency in which the harm was suffered, whichever is more appropriate.

Article 7.4.13   Agreed payment for non-performance
(1) Where the contract provides that a party who does not perform is to pay a specified sum to the aggrieved party for such non-performance, the aggrieved party is entitled to that sum irrespective of its actual harm.

(2) However, notwithstanding any agreement to the contrary the specified sum may be reduced to a reasonable amount where it is grossly excessive in relation to the harm resulting from the non-performance and to the other circumstances.

CHAPTER 8 — SET-OFF

Article 8.1   Conditions of set-off
(1) Where two parties owe each other money or other performances of the same kind, either of them ('the first party') may set off its obligation against that of its obligee ('the other party') if at the time of set-off,

    (a)   the first party is entitled to perform its obligation;

    (b)   the other party's obligation is ascertained as to its existence and amount and performance is due.

(2) If the obligations of both parties arise from the same contract, the first party may also set off its obligation against an obligation of the other party which is not ascertained as to its existence or to its amount.

Article 8.2   Foreign currency set-off
Where the obligations are to pay money in different currencies, the right of set-off may be exercised, provided that both currencies are freely convertible and the parties have not agreed that the first party shall pay only in a specified currency.

Article 8.3   Set-off by notice
The right of set-off is exercised by notice to the other party.

Article 8.4   Content of notice
(1) The notice must specify the obligations to which it relates.

(2) If the notice does not specify the obligation against which set-off is exercised, the other party may, within a reasonable time, declare to the first party the obligation to which set-off relates. If no such declaration is made, the set-off will relate to all the obligations proportionally.

Article 8.5   Effect of set-off
(1)   Set-off discharges the obligations.
(2)   If obligations differ in amount, set-off discharges the obligations up to the amount of the lesser obligation.
(3)   Set-off takes effect as from the time of notice.

CHAPTER 9 — ASSIGNMENT OF RIGHTS, TRANSFER OF OBLIGATIONS, ASSIGNMENT OF CONTRACTS

Section 1: Assignment of rights

Article 9.1.1   Definitions
'Assignment of a right' means the transfer by agreement from one person (the 'assignor') to another person (the 'assignee'), including transfer by way of security, of the assignor's right to payment of a monetary sum or other performance from a third person ('the obligor').

Article 9.1.2   Exclusions
This Section does not apply to transfers made under the special rules governing the transfers:
     (a)   of instruments such as negotiable instruments, documents of title or financial instruments, or
     (b)   of rights in the course of transferring a business.

Article 9.1.3   Assignability of non-monetary rights
A right to non-monetary performance may be assigned only if the assignment does not render the obligation significantly more burdensome.

Article 9.1.4   Partial assignment
(1)   A right to the payment of a monetary sum may be assigned partially.
(2)   A right to other performance may be assigned partially only if it is divisible, and the assignment does not render the obligation significantly more burdensome.

Article 9.1.5   Future rights
A future right is deemed to be transferred at the time of the agreement, provided the right, when it comes into existence, can be identified as the right to which the assignment relates.

Article 9.1.6   Rights assigned without individual specification
A number of rights may be assigned without individual specification, provided such rights can be identified as rights to which the assignment relates at the time of the assignment or when they come into existence.

Article 9.1.7   Agreement between assignor and assignee sufficient
(1)   A right is assigned by mere agreement between the assignor and the assignee, without notice to the obligor.
(2)   The consent of the obligor is not required unless the obligation in the circumstances is of an essentially personal character.

Article 9.1.8   Obligor's additional costs
The obligor has a right to be compensated by the assignor or the assignee for any additional costs caused by the assignment.

Article 9.1.9   Non-assignment clauses
(1)   The assignment of a right to the payment of a monetary sum is effective notwithstanding an agreement between the assignor and the obligor limiting or prohibiting such an assignment. However, the assignor may be liable to the obligor for breach of contract.
(2)   The assignment of a right to other performance is ineffective if it is contrary to an agreement between the assignor and the obligor limiting or prohibiting the

assignment. Nevertheless, the assignment is effective if the assignee, at the time of the assignment, neither knew nor ought to have known of the agreement. The assignor may then be liable to the obligor for breach of contract.

Article 9.1.10   Notice to the obligor
(1)   Until the obligor receives a notice of the assignment from either the assignor or the assignee, it is discharged by paying the assignor.

(2)   After the obligor receives such a notice, it is discharged only by paying the assignee.

Article 9.1.11   Successive assignments
If the same right has been assigned by the same assignor to two or more successive assignees, the obligor is discharged by paying according to the order in which the notices were received.

Article 9.1.12   Adquate proof of assignment
(1)   If notice of the assignment is given by the assignee, the obligor may request the assignee to provide within a reasonable time adequate proof that the assignment has been made.

(2)   Until adequate proof is provided, the obligor may withhold payment.

(3)   Unless adequate proof is provided, notice is not effective.

(4)   Adequate proof includes, but is not limited to, any writing emanating from the assignor and indicating that the assignment has taken place.

Article 9.1.13   Defences and rights of set-off
(1)   The obligor may assert against the assignee all defences that the obligor could assert against the assignor.

(2)   The obligor may exercise against the assignee any right of set-off available to the obligor against the assignor up to the time notice of assignment was received.

Article 9.1.14   Rights related to the right assigned
The assignment of a right transfers to the assignee:
   (a)   all the assignor's rights to payment or other performance under the contract in respect of the right assigned, and
   (b)   all rights securing performance of the right assigned.

Article 9.1.15   Undertakings of the assignor
The assignor undertakes towards the assignee, except as otherwise disclosed to the assignee, that:
   (a)   the assigned right exists at the time of the assignment, unless the right is a future right;
   (b)   the assignor is entitled to assign the right;
   (c)   the right has not been previously assigned to another assignee, and it is free from any right or claim from a third party;
   (d)   the obligor does not have any defences;
   (e)   neither the obligor nor the assignor has given notice of set-off concerning the assigned right and will not give any such notice;
   (f)   the assignor will reimburse the assignee for any payment received from the obligor before notice of the assignment was given.

Section 2: Transfer of obligations

Article 9.2.1   Modes of transfer
An obligation to pay money or render other performance may be transferred from one person (the 'original obligor') to another person (the 'new obligor') either
   (a)   by an agreement between the original obligor and the new obligor subject to Article 9.2.3, or
   (b)   by an agreement between the obligee and the new obligor, by which the new obligor assumes the obligation.

Article 9.2.2   Exclusion
This Section does not apply to transfers of obligations made under the special rules governing transfers of obligations in the course of transferring a business.

Article 9.2.3   Requirement of obligee's consent to transfer
The transfer of an obligation by an agreement between the original obligor and the new obligor requires the consent of the obligee.

Article 9.2.4   Advance consent of obligee
(1)   The obligee may give its consent in advance.
(2)   If the obligee has given its consent in advance, the transfer of the obligation becomes effective when a notice of the transfer is given to the obligee or when the obligee acknowledges it.

Article 9.2.5   Discharge of original obligor
(1)   The obligee may discharge the original obligor.
(2)   The obligee may also retain the original obligor as an obligor in case the new obligor does not perform properly.
(3)   Otherwise the original obligor and the new obligor are jointly and severally liable.

Article 9.2.6   Third party performance
(1)   Without the obligee's consent, the obligor may contract with another person that this person will perform the obligation in place of the obligor, unless the obligation in the circumstances has an essentially personal character.
(2)   The obligee retains its claim against the obligor.

Article 9.2.7   Defences and rights of set-off
(1)   The new obligor may assert against the obligee all defences which the original obligor could assert against the obligee.
(2)   The new obligor may not exercise against the obligee any right of set-off available to the original obligor against the obligee.

Article 9.2.8   Rights related to the obligation transferred
(1)   The obligee may assert against the new obligor all its rights to payment or other performance under the contract in respect of the obligation transferred.
(2)   If the original obligor is discharged under Article 9.2.5(1), a security granted by any person other than the new obligor for the performance of the obligation is discharged, unless that other person agrees that it should continue to be available to the obligee.
(3)   Discharge of the original obligor also extends to any security of the original obligor given to the obligee for the performance of the obligation, unless the security is over an asset which is transferred as part of a transaction between the original obligor and the new obligor.

Section 3: Assignment of contracts

Article 9.3.1   Definitions
'Assignment of a contract' means the transfer by agreement from one person (the 'assignor') to another person (the 'assignee') of the assignor's rights and obligations arising out of a contract with another person (the 'other party').

Article 9.3.2   Exclusion
This Section does not apply to the assignment of contracts made under the special rules governing transfers of contracts in the course of transferring a business.

Article 9.3.3   Requirement of consent of the other party
The assignment of a contract requires the consent of the other party.

Article 9.3.4   Advance consent of the other party
(1)   The other party may give its consent in advance.

(2)   If the other party has given its consent in advance, the assignment of the contract becomes effective when a notice of the assignment is given to the other party or when the other party acknowledges it.

Article 9.3.5   Discharge of the assignor
(1)   The other party may discharge the assignor.
(2)   The other party may also retain the assignor as an obligor in case the assignee does not perform properly.
(3)   Otherwise the assignor and the assignee are jointly and severally liable.

Article 9.3.6   Defences and rights of set-off
(1)   To the extent that the assignment of a contract involves an assignment of rights, Article 9.1.13 applies accordingly.
(2)   To the extent that the assignment of a contract involves a transfer of obligations, Article 9.2.7 applies accordingly.

Article 9.3.7   Rights transferred with the contract
(1)   To the extent that the assignment of a contract involves an assignment of rights, Article 9.1.14 applies accordingly.
(2)   To the extent that the assignment of a contract involves a transfer of obligations, Article 9.2.8 applies accordingly.

CHAPTER 10 — LIMITATION PERIODS

Article 10.1   Scope of the Chapter
(1)   The exercise of rights governed by these Principles is barred by the expiration of a period of time, referred to as 'limitation period', according to the rules of this Chapter.
(2)   This Chapter does not govern the time within which one party is required under these Principles, as a condition for the acquisition or exercise of its right, to give notice to the other party or to perform any act other than the institution of legal proceedings.

Article 10.2   Limitation periods
(1)   The general limitation period is three years beginning on the day after the day the obligee knows or ought to know the facts as a result of which the obligee's right can be exercised.
(2)   In any event, the maximum limitation period is ten years beginning on the day after the day the right can be exercised.

Article 10.3   Modification of limitation periods by the parties
(1)   The parties may modify the limitation periods.
(2)   However they may not
   (a)   shorten the general limitation period to less than one year;
   (b)   shorten the maximum limitation period to less than four years;
   (c)   extend the maximum limitation period to more than fifteen years.

Article 10.4   New limitation period by acknowledgement
(1)   Where the obligor before the expiration of the general limitation period acknowledges the right of the obligee, a new general limitation period begins on the day after the day of the acknowledgement.
(2)   The maximum limitation period does not begin to run again, but may be exceeded by the beginning of a new general limitation period under Art. 10.2(1).

Article 10.5   Suspension by judicial proceedings
(1)   The running of the limitation period is suspended
   (a)   when the obligee performs any act, by commencing judicial proceedings or in judicial proceedings already instituted, that is recognised by the law of the court as asserting the obligee's right against the obligor;

(b)   in the case of the obligor's insolvency when the obligee has asserted its rights in the insolvency proceedings; or

(c)   in the case of proceedings for dissolution of the entity which is the obligor when the obligee has asserted its rights in the dissolution proceedings.

(2)   Suspension lasts until a final decision has been issued or until the proceedings have been otherwise terminated.

Article 10.6   Suspension by arbitral proceedings

(1)   The running of the limitation period is suspended when the obligee performs any act, by commencing arbitral proceedings or in arbitral proceedings already instituted, that is recognised by the law of the arbitral tribunal as asserting the obligee's right against the obligor. In the absence of regulations for arbitral proceedings or provisions determining the exact date of the commencement of arbitral proceedings, the proceedings are deemed to commence on the date on which a request that the right in dispute should be adjudicated reaches the obligor.

(2)   Suspension lasts until a binding decision has been issued or until the proceedings have been otherwise terminated.

Article 10.7   Alternative dispute resolution

The provisions of Articles 10.5 and 10.6 apply with appropriate modifications to other proceedings whereby the parties request a third person to assist them in their attempt to reach an amicable settlement of their dispute.

Article 10.8   Suspension in case of force majeure, death or incapacity

(1)   Where the obligee has been prevented by an impediment that is beyond its control and that it could neither avoid nor overcome, from causing a limitation period to cease to run under the preceding articles, the general limitation period is suspended so as not to expire before one year after the relevant impediment has ceased to exist.

(2)   Where the impediment consists of the incapacity or death of the obligee or obligor, suspension ceases when a representative for the incapacitated or deceased party or its estate has been appointed or a successor has inherited the respective party's position. The additional one-year period under paragraph (1) applies accordingly.

Article 10.9   The effects of expiration of limitation period

(1)   The expiration of the limitation period does not extinguish the right.

(2)   For the expiration of the limitation period to have effect, the obligor must assert it as a defence.

(3)   A right may still be relied on as a defence even though the expiration of the limitation period for that right has been asserted.

Article 10.10   Right of set-off

The obligee may exercise the right of set-off until the obligor has asserted the expiration of the limitation period.

Article 10.11   Restitution

Where there has been performance in order to discharge an obligation, there is no right of restitution merely because the limitation period has expired.

INDEX

INDEX OF MATERIALS